TESTS AND MEASUREMENTS

TESTS AND MEASUREMENTS
Assessment and Prediction

Jum C. Nunnally, Jr.

ASSOCIATE PROFESSOR OF PSYCHOLOGY
UNIVERSITY OF ILLINOIS

McGRAW-HILL BOOK COMPANY, INC.

New York   Toronto   London

1959

TESTS AND MEASUREMENTS

V

47558

To the two persons who influenced me most in my early training
Professor B. Orman McDonald
Professor William Stephenson

Preface

This book is intended to serve as a comprehensive text for the use of students in tests and measurements courses, whether in the field of psychology or education. It can also serve as a helpful adjunct to graduate courses in measurement, and as a practical guide to psychological testing for teachers and administrators. For use in undergraduate courses, the material has been organized in such a way that some of the more difficult sections can easily be omitted if necessary. For example, if his students have had little or no training in statistics, the instructor may wish to omit all or parts of Chapters 6, 7, 8, and 9.

Tests and Measurements: Assessment and Prediction is based on four principles. The first of these principles is that the student must begin by learning some statistical concepts and procedures before he can thoroughly understand the measurement of human behavior. One of the major aims of this book is to make the statistical concepts relevant to such measurement both understandable and interesting. Although most students tend to be afraid of statistics and reluctant to learn about them, these negative attitudes are probably traceable more to poor methods of instruction than to the intrinsic nature of the subject matter. All too often statistical formulas are presented to classes without adequate preparation or explanation. In *Tests and Measurements,* the author has undertaken to provide the reader with some insights into why statistical methods are necessary and how they work.

The second principle upon which this book is based is that the reader should be given a broad acquaintance with the whole subject of measuring human behavior, not just with the measurement of individual differences. Therefore, measurement in various kinds of psychological research studies is discussed in Chapter 1; an introduction to psychophysics is given in Chapter 2; Chapter 17 specifically concerns measurement techniques for studies of personality and social psychology; and the ethics of performing research studies are discussed in Chapter 18. Although the major emphasis of the book is on studies of individual differences, these studies are presented in a context of general psychology; and as much material as possible has been introduced on measurement methods used in psychological experiments.

The third principle upon which this book is based is that the methodology of measurement is the proper subject matter for a tests and measurements course. Certainly a sound presentation of methodology is of more value to the students than a detailed description of particular tests and measurement techniques. For one thing, there are far too many tests and measurement techniques available to permit the reader to gain an acquaintance with even a fraction of them. Then, too, detailed study of particular tests and measurement techniques is of rather limited value, since we now know how to construct better instruments than most of those that are currently in use.

The fourth principle is that controversies about human measurement should be met head on rather than avoided. Under the guise of eclecticism, textbooks often hide from the reader the fact that there are differing points of view on many issues. If a person does not become acquainted with the major controversies in a field and does not learn about the conceptual and mathematical tools that are used in these controversies, he has at best only a shallow acquaintance with the subject matter. Consequently, the author has chosen to emphasize critical analyses of tests and of general approaches to measurement. It is hoped that these critical analyses will acquaint the reader with the major controversies in human measurement, will sharpen his ability to criticize measurement methods, and will help him make the decisions that he will face when applying his learning in actual testing and measurement situations.

The author is deeply indebted to those persons who read and criticized portions of the manuscript. Particular thanks are given to Doctors Lloyd Humphreys, Ted Husek, Charles Osgood, George Suci, and to Mr. Howard Bobren. The book owes a great deal to the patience and fine secretarial skill of Mrs. Freda Schell.

Jum C. Nunnally, Jr.

Contents

CHAPTER 1

The Foundations of Psychological Measurement

Psychological measurement is a close and important concern to all of us. The student who reads these pages for a course assignment is very much interested in one type of psychological measurement: the method of grading used by the instructor. The person who aspires to higher education needs the best possible measurement of his capabilities before wagering his future. A successful marriage depends on the personalities of the partners, and it would be worth a great deal to a young couple to have their compatibility measured in advance. Many millions of dollars are spent in measuring the public reaction to political candidates, new brands of soap, and television programs. In these and many other ways, psychological measurement is a part of everyday living.

In spite of the many needs for psychological measurement methods, few had been developed up to the turn of this century. It is surprising that men learned so much of the world around them without learning more about themselves. A technique was developed for measuring the circumference of the earth two thousand years before psychological tests came into general use. There are still many weak spots in the storehouse of psychological measurement methods. Important decisions must often be made about people on the basis of very crude "yardsticks." The slowness with which psychological measurement has developed is due in part to the complexity of the individual human. Some mistaken ideas about the purpose and substance of psychology have also retarded the development of measurement methods. These will be discussed in the following sections.

The Nature of Psychological Data. The development of psychological measurement and of psychology as a whole was delayed, in part, by some misunderstanding about the nature of the subject matter. The philosopher Kant once said that it would not be possible to have a science of psychology because the basic data could not be observed and measured. Modern psychologists would agree in part with Kant, agree to the extent that only certain kinds of psychological phenomena are open to observation and measurement.

1

Psychological science concerns itself with the study of human behavior, with the actions, judgments, words, and preferences of individuals. The study of such tangible behavior complies with the requirements of scientific research. However, there are other phenomena that are spoken of as being "psychological" which cannot be the substance of *direct* scientific study. Some of these are sensations, feelings, and images.

Throughout the history of philosophical thought there has been a tendency to divide psychological phenomena into those that are "physical" and those that are "mental." This division of phenomena is referred to as psychophysical dualism, the belief in separate mental and physical processes. Because of this unfortunate logical standpoint scholars have been drawn into many needless arguments about the "connections" between the mental and the physical.

By adopting a set of simple rules, the seemingly difficult problem of psychophysical dualism can be circumvented. The purpose of scientific effort is to test statements about the world of events—all those events that can be seen, heard, touched, or otherwise experienced in common. An illustrative scientific statement is, "Yellow fever is a virus infection." The phenomenon being studied might itself be impalpable, such as magnetism, atomic action, or the transfer of heat. But our knowledge of the phenomenon must always come from publicly observable events: the changing direction of a compass needle, the action of a Geiger counter, or the reading on a thermometer.

In order to accept a statement as either true or false, there must be a demonstration of evidence in the world of observable events. Only then can a statement be tested. The evidence must be such that it can be examined by others. The procedures for obtaining the evidence should be sufficiently clear to allow independent investigators to gather new evidence in respect to the problem. These are some of the major rules that have been adopted by scientists, and the rules demonstrate their worth by the progress that science has made during the last several hundred years.

Instead of trying to pass judgment on the whole field of psychology as to whether it is "mental" or "physical," it is more logical to examine particular kinds of statements in psychology to see whether they meet the requirements of scientific inquiry. In this way we will find many statements that are testable, as well as many statements that we will want to avoid because they are untestable.

Some testable and untestable statements in psychology can be illustrated if the reader will imagine that he has in his hand a large, red, juicy-looking apple. Take a bite of this make-believe apple. Does it taste good? If you had a friend there with you, would it taste "better" to him than to you? How much more pleasant would be his sensation—twice as much, or three times as much? This is an issue that cannot be studied directly. There is no way to measure your sensations directly. They are uniquely yours in a way that exempts them from direct observation by others. Lift the apple in your hand. Do you have a feeling of "weightiness" in response to the apple? How "large" is your feeling? This is another phenomenon that cannot be observed by others or measured directly.

There are some issues that could be studied in respect to the apple. Which would you rather have—an apple, an orange, or a pear? The way in which you respond to the question will demonstrate your preferences, and your preferences can be compared with those of other persons. How much do you think the apple weighs—7, 8, or 9 ounces? Your judgment can be compared with the weight of the apple, and a measure of your accuracy can be obtained.

Your subjective experiences—your feelings, sensations, and desires—cannot be observed by others, and as such cannot be subjected to measurement. Once you *do* something in respect to your feelings—make a judgment, state a preference, or even talk to others about the experience—then these behaviors meet the requirements of scientific inquiry, and measurement becomes possible.

It may seem like a trivial point to say that an individual's sensation of pleasantness is not open to scientific study but that his report of pleasantness is legitimate scientific data. However, failure to make this distinction forces the scientist into some knotty problems about the nature of his data. If it is claimed that the individual's sensation of pleasantness is being measured, then one can always inquire as to the proof that the individual really enjoys the apple. The answer is, of course, that there is no way to prove that the individual enjoys the apple or, for that matter, to prove that there is any sensation at all related to the apple. We have only the individual's word for liking or not liking the apple, and the verbal report, in this instance, is the basic datum with which the scientist must deal.

Being restricted to what the individual does, or says, does not foreshadow defeat in psychological work. There is much that can be learned about human behavior, and there are many ways in which one human action can be predicted from others. For example, the individual's stated preferences for fruits would likely be predictive of what he would purchase or what he would choose to eat. More importantly, the scores that a person makes on psychological tests can predict approximately how well he will perform in many real-life situations.

Emotional Barriers to Psychological Measurement. Psychological measurement efforts are often reacted to as being "nosey" activities—asking personal questions, embarrassing people with their shortcomings, and experimenting in emotionally laden matters. It gives most of us a twinge of anxiety to see ourselves portrayed as a set of statistics or to have our abilities compared with those of others. We like to think of ourselves as being unique in a way that exempts us from study.

Psychology has been held in disfavor by persons who think of it as a denial of "free will." Their argument is that if a person's behavior is predictable then the individual has no choice in his actions, no freedom of will. Psychology starts with no a priori viewpoints about the nature of man but looks instead for the regularities that occur in human behavior. When such regularities are sought, they are found in abundance. For example, a white object will nearly always be regarded as larger than a black one of the same size. Persons who make low scores on "intelligence" tests seldom manage to complete college training. If you are like most of us, you are consistent to some degree about the kinds of clothes that you buy, the types of people that you choose as friends, the place where you like to sit in a theater, and many other things that can be measured and studied.

Some people think of psychology as an attempt to intrude on religious and ethical beliefs. Because of psychology's behavioristic approach, it automatically prevents itself from investigating the individual's experiential world. Psychology can study the differences in ethical and moral practice among people but cannot reach decisions about which beliefs are more real or more correct.

The Need for Measurement. Some form of measurement is essential to all scientific studies. Without the precision of mathematical language and the deductive possibilities which it allows, it would be very difficult to express most statements in a way that would allow them to be tested. Consider the hypothesis that tornadoes occur on days when the atmospheric pressure is high and a sudden drop in temperature occurs. We would first want to inquire what is "high" pressure, high in relation to what, how much in an absolute sense. This part of the statement could be rephrased in terms of barometer readings. The question of "how much" would come again in respect to the phrase "sudden drop in temperature." How much of a drop is a sudden drop—10 degrees over a period of 30 minutes? We would need the measurement techniques provided by clocks and thermometers to make the original statement more specific. You can see that a hypothesis as simple as the fictitious one here requires several kinds of measurements. The problem would be all but impossible to state precisely without reference to measurement methods.

MEASUREMENT IN PSYCHOLOGY

There are a number of special fields in psychology. Some of these are clinical, social, physiological, and differential psychology. Research in all areas of psychology is dependent on adequate measurement methods. In some areas, the measurement problems have proved more difficult than in others. For example, the clinical psychologist finds it difficult to measure things like the improvement of patients in psychotherapy and the severity of emotional disorders. One of the most difficult problems for psychologists is to find ways to measure important human attributes.

Individual Differences and Psychological Processes. There are two basically different kinds of measurement problems encountered in psychology. These are the measurement of individual differences and the measurement of processes. The study of individual differences, differential psychology, is sufficiently broad to be considered a special field. As the name implies, differential psychology concerns the ways in which people differ from one another. People differ in terms of their walking speeds, ability to learn Latin, sensitivity to pain, susceptibility to hypnosis, and in countless other ways. Some of these individual differences are of little importance in our daily lives; others are of paramount importance for success and happiness.

A psychological process is a series of responses by one person. The process of reacting to alcohol is a useful example. First there is a decrease in pulse rate, an increased feeling of pleasantness, an increase in reaction time, and finally, gross loss of coordination. The characteristic changes would be the same for all persons regardless of the initial levels of pulse rate, reaction time, and so on.

Another example of the difference between processes and individual differences can be illustrated with a learning experiment. Any person who performs learning experiments with animals, say, with white rats, finds that some rats learn faster than others. Instead of being interested in individual differences among rats, the experimenter is usually more interested in the learning process. That is, he would like to determine the regularity of improvement and the variables which affect improvement, regardless of individual differences. The family of learning curves in Figure 1–1 illustrates the problem.

The curves in Figure 1–1 show the amounts of time taken by four rats to reach the goal in a maze on each of eleven trials. On the first trial it is apparent that there are individual differences among the rats in the time taken to reach the goal. Rat No. 1 took eighty seconds, and rat No. 4 took only fifty-five seconds. Also, we see that the order of the rats on the first trial is maintained in most of the other trials, showing that some of the rats are more capable in the particular type of learning problem.

A second type of information to be seen in Figure 1–1, and generally the most sought-after information in studies of this kind, is that the process of learning tends to be the same for all four rats. Regardless of individual differences at each trial, the rats as a group tend to learn in the same pattern. This group tendency can be seen better by looking at the curve of average times. This was obtained by adding together the times for the four rats at each trial and dividing by four. This curve shows that for the rats as a group the learning is much faster during the first several trials. The rate of learning for the group levels off after that, and only slight improvement for the group can be found after the eighth trial.

FIGURE 1-1. Hypothetical curves showing the amounts of time taken by four rats to reach the goal in a learning maze.

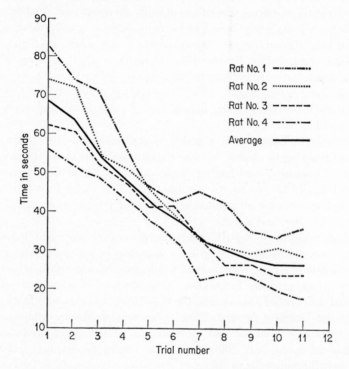

In studies of individual differences, the experimenter usually hopes that differences among people will be as large as possible. If such differences are small, there is nothing with respect to individual differences to study. In studies of processes, the experimenter usually hopes that individual differences will be as small as possible, because they only serve to complicate the regularity that he is seeking to measure.

Measurement in Differential Psychology. Measurement methods are particularly essential in differential psychology. Differential psychology concerns two kinds of problems: (1) the logic and methods of measuring individual differences, and (2) the study of how individual differences arise and how they relate to one another. The first concerns the tools for measuring individual differences; the second concerns the facts that have been established by applying the tools.

The remainder of the book will be more concerned with the subject matter of differential psychology than any other special area, and the emphasis will be on the measurement of individual differences. Attention will be given to some of the problems in the measurement of processes.

Although the major emphasis in this book is on the study of individual differences, we should not overemphasize the conclusions that can be obtained from studies of this kind. There are limits to what can be learned about human behavior from individual differences alone. Although studies of individual differences have proved very useful, it should be remembered that it is the study of processes with which psychology is more extensively concerned.

The study of individual differences has a wide appeal in the United States. Not only has much of the work in this field of study been done by persons in our country, but the subject of individual differences has a particular appeal for the American public. There is perhaps no other country in which a person can attract so much attention by being different or doing something unusual. There are contests to see who can eat the most pies, sit longest on a flag pole, and dance longest without falling from exhaustion.

One of the major reasons we are interested in differences among people is that this is a "land of opportunity," as the well-worn phrase puts it. There is more opportunity for an individual to use his ability to attain fame and fortune than in countries where either the class structure or the lower standard of living provides less room for the individual to get ahead. If a person is better looking, can sing better, is more intelligent, is a better athlete, he may be on the road to great personal gain. Consequently, people are usually eager to find some way in which they surpass others, even if it is in so remote a behavior as being able to hold their breath longer.

As evidence of our interest in individual differences, American magazines are replete with short, and usually inadequate, tests of vocabulary, popularity, marriage happiness, and many others. The mother is eager to see that little Johnny learns to walk before the neighbor's child. She wants to have his *IQ* measured, and hopes that he is a budding genius.

The study of individual differences has been given considerable attention during the last fifty years. One reason for the interest of psychologists in this type of work is the success that the testing movement has encountered. Some areas of psychology can be more properly regarded as sciences of the future. The groundwork is being laid, but the present storehouse of facts is not large. There is also a great deal yet to be learned about the measurement of individual differences. The measurement of personality characteristics has proven a particularly onerous stumbling block. Even considering the uncharted regions in the measurement of human behavior, the testing movement in America has reached an advanced stage of technical sophistication and proved practical importance.

MEASUREMENT SCALES

In the discussion to follow, we will speak of a "scale" as denoting the procedure, or "yardstick," with which a particular measure is obtained. Measurement scales are part of everyday living: the ruler as a scale to determine length, the thermometer to indicate temperature, and the achievement test to measure success in school. We customarily place numbers along scales, such as inches, degrees Fahrenheit, and test scores. However, these are not the same kind of numbers; they mean different things about "how much," and they have different mathematical uses. Some of the major kinds of measurement scales will be discussed in the following sections.

Labels. Labels, or tags, are used to signify that one object or person is distinct from another. The numbers on the backs of baseball players are labels. They tell nothing at all about quantities. The player numbered 44 is not necessarily twice as good as 22. If we add the labels for these two players, 66 is obtained. Does this sum have any meaning? Any other numbers would have served as well, or the players could be distinguished by different colors, alphabetical letters, or geometric designs. Labels have no mathematical properties and are not scales at all. Other examples of numbers used as labels are the numbers on theater seats, numbers used to designate highways, and the numbering of stamps in a collection. Not every set of numbers is necessarily a set of measures. The investigator must ensure that the numbers which he studies are really quantities rather than mere labels.

Categories. Categorization, or qualitative distinction, is the most elementary type of scientific datum. The biologist makes a distinction between insects that have wings and those that do not. The chemist classifies liquids into those that are acid and those that are alkaline. Mental patients are categorized into groups such as depressive and schizophrenic. Members of the general public are categorized in terms of their preferences for political candidates.

Categorization implies that the things in a category have something in common and that they differ in some characteristic from the objects in other categories. The difference can be illustrated with a geologist's collection of rocks. The geologist might first apply labels to his collection, numbering them from 1 to N, simply as a way of keeping track of all the specimens. Later he might categorize the rocks as to whether they are sedimentary or igneous in origin.

It was said previously that no mathematical significance could be placed on labels. Although this is a humble beginning, there are complex mathematical systems that work entirely with categorical data.

The number of categories used in particular problems may be only two, or, in some studies, the number of categories is large. An example of multiple categorization would be the description of people in terms of occupations: farmers, plumbers, lawyers, and so on.

When using categories, no distinction is made among the objects or persons within a category. We might think of the members of any category as being equated to the number one—one plumber, one schizophrenic, or one alkaline liquid. This would then give no information as to whether one plumber is better than another or whether one liquid is more alkaline than another. Also, from the categorizations alone, there would be no way of knowing that lawyers receive higher incomes than farmers and plumbers, or that any relationship exists among the categories.

The results of psychological studies are sometimes reported in terms of categories. There are a number of ways of statistically analyzing data of this kind, some of which will be mentioned in the chapters ahead. Chief among these procedures is the description of populations of people in terms of the frequencies that fall in various categories and the comparison of categories for the amount of overlap. Illustrating the former, mental hospital patients can be characterized as schizophrenic, paranoid, manic-depressive, or other. The latter type of procedure might be used to show that the members of one category of mental patients more frequently come from home environments of a particular kind than do the members of other categories of mental patients.

Ordinal Scales. The ordinal scale relates persons or objects to one another by ordering or ranking them in respect to an attribute. Course marks are sometimes reported as ranks. The person who performs best is given a rank of 1, second-best receives a rank of 2, and so on to the person with the worst performance. As a convention the ordering is symbolized as 1, 2, 3, . . . , N, with the understanding that the numbers mean first, second, third, . . . , Nth.

The essence of the ordinal scale is the concept of "greater than" portrayed by the symbol ($>$). Thus $a > b$ means that a is greater than b, or that b is less than a. To have an ordinal scale, it must be established that $a > b > c > d > e > . . . > N$ for N number of persons in respect to any particular attribute. The concept of "greater than" characterizing ordinal scales is a kind of information in addition to the concept of "different from" used with categories.

An ordering, or rank-ordering, constitutes a scale of measurement, but the use of such scales has definite mathematical limitations. The ordinary arithmetical operations of addition, subtraction, multiplication, and division make little sense with ordinal numbers. It is not sensible to add together the first and third man and equate this in any way with the fourth man, as the ordinary operations of arithmetic would lead us to expect.

Two important kinds of information are lacking in the ordinal scale. The first is that no information is provided as to how well the group performs as a whole. If there are six students and no ties in examination grades, there will be ranks 1, 2, . . . , 6 regardless of how well or how poorly the whole group performs. The ranks might have been determined within a group of geniuses, or the ranks might as easily have been obtained within a group of only moderately capable students.

The second important information that is lacking in the ordinal scale is that of the dispersion of performance. That is, there is no way of telling from the ranks alone how closely the second man approaches the first man, or how much better the first man performs than the man who is ranked last. If there are two classes and thirty students in each class, there will be ranks 1 through 30 in each class. There is no way of telling from the ranks whether the dispersion of ability is larger in one class than in the other. The students in one class might have performed much the same, and the students in the other class might have varied widely from one another in performance.

The most important type of mathematical operation that can be applied to ranks is that of correlation. In this way, it can be determined to what extent persons are ordered alike in two circumstances. It could be determined whether the persons who make grades near the top in history also make high grades in mathematics and additionally, an over-all numerical index of agreement could be found over the extent of both orderings. The ability to correlate two sets of measures satisfies the most basic requirement for evaluating tests. Correlational analysis will be discussed in detail in Chapter 5.

Interval Scales. If, in addition to an ordering of persons, a knowledge is obtained of the interval or the distance between persons, then an interval scale is produced. The results of a foot race could be reported in the form of an interval scale. The customary procedure is, of course, to state the exact running time for each participant. To illustrate the characteristics of interval scales, assume that the results are reported in terms of the interval between the first and second man, the second and third man, and so on. It could be said that the second runner came in one second behind the first, the third runner came in two seconds behind the second man, the fourth came in one second behind the third, and so on for all intervals.

Like ordinal scales, interval scales also provide no information about how well the people perform as a group. Because the results of the race were reported only in terms of intervals, we have no information about the absolute running times for the men. If we learn later that the first runner took ten seconds, then we know that the second man took exactly eleven seconds, the third man thirteen seconds, and so on for the other runners; but if the first man had taken twenty seconds, then we learn that the second man took twenty-one seconds, indicating that the group as a whole is much slower.

The important advantage of the interval scale over the ordinal scale is that knowing the interval allows for the determination of the dispersion, or spread, of the scores. The *range* of scores is the interval, or distance, between the person who stands highest and the person who stands lowest on the scale. Also, the *standard deviation* of a set of scores can be determined without a knowledge of the absolute level of measurements. (Measures of dispersion will be discussed in Chapter 3.)

The arithmetical operations of addition, subtraction, multiplication, and division can be used with interval scales only in respect to the differences between scores. For example, the interval between the men who finish the race first and second could be compared directly with the interval between those who finish third and fourth.

The ordinary Fahrenheit thermometer is an example of an interval scale. The zero point on the scale is arbitrary. It is not meaningful, for example, to say that 90 degrees is twice as warm as 45 degrees.

Ratio Scales. The final member in the hierarchy of measurement scales is the ratio scale. The ratio scale requires that the absolute measurement of each person be known. Then in the race that we used to illustrate interval scales, we might find that the first man took eleven seconds, the second man twelve seconds, the third man fourteen seconds, and so on for the remaining runners. Specifying the absolute level for running, or for any other attribute, is the same as saying that the zero point on the scale is known.

In addition to its own special virtues, the ratio scale has all the advantages of the less powerful scales. All of the operations of arithmetic as well as the tools of higher mathematics can be applied to ratio scales. As the name implies, one score can be divided by another, multiplied by another, subtracted from and added to any other.

Ratio scales are used quite frequently in everyday life. No simpler example is available than the weighing of two objects on a "scale." Comparisons of salaries, heights of individuals, numbers of rooms in buildings, and many, many other quantities are treated as ratio scales. It is so customary to deal with ratio scales that it is easy to make the mistake of assuming that all measures are of this kind. For example, it might be said that John is "twice" as handsome as Bill. It is difficult in this case to see how the ratio "twice" could be obtained, and it is reasonable to suspect that a ratio scale is being used where only an interval or even an ordinal scale is justified.

Test Scores as Scales. Most test scores are treated as though they are interval scales. Without such an assumption there would be no way of obtaining measures of dispersion. As will be shown later, the standard deviation and its companion statistic, the variance, are crucial to the gathering of test norms and to the determination of how well tests work.

It is not justifiable to treat most test scores as though they constitute ratio scales. The absolute scores that people obtain are largely artifacts of the ways in which tests are constructed. For example, a class instructor might decide to give five points for each correct answer, or he might decide on ten points instead. Such decisions markedly affect the absolute size of scores. For example, suppose that persons a, b, and c make scores of 20, 15, and 12 on a test. Then, if we assume that a ratio scale is logical in this case, it could be said that a demonstrates 1.33 times as much of the particular ability as does b. Suppose that the test were revised by adding five items which are so easy that a, b, and c get them all correct. Now, the scores for a, b, and c would be 25, 20, and 17 respectively. This changes the ratio between the score of a and b to 1.25. We see in this way that ratios computed from test scores are not usually meaningful.

In some instances, psychological measures are justifiably treated as ratio scales. Some of these would be the number of trials needed to learn a particular task, the length of time taken to respond to a visual signal, and the amount of perceptual distortion induced by a visual illusion. There have been some interesting attempts to deduce ratio scales for certain types of psychological measures, particularly for measures of attitudes and for measures of human judgment.

SUMMARY

Whether or not it is recognized and designated as such, psychological measurement is an important ingredient of everyday life. Systematic measurement methods were rather late in coming, and only during the last one hundred years has the problem been carefully studied. A major drawback to the development of measurement methods has been the failure to distinguish the kinds of psychological phenomena that can and cannot be measured. Psychological science is concerned with human behavior, with the actions, words, judgments, and preferences of people—all of which are open to measurement. Psychological science is not concerned with purely subjective phenomena; until the individual *does* something about his feelings, there is nothing to measure.

We are so accustomed to measuring physical objects and assigning numbers to them on the basis of ratio scales that it is easy to assume that all measurements are of that kind. However, many measurements, and particularly those in psychology, must be made on a cruder basis. Consequently, it is important to specify the type of measurement scale which is in use. This will indicate the kinds of mathematical procedures that can be legitimately employed.

Although we should be impressed with the need for measurement methods, this should not dim the importance of simple human observation and thought in the search for scientific lawfulness. Measurements are helpful to the scientist in explaining and exploring theories, but only the human observer can invent theories. No amount of elaborate measurement can make up for a lack of ideas on the part of the experimenter.

SUGGESTED ADDITIONAL READINGS

Boring, E. G. *A history of experimental psychology*. (Rev. ed.) New York: Appleton-Century-Crofts, 1950.

Goodenough, Florence L. *Mental testing*. New York: Rinehart, 1949, chaps. 1–6.

Lorge, I. The fundamental nature of measurement. In E. F. Lindquist (Ed.), *Educational measurement*. Washington: American Council on Education, 1951, chap. 14.

Murphy, G. *An historical introduction to modern psychology*. (Rev. ed.) New York: Harcourt, Brace, 1949.

CHAPTER 2

The Growth of Measurement Methods in Psychology

People have always been interested in the measurement of human attributes, and embryonic studies can be traced even to ancient China. However, it was only one hundred years ago that the first systematic attacks were made on problems of psychological measurement. During the nineteenth century, the field of psychological measurement was nourished by two major influences. First, psychological measurement borrowed heavily from the concepts and tools that had been applied so successfully in physics, chemistry, and astronomy. The nineteenth century was a period of great progress in the physical sciences, and it was reasoned by men of that day that the methods of physical science could be applied to the human mind. It was during this period that *psychophysics* was born: the precise and quantitative study of how human judgments are made. Psychophysics has a proud tradition, and it has had a wholesome influence on measurement methods in all areas of psychology. Because of the importance of psychophysics in its own right and because of the impact that it has had on psychological testing, the development of psychophysics and some of the measurement methods will be discussed in this chapter.

The second major influence on the development of psychological measurement methods was the clinical tradition growing out of medicine, psychiatry, and social welfare research. In these efforts there was an urgent need for methods of measuring emotional stability and intelligence. The first practical mental tests grew out of this tradition and were applied to the problem of classifying mental deficients in public schools.

It has been only during the last several decades that these two traditions have merged. The union of scientific technology and mathematics with the clinician's intuitive approach and his concern for people produced the modern methodology of testing.

In addition to the two major influences described above, a number of other historical trends had a prominent influence on the development of psychological measurement methods. There are many needs for psychological tests in education, and measurement methods have grown at the same rate that educational facilities have grown. Because of the many direct uses for statistical methods in the development and use of psychological tests, the early developments in the discipline of statistics were prominent influences on the growth of psychological measurement.

The theory of evolution had a very important influence on psychology as a whole and particularly on the field of psychological measurement. Although evolution developed in biology and had its most important influence there, it helped foster new concepts of human behavior and interested psychologists in measuring human adjustment and the inheritance of psychological traits.

More recently, the two great wars of this century had very important impacts on psychological measurement. In both conflicts psychological tests were needed for the selection and classification of armed forces personnel. Never before had psychological tests been used in such wholesale quantities, and they proved their worth so well that psychological testing received wide public acceptance.

Each of the major trends mentioned above will be discussed in some detail in this chapter. Only by understanding these historical roots can the modern methodology of psychological measurement be seen in its proper perspective.

PSYCHOPHYSICS

The Personal Equation. Considerable progress was being made during the eighteenth century in the development of scientific instruments: chronographs, telescopes, compasses, microscopes, and many others. Although scant attention was given to the place of the human observer in the use of these instruments, a fortunate mishap stirred interest in the problem. At the observatory at Greenwich, England, in 1796, an astronomer's assistant, named Kinneybrook, found himself consistently at odds with his superior about astronomical observations. It was Kinneybrook's job to observe the time of transit for certain stars (this consisted, essentially, of noting the time that a star passed one of the cross wires on a telescope). It was found that Kinneybrook differed with his superior on the average by more than one-half second. Although such an amount of time might seem trivial for practical purposes, it was sufficient to introduce serious error into astronomical calculations. The astronomer encouraged Kinneybrook to be more accurate in his observations; but in spite of his efforts, Kinneybrook retained his characteristic difference in observation time (see **2,** chap. 8).

Astronomers as well as other scientists became interested in Kinneybrook's difficulties. Astronomers began to compare their measurements with one another and found that there were consistent differences among them. It became necessary then to determine an individual's "personal equation," his characteristic tendency to over- or underestimate observations by a certain amount. This brought a recognition that people differ in their judgments, and that such individual differences can be measured and accounted for in scientific work.

The Limen of Sensation. Soon after interest had been focused on the personal equation, philosophers and the early psychologists began to speculate about the threshold of awareness, the *limen*. The limen is the point at which a visual object, or stimulus of any kind, comes into awareness. If you sit at late afternoon looking at the sky and wait long enough, stars will become visible. One minute you do not see them and the next minute you do. It is interesting to speculate about the precise moment at which the stars come into awareness, the *absolute limen*. Another example of the absolute limen can be made with the use of a watch. If you hold a watch at arm's length, you will not be able to hear the "ticking" (unless you have an unusually noisy watch). As you draw the watch closer, there is a point at which you can hear the ticking, which is the absolute limen.

In addition to the absolute limen, there is a *difference limen*, the difference in stimulation which makes the individual aware of a difference. The difference limen can be illustrated with a hypothetical experiment. Assume that you have two light bulbs, which we will refer to as S_t and S_l. The brightness of S_t is fixed at a particular level and is not changed throughout the experiment. Let the current be adjustable on S_l so that the intensity of light can be varied, and then make S_l the same brightness as S_t. If you increase the intensity of S_l, making it gradually brighter, there will be a point at which the subject will become aware of the difference between S_t and S_l. The difference in intensity of the two lights at that point is the difference limen, or as it is sometimes referred to, the *JND*, the just noticeable difference. Another kind of difference limen can be obtained by making S_t and S_l very different in intensity at the beginning of the experiment. Then S_l can be made gradually dimmer until the subject can no longer see a difference between S_l and S_t. When the difference limen is obtained in this way, it is referred to as the *JNND*, the just noticeable *not* difference. The *JND* and the *JNND* are usually not quite the same in experimental findings; therefore, the experimenter often averages these to obtain a better estimate of the difference limen.

During the first half of the nineteenth century, considerable study was made of the limen: studies of the sensitivity of touch, hearing, vision, and other sense modalities. One of the prominent persons in this work was Ernst Weber, a German physiologist. One of Weber's principal findings concerns the size of the difference limen at various levels of stimulation. If in the judgment of weights, a weight of 6 pounds is just noticeably different from a weight of 5 pounds, would a weight of 11 pounds be just noticeably different from a weight of 10 pounds? To carry the question further, would a weight of 101 pounds be "just noticeably different" from a weight of 100 pounds? Your everyday experience tells you that this is not the case, that the difference limen is dependent on the level of intensity of S_t.

Weber found that the *JND* tends to be a constant ratio of the intensity of S_t. If, in terms of the example above, a weight of 6 pounds is just noticeably different from 5 pounds (the *JND* is 1 pound at this level of intensity for S_t) the ratio would be 1.2. Then we would predict that the *JND* for an S_t of 10 pounds would be 2 pounds (a weight of 12 pounds would be just noticeably different). The *JND* can then be expressed in the form of an equation as:

$$JND = cS_t$$

The above equation, which is referred to as Weber's law, is approximately true for many different situations involving judgments. It has even been applied analogously to such situations as the willingness of an individual to invest money. For example, an individual might be willing to invest $100 in a radio for a $3000 car but would not be willing to spend that much on a radio for a $2000 car—the willingness to invest more money tending to be a function of the amount of money already invested.

Gustav Fechner. In the hands of Gustav Fechner, the rising interest in human judgment became the cornerstone for modern psychological measurement. Fechner went to the University of Leipzig when he was sixteen years old and remained there, studying, then teaching and doing research until his death seventy years later. Fechner went through an amazing gamut of careers. He took his university degree in medicine, but his subsequent livelihood and reputation were based on work in physics. He sought accomplishment as a philosopher; and, almost in spite of himself, he became a great psychologist. Fechner was what we might refer to today as an "odd ball." His philosophical speculations concerned the presence of consciousness in all things, even imputing consciousness to plants and inanimate objects. He wrote numerous pamphlets under the pen name of Dr. Mises. In a heraldic tone the pamphlets called on the sleeping world to arise to the new philosophy.

Fechner tried to support his metaphysical beliefs with scientific experiments. He seized on the studies of human judgment, and particularly the *JND*, as the starting point for his work. His research was based on the postulate that sensation cannot be measured directly but that it is legitimate to ask an individual whether a sensation is present or not and whether one sensation is more intense than another. This is still the logical foundation of psychophysics. Fechner set out on a long program of research on human judgment, and in the course of this, he invented the major methods of measurement and many of the procedures of analysis which are used today. He performed the now classical studies on lifted weights, visual brightness, and the sense of touch. Although he never proved his philosophical points, he demonstrated how the logic and methods of science could be used in psychological measurement. We will look at some of the methods that were either developed by Fechner or were suggested by his work.

PSYCHOPHYSICAL MEASUREMENT METHODS

The Method of Limits. The *method of limits* was used on the previous pages to explain the difference limen. In using the method a test stimulus, S_t, is compared to a variable stimulus S_l. One standard procedure is to place S_l equal to S_t, then increase S_l gradually until the subject recognizes the difference. Another procedure is to make S_l markedly more intense than S_t, and then gradually lower the intensity of S_l until the subject can no longer recognize a difference.

The method of limits is useful in designing mechanical equipment which requires the operator to detect differences in stimulus intensity of any kind. A radar scope embodies this principle. The operator must detect differences in amount of light on the scope. The equipment should be designed in such a way that the operator can most easily detect distant objects, such as a formation of airplanes.

The Method of Average Error. This psychophysical method differs from the method of limits in that the subject, instead of the experimenter, varies S_l; and the task is to equate two stimulus intensities rather than to judge when a difference is present. One procedure is to place S_l at a

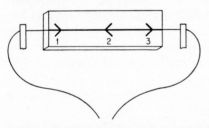

markedly different intensity from S_t. The subject is asked to adjust S_l until it appears to be the same as S_t. The classical use for the *method of average error* is in the study of visual illusions. Figure 2–1 shows the famous Müller-Lyer illusion.

In Figure 2–1 the arrowhead in the middle, 2, is midway between 1 and 3; however, the distance between 1 and 2 appears greater than

Figure 2–1. An apparatus for measuring the effect of the Müller-Lyer illusion.

that between 2 and 3. If 3 is attached to a cord and can be moved to the right and left by a subject, the method of average error can be used to determine the extent of the illusion. The arrowhead at 3 can be set far to the right and the subject asked to adjust it to a point where the two distances appear equal. The experimenter can then measure the difference between the two lines to determine the effect of the illusion.

The method of average error is often used to test depth perception. In this case two sticks are located in a frame placed about 20 feet from the subject. One stick, S_t, cannot be moved by the subject. A pulley arrangement permits the subject to move the other stick, S_l, forward and backward. The task for the subject is to align the two sticks (make them be at equal distances from himself). A person with good depth perception can align the two sticks within 1 or 2 inches, whereas some persons cannot bring the sticks closer than a foot from one another.

The Constant Method. Instead of using a variable stimulus, S_l, to compare with a S_t, the *constant method* uses a fixed set of stimuli, S_1, S_2, S_3, and so on, to compare in turn with one S_t. In laboratory work the number of comparison stimuli ranges from four to more than eight. In an experiment with lifted weights, six comparison stimuli could be used. If S_t is a weight of 200 grams, three of the comparison stimuli would weigh more than S_t, and the other three would weigh less than S_t. The subject would be presented one of the comparison stimuli and asked to judge whether it is heavier or lighter than S_t. Next, the subject would be given another of the six comparison stimuli and asked to judge whether it is heavier or lighter than S_t. The subject lifts S_t with one hand while holding the comparison stimulus in the other hand. Typically, the comparison stimuli would be given to the subject in a random order, to remove any unnecessary cues for judgment. Also, the subject would alternately lift S_t with the right and left hand to remove this source of bias. After the subject had

FIGURE 2–2. Psychometric function for the application of the *constant method* to the study of lifted weights.

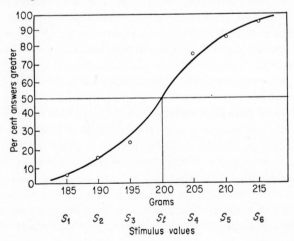

made many such comparisons, perhaps several hundred, the results could be pictured like that in Figure 2–2.

Figure 2–2 shows, as you would expect, that the per cent of answers "greater" grows as weights above 200 grams are considered, and that the percentage declines as weights less than 200 grams are considered. The subject hardly ever says that a weight of 185 grams is greater than S_t and almost always says that a weight of 215 grams is greater than S_t. A curve drawn through these points on the graph shows the typical psychophysical function.

The constant method can be used in a wide variety of psychophysical studies. Not only is it a useful way of determining thresholds, but the shape of the psychophysical function with different kinds of judgments is of interest.

The Method of Rank-order. In this method a number of stimuli are ordered in respect to an attribute. No one of the stimuli is specifically designated as the S_t. A simple example is to give an individual a number of objects and ask him to order them from heaviest to lightest. The *method of rank-order* is most frequently used when there are no measurable scales for the stimuli, as would be the case if an individual were asked to rank-order a number of foods in terms of preference. There would then be no intrinsic property of "likability" that could be measured, and consequently, the problem would be to determine the preference ordering for the one person. There would be no way of determining how "accurate" the individual is, as would be possible if lifted weights or visual intensities were being studied.

The method of rank-order is used in many studies of interests, attitudes, and preferences. The subject is asked to rank-order a number of activities in terms of his interests, a number of acquaintances in terms of preference, or a number of articles in terms of what he would purchase. The method is also used in tests of human ability, in which the individual is asked to rank-order a number of alternative answers to a question. Also, test scores are sometimes reported as ranks, the person making the highest grade receiving a rank of 1, the second highest a rank of 2, and so on for all the subjects.

The Method of Pair Comparisons. Like the method of rank-order, the *method of pair comparisons* is concerned with the relative ordering of the members in a set of stimuli. It differs from rank-order in that the subject is required to compare the stimuli two at a time, until each stimulus has been compared with every other. If we were studying food preferences and had as our "stimuli" apples, oranges, peaches, and a number of other fruits, the subject could be asked, first, "Which do you prefer, apples or oranges?" Next, the subject would be asked whether he prefers apples or peaches, and so on until apples are compared with each of the other fruits. There is a resemblance to the constant method in that apples are compared to a number of other stimuli. However, in pair comparisons, the subject is then asked to say whether he prefers oranges to peaches, and he continues to compare oranges with each of the other fruits. In all, the subject must make $n(n-1)/2$ judgments, where n is the number of stimuli being studied. If there are 10 fruits in the example, there will be 45 comparisons to be made.

The method of pair comparisons is usually considered the most exact psychophysical tool for many laboratory studies. It can be used to provide much the same information that can be obtained by the other methods; and, because of the many judgments which the subject must make in pair comparisons, the results are usually more reliable. Also, the method gives an indication of the definiteness with which the subject prefers some of the stimuli more than others. If an individual were to make pair comparisons among objects which he preferred equally or which he judged to be nearly equal in terms of an attribute, each object would be chosen about as many times as those with which it was compared. Such information could not be obtained in the method of rank-order, where the subject is forced to give a different rank to each stimulus. Due to the laboriousness of the pair comparisons procedure, its use is restricted to situations in which it is necessary to obtain rather exact information about a set of preferences or judgments.

The Place of Psychophysics in Psychology. We have had only a brief look at Fechner's contributions and some of the psychophysical methods which grew from his work. There are numerous other special methods, variants of the basic procedures, which are useful in studying particular problems. It is important to note that, as in nearly all the early work, in most current psychophysical studies, investigators are not primarily concerned with learning about individual differences. Instead, the purpose is to find laws about human judgment and preference that apply to everybody. In so far as large differences among people appear in psychophysical studies, they only serve to complicate the general lawfulness that is being sought.

In addition to the rich tradition of psychophysical research which still goes on in studies of human judgment, the psychophysical methods are used widely in physiological psychology, studies of perception, and the psychology of learning. Our particular concern is with the impact of psychophysics on the study of individual differences. Not only are the psychophysical methods used now in studies of individual differences, but the firm logical foundation of human measurement has been brought over into the development of psychological tests. We will not go into

The distribution of heads and tails is pictured in graph form in Figure 2–3. If the number of coins in each toss is increased from ten to one hundred, the curve will begin to smooth out to resemble that in Figure 2–4.

FIGURE 2–3. Graph of expected occurrences of "heads" and "tails" for 10 coins tossed 1,024 times.

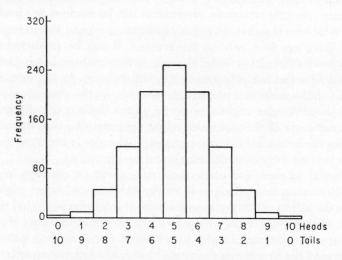

FIGURE 2–4. Smoothed curve showing expectancies of "heads" for a large number of coins tossed many times.

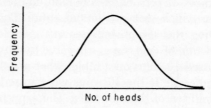

The bell-shaped curve in Figure 2–4 is encountered very often in practical work. It is referred to as the *normal distribution,* or it is variously called the *normal curve* and the *normal curve of error.* Much of the early development of statistics was concerned with the properties of the normal distribution.

Quetelet and the Normal Distribution. During the last hundred years numerous efforts have been made to apply statistical principles to the behavior of people. In the coming chapters we will see the key place that statistical methods play in the development and use of tests. During the first half of the nineteenth century, Adolph Quetelet, a Belgian statistician, undertook to gather a considerable amount of information about

European populations. He collected information on the number of children in families, the number of children born in different years, and the physical characteristics of people. He found that many of these characteristics distribute themselves in a shape much like the normal distribution. For example, he found that the chest measurements of soldiers were distributed like the normal distribution.

Because Quetelet knew that the normal distribution demonstrates the error in many types of predictions, he came to the conclusion that a normal distribution of human traits shows "nature's error" in the composition of human beings. It was his idea that "nature" aims at producing the average man, and that the extremes in either direction are "accidents of nature." We remember Quetelet not so much for this principle as for the influence he had on men to follow. He was one of the first persons to make systematic studies of individual differences, and he interested others in the application of statistical methods to the study of human behavior.

THE EFFECT OF THE THEORY OF EVOLUTION ON PSYCHOLOGY

Although the theory of evolution had its most direct influence on the science of biology, it also had an important impact on psychological measurement and psychology as a whole. Before the nineteenth century, the predominant view was that man is a static being, having since the day of creation a uniform and unchanging set of physical and mental attributes. Although Quetelet measured individual differences, he thought of these as "nature's mistakes" in producing the average man. It had always been noted that men differ from one another, but there had been no systematic attempt to study the part which individual differences play in everyday life.

Darwin. There were dissenters to the static theory of man and his surroundings, and there were even some, men such as Lyell and Lamarck, who theorized that life changes from generation to generation. It remained for Charles Darwin to amass the evidence to support the theory of evolution. He collected many examples from the animal kingdom showing the changing forms of life that develop in special environments. He saw that the mechanism of selection, or "survival of the fittest" as he called it, allows some animals to exist and forces others to die off. Therefore, the animals whose particular features make them more suited to an environment survive and pass on their genetic qualities to the next generation.

Darwin's major evidence for evolution was given in *The Origin of Species* published in 1859. It brought on several decades of argument among scientists as to the validity of the theory and the implications of the theory for scientific work. As the theory came to be accepted, it forced new viewpoints on scientific disciplines. It required biologists and botanists to think of animals and plants as being in a state of change, gradually progressing from one form to another to meet the changing environments. The theory also gave an impetus to the study of individual differences in psychology. It was reasoned that, if individual differences in plants and animals make for differential ability to adapt and survive, individual differences in humans would also have a functional significance. Further, if plants and animals inherit ancestral characteristics, some of the individual characteristics in humans might be accounted for on the same basis.

EARLY STUDIES OF INDIVIDUAL DIFFERENCES

Galton. The several lines of thought that we have traced—psychophysics, statistics, and the theory of evolution—converged in the psychological work of Sir Francis Galton. He was a member of a vanishing "breed," the gentleman scholar who, without formal university connections, dabbled effectively in a wide range of subjects. His interests ranged from criminology, psychology, biology, and anthropology, to the invention of numerous scientific devices. He invented the "supersonic" whistle and delighted himself by calling the dogs of London away from their incredulous masters. He invented composite photography, a procedure for combining a number of photographs into an average human appearance. He applied the method to the photographs of criminals, trying to obtain a composite of typical criminal features. He once practiced paranoia, going about imagining that everyone was talking about him. After several days he could imagine that even horses were plotting against him. In order to understand primitive religions, he built a religion of his own. He placed a comic picture of *Punch* on the wall and paid it all manner of homage and tribute in order to grasp the meaning of the idol in primitive worship. In addition to his many other activities, Galton also applied his genius to the study of psychological traits.

Galton was Darwin's immediate follower in the field of psychology. He developed an interest in the hereditability of individual characteristics and made studies of prominent men in England to support his views. In 1869 he reported his findings in *Hereditary Genius,* in which he tried to show that "greatness" runs in families. He came to believe that most important personal characteristics are inherited, not only the prominent physical characteristics, but also abilities and personality characteristics. He believed that criminality and psychological disorders are passed along from father to son by direct inheritance.

Galton founded the study of *eugenics,* the avowed purpose of which is the betterment of the human race through the control of mating. Although Galton never worked out the social problems which his program would involve, he was convinced that a world of superior humans could be developed by encouraging gifted couples to marry and by discouraging or preventing less gifted individuals from having children.

Galton realized that, before his program of eugenics could be undertaken, it would be necessary to learn more about the inheritance of individual characteristics. If it could be shown that a particular attribute, literary ability for example, is passed from father to son, then it should be possible to breed a generation of literary geniuses. However, if the attribute proved not to be inherited, there would be nothing that a program of eugenics could do to improve literary talent. Galton needed first to measure human characteristics before proceeding to study their hereditability, and it is because of this need to measure individual differences that Galton's contributions are of such importance to us here.

Galton coined the term "mental test" and set about to measure many different human attributes. He recognized the need for standardization in testing, that all subjects should be presented the same problems under uniform conditions. Galton's tests bore little resemblance to the ones which are most widely used today. He and his immediate followers in England made much of the philosopher Locke's dictum that all knowledge comes through the senses. They reasoned from this that the person with the most acute "senses" would be the most gifted and most knowledgeable. Most of Galton's tests were measures of simple sensory discrimination: the ability to recognize tones, the acuteness of vision, the ability to differentiate colors, and many other sensory functions. Galton also invented many instruments to use in his research, some of which are used in modified form today.

Galton began the first large-scale testing program at his Anthropometric Laboratory in the South Kensington Museum in 1884. Each visitor was charged threepence for having his measurements taken on a variety of physical and sensory tests, including height, weight, breathing power, strength of pull, hearing, seeing, and the color sense. In order to analyze the data obtained, Galton made use of statistical methods. With these, he determined averages and measures of variation. His particular need was for a measure of association, or correlation, to detect the amount of resemblance between the individual characteristics of fathers and their sons. He made the first attempts to derive the statistics of correlation, the procedures which are now widely used in the study of individual differences.

Pearson. Galton supported a younger colleague, Karl Pearson, in the development of statistical methods for the study of individual differences. Pearson was the genius in mathematical statistics that Galton was in studies of individual differences. He derived the correlation coefficient, partial correlation, multiple correlation, factor analysis, and laid the foundation for most of the multivariate statistics which are in use in psychology today (some of which will be seen in the chapters ahead).

Following the work of Galton, the last two decades of the nineteenth century saw a considerable expansion of studies of individual differences, in England and America. Prominent in this work was James McKeen Cattell, who studied with Galton and then undertook investigations in America. The tests continued to be largely of a sensory and motor type, measuring sensory speed and reaction time. Toward the end of the century, it came to be realized that these tests were not measuring intelligence. Scores on the tests bore almost no relationship to measures of intellectual achievement, such as school grades, refuting the hypothesis that sensory ability is closely related to intelligence.

THE FIRST PRACTICAL MENTAL TESTS

A brief summary will be given of the major developments in psychological testing during this century. Each type of test which is mentioned will be discussed in detail in later chapters.

At the turn of the twentieth century, some notable events in the history of psychological measurement occurred in France. It was there that the humanist tradition and the interest in medicine and social welfare were centered. After the French Revolution, terms such as "equality" and "the rights of man" showed the new interest in helping the downtrodden, the sick, and also the psychologically maladjusted. Medicine developed rapidly during the first part of the nineteenth century, partly because of the Napoleonic Wars and the need to treat wounded soldiers. Pinel released the insane from their dungeons and insisted that they were sick, not possessed by demons. Charcot, Janet, and Ribot founded the field of psychiatry and developed the first plausible theories of psychopathology. Freud drew his early knowledge from these men and went on to be the founder of psychoanalysis.

Binet. During the last quarter of the nineteenth century, the distinguished line of French investigators was joined by Alfred Binet. His early work was on the use of hypnotism in treating mental disorders; then near the end of the century, he turned to the problem of measuring intelligence. He was commissioned by the Minister of Public Instruction to construct tests for the measurement of intelligence in school children. The schools had become alarmed by the number of failures and needed some means of distinguishing the lazy or maladjusted from the children who lacked the fundamental capacity to learn.

Binet, working in collaboration with Simon, completed his first test in 1905. The test was not principally concerned with sensory and motor functions as had been the case with the tests of Galton and his immediate followers. Instead, it concerned the child's ability to understand and reason with the objects in his cultural environment. Consequently, the test items were such as the naming of objects, the completion of sentences, and the comprehension of questions.

The first Binet-Simon test had a range of questions from very simple ones, which even the dullest child might answer correctly, to questions which would indicate a superior level of ability. Practical work with the test indicated that some of the items were more difficult than had been anticipated, and some of the items proved to be insensitive to differences in ability. A revision of the test was made in 1908, in which the items were arranged in terms of age levels, with a group of items being designated as representing average intelligence for each particular age. The highest age level at which a child could perform adequately was called his *mental age*. Later, Stern suggested that the mental age be divided by the child's chronological age, which is essentially the *IQ* as it has come to be known.

The Binet-Simon tests aroused considerable interest in other countries, in England and especially in America. Several translations and revisions of the tests were made in America, including forms by Goddard (4) and Kuhlmann (6). The tests became very popular in studying school children, particularly in the understanding of psychological maladjustment and juvenile delinquency. The most prominent revision of the Binet-Simon test was completed by Terman (9) in 1916, the resulting form being referred to as the Stanford-Binet test. For the first time a considerable amount of research was done to select items which would be appropriate for each age level and which would differentiate age levels. Also, the large number of children which was tested provided norms for the interpretation of test scores.

Terman and Merrill presented a revision of the Stanford-Binet in 1937 (10). A truly heroic effort was made to construct a standardized measure of general ability. Several thousand children were tested in all parts of the United States to establish norms. This test has been used more frequently than any other comparable instrument and is still in wide use today. (The Stanford-Binet will be discussed in detail in Chapter 10.)

THE FIRST GROUP TESTS OF ABILITY

The Binet forms and their revisions are all individual tests, requiring an expert examiner to test one child at a time. During the First World War there was a need for classifying large numbers of recruits, to weed out men whose level of ability was so low that they would be a handicap to the service, and also to select more intelligent individuals for positions of responsibility. A special committee of the American Psychological Association, with R. M. Yerkes as chairman, began an investigation of testing procedures for the armed services.

Arthur Otis had been working on a group test of "intelligence," which he turned over to the committee. With some revisions, it was put to use. This test is referred to as the Army Alpha Test (7). It was a short form containing questions on arithmetic, reasoning, and general information. The test proved very successful, came into wide use in the armed forces, and is still used to some extent today. A companion test, the Army Beta (8), was constructed for use with individuals whose knowledge of English is scanty. The test instructions are given in pantomime, and the test items do not require the subject to use or understand English. The test requires the subject to solve geometrical puzzles and to analyze pictures. Although the Beta test was not so successful as the Alpha test, it set the stage for the nonlanguage tests which are in use today.

STANDARDIZED CLASSROOM EXAMINATIONS

The Essay Exam. The standardized classroom examination as we know it today came into wide use only during the last fifty years. Before that time it was customary for the instructor to give grades on the basis of his accumulated impressions of the student or on the basis of oral examinations. Grading in this way can be unfair to the student who is not popular with the teacher or who does not have the verbal facility to impress others. The first standardized examinations were of the "essay" type, in which the student writes about a number of problems or topics. Although grading is still somewhat subjective, the "essay" examination is standardized to the extent that all students receive the same questions, providing a uniform basis of comparison.

The Multiple Choice Examination. Progress in classroom examinations has moved in two directions, in the refinement of essay examinations and in the development of multiple choice tests. The advent of the multiple choice, or "objective" test, as it is sometimes called, ruled out the unreliability of instructors' impressions; and although there are abuses in the use of multiple choice tests, examinations of this kind are at least uniformly fair to all students.

Standardized Achievement Tests. A more recent trend in classroom testing is the use of achievement tests which are constructed by a group of specialists, instead of the teacher, and are applied to all of the children in a school system. This allows a comparison of the children in different classes of the same school and comparison among the children in different schools. Now the teacher can use standardized achievement tests for many different subject matters, ranging from reading ability to knowledge of geography.

THE DEVELOPMENT OF PERSONALITY TESTS

In line with the sequence in which tests were developed, we have talked so far about tests of ability, which concern how much an individual knows, how rapidly he can work, or how well he can solve problems. Tests of this kind are sometimes referred to as "cognitive" tests and have been contrasted with the variety of attributes which are "noncognitive" or not abilities in the strict sense. Cronbach (3) has distinguished these two kinds of attributes as being tests of "maximum performance" as opposed to tests of "habitual performance." You can see how these functions would differ if we were considering a test for "friendliness." It would not be a case of how friendly an individual could be if he tried, because most of us *know* how to be friendly. The question would be that of how friendly an individual habitually is in his dealings with others. Another synonym for noncognitive tests or tests of habitual performance is personality tests. Although the term has come to be used far too broadly to cover interests, attitudes, mental health, and many other matters, it is too firmly in use to be avoided.

Tests of ability were developed first and more firmly not because of a lack of interest in personality but because of the difficulty in measuring the noncognitive functions. Galton was as interested in the inheritance of personality as he was in the inheritance of abilities. However, the nearest he came to measuring personality characteristics was in a questionnaire study of "imagery," concerning the extent to which individuals can picture objects in memory. Binet was interested in tests of personality before constructing the first "intelligence" test, and among other devices, he designed a questionnaire test of "morality" for children.

Self-report Inventories. Psychologists were not only busy during the First World War developing "intelligence" tests, but they also tried to meet the need for tests of neuroticism and emotional instability. The number of recruits was too large to be seen individually in psychiatric interviews. R. S. Woodworth constructed a questionnaire which asked each recruit essentially the kinds of questions that would be used in an interview. The questions concerned the individual's adjustment in the home, school, and among friends. It was used primarily to sift out those men who needed further clinical study, but not, as similar inventories were often used afterward, to provide "measures" of personality. All the difficulties involved in the use of this instrument still continue to hinder the development of personality tests: the individual's inability or unwillingness to describe himself accurately and the difficulties in finding a valid set of items for use with even the most cooperative subjects.

Projective Tests. During the First World War, a Swiss psychiatrist named Hermann Rorschach was working on a novel line in the measurement of personality. The Rorschach Test (see 1), as it has come to be known, consists of 10 ink blots which the subject is required to describe and interpret. The test grew out of Freudian and other "depth" psychologies with their emphasis on unconscious motivation and the importance of symbolism. The purpose of the test is to get beyond what the subject knows about himself, and is willing to relate, to the "deeper" traits and urges which determine his overt behavior. Since Rorschach's pioneer research, numerous other projective techniques have been developed. In spite of the great difficulties in standardizing tests of this kind, the Rorschach and its followers have become the mainstay of the clinical psychologist.

THE PERIOD BETWEEN THE TWO WORLD WARS

As wars have so often been the gloomy milestones in historical developments, the direction of the measurement movement in psychology has changed with the two major conflicts of this century. We saw how the practical problems of the First World War encouraged the development of the first group tests of "intelligence" and personality. The products were inexpensive, convenient tests which could be applied to large numbers of people. Consequently, group tests came into vogue during the 1920s and 1930s and, unfortunately, were often applied uncritically to many problems. There was too little concern for testing the test, too little concern for determining the reliability and validity of the measures. Teachers often took the results of "intelligence" tests at face value and made major decisions about students on the basis of questionable measures. The general public became oversold on tests, and the *IQ* came to be regarded as an infallible and fixed mark on the individual. Numerous tests of personality purporting to measure "introversion," "marriage adjustment," "happiness," and many other complex attributes were constructed and sold with little research foundation. The uncritical overacceptance of tests during that period is not unlike a similar overenthusiasm that has occurred in the development of many other products: we have seen numerous medical discoveries regarded at first as cure-alls then later put to a more limited and more proper use.

FROM THE SECOND WORLD WAR TO THE PRESENT

A great conflict again presented needs for methods of classifying men. However, this time the need was on a much larger scale. Over ten million men and women were called into service, and they had to be allotted to a wide range of positions—jobs in airplane navigation, electronics, and meteorology, which had not existed a decade earlier.

Instead of having to construct only several group tests as had been the case in the previous conflict, psychologists were called on to construct numerous batteries of tests, some of them complicated beyond the extremes of what the early testers might have imagined. Psychologists were brought into the problem wholesale and spent several years in implementing the largest testing program that had ever been undertaken. In the process, the logic and methods of psychological measurement were considerably extended, and many researches were undertaken which would not have been possible without government support. The psychology of testing was pushed years ahead by the work which was undertaken in conjunction with the armed forces. Much of the work was methodological, concerning the best way to measure particular functions, in contrast to the pell-mell effort of earlier decades to compose tests without proper research foundation.

Now we find that the people who construct tests and the people who use them are more aware of the limitations of particular measures, more inquisitive about the research findings on an instrument, and more mindful of alternative approaches. A healthy skepticism has grown, and with it have come promising new lines of investigation in the measurement of individual differences. Testing has become a big business, with numerous firms devoting themselves to the development and sale of tests. Hundreds of psychologists and professional educators spend most of their time as measurement specialists. Psychological publications have hundreds of articles each year on specialized problems in measurement. However, there are still abuses in testing—tests being sold without proper research and a naïve acceptance by some persons of any scrap of paper which purports to be a test. In spite of the remaining abuses and in spite of the unsolved problems in many kinds of tests, psychological tests can now point to an increased efficiency and marked economy which they have brought to schools, the Armed Forces, psychological clinics, and more recently, to industry.

REFERENCES

1. Beck, S. J. *Rorschach's test:* Vol. 1. *Basic processes.* New York: Grune and Stratton, 1944.
2. Boring, E. G. *A history of experimental psychology.* (Rev. ed.) New York: Appleton-Century-Crofts, 1950.
3. Cronbach, L. J. *Essentials of psychological testing.* New York: Harper, 1949.
4. Goddard, H. H. A revision of the Binet scale. *Train. Sch.,* 1911, 8, 56–62.
5. Guilford, J. P. *Psychometric methods.* (2nd ed.) New York: McGraw-Hill, 1954.
6. Kuhlmann, F. A revision of the Binet-Simon system for measuring the inteltelligence of children. *J. Psycho-Asthenics, Monogr. Suppl.,* 1912, 1, 1–41.

7. Otis, A. S. *Otis Quick-Scoring Mental Ability Tests: Manual of Directions for Alpha Test.* Yonkers, N.Y.: World, 1939.
8. Otis, A. S. *Otis Quick-Scoring Mental Ability Tests: Manual of Directions for Beta Test.* Yonkers, N.Y.: World, 1939.
9. Terman, L. M. *The measurement of intelligence.* Boston: Houghton Mifflin, 1916.
10. Terman, L. M., and Merrill, M. *Measuring intelligence: A guide to the administration of the new revised Stanford-Binet tests of intelligence.* Boston: Houghton Mifflin, 1937.

CHAPTER 3

The Use of Scores and Norms

Test results are usually reported in some numerical form, for example, the total number of questions answered correctly on a true-false test. The numbers obtained in this way, before they are converted to any other form, are referred to as raw scores. Raw scores are seldom directly meaningful without some qualification as to how well other persons do or as to the established standards of performance. If Johnny tells his mother that he has made 22 in arithmetic and 48 in spelling, the mother might say, "That's good work in spelling, but we must do something about your arithmetic." But the 22 in arithmetic might have been the highest score; and if the spelling test consisted of 100 words, and the teacher expected the students to know the majority of them, a score of 48 would be an indication of poor performance.

MEASURES OF CENTRAL TENDENCY

The first thing that we need to learn about Johnny's performance is how well the students as a group performed on the two tests. This will tell us whether Johnny is above or below average. To simplify the problem, let us assume that there are only 11 students in the class and that they made scores on the two tests as follows:

	Arithmetic	*Spelling*
Johnny	22	48
Fred	12	52
Mary	14	49
Bill	12	51
Jane	14	55
Susan	14	52
Michael	17	50
Sharon	19	62
Harry	11	56
Patricia	15	52
Eric	20	75

By looking at the list of scores, it can be seen that Johnny did very well in arithmetic in comparison to the other students, but relatively poorly in

35

spelling. However, Johnny's mother would probably not have an opportunity to look at the list of scores; and it would be a clumsy way to make
comparisons if it were necessary to pass around the list to everyone who
was interested in the test results.

Mode. Some index is needed to let the mother know at once whether
Johnny did as well as the other children. One such index, called the *mode,*
is obtained quite simply by finding the score made most frequently by
the students. In the arithmetic test, more students made a score of 14
(Mary, Jane, and Susan) than any other score. The mode is 52 on the
spelling test. Although the mode is not as useful as some other measures,
it is sometimes used in testing as a measure of central tendency.

Median. Another measure of central tendency is obtained by seeking
the score which has an equal number of students above and below that
point. In the arithmetic test, the median is 14. Of the 11 students, five
made scores higher than 14 and six made scores of 14 or less. The *median*
is 52 on the spelling test, and there are three students whose scores fall
exactly at the median. If there is an even number of scores, if we show the
scores for 10 students instead of 11, the median falls between two scores.
If Fred had not taken the arithmetic test, the median would have fallen
between 14 and 15. The usual practice is to split the difference and say
that the median is 14.5. If Johnny's score of 48 were not considered on the
spelling test, the median would again lie between two scores, both of
which are 52. The median would then still be 52.

The median can be thought of as the score made by the "average person." This is different, as will be shown shortly, from the average score.
One advantage of the median is that it is easy to understand. The teacher
would find it relatively easy to explain this index to Johnny's mother, and
it would prove useful in discussing Johnny's class standing.

The reason that the mode and the median are not used more is that they
cannot serve as a basis for the derivation of other statistics which are
needed. If we start off with certain statistical measures instead of others,
it greatly simplifies the mathematical work to follow; and the mode and
median are poor starting points.

Mean. A measure of central tendency can be obtained which is both
easy to understand and can be used in numerous other mathematical
developments. The *mean* is obtained by adding all of the scores on a test
and dividing the sum by the number of persons tested. Introducing some
of the symbolism which will prove useful, let X stand for the raw scores
made on a test, N for the number of subjects, and M for the mean. Then
the formula for the mean is

$$M = \frac{\Sigma X}{N}$$

The summation sign (Σ) stands for the process of adding scores, the scores of Johnny, Fred, Mary, and so on, for the 11 students.

The symbolism can be made more specific by the use of subscripts to show the test on which the mean is being obtained. Letting the arithmetic test be referred to as test 1, the formula for the arithmetic mean can be more completely specified as

$$M_1 = \frac{\Sigma X_1}{N_1}$$

Different subscripts can be used to designate other tests, such as using the subscript 2 in referring to statistical operations on the spelling-test scores, and the subscripts 3, 4, 5, and so on, for other tests.

Applying the formula to the students' grades, a mean of 15.45 is found for the arithmetic test and a mean of 54.73 for the spelling test. A comparison can be made of the three measures of central tendency on the two tests as follows:

	Arithmetic	Spelling
Mode	14	52
Median	14	52
Mean	15.45	54.73

The three measures give similar results on both tests. Note that the mean on the spelling test differs by 2.73 from the median and the mode. Looking back at the scores, it can be seen that seven of the eleven people made less than the mean on spelling. This is due to Eric's performance in spelling, a score so divergent from the others as to affect the mean unduly. It is in situations like this that the mean can cause confusion in the interpretation of test scores.

When either one person or a small group of persons makes scores which are markedly higher or lower than the rest of the group, the median is often more useful than the mean for interpreting test results. Fortunately, such extreme cases as the example above are not often found in practice.

Deviation Scores. As a first step in transforming raw scores to a more useful form, each score can be expressed in terms of its distance from the mean. The transformed scores are referred to as deviation scores and are symbolized by a lower-case x:

$$x = X - M_x$$

The formula states that each person's deviation score is obtained by subtracting the mean from his raw score. The class grades can be transformed to deviation scores as follows:

Arithmetic	Spelling
x_1	x_2
6.55	−6.73
−3.45	−2.73
−1.45	−5.73
−3.45	−3.73
−1.45	.27
−1.45	−2.73
1.55	−4.73
3.55	7.27
−4.45	1.27
− .45	−2.73
4.55	20.27

Deviation scores tell whether an individual is above or below average. Because Johnny's deviation score in arithmetic is positive, we know that he is above the mean; because his deviation score is negative on the spelling test, we know that he is below the mean.

MEASURES OF DISPERSION

Before we can interpret a particular deviation score, we must learn how widely the scores are scattered above and below the mean. A deviation score of 2.00 would represent superior performance if all of the scores are closely packed about the mean. But if there are deviation scores that go as high as +100 and as low as −100, a deviation score of 2.00 would indicate near average performance. Consequently, we need an index of the spread, or scatter of scores about the mean in order to interpret particular deviations.

The Range. There are various indices of how widely a group is scattered, or of the dispersion, as it will be called. One very simple index, the *range*, is obtained by subtracting the lowest score from the highest score. The highest score on the arithmetic test is 22 and the lowest is 11. This gives a range of 11. The range on the spelling test is 27, showing that the dispersion of scores is greater than that in arithmetic. The range is a quickly obtained and often used index of dispersion. However, it lacks some of the properties that are needed for an acceptable measure. It is dependent on only two scores, the highest and the lowest. If Eric had not taken the spelling test, the range would be only 14 instead of 27. Also, the range lacks the mathematical properties which can lead to the development of other statistics (a point to which we will appeal quite often in choosing statistical measures).

The Average Deviation. An index of dispersion which is dependent on all of the scores instead of just two of them and which indicates the position of an individual in a group is the *average deviation*. As the name implies, it is obtained by finding how much the scores deviate on the average from the mean, as follows:

Arithmetic	Spelling	
$|x_1|$	$|x_2|$	$\Sigma|x_1| = 32.35$
6.55	6.73	$AD = \dfrac{32.35}{11}$
3.45	2.73	
1.45	5.73	
3.45	3.73	$AD = 2.94$
1.45	.27	
1.45	2.73	
1.55	4.73	$\Sigma|x_2| = 58.19$
3.55	7.27	$AD = \dfrac{58.19}{11}$
4.45	1.27	
.45	2.73	
4.55	20.27	$AD = 5.29$

The symbol $|x_1|$ indicates that we are dealing with absolute deviations, paying no attention to the signs.

One method of transforming deviation scores to a more useful form is to divide each of them by the average deviation (AD). This conversion will give Johnny a score of 2.23 in arithmetic and -1.27 in spelling. When the distribution of scores is *normal*, scores transformed in this manner will lead to a precise indication of where an individual stands in a group. However, developing this measure further will not be worth the effort. There are more desirable measures of dispersion which can be used; the range and AD have been discussed to provide a background for the measure now to be developed.

The Standard Deviation. The AD has a serious fault: it is based on absolute scores. It is very difficult to work mathematically with absolute scores; and consequently, if the AD is used in some of the early statistical work, it severely limits the development of other measures. However, we will also find ourselves blocked if we seek a measure of dispersion by working with the deviation scores. The sum of these is always zero in any set of scores. Therefore, equations based on the sum of deviation scores "fall apart" and leave nothing with which the mathematician can work.

An alternative to using either x scores or $|x|$ scores is that of working with the squared deviations. These will all be positive, and it also happens that they provide an excellent starting place for the derivation of many other statistics. The squared deviations on the two tests are

$x_1{}^2$	$x_2{}^2$
42.90	45.26
11.90	7.45
2.10	32.83
11.90	13.91
2.10	.07
2.10	7.45
2.40	22.37
12.60	52.85
19.80	1.61
.20	7.45
20.70	410.87
$\Sigma x_1{}^2 = 128.70$	$\Sigma x_2{}^2 = 602.12$

The *mean square deviation* can be obtained by summing the squared deviations and dividing by the number of persons who took the test. This statistic is called the *variance* and is symbolized as σ^2:

$$\sigma^2 = \frac{\Sigma x^2}{N}$$

An even more useful statistic is obtained by taking the square root of the variance, which is then called the *standard deviation:*

$$\sigma = \sqrt{\frac{\Sigma x^2}{N}}$$

Applying the formula to the arithmetic and spelling tests, the following variances and standard deviations are found:

Arithmetic	Spelling
$\sigma^2 = \dfrac{128.70}{11}$	$\sigma^2 = \dfrac{602.12}{11}$
$\sigma^2 = 11.70$	$\sigma^2 = 54.74$
$\sigma = 3.42$	$\sigma = 7.40$

Subscripts can be used with the variance and standard deviation formulas to indicate which test is being studied, like using σ_1 to refer to the standard deviation of the scores on a particular test.

The standard deviation and variance can be obtained without actually going through the step of converting from raw to deviation scores, as follows:

$$\sigma^2 = \frac{\Sigma(X - M)^2}{N}$$

$$\sigma^2 = \frac{\Sigma X^2}{N} - \left(\frac{\Sigma X}{N}\right)^2$$

Identical results will be obtained by either approach, showing here at an early stage the mathematical maneuverability that is gained by working with squared deviations.

THE EFFECT OF LINEAR TRANSFORMATIONS ON THE MEAN AND STANDARD DEVIATION

If an arbitrary number were added to each of the raw scores in a distribution, how would this change the mean and standard deviation? For example, we could add the number 5 to each of the arithmetic scores mentioned earlier. The new mean would then be 5 more than the original mean. The proof of this is simple:

$$M_X = \frac{\Sigma X}{N}$$

$$M_{(X+C)} = \frac{\Sigma(X+C)}{N}$$

$$= \frac{\Sigma X + \Sigma C}{N}$$

$$= \frac{\Sigma X}{N} + \frac{\Sigma C}{N}$$

$$= \frac{\Sigma X}{N} + \frac{NC}{N}$$

$$= \frac{\Sigma X}{N} + C$$

$$= M_X + C$$

where C stands for any *constant*, such as 5

$M_{(X+C)}$ stands for the mean of the scores after the constant is added to each score in turn

If then the mean of the original scores is 10, and we add 5 to each of the scores, the new mean is 15. (The student should work out the simple proofs on his own. Not only will they prove relatively "painless"; but by thoroughly understanding the steps in the simple proofs, it will be easier to follow more complex statistical developments.)

Next we can determine what happens to the standard deviation when a constant is added to each of the scores. We could derive this from the raw score formula; but since we know that the standard deviation is the same whether it is determined from raw or deviation scores, it will be simpler to work with the deviation score formula.

$$\sigma^2_{(x+C)} = \frac{\Sigma[(x+C) - M_{(x+C)}]^2}{N}$$

What the formula shows is that from each new score, which will be the original deviation score plus the quantity C, is subtracted the mean of the new scores. The mean of the original deviation scores is zero by definition. Then the mean of the new scores is C, so we can rewrite the formula as

$$\sigma_{(x+C)} = \sqrt{\frac{\Sigma(x+C-C)^2}{N}}$$

which reduces to

$$\sigma_{(x+C)} = \sqrt{\frac{\Sigma x^2}{N}}$$

This is the same formula used to obtain the standard deviation of the original scores. We have then proved that the standard deviation is unchanged if we add or subtract a constant from each of the scores. If then the standard deviation of a set of scores is 2, and we add 5 to each of them, the new standard deviation is also 2.

Next we can see what will happen if each of the scores is multiplied by a constant. The mean would then become

$$M_{(CX)} = \frac{\Sigma(CX)}{N}$$

Because a constant term can always be moved to the left of a summation sign,

$$M_{(CX)} = \frac{C\Sigma X}{N}$$

$$= C\left(\frac{\Sigma X}{N}\right)$$

$$= CM_X$$

We have proved that if each score is multiplied by a constant, the mean of the new scores equals the mean of the old scores times the constant. If then the mean of the original scores is 10, and we multiply each score by 3, the new mean is 30.

The effect on the standard deviation of multiplying each score by a constant is as follows:

$$\sigma_{(Cx)} = \sqrt{\frac{\Sigma(Cx)^2}{N}}$$

$$= \sqrt{\frac{\Sigma C^2 x^2}{N}}$$

$$= \sqrt{C^2\left(\frac{\Sigma x^2}{N}\right)}$$

$$= C \sqrt{\frac{\Sigma x^2}{N}}$$

$$= C\sigma_x$$

The standard deviation of the new scores will be C times as large as the old standard deviation. If then the standard deviation of the original scores is 2, and we multiply each score by 3, the new standard deviation is 6. The student should satisfy himself that the variance will increase by the square of the constant.

We have taken the time to derive these results for several reasons. The mean and standard deviation will be seen many times in the discussion of test results, and it is important to understand their properties. Knowing how these statistics are affected by linear transformations will allow us to make many computational short cuts without having to re-compute mean and standard deviation. Also, the simple proofs which are involved here demonstrate some of the manipulations which, when applied to more complex equations, permit us to derive many useful results.

SCORE DISTRIBUTIONS

The Normal Distribution. The standard deviation is most easily interpreted when working with a normal distribution of scores. The normal distribution, or *normal curve,* as it is sometimes called, was mentioned in Chapter 2, but no fuller explanation was given at that time. The normal distribution refers to the way in which the score frequencies fall. Instead of listing test scores, as we did with the arithmetic and spelling tests, the same information could have been given by specifying the number of persons who obtained each score. Using the symbol f to stand for frequency, frequency distributions for the two tests are as follows:

Arithmetic			Spelling	
X_1	f		X_2	f
22	1		75	1
21	0		..	.
20	1		..	.
19	1		62	1
18	0		..	.
17	1		..	.
16	0		56	1
15	1		55	1
14	3		54	0
13	0		53	0
12	2		52	3
11	1		51	1
			50	1
			49	1
			48	1

The frequency distributions are presented graphically in Figure 3–1. There are not enough scores to indicate much about the distribution form for either test. However, when there are many scores instead of just eleven, the shape of the distribution begins to become apparent. If we had given the arithmetic test to 200 students, the distribution of scores in arithmetic might have looked like that in Figure 3–2. In Figure 3–2 it

Figure 3–1. Frequency distributions for arithmetic and spelling tests.

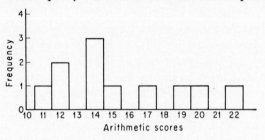

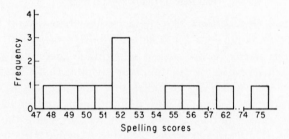

Figure 3–2. Hypothetical frequency distribution of arithmetic scores for 200 students.

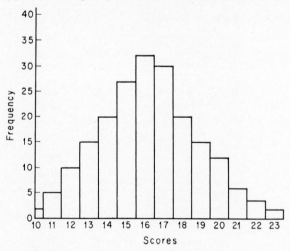

can be seen that most of the scores are clustered around 16, and that scores become fewer and fewer as we go either toward high scores or toward low scores.

As the scores in Figure 3–2 are drawn, they resemble the normal distribution. The standard deviation tells the number of persons whose scores fall in different regions of the normal curve. Figure 3–3 shows

FIGURE 3–3. Per cents * of subjects in various regions of the normal distribution.

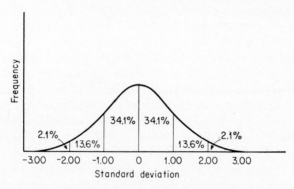

* **The per cents add up to 99.6 instead of 100 because a fraction of 1 per cent of the cases lies above and below three standard deviations.**

that approximately 68 per cent of the persons make scores between plus one and minus one standard deviations and 95 per cent of the scores fall between plus two and minus two standard deviations. A detailed breakdown of the percentages of scores in various regions of the normal distribution is presented in Appendix 3. It will prove useful in interpreting the many statistics based on the normal distribution.

Standard Scores. A very useful type of score can be obtained by dividing an individual's deviation score on a test by the standard deviation of the scores.

$$z = \frac{x}{\sigma_x} \quad \text{or} \quad z = \frac{X - M_x}{\sigma_x}$$

where z symbolizes the standard score.

Applying the formula to Johnny's arithmetic score we find

$$z = \frac{22 - 15.45}{3.42}$$

$$= \frac{6.55}{3.42}$$

$$= 1.9$$

An individual's standard score indicates his place in the frequency distribution (if the distribution of scores is approximately normal). If a person has a standard score of 2.1, this indicates that his score is above two standard deviations, and that about 98 per cent of the subjects made lower scores. Similarly, a person who makes a standard score of less than −1.0 is lower than 84 per cent of the subjects.

When the raw scores on different tests are converted to standard scores, they have the same mean, which is zero in all cases. What is the standard deviation of a set of standard scores? Because of the way in which standard scores are obtained, the standard deviation of any set of standard scores is 1.00.

Converting raw scores to standard scores makes results comparable from test to test. If an individual makes a standard score which is positive on two tests, then we know that he did better than average on both tests. If he makes a standard score of 1.00 on one test and 1.50 on another, we know that he performed better on the second test.

Transformed Standard Scores. For practical purposes, it is often useful to express test scores by a modification of z scores. A teacher might have difficulty in explaining to a student's mother that a standard score of zero meant average performance rather than zero performance. Also, the negative values which are obtained with standard scores are difficult for some persons to understand. Starting with a set of standard scores, and knowing what we do about transformations, we can derive a new set of scores with any mean and standard deviation that we like. If we desire to have the scores in such a form that the mean is 100 and the standard deviation is 10, the first step is to multiply all the standard scores by 10. Then 100 is added to each of the resulting scores. If it is desired to compare the scores on two tests which have different means and standard deviations, the mean and standard deviation of one test can be made the same as the other. It proves much easier to make transformations directly on raw scores rather than having to compute standard scores first. A formula for this is given in Appendix 2.

Rank-order Scores. In Chapter 1, it was said that psychological measures are sometimes expressed in the form of ranks. Ranks are often used to describe test scores when the number of subjects is not large. If a mother is told that her daughter made the fifth highest score in a class of eleven, she can easily understand how well the daughter performed in comparison to the other children.

The scores on the arithmetic and spelling tests can be expressed as ranks. Because Johnny made the highest score on the arithmetic test, his score would become rank 1. Eric would have rank 2, Sharon would have rank 3, and so on. When several persons make the same score, the individual is given the average of the ranks for the group. There are three persons who have scores of 14 in arithmetic. They must share the ranks of 6, 7, and 8. The mean of these three ranks is 7, and consequently all three persons would be given a rank of 7. There are two people with scores of 12, and they must share the ranks of 9 and 10. They are each given a rank of 9.5. The lowest score, that made by Harry, is then given a rank of 11.

Percentile Ranks. When the number of scores is large, if we are treating 200 scores instead of 11, it proves useful to make a conversion of ranks. One useful conversion is to express each individual's score in terms of the per cent of scores which are lower. If an individual ranks fourth among 200 persons, then 196 persons rank lower. Dividing 196 by 200, we find that the individual has a percentile score of 98. Because several or more persons will usually make the same score, a modification of the basic formula is often used to take account of tied ranks. The formula is to divide the number of people below a particular score, plus half the number of people who make the score, by the total number of subjects. Scores obtained in this way are referred to as "midpoint percentile ranks."

Percentile scores, like ranks, are useful in explaining test results to individuals who have little background in the statistics of testing. However, they are awkward for other statistical manipulations that might be needed. Percentiles provide no indication of the distance between scores. There might be a wide gap in raw scores between the person who has a percentile score of 70 and the person who has a percentile score of 71, but this would not be seen from the percentile scores alone. Percentile scores underemphasize the differences between scores on the extremes of the distribution. Looking back at Figure 3–3, you can see that only about 2 per cent of the cases fall between standard scores of 2.00 and 3.00. These standard scores would be equal to percentile ranks of about 97 and 99. Although the scores appear to be separated by only a trivial amount when expressed in terms of percentiles, we can see that in terms of standard scores there is a wide separation.

FIGURE 3–4. Frequency distribution of percentile scores.

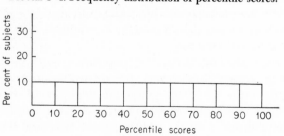

What is the distribution form of a set of percentile scores? An equal per cent of the subjects make scores between 99 and 90 percentiles as between the 89 and 80 percentiles, and so on. Consequently, the frequency distribution is flat, or rectangular as it is called (see Figure 3–4).

NORMS

Although standard scores or percentile scores would give a good indication of where Johnny stands in relation to his 10 classmates, it would still be a question as to how well Johnny performs in relation to the students in other schools. It may be that Johnny is in a particularly bright class, in which average performance means high performance in comparison to other classes. It might be that Johnny goes to school in a "well-to-do" neighborhood where the children as a group are well above the community average. To dramatize the specificity of scores in a particular setting, we can imagine the problems involved in testing a class composed of geniuses. Because of the mechanics of obtaining standard scores and percentiles, half the students would inevitably come out "below average." But, of course, below average performance for geniuses would mean superior performance in a group of less gifted children.

Normative Populations. In order to understand how well a child performs on a test, it is often necessary to compare his score with the scores made by children in previous years and the scores made by children in a range of localities. In order to interpret the test score made by an applicant for a particular branch of the Armed Forces, it would be necessary to compare his score with the scores of many other applicants. The larger group to which an individual is compared is called a *normative population.*

The collection of people which constitutes a normative population is determined by the use to which the scores will be put. If achievement test scores are being used to place students in special high school study programs in a particular city, the normative population should contain students from all of the grammar schools in the city. If a selection test for the Armed Forces is being used to select individuals for pilot training, the normative population should contain the individuals who have previously applied for pilot training.

On some occasions, the normative population must be quite large. When selecting students for college, the normative population consists, at least hypothetically, of all the graduating high school students in the United States. Later we will see that in order to interpret the scores on a particular "intelligence" test, the test was given to several thousand children in all parts of the country. In other testing situations, the normative population may be quite small. To interpret the results of a course examination, the teacher may need only to make comparisons with the scores made by several previous classes.

Scoring in Respect to Norms. It is often more meaningful to compare an individual's test score with the scores obtained from a normative population rather than with some smaller and less representative group. In this case, an individual's standard score would be determined by a comparison with the mean and standard deviation of the normative population. Similarly, percentile scores would be determined by the scores found in the normative population. Instead of going through the labor of actually computing such scores for each new individual, it is easier to compose a table which allows a direct conversion of raw scores to standard scores or percentile scores.

Sampling of Scores. The group of persons actually tested is usually small in comparison with the total number of persons in the normative population. Seldom will there be test scores for all of the individuals who could conceivably be included. Even several thousand children is a small group in comparison with the many millions in this country. The norms obtained from a sample are then only estimates of the norms which would be obtained from the entire normative population.

Sampling Bias. When choosing a sample for constructing norms, it is important to select a group which is as representative as possible of the normative population. The sample would be biased if all of the tests were given at one school, because, as we said earlier, the particular school might be above or below average for the community as a whole. If the sample is meant to represent all of the children in the United States, it must be ensured that there is a balance of children from all sections of the country, that there is a proportionate representation of urban and rural children, and that all races and ethnic groups are included.

One way of ensuring a representative sample is to choose the subjects randomly from the normative population. This might be feasible in establishing norms for the performance of students in one city. It would be possible to randomly select, say, 500 of the children as a sample. On any larger scale it is not feasible to gather a completely random sample. It is at least conceivable that a sample of the children in the United States could be obtained by selecting randomly from all of the millions of children. But this would be prohibitively expensive and time consuming. It might be necessary to go several hundred miles just to test one subject who, because of the sampling procedure, was chosen from a remote region. When, as is usually the case, it is not feasible to use a completely random sample, there are alternative sampling methods which can be applied. Some of these will be discussed in Chapter 13.

Sampling Error. Regardless of how representative the sample, results obtained from a sample can only estimate the true norms in the population. If we find the mean and standard deviation of a test in a sample, it must be considered how much these estimates are likely to be in error. As in all sampling problems, the larger the number of cases (more items in the sampling of content and more persons in the sampling of scores) the less the estimates will be in error.

The Sampling Distribution of the Mean. In an ideal situation, it is possible to determine the error that will be involved in making estimates from a sample. In this situation, it would be necessary to know in advance the statistics, here the mean and standard deviation, which would be obtained in the entire population. This would be the case where tests were given to all of the subjects in a population. Samples of the tests could be drawn randomly just to see how much the mean and standard deviations of the samples would depart from the actual mean and standard deviations which are known to exist in the population. We could draw out samples of different sizes to see how much more error is involved in the ones which have a relatively small number of people.

If we drew 100 samples with 50 test scores in each, the *sample means* could be plotted in a frequency distribution and compared with the *population mean.* We would find a distribution resembling that in Figure 3–5. In Figure 3–5 we see that the distribution of means is like

FIGURE 3–5. Distribution of sample means about the population mean.

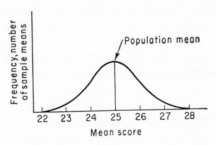

the normal distribution. If the sample is not biased, the mean of the sample means will approximately coincide with the population mean. Figure 3–5 shows that the means obtained from samples cluster about the population mean, and the means which are extremely different from the population mean will be found infrequently.

Another example could be made in which each of the 100 samples would contain the scores of 200 persons. The 100 means could be obtained and plotted like those in Figure 3–5. Again we would expect to find a near normal distribution, with the mean of the sample means very close to the population mean. However, because each sample now contains 200 instead of 50 persons, we would expect to find the distribution of means clustered more tightly about the population mean. Because of the greater stability obtained from a sampling of 200 persons, it would be surprising to find sample means which deviated by as much as 2 score points from the population mean.

In the same way that a standard deviation can be computed for any group of scores, a distribution of means can also provide a standard deviation. We would expect the standard deviation of the means for the samples of 50 persons to be larger than the standard deviation of the means for the samples of 200 persons. In fact it would be about twice as large.

If, as in our ideal example here, we knew the mean and standard deviation of the population, we could determine what would be the standard deviation of the means for a particular sample size, without going to the trouble of drawing samples and computing means. The standard deviation of the means, usually called the *standard error of the mean,* would be very useful in specifying the accuracy of norms. For example, if we know that the population mean is 25 and the standard error of the mean is 1, then we can tell how rarely means of a particular size could be obtained from samples. Working backward, if we know the standard error of the mean for a particular sample size and know the mean of one sample, we can state the likelihood with which the population mean will differ from the sample mean by any number of score units.

Unfortunately, in nearly all practical work with norms, only the mean and standard deviation can be obtained for one sample. There are statistical techniques for working backward from sample values to the standard error of the mean. A standard error can also be obtained for the standard deviation, to determine the extent to which the standard deviation obtained from a sample is likely to be divergent from the population standard deviation. To explain these procedures in detail would take us far afield from the central topics of tests and measurements. The purpose here is to make the reader aware of the existence of sampling error and its influence on norms. There are numerous books devoted primarily to sampling error (see **1, 2, 3**), where detailed procedures are given for estimating the accuracy of norms.

Age Norms. We discussed previously how percentile scores and standard scores could be used to express norms. In some situations it is desirable to express norms in terms of children's ages. One such set of norms could be obtained by testing the vocabulary of children at all ages from four to twelve years. For this purpose, a list of 100 words varying in difficulty could be used. The mean score could be obtained for each age group separately. A graphic plot of these might look like that in

Figure 3–6. Figure 3–6 shows, for example, that seven-year-old children have a larger vocabulary than five- and six-year-old children, as would be expected. Age norms would prove useful in interpreting the vocabulary score made by a particular child. Suppose that he is seven years old and has a vocabulary score of 25. The mean score for the seven-year-olds in the normative sample is 30. We can then look to find the age group which corresponds to a score of 25. Although there is no age group whose mean falls exactly at this point, we can work as though the curve were continuous throughout all age levels and determine the fractional age group that would correspond to a particular score. Reading from Figure 3–6, it can be seen that an age of approximately 6.5 would correspond to a score of 25. It then can be said that the seven-year-old boy has the vocabulary of a six and one-half year old. Age norms fit in well with the way in which we customarily think about the progress of children, and they are, therefore, very useful in the interpretation of test scores.

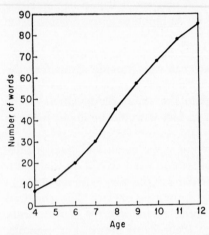

FIGURE 3–6. Mean vocabulary scores of children at each age from four to twelve years.

Mental Age. Age norms are employed with some of the "general intelligence" tests, such as the Stanford-Binet. By comparing a child's score with age norms, it can be determined whether he is more or less "intelligent" than the average child of his age. A score which is compared in this way with age norms is referred to as a *mental age*. If a six-year-old child performs as well as the average seven-year-old child, he is said to have a mental age of seven. Similarly, the six-year-old who performs only at the level of the average five-year-old would be said to have a mental age of five.

The term mental age is somewhat misleading. It gives the impression that the score which a child makes on an intelligence test is a direct measure of total ability. Although tests of this kind have worked well in practice, it is not reasonable to believe that they measure all that could be considered intelligence. Even though there is a tendency for children to score much the same on different intelligence tests, especially those which depend heavily on the use and understanding of language, the correspondence is far from perfect. Therefore, a child's mental age is partly a function of the test which is employed.

Grade Norms. A set of norms which is very similar to age norms can be obtained by finding the mean scores for children in various grade levels. If a standard spelling test were given to children in the fourth through eighth grades, the means could be plotted by grades much as they were plotted by ages in Figure 3–6. Comparing an individual's score with grade norms gives the teacher an indication of how well the pupil is progressing.

Quotient Scores as Norms. By dividing an individual's mental age by his chronological age, a score is obtained which is called an *intelligence quotient,* or as it has come to be known, the *IQ*. If an eight-year-old child does as well on an intelligence test as the average ten-year-old, then he would have an *IQ* of 125. The formula for obtaining the *IQ* is then

$$IQ = \frac{MA}{CA} \times 100$$

where *MA* stands for mental age

CA stands for chronological age

In spite of the wide use and popularity of the *IQ* there are a number of misleading connotations which it bears. Because the *IQ* is a ratio, a ratio of *MA* to *CA*, it suggests that a ratio scale is available for intelligence. Not only is it questionable whether or not the term intelligence should be used with the available tests, but it is certainly unwise to consider *IQ* scores as constituting a ratio scale. How unwise this is becomes evident when we consider the *IQ* of a child who got none of the items correct on the test. Such a child would certainly be retarded, but it makes no sense to say that his intelligence is zero.

The *IQ* is misleading when applied to adults. It has been found that an individual's score on an intelligence test grows until the late teens and then levels off. If a twenty-year-old individual has an *IQ* of 150, this cannot be interpreted to mean that he has a level of ability equal to that of the average thirty-year-old.

The *IQ* is most correctly considered as a transformed standard score. The mean *IQ* on the Stanford-Binet is approximately 100 (as it should be if the test is properly standardized) and the average standard deviation is approximately 16. This is the same distribution that would be obtained by multiplying a set of standard scores by 16 and then adding 100 to each. However, if the *IQ* is to be construed as a transformed standard score, it is necessary that the standard deviation be the same for all tests which use such scores. This is unfortunately not the case. In other words, if one person makes an *IQ* of 120 on Test A, and another individual makes an *IQ* of 115 on Test B, it is entirely possible that the latter individual has a higher standard score (due to a difference in standard deviations of *IQ*'s on the two tests).

If Bill tries all 40 items and gets 24 correct, the correction would be

$$R_c = \frac{24 - .2 \times 40}{.8}$$

$$= 20$$

Both of the boys "knew" twenty of the questions. John guessed at ten of the items and got the expected percentage correct, achieving a score of 22. Bill was more willing to guess. Because he guessed on 20 items, he obtained a score of 24. The example illustrates the situation in which the correction for guessing is most necessary, when the subjects are allowed to attempt as many items as they choose. If a test is constructed on that basis, the correction for guessing should be applied to the scores. However, there is usually little reason for allowing subjects to answer only as many questions as they choose. It is much easier to instruct them to answer all questions whether they know the answers or not. Then T becomes the same for all students; and if one student gets more items correct than another, he will maintain a higher score after the correction is made.

It should be remembered that the correction for guessing is only an estimate based on the *expected* effect of guessing. If an individual flipped a coin to decide the answers on a true-false test, the expectation is that he will get 50 per cent correct. However, this would be so only on the average. Luck might have it that the individual would get all of the items correct or none of them correct. The effect of guessing is then not only to distort the scores, overestimating the scores of the persons who know the least, but it introduces a certain amount of randomness, or "error," into the scores. This and other sources of error in test scores will be discussed in Chapter 6.

REFERENCES

1. Dixon, W. J., and Massey, F. J. *Introduction to statistical analysis*. New York: McGraw-Hill, 1951.
2. Lindquist, E. F. *A first course in statistics*. (Rev. ed.) Boston: Houghton Mifflin, 1942.
3. Walker, Helen M. *Elementary statistical methods*. New York: Holt, 1943.

CHAPTER 4

The Evaluation of Psychological Measures

In these times, it would be difficult to find someone who has not had first-hand experience with psychological measures. Course examinations in school are examples of psychological measures. The aptitude tests which you might have taken in applying for college, for a branch of the Armed Forces, or for a particular job are psychological measures. You might have taken personality inventories which classify you as an "extra-vert" or "introvert," or seen ink blot and other less direct personality tests. You have probably taken sensory tests of various kinds, for example, the test for acuity of vision that is required in many states for a driver's license. Perhaps you have participated in psychological experiments in which you were required to place pegs in a peg board, react as quickly as possible to a light signal, or solve a problem in the shortest possible time. These are all within the area of psychological measurement.

Testing the Test. Tests should be held suspect until their worth is proved. Tests that purport to measure intelligence, anxiety, and social adjustment may not measure those characteristics at all. If there are a number of ways in which a measure can be obtained, a method is needed for deciding the relative merits of the different approaches. This takes us into the subject of test validation.

Psychological measures differ markedly in the extent to which their usefulness is self-evident. On one extreme, tests of auditory acuity have a relatively direct meaning and importance. If the tests indicate that a person has very low acuity, he would probably fail in a job that required good hearing. Also, it is a safe bet that this person would have difficulty in receiving phone messages, in working as a telegrapher, and in trying to understand radio programs.

At the opposite extreme, where the meaning of the test results is not at all self-evident, are some of the personality tests. What does it mean when an individual describes an ink blot as looking like a butterfly? In this case it is necessary to show a connection between the test response and what the individual does in daily life. It is necessary to show that the test predicts something, in the broad sense of the word.

Starting with the distinction between measures that stand for themselves and those which must prove their ability to predict, the outline
in Table 4–1 shows how different kinds of psychological measures are
constructed and appraised.

TABLE 4–1. OUTLINE OF VALIDATION PROCEDURES FOR THE USE OF PREDICTORS
AND ASSESSMENTS

	Predictors	Assessments
Purpose	Prediction of behavior	Measurement of behavior
Standard of validity	Demonstration of predictive power	Demonstration of representative- ness
Validation procedure	Correlation with an assessment (a criterion)	Sampling of content
Construction	Hypothesis; collection of items; finding the best items	Definition: a. Actions to be measured b. Persons who stand high and low in the measure
Examples	Aptitude tests Personality tests General intelligence tests Special ability tests: musical aptitude, art judgment, manual dexterity, etc.	Achievement tests School examinations Job ratings Work records Work samples All criteria for evaluating predictors
	Attitude tests Interest tests Opinion surveys	

The remainder of the book will be largely devoted to filling in the outline
in detail.

EVALUATION OF ASSESSMENTS

Assessments [1] are measures in their own right. If the instructor in a
particular course gives you a final grade of *A*, then you have been as-

---

[1] The reader should be careful to distinguish the meaning of the term "assessment"
as it is used here from the misleading use of the term that often appears in the psychological literature. For example, the term "personality assessment" is often used
when the instruments themselves are really predictor tests. Some psychologists use the
term "content validity" to refer to the procedures which are described in this chapter
for the validation of assessments.

sessed, or measured, in your course achievement. When an employer promotes one of his salesmen, the salesman has been assessed in regard to his performance. When the manager of a baseball team retains some of his players and sends others to a minor league, the players have been assessed by the manager. In each of these cases, the measure of performance is determined by someone who has the right, or the responsibility, to decide what is good and bad in the particular situation. The course instructor decides that a test of a particular form will best measure what he wants to be measured. Perhaps the salesman is promoted because he sells more articles than other salesmen. The baseball players might be retained in terms of a statistical complex of batting average, number of errors, runs batted in, or whatever else the manager chooses to consider. An assessment has an immediate importance, at least to the person who is being assessed and who stands to gain or lose from the outcome.

The Standards for an Assessment. We might disagree with the way in which particular assessments are made, arguing, in terms of our previous examples, that there are better ways to construct course examinations, better ways in which to decide on the promotion of salesmen, and better ways to determine the effectiveness of baseball players. What evidence could we use in our arguments? The most pertinent point to make in criticizing an assessment is to question the extent to which the assessment represents important types of performance.

The course examination might be criticized by examining the content of the questions and comparing these with the subject matter of the course. If the examination is in American history, it might be possible to point out that no questions are included on the effect of the mechanical revolution on American culture, or other omissions of this kind might be noted. Another point of criticism would be to argue that certain of the examination questions concern issues which are less important than others that might be included. The standard that an assessment should meet is that of *content representativeness* for the achievement which it seeks to measure.

Similar arguments could be made about the representativeness of the yardsticks used in assessing the salesmen and the baseball players. We might argue with the sales manager that there are other things to consider in addition to the number of sales made. It might be pointed out that it helps the company more when sales are made of particular new products, ones that the company wants to introduce to the public. Another argument might be that some salesmen build more good will in their work, perhaps forsaking some sales to gain the long-range trust of the client. We might argue with the baseball manager that he fails to include some important types of performance in his assessments, that factors such as how well players stand up in "close" games, how many errors a player causes for the other team, and how much the player contributes to team morale should also be considered.

The Sampling of Content. Using the word "content" to stand broadly for all of the possible things that could be taken into consideration in making an assessment, it is apparent that the content of an assessment is only a sample of the total content which could be considered. It is a sample in the sense that the number of items or points of consideration in the assessment is very small in comparison with the many that are involved in most complex performance situations. The history examination conceivably could include every fact stated in the textbook, plus those given in the class lectures, plus the many questions that could be asked about the relationships between the facts.

Although the course examination is a sample of the total course material, it is seldom a randomly chosen set of questions. If the purpose were to select randomly chosen bits of the things that met the student's eye during the semester, it would be sensible to use questions like, "What is the middle initial of the author of the text?" "Where was the text printed?" "Whose picture is on page 75?" Of course, materials of this kind would not be likely to find their way into an examination, and the reason is that the sampling is restricted to items that are judged to be important by the instructor. We will talk at greater length about the sampling of content when classroom examinations are considered in Chapter 8.

Defining an Assessment. The sampling of content for an assessment inevitably involves human judgment and human values. That is why the outline in Table 4–1 states that the construction of an assessment begins with a definition, a definition of what is desirable in a particular performance setting. Sometimes the valuing is done by one person only, and it can be done arbitrarily if he chooses. The business executive who takes the responsibility of hiring and firing, promoting and demoting, may use only his own impression of the individual's achievement. In this case, the assessment is defined in terms of the personal likes and dislikes of one individual.

In other situations, the assessment is defined cooperatively by a number of persons. Some of the school achievement tests illustrate this. The test might be the joint product of, say, a number of history teachers, who try to come to an agreement about the important course material. The definition, or the statement of what is valued, might be explicitly set out in outline form and rules might be established as to how the examination questions should be presented. Regardless of how explicitly the assessment is defined or the extent to which the assessment is a joint effort, the assessment stands as a definition of what is "good" or what is valued in a particular situation.

An assessment can be defined most explicitly if it is possible to state the actions, or behaviors, which constitute successful performance. The several illustrative assessment situations which we have spoken of so far were defined in terms of actions. For the salesman, successful actions consist of selling products. Success for the history student depends on answering the examination questions correctly. The successful baseball player performs the actions of making hits, stealing bases, and making put-outs. When assessments are defined in terms of actions, it is relatively easy for people to examine and discuss the assessment content.

In many assessment situations, the actions which make for successful performance are difficult to state. What actions are involved in being a successful floorwalker in a department store, naval captain, or chef? Members of these professions are certainly assessed in terms of performance and some given positions of more and some of less responsibility. Occupations such as these are difficult to define in terms of concrete actions, and there are often legitimate reasons for disagreeing about who is successful and who is unsuccessful in each. It would be hard to defend the salesman who never sold an article; but even though you might find the products of a particular chef to be less than desirable, there may be others who relish his fare.

If the assessment cannot be explicitly defined in terms of actions, then it must at least be definable in terms of persons, in terms of those who are relatively successful and unsuccessful. We would want to know whether the people who judge the effectiveness of naval captains agree about the assessment of each of the captains. If the assessment rests with a group of higher-ranking officers, each of them could be asked to rate or rank-order 50 naval captains as to their performance. If the separate ratings agree highly, if Captain Smith is rated high by all of the judges and Captain Green is rated as relatively ineffective in his duties, and so on for the captains in between, it can be said that there is a *reliable* assessment being made. We would then know that the same or very similar actions are probably being considered by each of the judges, even though the judges are not capable of stating what these actions are.

Criterion Research. If the ordering of people on the assessment proves to be reliable, there is something that the measurement specialist can do to make the assessment more explicit. He can perform research to learn some of the actions which constitute successful performance. The behavior of 50 successful naval captains could be studied and compared with that of 50 captains who had been judged to be relatively unsuccessful in their duties. Studies could be made of the way in which the successful captains organize their commands, the kinds of responsibility which they designate to particular officers, the systems of communications which they set in operation for handling emergencies, and so on for the many places in which successful officers might differentiate themselves from unsuccessful officers.

The set of "critical behaviors" or "critical incidents" which are found could be used in an assessment rating scale, like the following:

	Yes	No
Does the officer supervise the ship's navigation rather than leave it to other officers?	_____	_____
Does the officer instruct his men about their behavior when off the ship?	_____	_____
Does the officer try to keep informed on new technical developments?	_____	_____
Does the officer discipline his subordinates in the company of crew members?	_____	_____
Does the officer consider the grades made by the men in specialized courses when recommending promotions?	_____	_____

A longer list of actions or behaviors of this kind could be used by judges in making assessments. Although such a list of critical behaviors would not be completely satisfactory to all of the judges nor would there be assurance that important actions were not being overlooked, the list would be at least a start in making the assessment more explicit.

EVALUATING A PREDICTOR

The score that an individual makes on a predictor test has no necessary importance in its own right. Consider the following type of test material.

Circle every group of dots that has exactly four dots.

Do as many as you can in ten seconds.

```
...  ....  ....  ..  ....  ..  .....  ....  .....  ...  ....  ....  ...  ....
......  ....  ....  ........  ......  ....  ...  ....  .....  ..  .  ....  ....
...  ....  ....  ...  ..  ...  .........  ...  ....  ...  ....  ..  ....  ....
...  ......  ....  ........  ...  ..  ......  ....  ....  ......  ....  ......
........  ....  ......  ...  ....  ......  ....  ......  ...  ....  ...  .....
```

Although scores on a test of this kind would have no obvious meaning, it can be shown that they would predict performance on certain clerical jobs. Employers would, of course, have little interest in the ability of prospective employees to circle groups of dots. Their purpose is to select applicants who will later prove to be good workers. The purpose of tests of this kind is to predict, or forecast, how well individuals will perform, or how highly they will be assessed, in important situations. The assessment which a particular test is intended to predict is called the *validation criterion*.

It should be understood that the term "prediction" [2] is being used in the broad sense to encompass functional relationships of all kinds. A test could conceivably be used to "predict" what people have done in the past, in the same way that the detective gathers clues to "predict" who committed a crime. Also, tests could be used to "predict" how people behaved when they were children. Tests are often used to "predict" a current condition rather than to predict in the stricter sense, or to forecast future behavior. A typical example is a test for brain damage. The purpose is to "predict" the present condition of brain damage, and the proof of the "prediction" would be borne out by detailed physiological investigations.

The Statistics of Prediction. No test is a perfect predictor and, as we shall see later, nearly all predictors entail more error than accuracy in forecasting performance. The relative accuracy of predictor tests is determined from statistical analysis: statistical descriptions of the number of people who are properly and improperly classified, statistical estimates of the per cent of persons who can be safely forecast at particular levels on the assessment, and statistical estimates of the amounts of money that can be saved by using a predictor. Because of the need for statistical measures in determining the utility of predictor tests, the next several chapters will concern the statistical models which are most often used in testing.

Construction of a Predictor. A predictor test begins with a hypothesis, a hypothesis that test materials of a particular kind will predict a particular assessment. We might hypothesize that numerical problems will predict how well individuals will perform in mechanical engineering school. The task would then be to assemble a large number of numerical problems such as:

$$(a) \ \frac{268}{32} = \underline{\hspace{2cm}} \qquad (b) \ 14 \times 64 = \underline{\hspace{1.5cm}} \qquad (c) \ \begin{array}{r} 95,342 \\ -25,983 \\ \hline \underline{\hspace{1.5cm}} \end{array}$$

A large collection of items of this kind would be called an *item pool*. The problem is then to select from the item pool the minimum number of items which afford the best prediction of an assessment. This is done by statistical procedures of item analysis, which will be discussed in Chapter 8.

Examples of Predictors. Most of the measures which psychologists construct are predictors. There are very few places in which the psychologist

---

[2] Different terms are often used to refer to functional relationships with past, current, and future events. Functional relationships with past events are more properly termed "postdiction." Functional relationships with current statuses are often called "diagnosis." Whereas the proper meaning of the word "predict" is to forecast future behavior, it will be used here to refer to all three kinds of functional relations.

has the responsibility of deciding what is good and bad in particular performances, the exception being when the psychologist gives grades to his own students. All the aptitude tests are predictors; they are meant to forecast how well people will perform as salesmen, students, naval captains, artists, etc. All personality tests are predictors. They are meant to predict the likelihood that a person will have a "nervous breakdown," enter a mental hospital, or how he will react in emergencies, how effective he will be in positions of leadership, and how successful he is likely to be in marriage.

The so-called intelligence tests were initially instruments of the predictor type. Although some have tried to argue that these tests are measures, i.e., assessments, of intelligence, the domain of all possible actions that could be called intelligent behavior is not agreed on by different investigators, and the domain is too large to permit an adequate sampling.

Whether an instrument is classified as an assessment or as a predictor often depends on the way in which it is used. On a test of attitudes toward Eskimos, for example, an individual answers "yes" to questions such as, "Do you think that Eskimos are as intelligent as other people?" "Would you be willing to have an Eskimo as a personal friend?" "Would you be willing to make a donation for helping Eskimos?" It could then be said that the individual responds as though he is favorable to Eskimos. Consequently, the instrument could be considered an assessment of verbal report. However, there is no guarantee that the individual would actually behave in a friendly manner toward Eskimos, that he would treat them as intelligent persons, make friends with them, or donate money for their aid. Therefore, the instrument is being used as a predictor of how people will behave.

An interest test can demonstrate what an individual says that he likes to do, but the verbal report alone gives no assurance that the individual will actually seek out the things which he professes to enjoy. The individual who says that he likes classical music may never attend a concert and may habitually switch the radio from a presentation of Beethoven to other forms of musical fare. Similarly with the responses given in an opinion survey, it is not necessarily so that an individual will behave as though he holds a stated conviction.

When an instrument tries to determine only an individual's verbal response, it can be said that an assessment is being made. Any effort to use the response as an indication of how an individual behaves in other situations or how he will react in the future means that the instrument is being used as a predictor.

Numerous studies have found relationships between what people say and what they do later, but the important point here is that it is necessary to prove such relationships rather than take them for granted. Also, what people say they like, think, and feel is an important type of information regardless of whether it predicts or is used to predict subsequent actions.

When Not to Construct Predictor Tests. Predictor tests have proved themselves useful in countless practical situations. They have been particularly useful in the selection and assignment of people in schools, in the Armed Forces, in government agencies, and more recently in industry. Care must be taken that the demand for new tests does not bring forth poorly standardized and improperly evaluated instruments.

The test constructor must be cautious at the outset not to launch a program of research which has little chance of ending in success. Before the construction of predictor tests is undertaken, the nature of the assessment, or criterion, should be examined. It is most fortunate if the assessment is defined in terms of easily observed actions. If the assessment cannot be specified in terms of actions, it is essential that the assessment at least be expressed in terms of the persons who stand high and who stand low in the particular performance. It is very important in this latter case to make sure that the ratings of persons are reliable. If neither the actions can be specified nor the people be reliably rated, it is a waste of time to work on the construction of predictor tests. There will be no way to evaluate the tests which are constructed. In some situations, the best service that the test constructor can perform is to tell the people who want predictor tests that it would be futile to begin such work until more systematic assessments are developed.

CONSTRUCT VALIDITY

The distinction between predictors and assessments will serve to judge many, if not most, of the instruments in psychology. If a measure can be unambiguously categorized as either a predictor or an assessment, the rules for constructing and validating the measure are reasonably clear. There is a third category of measures that does not fit completely into either of the two basic divisions. Measures of this kind are encountered most often in psychological experiments. In a typical experiment, the purpose is to test the hypothesis that difficult learning tasks raise anxiety. In order to test the hypothesis, it is necessary to measure anxiety. The measure of anxiety cannot be regarded as a predictor, because the purpose is not to predict some other action but to measure anxiety then and there. Neither can the measure be an assessment, because there is no agreed-on set of "anxiety actions," or content, to be sampled.

Construct validation consists of defining a measure in terms of numerous research findings. This is essentially the way in which intelligence tests have gained meaning. Enough research has been done with these instruments to know how the underlying function grows with the child and how intelligence test scores relate to numerous other variables. This gradual defining of an instrument in terms of what it does is the major approach to validating some psychological measures. It is not a sure nor an easy course, and psychologists are not entirely in agreement as to what constitutes construct validity. There is also a danger that instruments which should be considered as either predictors or assessments and validated as such will hide under the cloak of construct validity. Construct validity should be considered a last resort, when the instrument is not specifically intended to predict performance or when the instrument cannot stand alone as a self-evident measure of what is intended. However, there are some instruments which can be judged only by accumulated research experience.

OTHER LOGICAL CONCEPTS

The logic which has been presented here for the evaluation of psychological measures is not one that would be agreed on by everyone in the field of testing. There are numerous other logical classifications which have been used in explaining the usefulness of measures. Some of these constructs will be listed and compared with the logical scheme described above.

Face Validity. Face validity refers to whether or not the test content "looks" as if it measures what is meant to be measured. This is certainly one of the important properties of an assessment, such as a school examination; but this standard of validity has often been applied to predictor tests. Personality inventories have sometimes been claimed to be valid because they have face validity. This is a poor way to evaluate a predictor. Indeed, with personality tests, the more the test items bear an obvious relationship to what is being predicted, the more easily the test can be "faked" by the subjects.

Predictor tests should not be judged in advance because they do or do not have face validity. Sometimes the most unlikely looking test will prove to be an adequate predictor. We said earlier that a predictor test represents a hypothesis. One of the prime rules in science is never to exclude a hypothesis before it has been tested. There are numerous cases in which scientific progress was held up because of a refusal on the part of some to let a hypothesis be tested. Some of these were the germ theory of disease, the heliocentric theory of the solar system, and the law of "falling bodies." Predictor tests can only be judged empirically, by the strength of their relationships with assessments.

Correlations between Predictors. A not uncommon practice has been to correlate a new predictor test with a better-established predictor test.

If the correlation is high, this is taken as evidence that the new test is "valid." The difficulty with this procedure is that a new test can correlate highly with an older test but not correlate at all with the assessment it is meant to predict. For example, the older test might correlate .60 with a particular assessment. The new test might be found to correlate as high as .70 with the older test. It is possible in this case for the new test to correlate zero with the assessment. It is always much more to the point to correlate a predictor directly with the thing it is meant to forecast.

There are only two cases in which correlating one test with another will provide definite information. If the correlation between the two tests is nearly perfect, close to .90, then the two tests are almost identical and should be approximately equal in predictive effectiveness for any assessment. On the other extreme, if the correlation between the two tests is very low, approaching zero correlation, it is certain that the two tests are measuring different things.

We can get some information from correlating one assessment with another of its kind. For example, we might try out two achievement tests which are both intended to assess the student's knowledge of history. If scores on the two tests do not correspond, if the correlation is not high, we would wonder about the differences in content which made one measure different from the other. This might lead to a better appraisal of the subject matter, a more explicit outline of the major topics, and eventually to a more comprehensive achievement test. However, the observation that two assessments correlate is not necessarily an indication that the assessments are "good." For example, one instructor could measure course achievement in history by seeing how far the students could throw the textbook. Another instructor could use as a test how far the students could throw their notebooks. The two measures would correlate highly, but neither would have anything to do with history.

Factorial Validity. A primary concern of measurement specialists is to find tests that measure some common function and thus define what is called a factor. Factor analysis is the statistical procedure for isolating these common functions and will be discussed in Chapter 9. It has been found, for example, that tests like reading comprehension, vocabulary, and word problems have in common a factor of *verbal comprehension*. Other groups of tests define reasoning, memory, and perceptual factors. Factor-analysis studies help us to understand the nature of human attributes and provide a very useful classification scheme for available tests.

If a test is described as a measure of *verbal comprehension*, some proof should be offered that the classification is correct. The proof consists of correlating the test with the factor which it is intended to measure. It is sometimes found in this way that a test which is intended to measure a particular factor is in fact more related to some other factor. Although it is quite useful to learn the factor composition of particular tests, the term "factorial validity" should be accepted with some caution. Even if a test has high factorial validity, it may be invalid as a predictor of particular criteria. Factorial validity indicates only that a test is properly classified but not necessarily that it is good or useful for any purpose.

RELATIONSHIPS AMONG VALIDITY CONCEPTS

Although most measurement specialists recognize predictive validity and content validity, there is some controversy as to how these concepts apply to currently available tests. For example, there are some who claim that intelligence tests should be judged by content representativeness, or content validity (see **4**, chap. 7). The point of view given here is that intelligence tests must be validated by standards of predictive and construct validity rather than by standards of content sampling. Whereas the point advocated here is that most tests of personality should be regarded as predictor tests and validated as such, there are those who argue for face validity. (See **1, 2, 3, 4, 5** for alternative points of view about test validation.)

Some measurement specialists regard factor analysis as an end in itself and factorial validity as the key standard for test validation. The point of view advocated here is that factor analysis is very useful in classifying and exploring the nature of tests, but that factor analysis should be considered only the first step in determining the practical usefulness of particular instruments.

Even if a test can be classified clearly as a predictor or as an assessment, this does not mean that the standards and procedures that apply to other kinds of measures are not useful. For example, some of the validation procedures that apply to predictor tests are useful with assessments, such as with achievement tests. Although achievement tests, and all assessments, must ultimately be judged by standards of content representativeness, it is helpful to learn whether the tests correlate well with other achievement tests and whether the tests predict later achievement.

Factor analysis is useful in exploring the content of achievement test batteries. For example, a factor-analysis study of achievement tests might show that a test which is intended to measure general knowledge of the social sciences is overly slanted toward economics or toward some other special field. This information would help the investigators to revise the test in such a way as to include a broader coverage of social science material.

Whereas a predictor test must ultimately be judged by its ability to predict (in the broad sense of the word) important behavior outside the testing situation, other standards are useful. An effort to understand the content of predictor tests and to hypothesize what the tests measure are natural ways of exploring the nature of human abilities. As was said previously, factor analysis plays an important part in helping us understand the nature of human abilities as it is reflected in predictor type tests. Also, it is often helpful to correlate one predictor test with a number of others in order to get some hunches regarding practical uses for an instrument.

Construct validation requires not only some of the procedures used with assessments and predictors but also some other procedures as well. The major approach is to determine whether the experimental evidence obtained from applying an instrument fits the "construct," or the theory, for which the instrument was designed. For example, in the construct validation of an instrument to measure "anxiety," it is important to determine whether or not the instrument gives results that are in compliance with a theory about anxiety. If the theory holds that anxiety increases in particular kinds of frustrating situations, an experiment can be undertaken to determine whether people who are placed in the situation obtain higher anxiety scores than people who are not placed in the situation. Many such experiments will help to determine whether an instrument measures a particular construct, such as the construct of anxiety in the example.

It is primarily important to keep in mind that an instrument is validated for particular uses rather than in a general sense. For example, the test which predicts one job performance well is not necessarily a good predictor in general. In fact, it may have no validity at all for predicting other kinds of vocational accomplishment. A mathematics examination may have good content representativeness for a particular unit of instruction, but the test will not necessarily be good for other uses. If, as in the example above, a test proves to have construct validity for the measurement of anxiety, it is not necessarily the case that the test will be predictive of marriage happiness or any other set of behaviors that might be predicted. The proper aim, therefore, is to try to determine how well an instrument serves some function, or set of functions, rather than to try to prove that an instrument is generally "good."

SUMMARY

There is still some controversy as to how psychological measurements should be validated. Although they may not use this particular nomenclature, most psychologists recognize the categories of "predictors" and "assessments." If an instrument is used as either a predictor or an assessment, the rules for validation are relatively clear. Primarily, a predictor must demonstrate functional relations with important behaviors outside the testing situation, and an assessment must rest on sound methods of content sampling. In addition to the primary validation procedures for predictors and assessments, some auxiliary empirical and statistical procedures are useful.

Some instruments can neither be classified entirely as predictors nor as assessments. These types of instruments are often used in psychological experiments. If the instruments measure what they are purported to measure, they should demonstrate construct validity. There is considerable controversy about construct validity—whether it is a meaningful concept, and if so, how it is to be studied. Construct validation is essentially a "bootstrap" operation in which an instrument that initially has little meaning in its own right gains meaning through continued use and research.

REFERENCES

1. Anastasi, Anne. The concept of validity in the interpretation of test scores. *Educ. psychol. Measmt.*, 1950, **10**, 67–78.
2. Cronbach, L. J., and Meehl, P. E. Construct validity in psychological tests. *Psychol. Bull.*, 1955, **52**, 281–303.
3. Cureton, E. E. Validity. In E. F. Lindquist (Ed.), *Educational measurement*. Washington: American Council on Education, 1951.
4. Goodenough, F. L. *Mental testing*. New York: Rinehart, 1949.
5. American Psychological Association, Committee on Test Standards. Technical recommendations for psychological tests and diagnostic techniques. *Psychol. Bull.*, 1954, **51**, No. 2, Part 2.

CHAPTER 5

Predictive Efficiency of Tests

Predictor tests are used to improve the "bets" that are made about how individuals will perform in particular situations. As background for understanding how tests are used, let us first look at a situation in which there is no test available for making predictions. Imagine that we are trying to predict the grade averages of graduating college students. The grade averages are at hand, the mean and standard deviation are known, but there is no indication as to which student made which grade average. Also, we do not know any of the students personally and have no information about their individual capabilities. Imagine then that someone calls off the name of each student in turn and you are required to guess the grade average of each. With this complete lack of information about the ability of the individual students, what would you guess for Bill Smith, Mary Jones, Tom Wilson, and each student as his name is read off?

Would the predictions be most accurate by betting that the whole group made low scores, that some made high and others low scores, or should the bets be made on some random basis? You would lose by choosing any of these courses. The proper course would be to bet that all of the students made exactly the same grade, the mean. The mean is the point about which the sum of squared deviations is a minimum; and without a knowledge of the ability of individual pupils, the over-all amount of error will be least by predicting that all students make average grades.

Why should you make a series of bets that are sure to be largely in error? Only a minority of the grades will be exactly at the mean, and the standard deviation may indicate that some of the grades vary considerably from that point. The reason is that, in spite of some large errors in prediction that are bound to occur, the over-all amount of error in prediction would be even larger if any system of betting were employed other than betting at the mean for all students. We know this is so because of mathematical proofs, and we must learn to accept mathematical proofs even if they do not correspond with common-sense expectations. Procedures of statistical estimation are always on the conservative side, allowing bets to venture away from the mean as more and more information is obtained about particular persons. Only in the case of a perfect predictor test would the bets vary as widely as the actual assessment scores.

Statistical Methods in Scientific Activity. Perhaps it would be wise to consider for a moment why there is need for statistical procedures in scientific enterprise. In classical mathematics, the kind that you encountered in introductory algebra, simultaneous equations like the following are often found:

	X	Y
a.	2	1
b.	4	2
c.	8	4
d.	10	5

Each pair of numbers above forms an equation. Equation *a* says that when X is 2, Y is 1, or, in other words, that X is twice as large as Y. Equation *b* says that when X is 4, Y is 2, which shows again that X is twice as large as Y. Equations *c* and *d* also affirm that X is twice as large as Y. The same relationship would be found by adding the four equations together. When a number of equations all supply the same information, they are said to be *equivalent*.

One of the exercises in elementary algebra is to make a graphic plot of equations like those above. This is done in Figure 5–1. Any set of two-variable equations, called a *bivariate relationship*, can be plotted as in Figure 5–1 by locating the point for each equation in terms of the values on the X and Y axes. In Figure 5–1 all of the points lie on a straight line.

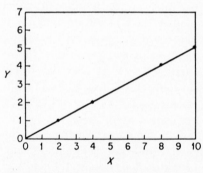

FIGURE 5–1. Graphic demonstration of functional relationship between variables X and Y.

Now let us consider some equations that concern real-life things rather than abstract mathematical relations. Turning back to the earlier example of the prediction of college grade averages, imagine that a predictor test is in use. Let us say in this case that a vocabulary test was administered to incoming freshmen and that the scores are to be compared with grade averages when the students reach graduation.

In order to find out how well the predictor test works, we would want to compare vocabulary scores with grade averages. Comparisons could be made of the raw scores on the two variables, but, because the size of raw scores is dependent on the method of test construction used, this would cause some confusion. The important consideration is whether the students who make high vocabulary scores also make high grade averages and whether the students who make low vocabulary scores also make low grade averages. Consequently, it is most meaningful to express both vocabulary and grade average in standard score units. To simplify the comparison, we will deal with only nine students. Means and standard deviations are obtained on vocabulary and grade averages for the nine students only. Standard scores are determined for the nine students on vocabulary and grade average, with the following results:

Student	Vocabulary (z_x)	Grade average (z_y)
a.	1.55	1.18
b.	1.16	1.77
c.	.77	.59
d.	.39	−1.18
e.	.00	.59
f.	− .39	− .59
g.	− .77	− .59
h.	−1.16	− .59
i.	−1.55	−1.18

Just as in the earlier example we considered each pair of numbers as constituting an equation, each pair of standard scores above also forms an equation. Person *a* has a vocabulary standard score (z_x) of 1.55 and a grade standard score (z_y) of 1.18. Then, by dividing 1.55 into 1.18, a ratio of .76 is found. In the previous example, only one equation was necessary to determine the over-all relationship between two variables. If that were so in the present example, we could say that each person's grade standard score is exactly .76 times as large as his vocabulary standard score. Let us go on to see what relationships the other equations specify. The equation for person *b* indicates that the ratio is 1.53, *c* indicates .77, and *d* indicates −3.03. It is obvious that these equations provide very different indications of the over-all relationship between vocabulary (z_x) and grades (z_y). When, as in the example here, simultaneous equations do not agree with one another, they are said to be *nonequivalent*.

Correlation. Nonequivalent relations are the typical and not the unusual scientific finding. Whether the subject matter is physics, chemistry, biology, or psychology, the numerous observations tell different stories about the form of a particular relationship. In some investigations, where the variables are simple and easily controlled, the divergence from equivalence is very small. In more complex problems, such as predicting how individuals will perform on a particular job, the divergence from equivalence is usually considerable. Statistical methods were developed as a means of dealing with nonequivalent equations.

A graphic comparison is made of vocabulary and grade standard scores in Figure 5–2 (the "best-fit" line in the figure will be explained shortly). It is obvious that the points do not lie on a straight line, but there is a tendency for the two variables to go together. How would you summarize the relationship? We might use only our impression and say that there is a "strong correspondence" or a "moderate correspondence." A better approach is to use a statistical statement of the degree of relationship between vocabulary and grade averages.

FIGURE 5–2. Comparison of standard scores on a vocabulary test with grade point averages expressed as standard scores.

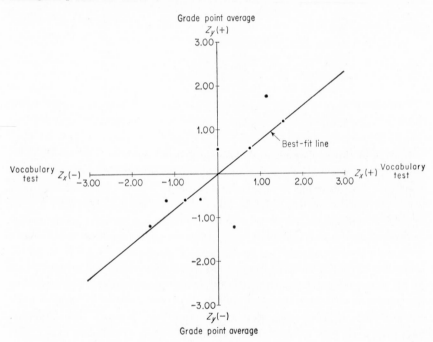

There are a number of ways in which statistics can be developed for the problem here. One that might seem reasonable at first thought is to add together all of the vocabulary standard scores and divide this sum into the sum of the grade standard scores. This method worked with the equations in the earlier example, but it will not do here. As you will remember from Chapter 3, the sum of standard scores on any variable is zero. Consequently, we would get zero equals zero as a summarizing equation, which is certainly true, but does not provide the needed statistic.

Previously it was shown that working with squared scores and squared deviations leads to some very useful results. We will appeal to that principle again by looking for a summary equation which leads to the smallest sum of squared errors in prediction. That is, we will seek a ratio between vocabulary and grade standard scores, such that the sum of the squared errors in predicting grades will be at a minimum. This means that we are seeking an equation like the following:

$$z_y' = bz_x$$

such that

$$\Sigma(z_y - z_y')^2 = \text{a minimum}$$

where b is a constant

  z_y is a grade standard score

  z_x is a vocabulary standard score

  z_y' is an estimate of a grade standard score

The equation above is referred to as a linear equation: no matter what value we choose for b, it results in a straight line of relationship. Of the infinite number of values that could be chosen for b, there is only one that satisfies the "least squares" criterion. The method for determining the correct b value is derived quite easily from elementary calculus. The method which is derived in this way can be applied to the present problem. The first step is to multiply each vocabulary standard score by its corresponding grade standard score, as follows:

$$
\begin{array}{rcr}
1.55 \times & 1.18 = & 1.83 \\
1.16 \times & 1.77 = & 2.05 \\
.77 \times & .59 = & .45 \\
.39 \times -1.18 = - & .46 \\
.00 \times & .59 = & .00 \\
- .39 \times - & .59 = & .23 \\
- .77 \times - & .59 = & .45 \\
-1.16 \times - & .59 = & .68 \\
-1.55 \times -1.18 = & 1.83 \\
\end{array}
$$

$$\Sigma z_x z_y = 7.06$$

$$b = \frac{\Sigma z_x z_y}{N}$$

$$= \frac{7.06}{9}$$

$$= .78$$

The final steps are to sum the standard score cross products $(\Sigma z_x z_y)$, and divide the result by the number of persons (N). This is all that is necessary to obtain b, the value which satisfies the "least squares" criterion. In this case b is .78, which means that the best (least squares) estimate of each grade standard score is obtained as follows:

$$z'_y = .78 z_x$$

Then the estimated grade standard score for person a is

$$z'_y = .78 \times 1.55$$

$$= 1.21$$

Person a actually has a grade standard score of 1.18; consequently, the estimate is in error by .03 score units. Although there will be errors in prediction by using b to summarize the relationship, the sum of the squared errors will be less than that obtained from any other linear equation.

Because the prediction equation above is a linear formula, b can be used to draw a "best-fit" line as is done in Figure 5–2. For every unit the line moves over the vocabulary axis, it moves up .78 units on the grade average axis. Those who have studied trigonometry will recognize b as the tangent of the angle formed by the best-fit line and the vocabulary axis.

When the constant term, b, is sought by the "least squares" criterion in respect to standard scores, it is given a special name: the *correlation coefficient*. Also, when dealing with standard scores, the symbol r is usually employed instead of b. Then we can rewrite the best-fit equation as follows:

$$z'_y = r z_x$$

To obtain the best estimate of the grade standard scores, we multiply each vocabulary standard score by the correlation coefficient.

When the constant term is found for standard scores, it not only serves to place the best-fit line, it has descriptive value of its own. The correlation coefficient, r, varies in different problems from $+1.00$ through zero to -1.00. If the correlation is $+1.00$, it means that there is a perfect correlation. Then the prediction equation becomes

$$z'_y = z_x$$

and the predicted standard scores will be exactly the same as the actual grade standard scores. As the correlation coefficient goes downward from

+1.00, the predictions become poorer and poorer. When the correlation reaches zero, the prediction equation is as follows:

$$z'_y = rz_x$$

$$= 0z_x$$

$$= 0$$

Because the mean of a set of standard scores is zero, a zero correlation leads to the prediction that all scores fall at the mean of the assessment. A negative correlation means that high scores on one variable go with low scores on the other variable and vice versa.

Although the formula for the correlation coefficient, r, above is relatively easy to understand, it is not the easiest approach to computing the correlation. If scores are standardized over several hundred persons, rather than over the nine cases employed above, it results in considerable work. Therefore, it is easier to compute the correlation coefficient from deviation scores or from raw scores. Some manipulations of the basic formula will show how this is done.

$$r = \frac{\Sigma z_x z_y}{N} \tag{5-1}$$

$$= \frac{\Sigma \left(\frac{x}{\sigma_x}\right)\left(\frac{y}{\sigma_y}\right)}{N}$$

$$r = \frac{\Sigma xy}{N\sigma_x \sigma_y}$$

$$= \frac{\Sigma xy}{\sqrt{\Sigma x^2}\sqrt{\Sigma y^2}} \tag{5-2}$$

Formula (5-2) can be used to compute the correlation coefficient from deviation scores. Next we can replace each x value in Eq. (5-2) by $X - M_x$ and each y value by $Y - M_y$ and obtain the following raw score formula:

$$r = \frac{N\Sigma XY - (\Sigma X)(\Sigma Y)}{\sqrt{N\Sigma X^2 - (\Sigma X)^2}\sqrt{N\Sigma Y^2 - (\Sigma Y)^2}} \tag{5-3}$$

It must be remembered that the correlation coefficient specifies the relationship between two sets of standard scores. Either the computations begin with standard scores, as in Eq. (5-1), or the standardizing is done in the computations, as in Eqs. (5-2) and (5-3). The three formulas above will give exactly the same correlation coefficient. Although Eq.

(5–3) looks complicated, it is actually the easiest way to obtain the correlation coefficient if an automatic calculator is available.

It is not only easier to compute the correlation coefficient from deviation scores and raw scores, it is often convenient to form the prediction equation from deviation scores and raw scores.

The standard-score formula

$$z'_y = rz_x \tag{5-4}$$

can be converted to the deviation score formula

$$y' = r\frac{\sigma_y}{\sigma_x} x \tag{5-5}$$

where y' is the estimated deviation score on the assessment (grades)
x is the actual deviation score on the predictor (vocabulary)
r is the correlation between predictor and assessment
σ_y is the standard deviation of the assessment
σ_x is the standard deviation of the predictor

Formula (5–5) could be used to predict students' deviation scores in college grades from their deviation scores on the vocabulary test. Thus, if a student has a vocabulary deviation score of 3 and the correlation is .50, and the standard deviations for vocabulary and grades are 2 and 1 respectively, the prediction is as follows:

$$y' = .50 \times \tfrac{1}{2} \times 3$$
$$= .25 \times 3$$
$$= .75$$

The prediction is that he will score .75 deviation score units above the mean of grade averages. Let us say that he actually makes a deviation score of 1.25 in grades, and therefore, the prediction is in error by .50 deviation score units.

The prediction equation can also be expressed in raw score terms:

$$Y' = r\left(\frac{\sigma_y}{\sigma_x}\right)(X - M_x) + M_y \tag{5-6}$$

where Y' is an estimated raw score on the assessment (school grades)
X is an actual raw score on the predictor (vocabulary)
σ_y is the standard deviation of the assessment
σ_x is the standard deviation of the predictor
M_y is the mean of the raw assessment scores
M_x is the mean of the raw predictor scores

Although Eq. (5–6) looks complicated, it is a straightforward extension of Eqs. (5–4) and (5–5). Formula (5–6) might predict that a person with a raw vocabulary score of 20 will make a raw grade average of 4.0.

Both Formulas (5–5) and (5–6) can be used to plot best-fit lines. Formula (5–5) would be used if deviation scores are plotted, and Formula (5–6) would be used if raw scores are plotted. The correlation coefficient and the three prediction equations above are the basic statistical procedures needed for the validation and use of predictor tests.

The correlation coefficient is, of course, not used to predict grade averages that are already known, but to forecast the grade averages of incoming freshmen. If subsequent groups of incoming freshmen are students of about the same caliber as their predecessors, the correlation between vocabulary and later grades will be approximately the same. Therefore, it is safe to use the first correlation to forecast the grade averages of incoming freshmen.

The Standard Error of Estimate. Another way to understand correlational analysis is to think in terms of the errors of prediction. Figure 5–3 shows a typical comparison of raw scores on a test and on an assessment. (Whereas in the earlier example the correlation was .78, here the correlation is .50.) Here we will assume that the best-fit line is known to begin

FIGURE 5–3. Scatter diagram of vocabulary scores and school grade averages.

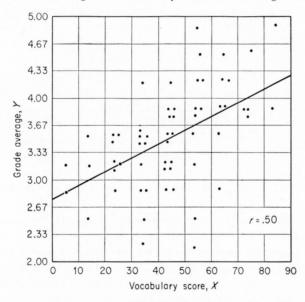

with, as shown in Figure 5–3, and see how it is used to make predictions. When a bivariate relationship is pictured like that in Figure 5–3, it is referred to as a scatter diagram. The points are plotted in terms of intervals instead of discrete scores. That is, all of the vocabulary scores from 0 through 9 are plotted in the first column, all of the scores from 10 through

19 are plotted in the second column, and so on for all intervals. Each column is referred to as an "array," and there are as many arrays as there are intervals on the vocabulary axis.

In order to predict any student's grade, simply find his score on the vocabulary axis and then move upward to the best-fit line. Then move parallel to the vocabulary axis to the predicted grade average. If a student makes a vocabulary score of 10, the prediction is that he will make a grade average of approximately 2.92. If a student makes a vocabulary score of 80, the prediction is that he will make a grade average of approximately 4.12. In each case we predict as though all of the points lay on the best-fit line, but, in fact, the points in each array scatter above and below the line. This tells us that a prediction from any point on the vocabulary axis about how well an individual will perform in school is likely to be in error in proportion to the scatter of the Y points about the prediction line. If the scatter about the best-fit line is large, then prediction will be poor; as the scatter lessens, the prediction becomes better and better.

In Chapter 3, the standard deviation was given as a measure of dispersion. The same kind of measure can be used in the scatter diagram to describe the error in predicting grades from vocabulary scores. A measure of the standard deviation type could be determined for any one array by subtracting the predicted grade average (at the point of the best-fit line) from each of the grade averages actually found. We could then find the standard deviation of the prediction errors. A like measure could be obtained for each of the arrays, and these could be averaged to determine an over-all estimate of the dispersion about the best-fit line. The method used in practice is slightly different from this procedure. Instead of finding the separate dispersions and averaging them, all of the deviates are determined about their respective points of prediction, and these are placed in the conventional standard deviation formula. The resulting value is called the *standard error of estimate* and will be symbolized as σ_{est}.

The standard error of estimate is an absolute measure of error in predicting Y, but the units in which the assessment is expressed are often arbitrary functions of test construction practices. If, for example, the assessment is a course examination, the grades could range from 1 to 10, 50 to 100, or assume any other range in accordance with the system of grading used. Consequently, it is necessary to compare the standard error of estimate with the standard deviation of the assessment before the efficiency of prediction can be determined.

As was mentioned previously, if no knowledge were had about the assessment scores of particular people, the best bet would be that they all fell at the mean of Y. These bets would be in error in accordance with the size of the standard deviation of assessment scores which is actually obtained. The standard deviation of Y would specify the likelihood with which predicted scores would fall within certain intervals on the assessment continuum. Then, as would be expected, when the correlation between the test and the assessment is zero, the standard error of estimate will be the same as the standard deviation of Y. As the correlation becomes larger and larger, σ_{est} becomes comparatively smaller than σ_y. The ratio of these two measures of dispersion leads to a very useful index of predictive efficiency.

It is easy to picture what the scatter diagram will look like as the correlation becomes larger and larger; the area of scatter will become progressively more narrow. This progressive narrowing can be seen in Figure 5–4.

The correlation coefficient concerns the squares of σ_y and σ_{est}. The squares are used because the resulting formula indicates how the best-fit line should be drawn, as well as indicating the degree of relationship between the two variables. As was previously noted, the square of any standard deviation type value is called the variance. The ratio of the two squared values is then a variance ratio, a term that will be seen quite often in testing theory. If this ratio were used as a measure of

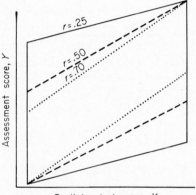

FIGURE 5–4. Areas of scatter for different size correlations.

relationship, it would read "backwards": a high ratio would indicate a weak relationship, and a low ratio would represent a strong relationship. This difficulty is overcome by subtracting the ratio from 1, resulting in the following formula:

$$r^2 = 1 - \frac{\sigma^2_{est}}{\sigma^2_y} \tag{5-7}$$

$$r = \sqrt{1 - \frac{\sigma^2_{est}}{\sigma^2_y}} \tag{5-8}$$

The letter r stands for the correlation coefficient, r^2 is said to be the "per cent of variance explained," and $1 - r^2$ is spoken of as the "per cent of variance unexplained." It is perhaps easier to visualize the meaning of r^2 than r itself, but as was shown previously, the correlation coefficient is directly useful in making predictions.

Although σ_{est} does not appear directly in Formulas (5–1), (5–2), or (5–3), it can easily be derived after the r is obtained. Formula (5–7) can be suitably transformed as follows:

$$\sigma_{est} = \sigma_y\sqrt{1 - r^2} \qquad\qquad (5\text{--}9)$$

Nonlinear Relationships. We have spoken so far only about linear relationships. Formulas (5–1), (5–2), and (5–3) indicate the linear correlation between two sets of scores, and Formulas (5–4), (5–5), and (5–6) place the best-fitting straight lines in scatter diagrams. Formulas (5–7), (5–8), and (5–9) were used to illustrate the dispersion about the best-fitting straight line. A possibility that has not been mentioned so far is that the bivariate relationship might not be linear. A relationship is linear if the points in each array spread equally above and below the best-fit straight line. Technically, the relationship is linear if the mean assessment score for each array falls exactly on the best-fit line.

In any particular scatter diagram, the array means can be plotted and compared with the best-fit straight line. It is expected that the array means will diverge from the line by small amounts if only because of sampling error. However, in the use of psychological tests it is rare to find that the array means show some systematic trend other than a

FIGURE 5–5. Scatter diagram illustrating a curvilinear relationship.

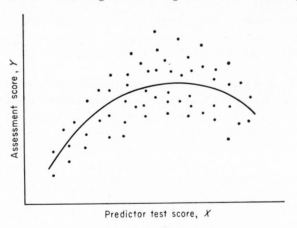

Predictor test score, X

straight-line function. When this happens, the relationship is called curvilinear, an example of which is shown in Figure 5–5. Figure 5–5 shows that assessment scores increase with predictor test scores up to a point and then start to decline. Then the people who make very high scores on the test do less well, as a group, on the assessment than the people who make only moderately high test scores. Although curvilinear relationships are sometimes found in psychological experiments, such a marked departure from linearity as the one shown in Figure 5-5 is rarely found in using predictor tests.

Formula (5-7) was illustrated with a linear relationship, but it can be applied equally well to curvilinear relationships like that in Figure 5-5. The only difference is in the way that the standard error of estimate is obtained. Instead of computing the statistic about the best-fitting straight line, σ_{est} can be obtained about the array means. The mean assessment score in each array is subtracted from the assessment scores in each array. The differences are then squared and summed over all arrays. The resulting sum is divided by the number of individuals. This is then the squared standard error of estimate taken about the array means. When this is placed in Formula (5-8), it gives a general index of correlation which is independent of the form of the relationship. Formula (5-8) is a measure of correlation that can be used on relationships of all kinds. When the standard error of estimate is obtained about the best-fitting straight line, the resulting statistic is called the correlation coefficient and symbolized as r. When the standard error of estimate is obtained about the array means, the resulting statistic is called the *correlation ratio* or *Eta*.

It must be kept in mind that the linear correlation formulas will place the best-fitting straight line in the scatter diagram regardless of whether the relationship is actually linear. Before applying the linear correlation formulas, the scatter diagram should be inspected to see if the relationship is reasonably linear. If there is only a moderate curve in the relationship, the linear formula will still do an adequate job of describing the trend. However, if there is apparently a marked tendency toward curvilinearity, a test of statistical significance should be made (see 3, pp. 255–262). Then if the departure from linearity is statistically significant, either the correlation ratio should be applied or people should be told that the linear correlation formula was applied to a curvilinear relationship. When correlations are stated in research reports, readers will assume that the relationships are reasonably linear. Among the other assumptions which are made in employing the correlation coefficient, r, linearity of relationship is the most important.

If a linear relationship is found between predictor and assessment, this provides at least a practical justification of the original assumption of an interval scale for the predictor test. A linear relationship means that equal intervals on the predictor correspond to equal intervals on the assessment. Because a linear relationship is the usual and not the unexpected finding in working with predictor tests, this shows that for practical purposes the assumption of an interval scale and the use of the statistics which depend on this assumption are often justified.

In order to use σ_{est} as a measure of the error in making predictions, the bivariate relationship should have several characteristics in addition to linearity. Earlier in the chapter there was a discussion of the errors of prediction in terms of the array dispersions. A possibility which was not mentioned at the time is that the array dispersions are not equal. An example is shown in Figure 5–6. Although relationships similar to the

FIGURE 5–6. **Scatter diagram in which array dispersion increases with test score.**

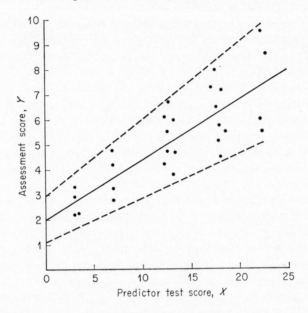

one in Figure 5–6 are sometimes found in practice, it is usually considered an undesirable condition. The σ_{est} obtained for this relationship would be an underestimate of the error in predicting from high X scores, and an overestimate of the error in predicting from low X scores. The assumption in using the correlation coefficient is that the dispersion about the best-fit line is the same for all of the arrays on the X axis. The presence of equal array dispersions is referred to by the rather formidable name of *homoscedasticity*.

Not only is it desirable to have equal array dispersions, it is helpful if the points in each array are normally distributed about the best-fit line. This means that the points are more numerous where the best-fit line crosses the particular array and progressively less numerous in moving upward or downward from the best-fit line, in accordance with the frequencies expected from the normal distribution. Normality of array dispersions is necessary if the σ_{est} is used as a standard deviation type measure. Only if the distribution is normal will 68 per cent of the cases fall between plus and minus 1 standard error, and so on for all other segments of the distribution.

If array dispersions are normal, the standard error of estimate can be used to determine the probability with which predicted assessment scores will deviate from actual assessment scores by particular amounts. If, for example, a predicted score is 40 and the σ_{est} is 5, the odds are only 5 in 100 that the actual assessment score is greater than 50 or less than 30 (remember from Chapter 3 that only 5 per cent of the cases are beyond plus 2 and minus 2 standard deviations of the normal distribution). If the array dispersions are not normal, σ_{est} will lead to inaccurate probability statements. It is fortunately the case that array dispersions are almost always normal.

Another feature which is desirable in the correlation problem, but not absolutely necessary, is that each of the two variables has normal distributions of scores. In practice it is found that highly skewed variables and other forms that differ markedly from the normal are often accompanied by one or more of the several undesired features in the bivariate relationship, such as nonlinearity.

Regression. Looking back at Eq. (5–4), it can be seen that the best prediction is always that an individual will make a standard score nearer the mean of the assessment than his standard score on the predictor— except in the case of a correlation of 1.00. Also, because each of the standard scores on the predictor is multiplied by a constant, r, the standard deviation of the predicted scores will always be smaller than the standard deviation of the real assessment standard scores. Because of the need to make bets nearer the mean of Y than σ_y would indicate, the best-fit line is often referred to as the *regression line* and Eqs. (5–4), (5–5), and (5–6) as *regression equations*.

The observed tendency for predictions to regress toward the mean was the original stimulus for developing the correlation coefficient. For example, it was noted that the sons of very tall fathers tended to be shorter than their fathers, and that sons of very short fathers tended to be taller than their fathers. There is a simple reason why the regression tendency occurs. The people who make the highest scores on the predictor test can either make the highest assessment scores or they can vary downward toward the mean. Consequently, the array means of the extremes on the predictor regress toward the assessment mean. The in-between arrays tend to follow suit, resulting in the general tendency of regression toward the mean.

The slant, or slope, of the best-fit line is evidence of the regression tendency. The slope indicates the number of units of X that are required to advance a unit of Y. When dealing with standard scores, the correlation coefficient is the slope of the best-fit line. For example, when there is a correlation of .50, the best-fit line moves over two units on the predictor axis before going up one unit on the assessment axis.

Correlational analysis can be used to predict the X's from the Y's as well as the Y's from the X's. It is arbitrary which variable is labeled X and is placed on the horizontal axis rather than labeled Y and placed on the vertical axis. In the example above, the height of fathers could be predicted from the height of sons. The correlation coefficient will be the same regardless of which variable is labeled X. Also, we could predict test scores from grade point averages, although there would be no practical purpose served. Correlation Formulas (5–1), (5–2), and (5–3) would be unchanged, and we would obtain the same coefficient of .78 that was determined earlier. Regression, correlation, and standard error of estimate formulas (5–4) through (5–9) would be altered by substituting Y's for X's and Y subscripts for X subscripts, and vice versa. In most testing problems it is important to estimate the assessment from the predictor test, but not vice versa. Consequently, the assessment will be labeled Y and shown on the vertical axis throughout the text, and the regression problem will be treated in terms of the prediction of assessment scores.

Linear Transformations. One important property of the correlation coefficient is that it is completely insensitive to linear transformations of the predictor and assessment scores. A linear transformation consists of adding a constant amount to each score, subtracting a constant amount, multiplying or dividing each of the scores by a constant amount. For example, the correlation in Figure 5–3 would remain .50 if the number 10 million were added to each of the scores on the predictor test and each of the assessment scores were multiplied by 20 billion. The reason why the correlation coefficient is insensitive to linear transformations is that it is a measure of the relationship between two sets of standard scores. Either standard scores are used in the correlation formula or the conversion to standard scores is done in the deviation score and raw score computational formulas.

THE STATISTICAL SIGNIFICANCE OF CORRELATIONS

Before correlation coefficients are used in any way, they should be tested for statistical significance. In undertaking a correlational analysis, the interest is usually in determining the relationship between two variables, here predictor test and assessment scores, in a whole population, or universe, of people. We are seldom interested in only the relatively small sample of persons whose scores are actually used to compute the correlation. Therefore, we must question the precision with which a correlation coefficient determined from a sample of persons mirrors the real correlation between variables in the whole universe of persons.

To illustrate the influence of sampling error on correlation coefficients, imagine that we are trying to learn the correlation between height and weight for British male adults. It would be exceedingly laborious to measure the height and weight of every male above twenty-one years in England; and it would be no small amount of work to compute the correlation. If a research worker set out to learn the correlation between height and weight, he would probably work with only a sample from the universe. The sample might be quite large, say over ten thousand men, or perhaps only a few dozen men would be used instead.

FIGURE 5–7. Distributions of sample correlations when the universe correlation is .00. (*N* is the sample size.)

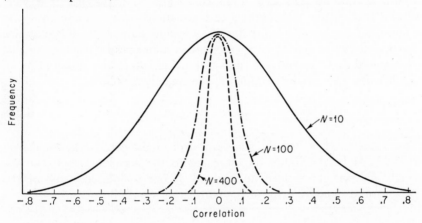

Even if the universe correlation is zero, the correlation found for a particular sample probably would not be exactly zero. We might draw a number of different samples of persons, say all of them with 100 persons, and run the separate correlations. It would be expected that these correlations would range around zero. There would be no reason to expect more positive than negative coefficients or vice versa. The dispersion of the coefficients about zero would be dependent on the *N* or sample size. That is, the correlations obtained from successive samples would crowd nearer to zero when the sample size is large—assuming again that the universe correlation is exactly zero. The distributions of coefficients that would be obtained for different sample sizes would look like those in Figure 5–7. Because the true correlation is zero in Figure 5–7, all of the non-zero coefficients are due to chance. On occasion these chance coefficients can be quite large. Notice that with an *N* of 10, correlations greater than +.50 and less than −.50 would occur appreciably often purely by chance.

Before any effort is made to interpret a particular correlation, some assurance must be obtained that the coefficient is significantly different from zero. Otherwise the correlation may represent a chance sampling of people from a universe in which the true value is zero. One way to gain some confidence in particular correlations is to learn the odds, or the probability, with which the correlation could have been obtained by chance alone. If the probability is very low, say 1 in 100, or at the .01 level as it will be called, then it is relatively safe to assume that the correlation is not merely a chance relationship.

The Standard Error of the Correlation. In Chapter 3 it was shown how the normal curve can be used to determine probabilities. For example, it was said that only 32 per cent of the cases would be beyond plus and minus 1.00 standard deviations, and that only 5 per cent of the cases would lie beyond plus and minus 2.00 standard deviations. If it were known that chance distributions of correlations such as those shown in Figure 5–7 are normally distributed, it would be possible to determine the probability of getting correlations of certain sizes by chance. All that is required is to obtain the standard deviation of the distribution of coefficients. This can be obtained approximately as follows:

$$\sigma_r = \frac{1}{\sqrt{N-1}} \qquad (5\text{--}10)$$

The statistic σ_r is called the standard error of the correlation coefficient. Its use can be illustrated by returning to the correlation between the height and weight of men in England. If our sample consisted of 101 persons, the standard error of the correlation would be:

$$\sigma_r = \frac{1}{\sqrt{101-1}}$$

$$= \frac{1}{\sqrt{100}}$$

$$= \frac{1}{10}$$

$$= .10$$

This means that, if the universe correlation is zero, the standard deviation of correlations obtained with samples of 101 persons will be .10. Then we would expect 68 per cent of the correlations obtained by chance not to exceed plus or minus .10—in other words, only 32 per cent would exceed these points. Thus, if a correlation is obtained for a sample of size 101, the σ_r allows us to determine the odds that the sample was drawn from a population which has a correlation of zero.

It is customary not to accept a finding as statistically significant unless it is at the .05 level or beyond. Looking at the per cents of cases in various areas of the normal distribution in Appendix 3, it is found that 5 per cent of the cases lie beyond plus and minus 1.96 standard deviations from the mean. By multiplying 1.96 times the σ_r for a particular sample size, the .05 level for correlation coefficients can be determined. When the N is 101 and, consequently, the σ_r is .10, the .05 level would be represented by correlations greater than $+.196$ and less than $-.196$. Because it is customary to use only two decimal places for correlations, the .05 level would be set at correlations of $+.20$ and $-.20$. Then if with a sample size of 101 persons a correlation as large as $+.20$ or $-.20$ is found, it can be said that the odds are less than 5 in 100 that the sample was drawn from a population in which the correlation was zero. This is another way of saying that the particular correlation is significant at the .05 level. In a similar way it can be found that correlations of .26 or above and correlations of $-.26$ or below are significant at the .01 level for a sample size of 101 (see Appendix 3). The standard error of the correlation can be found for any sample size by substituting the N in Formula (5–10).

Because of an untenable assumption, the standard error of the correlation has only limited use. The formula assumes that when samples are drawn from a universe in which the correlation is zero the sample correlations will be normally distributed. This is not quite true for any size of sample, and it is a particularly bad assumption for samples with less than thirty cases. The σ_r offers a good approximation to the needed error term under two conditions: (1) when the problem is to determine the significance of a particular correlation from zero correlation, and (2) when the sample size is reasonably large, say with an N of 100 or more.

Although σ_r provides a good estimate of the sampling error of correlation coefficients under the conditions stated above, there are more precise error formulas that can be used (see 1, 2, 3, 6). The standard error of the correlation coefficient was described in order to illustrate tests of significance. Rather than go more deeply into the statistical checks which can be applied, we will discuss the implications of significance tests for measurement programs.

Before any practical decisions are made about the usefulness of a predictor test, it must first be determined whether or not the test is significantly related to the criterion variable. Unless the correlation is based on a very large number of cases, say over 300, there is considerable sampling error. Any decisions about using a test should be tempered by the size of the sampling error as well as by the size of the obtained correlation. Samples of less than a hundred persons have so much sampling error that they do not offer firm enough evidence for the acceptance of tests. It is only as the sample size gets to be larger than several hundred persons that we can have confidence in the indicated validity.

If the problem in a testing program is to decide whether or not to use a particular test, it must first be determined if the test-assessment correlation is significantly different from zero. If the correlation is not significantly different from zero, the predictor test should be held suspect. It is always possible to gather a larger sample and examine the significance of the new correlation. The burden should always be placed on the test to prove its utility.

In some testing situations there is a minimum validity that a test must have in order to be usable. For example, it might be the case that the expense of using a test can be justified only if the test-assessment correlation proves to be greater than .30 in continued use. If on the first sample of test responses a correlation of .55 is found, a statistical check can be made to see if the correlation is significantly greater than .30.

Another problem that will occur quite often in testing is that of deciding whether one test works better than another in predicting a particular assessment. For example, a vocabulary test and an arithmetic test could be given to fourth-grade students. It might be found later that the vocabulary test and the arithmetic test correlate .60 and .40 respectively with school grades. If the intention is to use only one test to assign children to class sections, it would have to be determined whether the apparent difference in predictive power could likely be due to chance.

THE INFLUENCE OF THE DISPERSION ON CORRELATIONS

An important property of the correlation coefficient is that its size is directly related to the standard deviation of the assessment. Looking back at Figure 5–3, what would happen to the correlation if only the people with grade averages above 2.67 were considered in the calculation? This would certainly reduce the standard deviation of grades, Y, but it would have relatively little influence on σ_{est}. Remember that the assumption of equal array dispersions requires that σ_{est} will be the same regardless of the region of predictor scores being considered. If only the people who score above 2.67 in grades were considered in the computations, the correlation would be smaller. Look back at Formula (5–7) and you will see that this is the only possible result. Whenever the dispersion of ability on the assessment is altered, the correlation changes. Be careful to note that the change in dispersion must be a change in sampling such that the range of "real ability" varies. As you remember, changing the size of the standard deviation by a linear transformation of the assessment scores will have no influence on the correlation. Whereas σ_{est} tends to be the same in different samples of persons, the correlation varies with the assessment dispersion.

Because of the influence of the assessment dispersion on validity, the standard deviation of the assessment scores should be compared with that which is generally found in the assessment situation. If the dispersion used in validation work is different from the usual dispersion found, then a statistical correction gives an estimate of what the test validity would be with a more representative dispersion of assessment scores (see **5**, pp. 169–176).

The influence of the dispersion on test validity relates to an interesting and often misunderstood observation: intelligence tests become less successful predictors as higher educational levels are reached. The tests correlate around .70 with grammar school grades, around .60 with high school grades, around .50 with college grades, and they tend to correlate only slightly with the grades of students in graduate school. The reason for the progressive decline in validity is that the dispersion of intellectual ability is gradually being decreased. The less able students are dropped out year by year. By the time graduate school is reached, there is relatively little dispersion of intellectual ability. Tests can "commit suicide," if, as is often the case, the tests are used at various stages to determine who should continue in school. Theoretically the stage could be reached where the test correlates zero with the assessment which it has been so successful in predicting over the years. This is much like the physician who advises his patients so successfully on how to remain well that he finds himself with no ailments to treat.

THE SELECTION OF PERSONNEL

The statistical tools which have been discussed in this chapter are all aimed at answering the question, "How good are particular tests?" In many situations, an ability test which correlates .50 with its criterion will be considered as showing "good prediction." To find personality tests of equal predictive efficiency would be considered a mark of outstanding success. However, as you know by now, a correlation of .50 means that only 25 per cent of the variance in the assessment can be explained by the predictor. Another way of looking at it is that a correlation of .50 substituted in Formula (5–9) shows that the standard error of estimate will be .87 as large as the standard deviation of the assessment. On the face of it, this seems like rather poor prediction and a discredit to psychological tests.

If near perfect correlation were the standard for psychological tests, then nearly all of them would be considered very poor. However, a test need not correlate highly with an assessment to perform the job that is needed in many situations. How this is done can be demonstrated with a typical personnel-selection situation. The number of people who apply for a job is usually larger than the number who are selected. The ratio of these is referred to as the selection ratio:

$$\frac{\text{number selected}}{\text{number who apply}} = \text{selection ratio}$$

If it were necessary to hire all of the people who applied, the selection ratio would be 1.00 and there would be no room for the use of psychological tests. Of the people who are selected for a job, some will succeed and some will not succeed. The unsuccessful employees may be released, shifted to other jobs, or remain on the job at an unsatisfactory level of performance. The number who succeed provides another important ratio:

$$\frac{\text{number who succeed}}{\text{number selected}} = \text{success ratio}$$

To illustrate the importance of the selection ratio and the success ratio, consider a hypothetical situation in which 100 persons are selected at random from the group that applies for a job. Imagine that a predictor test has been given to the entire group that applied, which, of course, could not have affected the random selection of persons. Suppose that the selected group is placed on the job and only 54 per cent of the people prove to be successful enough to continue. Later it is found that the predictor test correlates well with job performance scores. This prediction situation is illustrated in Figure 5–8.

Instead of using dots, numbers of subjects are recorded in the scatter diagram in Figure 5–8. Because 100 persons are shown, the numbers can also be interpreted as per cents. As would be expected from the meaning of the correlation coefficient, smaller and smaller per cents of failure are found as higher scores are made on the predictor test. None of the people who make a score of 20 or below succeeds on the job. Of the people who score 50 on the predictor test, 50 per cent succeed. None of the people who score as high as 70 on the predictor fails on the job.

The information in Figure 5–8 tells us that it would be foolish to go on selecting in a random manner, that the test can be used to improve the selection of employees. Just how successful the test can be in selecting the applicants is a function of the selection ratio. In this validation problem, 25 per cent of the subjects made scores of 70 or higher, and all of those succeed on the job. Because the group was randomly selected, it might be expected that, on the average, an equal per cent of all new applicants would make scores in that range. Suppose that 100 persons are needed for the job exemplified in Figure 5–8. Then, in order to select a group in which no failures are likely to be found, the number applying would have to be 400.

FIGURE 5–8. Relationship of predictor test scores to job success.

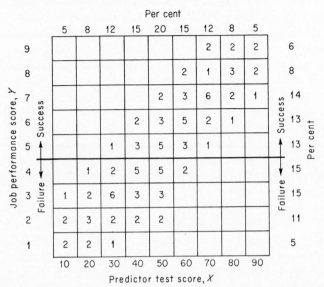

Usually it is not possible to find a combination of the proper correlation, selection ratio, and success ratio to obtain persons who all will succeed. But it is possible, often with only moderate-sized correlations, to choose a substantial preponderance of successes (see **4**).

If the success ratio is large, there is no great need for an improvement in selection procedures. The extent to which the test raises the success ratio is the measure of the test's utility in a particular situation. If the selection ratio is large, there is nothing that a predictor test can do to improve selection. One obvious way to improve the selection situation is to obtain as many applicants as possible for the job, assuming that the new groups of applicants are of the same ability levels as the ones who have been applying. In many situations, an improvement in successes of only 10 per cent will save thousands of dollars ordinarily wasted in training persons who will not succeed, as well as sparing the persons concerned the pains of failure.

In some selection situations, the success ratio tends to remain the same after predictor tests have been brought into use. This is often the case in school programs, where a certain per cent of the students are failed out as a matter of custom. If a valid predictor test is used in selection, either the number of failures decreases or the standards for success shift upwards.

Tests are used as often in vocational guidance as in selection. In vocational guidance there is no selection ratio to consider. Some good advice must be given to each individual. For example, a student might consider going into engineering on the basis of high scores on certain ability tests and the results of an interest inventory. When it is necessary to make a decision about each person, not just select the special group who score very high on a predictor test, the error in prediction is considerably larger. Even if the predictor-assessment correlation is as high as .87, the standard error of estimate is one-half the size of the assessment standard deviation. Consequently, when it is necessary to advise separate individuals, much more confidence can usually be felt when dealing with persons from either extreme of the test continuum. Persons who make very low scores can safely be dissuaded from entering the particular vocation or school program, and persons with very high scores can safely be encouraged to follow their ambitions.

Looking back at Figure 5–8, it is obvious that persons who score no higher than 30 on the predictor test would be well advised not to apply for that job; and persons who score as high as 60 could safely be advised to apply. The error in advising grows as we get into the "indifferent zone" of scores between 30 and 60. If a person has a score of 50, giving advice on the basis of the test alone would be no better than flipping a coin.

The region of maximum error in making decisions is not always in the middle of the predictor test continuum. If the job is very simple and, consequently, most persons succeed, the "indifferent zone" lies in the lower-score section of the predictor. If the job is so complex that only a minority succeed, the "indifferent zone" will lie in the upper-score regions. The farther people are on the predictor test continuum in either direction from the point of complete "indifference," where 50 per cent succeed and 50 per cent fail, the safer it is to advise them or make decisions about them.

REFERENCES

1. Dixon, W. J., and Massey, F. J. *Introduction to statistical analysis.* New York: McGraw-Hill, 1951.
2. Lindquist, E. F. *A first course in statistics.* (Rev. ed.) Boston: Houghton Mifflin, 1942.
3. McNemar, Q. *Psychological statistics.* New York: Wiley, 1949.
4. Taylor, H. C., and Russell, J. T. The relationship of validity coefficients to the practical effectiveness of tests in selection: discussion and tables. *J. appl. Psychol.*, 1939, **23**, 565–578.
5. Thorndike, R. L. *Personnel selection: test and measurement techniques.* New York: Wiley, 1949.
6. Walker, Helen M. *Elementary statistical methods.* New York: Holt, 1943.

CHAPTER 6

Reliability of Measurements

Reliability concerns the *precision* of measurement regardless of *what* is measured. Some random error is involved in all scientific measurements. For example, a metal ruler expands and contracts with changing temperatures. This introduces some error into measurements and, consequently, lowers the precision of measurements made with this ruler. Measurement error of this kind tends to obscure scientific lawfulness. For example, if there is a close relationship between electrical resistance and length of a wire, the relationship would be somewhat obscured by measuring wire with the unstable metal ruler. This is why precise measurements can be made only by holding temperature constant or by using a measuring instrument that does not vary with temperature. Psychological measures also contain a portion of random error analogous to that of the metal ruler. In this chapter we will discuss some of the ways of detecting and eliminating measurement error from tests.

A careful distinction should be made between test validity and test reliability. A test can have high reliability and not be valid for any particular purpose. For example, we might use the weight of individuals to predict college grades. Whereas weight may be measured very precisely, and thus be highly reliable, weight would be invalid as a predictor of college grades. As will be shown in the pages ahead, the opposite is not true. In order for a test to be highly valid, it must be highly reliable also. High reliability is a *necessary* but not *sufficient* condition for high validity.

Measurement Error and Predictive Efficiency. Figure 6–1 shows a hypothetical relationship between a predictor test and an assessment. As would be the case only in hypothetical circumstances, the test predicts the assessment perfectly, and consequently, all of the scores lie on a straight line. Let us see what happens when some error is introduced into the test scores. What we will do is to flip a coin for each score in turn; if it turns up "heads," we will add three points to the score; and if it is "tails," the

Figure 6–1. Relationship between a predictor test and an assessment before measurement error is added.

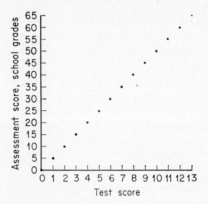

score will be left as it is. Flipping the coin for each of the test scores in turn, we find the following:

Original score	Coin flip	New score
0	H	3
1	T	1
2	H	5
3	H	6
4	H	7
5	T	5
6	T	6
7	H	10
8	H	11
9	H	12
10	T	10
11	T	11
12	H	15
13	T	13

In Figure 6–2 the new scores are plotted, with the included error component, against the assessment. The assessment scores have, of course, not been changed by the random additions to the predictor test scores. In Figure 6–2 it can be seen that there is no longer a perfect correlation. The effect of adding error to the scores is to lower the correlation. Starting off with a perfect relationship, there is no way for the relationship to change except to a lower correlation. The important point is that the addition of random error will tend to lower the correlation no matter what it is originally. If we had pictured a scatter plot with a correlation of .50, the random addition of score points would have tended to make the correlation nearer zero. Likewise, if we had a correlation of −.50, the random addition of score points would have tended to make the correlation nearer zero.

Random error works to make an observed relationship less than it would be if the randomness were not present. This is why we speak of error, or unreliability, as *attenuating*, i.e., lessening, a correlation. With as few scores as those in the example above, it is possible that the random changes in scores would either leave a correlation unchanged or could, in

FIGURE 6–2. Relationship between a predictor test and an assessment after measurement error is added.

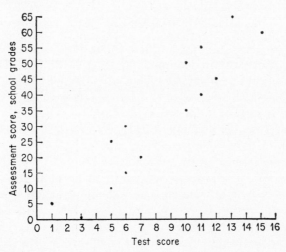

a very rare circumstance, make the correlation larger. However, the odds are against anything but a lowering of the correlation; and if the number of subjects is as large as it is in most testing situations (over 100 persons), it can be predicted not only that the correlation will be lower, but with fair accuracy, just how much it will be altered.

A rule can be stated which will help us in discussing test reliability: *If a subgroup of individuals is randomly chosen from a larger group, any differential treatment of the subgroup which tends to make the members all score higher or all score lower than if the differential treatment had not been applied will tend to lower the correlation between the scores of the total group and any other variable.* There are many ways in which test scores can be randomly altered in this way. Suppose that you are developing a test to predict school grades and that the whole group which you intend to test contains several hundred students. If some of the students are tested when they are tired, say after a long train trip, and others are tested after a good night's rest, the scores of the "tired" group will tend to be lower. If some of the students are tested in a quiet, well-lighted room and others are tested in a gloomy room adjacent to noisy machinery, the grades of the students in the less comfortable situation will tend to be lower. If the test instructions are given to one subgroup in a complete and clear manner, and if the test instructions are given to another subgroup in an incomplete and confusing manner, the grades of the latter subgroup will tend to be lower. If in each of these circumstances it can be thought that the students fall into the subgroups on a near random basis, the resulting influences on test scores will cause unreliability and will lower the ability of the test to predict school grades.

THE THEORY OF MEASUREMENT ERROR

It is easy to introduce error into test scores purposely, as was done in the example above, and to determine the effect it will have. However, in nearly all practical situations, error is not purposely introduced into scores, and the problem instead is to try to determine the amount of error which has occurred in spite of the tester's best efforts.

Samples of Tests. In a number of places so far in this book, we have had to think of the content of a test, particularly of an assessment, as being a sample from a larger collection, or universe, from which items could conceivably be drawn. It was said that a sampling logic for test content is not as easy to maintain as is a sampling logic for universes, or populations, of persons. However, here again it will be necessary to discuss content sampling to provide measures of reliability.

Any test can be thought of as one test in a universe of possible tests. If an achievement examination is being constructed, say to measure progress in spelling, many different tests of the same length could conceivably be made. Similarly with a predictor test, the individual form can be thought of as only one from a universe of tests which could be composed. Whether the test is an assessment or a predictor, the purpose is to estimate the score that the individual would make if he were given the entire universe of tests. If the score that an individual makes on one sample test is markedly different from that which he would make on another sample test, this would mean that either one or both tests are unreliable.

The Estimation of "Universe" Scores. The problem is to estimate an individual's score on a hypothetical universe of tests from the score which he makes on a sample test. (To keep in step with accepted terminology, universe scores will be referred to as "true" scores.) The most accurate way to estimate a "true" score would be to give the individual a large number of tests, say, 100 spelling tests over a period of several months, and then average the scores. It is expected that the errors would average out over time and over the different situations in which tests are administered. The individual who is lucky on one day and manages to guess some of the items would probably be unlucky on another day. The individual who is in either a poor mood or poor physical condition on one day would probably be more fit on another day. Similarly for the other sources of error variance, the errors would tend to average out. Consequently, the average score over the 100 test administrations would tend to correspond closely to an individual's "true" score.

Although measurement error would be considerably reduced if a large number of similar test forms could be used, this would be a thoroughly impractical procedure. In order to obtain estimates of "true" scores without this labor, some assumptions must be made. If sample tests all containing the same number of items were administered to a group of persons, the assumptions would be these:

1. All sample tests have the same standard deviation.

2. All sample tests correlate the same with one another (it does not matter what the correlation is).

3. All sample tests correlate the same with the universe scores (it does not matter what the correlation is). These three assumptions are all that are required to deduce mathematically the formulas for determining the influence of measurement errors on test scores. This mathematical development is given in Appendix 4 for the reader who is interested.

The Reliability Coefficient. A useful measure, if it could be obtained directly, would be the correlation of the scores from a sample test with the correlation of the universe or "true" scores. This would be symbolized as

$$r_{1u}$$

where r stands for the correlation coefficient
subscript 1 stands for test 1
subscript u stands for universe or "true" scores

If the assumptions above are valid, then r_{1u} can be determined from the correlation of any two of the sample tests. (Each of the sample tests could be labeled 1_a, 1_b, 1_c, and so on. The correlation between any two of these tests will be symbolized as r_{11}, and we will keep it in mind that the letters a and b are omitted to simplify subscripts.) Then it is proved in Appendix 4 that

$$r_{1u} = \sqrt{r_{11}} \qquad (6\text{-}1)$$

The correlation of two sample tests is called the *reliability coefficient*. Because its square root is an estimate of the correlation of either of the sample tests with the "true" scores, the reliability coefficient is said to be the per cent of non-error variance (this would be the same as the square of r_{1u}, and you will remember that the square of a correlation coefficient has meaning as a per cent of "variance explained").

The exactness of Formula (6–1) hinges on how well the assumptions above hold in particular testing situations; and because we are sure that they will not hold precisely, we must question the accuracy with which r_{1u} is estimated in practical circumstances. First we will go on to develop measurement error statistics and return in the latter part of this chapter to consider the practical problems in the estimation of reliability.

The scores that people actually make on a test can be used to estimate their universe or "true" score as follows:

$$x_u = r_{11}x_1 \tag{6-2}$$

where x_u is the individual's estimated "true" deviation score

x_1 is the individual's deviation score on test 1

r_{11} is the correlation between any two sample tests from a content universe

If an individual has a test deviation score of 10 and the reliability of the test is .90, the best estimate of his "true" score is 9. If another individual has a test deviation score of -20, his estimated "true" score is -18. The best estimate of the standard deviation of "true" scores is then

$$\sigma_u = \sigma_1\sqrt{r_{11}} \tag{6-3}$$

where σ_1 is the standard deviation of test 1

r_{11} is the reliability coefficient

σ_u is the estimated standard deviation of "true" scores

Unless the test is perfectly reliable, the standard deviation of "true" scores will be less than the standard deviation of the sample, or obtained, scores. "True" scores are of more theoretical than practical interest. People will retain their same relative score positions in respect to one another on the "true" score continuum as they have on the test actually being used.

Standard Error of Measurement. Formula (6–2) provides only an estimate of "true" scores. The precision of the estimate is dependent on how well the reliability coefficient is determined. Some methods of estimating the reliability coefficient will be discussed in the following sections. Even if the reliability coefficient is determined in the most rigorous manner, there is still an element of error in the estimation of "true" scores.

Looking back at Formula (6–2), it can be seen that "true" scores are estimated from the reliability coefficient, which is a special kind of correlation coefficient. In Chapter 5 it was shown that the correlation coefficient not only provides a way of estimating one set of scores from another, it indicates the amount of error involved in the estimation: the standard error of estimate. The reliability coefficient can be used in a similar way to estimate the error dispersion of sample scores about "true" scores:

$$\sigma_{meas} = \sigma_1\sqrt{1 - r_{11}} \qquad (6\text{-}4)$$

where σ_{meas} is the standard error of measurement

σ_1 is the standard deviation of test 1

r_{11} is the reliability coefficient

Using the example above of a test with a standard deviation of 10 and a reliability coefficient of .90, the standard error of measurement would be obtained as follows:

$$\sigma_{meas} = 10\sqrt{1 - .90}$$
$$= 10\sqrt{.10}$$
$$= 10 \times .333$$
$$= 3.33$$

It must be kept in mind that the standard error of measurement ranges about the estimated "true" score for an individual, not, as is often mistakenly assumed, about the obtained, or sample, score.

The score that a person makes on a test should never be taken as an exact point. First, it is necessary to recognize that measurement error tends to push scores out in both directions from the mean. High scores are usually overestimates of ability and low scores are underestimates. Second, measurement error introduces a zone of uncertainty about each estimated "true" score, the size of which is indicated by the standard error of measurement. Consequently, an individual's score should be considered as lying somewhere in a band along the score continuum. The width of the band which is used depends on the precision with which scores will be interpreted. If we set the odds as 1 in 100 that the individual's score will not be overestimated or underestimated, the individual can be considered to lie in a band stretching 2.56 standard errors of measurement (see Appendix 3) above and below his estimated "true" score.

The use of the standard error of measurement to set confidence intervals can be illustrated with the example above in which "true" scores for two persons are estimated to be 9 and −18 respectively and the standard error of measurement is 3.33. The .01 confidence level would then lie 8.52 (2.56 times 3.33) score units above and below each estimated "true" score. For a person with an obtained deviation score of 10 and an estimated "true" score of 9, the confidence band would stretch from .48 to 17.52. In other words, if the individual were given 100 sample tests which met the assumptions given earlier, we would expect to find only 1 of the 100 scores either less than .48 or greater than 17.52. Because most test scores are reported as integers, the confidence zone limits could be rounded to the nearest whole numbers of 0 and 18. The .01 confidence band for a person with an obtained score of −20 and an estimated "true" score of −18 would extend from −26.52 to −9.48.

The measurement error confidence band is often indicated by stating the individual's score as so much plus or minus 2.56 standard errors of measurement. For example, an *IQ* might be reported as 120 plus or minus 10. However, a common mistake is to space the confidence zone symmetrically about the obtained score rather than about the estimated "true" score. The correct procedures are either to space the confidence zone symmetrically about the estimated "true" score or asymmetrically about the obtained score. Illustrating the former, the scores in the example above could be phrased as 9 plus or minus 8.52 and −18 plus or minus 8.52. The latter approach would be to say that the scores are 10 plus 7.52 or minus 9.52 and −20 plus 10.52 or minus 6.52. Only if an individual's obtained score is exactly at the mean and, consequently, the deviation score is zero, would the confidence zone be symmetrical. Then with a standard error of measurement of 3.33 in the example above, the score would be stated as 0 plus or minus 8.52.

The Correction for Attenuation. It was said earlier that unreliability tends to attenuate, or lower, the correlation of a test with any other variable. The theory of measurement error (see Appendix 4) allows us to estimate how much the unreliability influences the predictive power of a test. For example, if we have correlated the scores on a test with a set of assessment scores and if we have made an estimate of the test reliability, a prediction can be made as to what the test assessment correlation would be if the predictor were made perfectly reliable:

$$r_{u2} = \frac{r_{12}}{\sqrt{r_{11}}} \tag{6-5}$$

where r_{11} is the reliability estimate for test 1

r_{12} is the correlation of test 1 with the assessment, 2

r_{u2} is the estimate of how much 1 would correlate with 2 if the test were made perfectly reliable

Formula (6–5) can be illustrated in the situation where a test correlates .50 with an assessment and the test reliability is estimated as being .81:

$$r_{u2} = \frac{.50}{\sqrt{.81}}$$

$$= \frac{.50}{.9}$$

$$= .56$$

We would expect then that as the test is made more and more reliable its predictive validity will move toward .56.

The correction for attenuation is often said to estimate the "true" relationship between a test variable and an assessment; however, because of the assumptions which must be made, such estimates should always be taken with a "grain of salt." Where the correction for attenuation is helpful is in indicating the improvement in predictive validity that might follow from an improvement in test reliability. In the early stages of a testing program, it is often necessary to compose short and relatively unreliable tests. The correction for attenuation provides a helpful suggestion as to how well particular tests will work if they are lengthened and more highly standardized.

Whereas it is important to consider the measurement error in predictor tests, it is equally important to consider the measurement error in the assessments they are meant to forecast. In many situations, the assessment is less reliable than the predictor test. This is particularly so when the assessment consists of impressionistic ratings by foremen and supervisors. The reliability of the assessment can be used in the correction for attenuation as follows:

$$r_{1u} = \frac{r_{12}}{\sqrt{r_{22}}} \qquad (6\text{–}6)$$

where r_{1u} is the correlation of a test with a completely reliable assessment

r_{12} is the correlation of a test with obtained assessment scores

r_{22} is the reliability of the assessment

If a predictor test correlates .32 with an assessment, and the reliability of the assessment is .64, the correction for attenuation would be as follows:

$$r_{1u} = \frac{.32}{\sqrt{.64}}$$

$$= \frac{.32}{.8}$$

$$= .40$$

Whereas the correction for attenuation due to the unreliability of the predictor test is only an indication of the increased validity that might come from improving the predictor, the correction due to the unreliability of the assessment indicates how well the test "really" works at present. Predictor tests often work much better than the test-assessment correlations indicate. If, as is often the case, assessments are relatively unreliable, the predictors actually do a much better job than the correlations show. It is then quite sensible to correct for attenuation due to the assessment unreliability, as shown in Formula (6–6), to estimate the "real" test validity.

Finally, a double correction for attenuation can be made which considers the unreliability in both the predictor and the assessment:

$$r_{uu} = \frac{r_{12}}{\sqrt{r_{11}}\sqrt{r_{22}}} \qquad (6\text{--}7)$$

where r_{uu} is the correlation between a perfectly reliable predictor and a perfectly reliable assessment, and other symbols retain the meanings given above

For example, if a test correlates .36 with an assessment, and if the reliabilities of the predictor and the assessment are .81 and .64 respectively, the correction would be as follows:

$$r_{uu} = \frac{.36}{\sqrt{.81}\sqrt{.64}}$$

$$= \frac{.36}{.9 \times .8}$$

$$= \frac{.36}{.72}$$

$$= .50$$

The correction for attenuation can be made to estimate not only what a correlation would be if the test were made perfectly reliable, it can be used to estimate how much the predictive validity will rise if the reliability is raised by any particular amount (see Appendix 9).

SOURCES OF UNRELIABILITY

It was stated that any random influence on test scores will cause unreliability. There are many ways in which this can happen in practice. Some of the most prominent sources of unreliability are discussed in the following sections.

Poorly Standardized Instructions. If parts of the test instructions are given orally by the tester, there is always the possibility that testers will vary the instructions to an extent which will introduce measurement error into the scores. The tester who gives inadequate instructions, failing, for example, to mention that the subjects can go back later to questions which are left blank initially, will penalize his group. If the tester is too lenient in setting the time limit for a test, the group will make higher scores than would have been the case with a strict adherence to time. If the test instructions vary in any way from group to group, the results of the test will tend to be unreliable.

When test instructions are not written out as part of the examination booklet, a standard set of instructions should be made for all testers to read to their groups. In addition, all testers should adhere strictly to time limits and other standardized procedures.

Errors in Scoring Tests. On multiple choice tests, the errors in scoring are purely mechanical. If the test is scored "by hand," it is possible to accidentally score some "correct" answers as "incorrect" and vice versa. Also, errors can be made in counting up the number of "correct" and "incorrect" answers for each person. If tests are machine scored, an improperly functioning machine can add a considerable amount of measurement error to test scores.

The errors in scoring an "essay" examination are more subtle in character, but they also make for unreliability. One of the prime sources of unreliability in scoring essay examinations comes from the different grading standards used by different instructors. If three instructors teach different sections of the same course, they will probably have at least slightly different ideas about what kinds of answers merit good and bad marks. If each instructor grades his own examinations, the grade that a person gets is partly dependent on the instructor he happens to have.

Measurement error is also "built in" the individual instructor. If an instructor regrades a set of essay examinations after a period of time, and there are no identifying marks to indicate what the earlier grades were, the grades will be somewhat different the second time. Another source of measurement error is that the instructor often changes his standards as he goes through a set of essay examinations. He might have strict standards at first; but as he goes through the papers and sees that none of them measure up, he is likely to become more lenient. Consequently, the grade that a student obtains is dependent on the chance appearance of his test in the order in which they are graded. Some ways of improving the reliability of essay examinations will be discussed in Chapter 8.

Errors Due to Testing Environment. An effort should be made to test subjects under uniform conditions. Carried to extremes this rule becomes impossible to follow. However, gross differences in testing environment can be removed, such as testing one group in a poorly lighted, noisy room and testing others in more comfortable surroundings.

Errors Due to "Guessing." In Chapter 3, we discussed the effect of guessing on multiple choice tests and the inequities in scoring which can result from a failure to make corrections for guessing. The correction formula presented there is true only on the average. It is not capable of specifying exactly how much an individual knows. Some individuals may be "lucky" enough to guess considerably more than the expected number of items, and other individuals may guess fewer correct than would be expected on the average. Therefore, guessing on multiple choice tests adds a certain portion of unreliability to test scores. Also, because the individuals who know the least do the most guessing (assuming that everyone tries every item), guessing tends to make lower scores less reliable than higher scores.

A free-response test, one in which the subject supplies the correct answer, is theoretically more reliable than a multiple choice form. However, there are few subject matters which can be cast in the free-response form, the requirement being that there be only one word or term which represents the correct answer. The point to consider is that multiple choice tests become more reliable as the number of alternative answers is increased. If the subject matter permits, a test will be more reliable if five or six alternatives are used for each item instead of only two or three.

Errors Due to the Sampling of Content. If the object is to estimate an individual's score on a universe of content, the sampling of content for a particular test will introduce some unreliability. Every student has had the feeling that he was "lucky" on a particular test, that of the many topics in the course, the instructor happened to ask about things which he knew. Another student, with the same level of understanding about the whole course material, may have been "unlucky" in that he happened not to know about the particular questions.

As in all sampling problems, the more items there are, the less unreliability will come from the sampling of items. Generally speaking, longer tests are more reliable than shorter tests. In order to reduce the unreliability due to sampling error, as many items as possible should be used (and also the items should range broadly over the subject matter). However, this is somewhat in opposition to reducing the unreliability due to guessing by making as many alternatives for each item as possible. Due to the difficulties in composing tests, and the limited amount of time available for testing, some compromise must be reached between the need to have both many items and many alternative answers for each item. That is why many standard tests have sought a compromise solution in using about four or five alternatives, with as many items as time will permit.

Errors in the Individual. A large portion of the measurement error in most tests is due to "chance" fluctuations in the individual which raise or lower his score. A fly lighting on the student's test, a broken pencil, a momentary distraction, a concern about the next school dance, a mistake in marking the answer sheet, and many more such "chance" events can influence test scores. Although such "chance" influences tend to average out over a long, well-standardized test, there always remains a component of unreliability due to errors in the individual.

Errors Due to Instability of Scores. In most testing situations, an individual's score is expected not only to represent his immediate standing but his standing for some time to come. The stability which is expected of scores is relative to the type of test. If students are given the same examination or a similar examination several weeks after the first testing, it is expected that the two sets of scores will correlate highly. Scores on intelligence tests are expected to remain relatively stable over long periods of time. If a child's *IQ* goes up or down by as much as 10 points over a period of two years, it makes the test very difficult to use. On the other hand, there are measures which are expected to change in relatively short periods of time. If an experiment is being conducted to alter the attitudes of a group of students towards some political issue, it is expected that a test of attitudes given after the experiment will show differences from a test given before the experiment. Whenever a psychological process is being studied or when individuals participate in an experiment, it is expected that changes of some kind will occur. If measures remain absolutely stable during the study, then there are no research findings to report, except to say that nothing changed.

Instability of test scores acts much like the other sources of error to reduce the reliability. If intelligence test scores obtained in the fourth grade are used to place children in special classes in the eighth grade, and if the scores have fluctuated markedly during that time, the test scores will do a poor job of classifying the children. If a child is being placed in a special class because the earlier testing showed an *IQ* of 125 and if a test given four years later shows an actual *IQ* of only 110, the original test score would give a faulty picture of the child's ability. It is theoretically possible that earlier scores will be more predictive than scores obtained at the time when decisions are made about people, but this is almost never found in practice. The safest assumption is that if scores are used over a period of time as an indication of an individual's standing, and the scores are found to be unstable, the instability makes for unreliability.

ESTIMATING THE RELIABILITY COEFFICIENT

What has been said so far about the sources of measurement error and the influence of measurement error on test scores depends on the theory of reliability, the conditions of which were given earlier. However, the theory is an idealization of the practical circumstances in which tests are used, and consequently, we can only estimate the reliability coefficient rather than determine it directly. There are a number of ways of estimating the reliability coefficient, each of which has its own advantages and disadvantages.

Retest Method. The simplest approach to determining the reliability coefficient is to give the same test on two occasions. The correlation between the two sets of scores will be an estimate of the reliability coefficient, r_{11}, as it was denoted earlier.

There are two important disadvantages in using the retest method. The first is that the obtained reliability coefficient will reflect little of the error due to the sampling of content. The second is that the individual's memory of his answers to the first test administration is quite likely to influence the answers which he gives on the second test administration. Such influences should dwindle as the time between the two test administrations is lengthened, and therefore, it is wise to wait at least several weeks before retesting. However, it is possible that memory will affect the second administration to some extent even if there are several years between testings. Memory works to make the two sets of test scores correlate highly, and consequently, the reliability coefficient is usually an overestimate when determined by the retest method.

Equivalent-form Method. Instead of using the same test on two occasions, it is better to use two "equivalent" forms (also called "comparable" forms and "parallel" forms). That is, instead of making up only one test form, two forms can be constructed which are very much alike. If, in constructing either an achievement test or a predictor, explicit sampling procedures have been used (test items have been sampled from a large collection of relevant items), an equivalent form can be obtained by the random selection of new items. However, in the construction of most tests, the sampling is not so exact: the items are simply collected across a broad range of the hypothetical universe of content without an explicit sampling. Then, to obtain an equivalent form, the test constructor must try to make up a test that "looks" as much like the first form as possible. Sometimes this is a fairly easy task, for example, where the test contains spelling items, vocabulary items, or arithmetic items. But in some of the other tests of ability, and in many of the personality tests, it is difficult to compose equivalent forms.

When the reliability coefficient is obtained from equivalent forms, it will manifest more of the sources of measurement error, and more accurately, than any other method. It will contain all of the sources of measurement error found in the retest method and, in addition, will give an indication of the amount of error due to the sampling of content. Although the memory of one test form may give the individual a slight advantage on taking the equivalent form, the effect of memory on the equivalent form reliability coefficient is slight. Were it not for the expense and the difficulties of making up equivalent forms, this method of reliability estimation would almost always be preferable to the retest method.

Subdivided-test Method. Instead of making up equivalent forms, a compromise procedure has been to obtain "part scores" for different sections within the same test. The most popular of such procedures, referred to as the "split-half" method, is to give the individual one score on all of the even-numbered questions in the examination and another score on the odd-numbered items. The two halves of the same test can then be correlated to obtain an estimate of the reliability coefficient. A statistical correction then must be made to estimate the reliability of the whole test, not just of the half-tests (the correction is given and discussed in Appendix 5).

Practical considerations have caused the subdivided-test method to be used as extensively as it has. In many situations it is either too expensive to compose equivalent forms, or it is not possible to obtain the same subjects for a second test administration. However, there are some serious flaws in the use of the subdivided-test method. Although the method determines some of the error due to the sampling of content, it does not do this as well as the equivalent-form method. The subdivided test shows none of the error due to instability over time, because both halves of the test are given at the same time. For these reasons, the subdivided-test method usually gives an overestimate of the reliability.

It is particularly misleading to use the subdivided-test method on a highly "speeded" test (see 1, pp. 110–114). Such a test would be, for example, one in which the subjects are asked to complete as many simple arithmetic problems as possible in a short period of time. If the problems are very simple, it is a test of how fast the individual can work. Then each person is likely to get nearly all of the items correct as far as he goes, and individuals will differ mainly in terms of how far along in the items they are when time is called. This works to make the individual's scores very much alike on the split-halves. The odd and even scores will be alike on most of the items up to the point at which time is called, because most of them will be correct. Also, the odd and even items will be alike beyond that point, because they would all be incorrect. The split-half reliability estimate obtained on a purely speeded test, such as the one illustrated here, would be completely meaningless. Fortunately, there are very few tests which are purely concerned with speed. Most tests have some time limit simply as a practical way of getting the test completed, but time, as such, might be only a trivial influence on the scores. However, we should always be wary of split-half reliability estimates obtained on highly speeded tests.

Item-interrelationship Methods. The individual who works in the field of testing will encounter special methods of reliability estimation based on homogeneity, or amount of correlation among the item responses within one test (see **2,** pp. 385–389). Because these methods work within the items on one test, they provide no indication of the fluctuation in scores over time. What these formulas do is to provide a conservative estimate of the subdivided-test type of reliability. The item-interrelationship formulas are the preferred procedures when the retest method is not advisable and when equivalent forms are not available.

Measurement of Stability. Most psychologists prefer to consider the measurement of stability of scores over time as a separate problem from the measurement of the other sources of error variance. As was said previously, stability is expected of some instruments and not of others. Also, whether or not it is necessary for test scores to remain stable depends on the way in which the test is used. If an instrument is used over a number of years to make predictions, then stability of scores is essential.

It should be obvious that stability can be measured only by the retest and the equivalent-form techniques and not by the subdivided-test and item-interrelationship techniques. Stability can be measured either by retesting or, preferably, by administering equivalent forms over the range of time in which the test is used to make predictions. The measurement of stability is of more theoretical interest than practical importance. It is usually unsafe to use test scores obtained at one time to make predictions or counsel individuals at a much later time. It is better to give tests at the time when decisions must be made about individuals. The measurement of stability is primarily important in helping us understand how human attributes develop and change.

In using either the retest or the equivalent-form techniques for measuring reliability, it is customary to space the test administrations several days to a month or more apart. This is done not so much to measure stability over time but to measure "errors in the individual." It is reasonable to expect day-to-day fluctuations in moods and physical conditions to influence test scores. If the two test administrations occurred on the same day or only several days apart, it would provide an insufficient basis for measuring the errors due to fluctuating moods and physical conditions. Also, if the time span between administrations is very short, individuals will remember the first test and will tend to repeat their work habits, guessing behavior, and characteristic mistakes on the second test.

THE HANDLING OF MEASUREMENT ERROR
IN A TESTING PROGRAM

Because of the tendency for errors of measurement to lower test validity regardless of the sense in which validity is determined, unreliability is "bad" in any measurement situation. No definite rule can be stated as to how high the reliability coefficient should be for a test, but in general one suspects a test that has a coefficient less than .80. Some of the better-standardized instruments have reliability coefficients over .90.

It must be remembered that measurement error is important only because it attenuates test validity. If a predictor test has a high correlation with its criterion, reliability is no problem. The test constructor is concerned with measurement error when a test fails to predict its criterion. It is sometimes found that the low predictive power of the test is due to unreliability from one or more of the error sources described previously. By removing some of the sources of measurement error, the predictive power of the test can be increased.

Increased Standardization. Rather than worry about unreliability after it has occurred, it is primarily important to remove as many sources of measurement error as possible when the test is being constructed. Anything that works to standardize the test instructions and procedures of administration, prevents errors in scoring, equates testing environments, and lowers the influence of guessing, will make a test more reliable. Errors in the sampling of content can be lowered to some extent by either an actual sampling of items or a careful effort to range the items across a defined universe of materials. However, even with the best sampling of items, there will be some sampling error due to the limited number of items in any test.

It is often erroneously assumed that the need for test standardization requires that tests should be given under the most comfortable conditions possible. The requirement is that all subjects should be treated in the *same* way. A particular test may be most valid if the subjects are told little about the instrument or if they are purposely confused. It may also promote test validity if the subjects are purposely distracted and harassed while the test is being administered.

Increasing the Number of Items. After all efforts have been made to increase test standardization, the reliability can be raised by making the test longer. The increased length will act to reduce the errors due to "guessing," the errors due to the sampling of content, and the errors in the individual. If we make several reasonable assumptions about the effect of lengthening a test, it can be predicted how much the reliability will be raised by increasing the number of items (the formula is presented and explained in Appendix 5).

Residual Errors. In spite of the tester's best efforts, there will remain some measurement error, and there will be considerably more in some tests than in others. In some of the personality inventories where the individual is asked vague questions, the scores will inevitably be unreliable. Similarly, nothing can be done to remove errors due to instability over time, which are errors only in the sense that they hinder predictions.

If the trait being measured fluctuates over short periods of time, the test will be of little use in predicting behavior. For example, it is relatively meaningless to give interest tests to grammar school students, if the purpose is to use the results in planning future training. The things that children say they will want to study and work at professionally undergo marked changes in relatively short periods of time.

Interpretation of Reliability Coefficients. All commercial tests should report complete reliability data (see **4**). If the test manual either gives no reliability information or states a reliability coefficient without saying how it was determined, the test should be viewed with suspicion. In particular, the manual should tell the standard deviation of scores for the group on which the reliability estimate was made. The reliability estimate is a correlation coefficient, and like all correlations, its size is directly dependent on the dispersion, or standard deviation, of scores. The reliability coefficient is directly meaningful only when the standard deviation of test scores is the same as the standard deviation for the group with which the test will be used. It was said in Chapter 5 that the standard error of estimate tends to remain unchanged with changes in test dispersion, but that the correlation coefficient tends to change with the dispersion. Similarly, the standard error of measurement tends to remain the same with changes in the dispersion of test scores, and the reliability coefficient becomes larger as more diverse groups are studied.

If a test is being constructed to predict success for college applicants, and a reliability study is being made of the test, the group used in the reliability study should have a standard deviation of test scores which is very nearly the same as that of the total group of applicants. If the reliability study is made on a group of freshmen, this will not include the individuals who were refused admission, and consequently, the standard deviation of scores in the reliability study will be too small. The reliability coefficient will then be an underestimate. If the standard deviations are known both for the whole group and the subgroup which is used in the reliability study, statistical corrections can be made (see **3**, pp. 96–99; **2**, p. 392).

There have been cases where the erroneously high reliability coefficients which have been reported in test manuals were obtained by computing the coefficients on groups of subjects more diverse than those in which the tests are actually to be used. This has been done most frequently in determining the reliability of raw scores or mental ages on intelligence tests by using groups of children ranging in age from, say, nine through twelve years. This makes the standard deviation of scores much larger than if a representative sample is obtained at one age level only.

If a test is to be used consistently, and especially if it is a commercially published instrument, thorough reliability studies should be made. The results should then be fully reported, including (1) the method used to estimate the reliability coefficient, (2) the standard deviations of scores, (3) the standard error of measurement, and (4) a description of the sample of persons used in the reliability study.

REFERENCES

1. Anastasi, Anne. *Psychological testing.* New York: Macmillan, 1954.
2. Guilford, J. P. *Psychometric methods.* (2nd ed.) New York: McGraw-Hill, 1954.
3. Thorndike, R. L. *Personnel selection: test and measurement techniques.* New York: Wiley, 1949.
4. American Psychological Association, Committee on Test Standards. Technical recommendations for psychological tests and diagnostic techniques. *Psychol. Bull.,* 1954, **51**, No. 2, Part 2.

CHAPTER 7

Multivariate Prediction

The use of one predictor test to forecast an assessment was discussed in Chapter 5. In many testing programs there will be several predictor tests used, and there are often several assessments to which the predictors are applied. A typical situation is the selection of students for graduate school. A battery of tests might be employed, including, say, vocabulary, mathematical reasoning, mechanical aptitude, knowledge of current events, and a personality test of introversion. The tests could be used to select students for different graduate schools, such as engineering, psychology, mathematics, journalism, physics, and others. Multivariate prediction problems are much more complicated than the relatively simple strategy of using only one predictor test. This chapter will discuss some of the general principles and techniques for dealing with multiple measurements.

Multiple Correlation. First we will discuss the situation in which several tests are used to predict one assessment. It is generally the case that scores from two or more tests can be combined in such a way as to improve the predictions that can be made from one test alone. Much the same is done in everyday life when we gather different kinds of information before making decisions. Suppose, for example, that you are thinking of buying a certain make of automobile. For one source of information you might talk with a person who owns one of the automobiles to get his reactions. Not being satisfied with the one source of information, you might discuss the automobile with a mechanic, take a trial drive, and consult the reports of consumers' magazines. If all of these sources of information gave favorable indications about the automobile, you would feel much more confident in making the purchase. In this instance you would be using a number of sources of information to predict future satisfaction with the particular make of automobile. In like fashion, drawing information from a variety of tests enables us to make a better prediction of the performance of individuals.

In order to discuss the use of a battery of tests to predict an assessment, it will be helpful to return to the concept of "variance explained" as it

114

was mentioned in Chapter 5. There it was said that the squared correlation coefficient indicates the per cent of the assessment variance which can be "explained" by a predictor test. Partitioning variance in this way has its most direct meaning in the mathematical statistics of prediction, and it is sometimes difficult to see its common-sense meaning. In Chapter 5 the per cent of variance *not* explained was stated as

$$\text{Per cent of variance } not \text{ explained} = \frac{\sigma^2_{est}}{\sigma^2_y}$$

(More properly, it is a variance ratio, a fraction rather than a per cent; but we customarily read ratios of variances without the decimal point, or, in other words, as per cents.) By subtracting the per cent of variance not explained from 1.00, the per cent of variance explained is found:

$$\text{Per cent of variance explained} = 1 - \frac{\sigma^2_{est}}{\sigma^2_y} = r^2$$

Another way of looking at the problem is that there are individual differences in assessment scores and that the size of these individual differences is indicated by the variance. The strategy is to use the individual differences on the predictor test to predict individual differences, or the variance of individual differences, in assessment scores. The larger the per cent of variance explained, r^2, the more effective the test is in predicting individual differences on the assessment.

One way to understand the prediction problem is to think in terms of geometric designs showing the amount of overlap of predictor tests with the assessment. Here we will use squares to represent the variances of the predictors and the assessment. Imagine that our purpose is to predict college grade averages, and the first test that we employ, a vocabulary test, correlates .50 with grade averages. This means that 25 per cent of the assessment variance is explained by one predictor, vocabulary. The overlapping variance can be illustrated as in Figure 7–1.

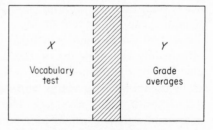

FIGURE 7–1. Variance diagram showing correlation of .50 between a test and an assessment.

The vocabulary square has been placed over 25 per cent of the area of the grade average square. The same picture would be obtained by laying one cardboard square over 25 per cent of the area of another cardboard square.

Variance diagrams like that in Figure 7–1 begin to show their usefulness when we consider the application of more than one predictor test.

Suppose that in addition to the vocabulary test, an introversion test is given to the college students. It correlates .50 with grade averages and zero with vocabulary. In other words, introversion explains *another* 25 per cent of the grade average variance. A diagram showing the overlap of both vocabulary and introversion on grade averages is shown in Figure 7–2. The vocabulary and introversion tests together explain 50 per cent of the variance of grade averages.

FIGURE 7–2. Variance diagram showing two tests which each correlate .50 with an assessment. The correlation between the two tests is .00.

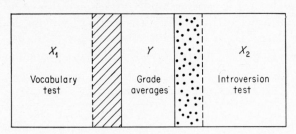

The combined variance explained by a number of predictor tests can be used to form a correlation coefficient. It is called the multiple correlation, and it will be labeled with a capital R instead of with the lower case r that is used for the bivariate, or "simple" correlation. The symbol for multiple correlation in its complete form is $R_{y \cdot 123 \cdots p}$. The symbol means the correlation of all the tests 1, 2, 3, up to p, with the assessment Y. The multiple correlation for the problem in Figure 7–2 would be symbolized as $R_{y \cdot 12}$. In Figure 7–2 the 50 per cent of the variance explained means that there is a multiple correlation of approximately .71, obtained by finding the square root of .50.

If a third test is found which correlates zero with both vocabulary and introversion, the variance of the assessment which it explains can be added to that explained by the other two. Imagine that a mathematics test is used which correlates zero with both vocabulary and introversion and .30 with grade averages. The three independent portions of the assessment variance would then sum to .59. The multiple correlation of vocabulary, introversion, and mathematics with grade averages is then .77, the square root of .59.

If we could continue to find new tests which correlate zero with the tests already being used and which correlate to some extent with the assessment, the per cents of variance explained would accumulate until the assessment is predicted perfectly. In this unusual circumstance in which the tests all correlate zero among themselves, the multiple correlation can be obtained very easily. The squared multiple correlation equals the sum of the squared correlations of the predictors with the assessment.

Correlated Tests. The strategy of employing a battery of tests to predict an assessment is more complicated than the description given so far. If correlations among predictor tests were in fact zero, the multiple correlation would be easy to compute and easy to understand. However, correlations among tests are almost never zero, and in most cases, the correlations are substantial. Then the portions of variance explained by the different predictor tests are no longer independent and can no longer be summed to obtain the squared multiple correlation. Going back to the illustration in Figure 7–2, imagine that vocabulary and introversion each correlates .50 with grade averages but, now, imagine that the correlation between vocabulary and introversion is .50 instead of zero. The overlapping variances are shown in Figure 7–3. In Figure 7–3 each vari-

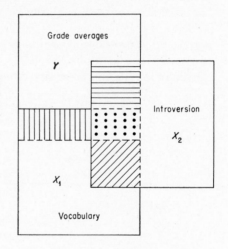

FIGURE 7–3. Variance diagram showing two tests which correlate .50 with an assessment and in which the correlation between the two tests is also .50.

able overlaps 25 per cent of the areas of the other two variables. Vocabulary covers 25 per cent of the area of grade averages and 25 per cent of the area of introversion. Similarly, introversion covers 25 per cent of grade average area and 25 per cent of the vocabulary area. With the addition of the correlation between vocabulary and introversion, Figure 7–3 cannot be used to obtain the multiple correlation directly. However, the diagram will prove useful in showing how a solution is obtained.

In Figure 7–3 there are three areas in which grade average is overlapped by at least one of the predictors. The area with vertical lines is a part of the assessment that is explained by vocabulary alone. The area with horizontal lines is a portion of the assessment that is explained by introversion alone. The dotted area is a portion of the variance of the assessment that is explained in common by vocabulary and introversion.

In Figure 7–2 where there was no overlap between vocabulary and introversion, the areas of overlap with grade averages could be added to obtain a squared multiple correlation of .50. Because the predictors do overlap in Figure 7–3, it would not be correct to add the per cents of variance each has in common with grades. Instead, the correct estimate of the variance of grades explained by the two predictors must be somewhat less than the 50 per cent that was obtained from Figure 7–2. To the extent that the tests correlate among themselves, the squared multiple correlation of the tests with the assessment will be different from the sum of the squared simple correlations of the tests with the assessment.

First we will look at some examples of multiple correlations obtained where the correlations among predictor tests are not zero. Then, we will go on to see how the multiple correlation is obtained in the general case. The symbol r_{y1} will stand for the correlation between the assessment and predictor test 1. The symbol r_{12} will stand for the correlation between the tests 1 and 2. Considering two tests each of which correlates .50 with an assessment, the multiple correlation for varying degrees of relationship between the tests can be seen as follows:

$$(1) \quad \begin{aligned} r_{y1} &= .50 \\ r_{y2} &= .50 \qquad R = .71 \\ r_{12} &= .00 \end{aligned}$$

$$(2) \quad \begin{aligned} r_{y1} &= .50 \\ r_{y2} &= .50 \qquad R = .62 \\ r_{12} &= .30 \end{aligned}$$

$$(3) \quad \begin{aligned} r_{y1} &= .50 \\ r_{y2} &= .50 \qquad R = .58 \\ r_{12} &= .50 \end{aligned}$$

$$(4) \quad \begin{aligned} r_{y1} &= .50 \\ r_{y2} &= .50 \qquad R = .54 \\ r_{12} &= .70 \end{aligned}$$

$$(5) \quad \begin{aligned} r_{y1} &= .50 \\ r_{y2} &= .50 \qquad R = .53 \\ r_{12} &= .80 \end{aligned}$$

In the examples above, it can be seen that the multiple correlation dwindles as the correlation between the tests grows larger. When the correlation between the two predictor tests is .30, the multiple correlation drops to .62. When the correlation between the tests reaches .70, the multiple correlation goes down to .54. From that point on the multiple correlation drops off very slowly, going down only 1 point as the correlation between the two predictor tests goes from .70 to .80.

The multiple correlation would reach .50 only when the correlation between the two predictors became 1.00. A perfect correlation between the two tests could be pictured by placing the variance square for vocabulary completely over the variance square for introversion. Then they would both necessarily overlap the grade average area in exactly the same place and the same amount. Consequently the multiple correlation would have to be the same as the simple correlation of either predictor with grade averages.

The multiple correlation will always be at least as large as the largest correlation between any of the predictor tests and the assessment. That is, if one of the tests correlates .50 with the assessment, no matter what other correlations are found, the multiple correlation cannot be smaller than .50. This is another way of saying that when using multiple correlation the addition of tests to a battery cannot lower the predictive efficiency that is already present.

Multiple Regression. Now that some background has been obtained on multiple correlation, the technical aspects of the problem can be discussed. The use of the correlation coefficient was discussed in Chapter 5 in respect to the regression equation, or the equation for the best-fit line. The standard score form of the regression equation was given as

$$z'_y = r z_x$$

When there is more than one variable to be used in predicting an assessment, the regression equation can be extended as follows:

$$z'_y = \beta_1 z_1 + \beta_2 z_2 + \beta_3 z_3 + \cdots + \beta_p z_p \qquad (7\text{--}1)$$

where z'_y is an estimated standard score on an assessment (college grades)

z_1 is the standard score actually obtained on the first predictor (say, vocabulary)

β_1 is the weight for the first predictor

What the above equation says is that, for any p number of tests, there are weights by which to multiply the standard scores of the predictors such that the composite scores will give the best estimate of the assessment. The least-squares criterion is used as the standard for a "best estimate." The problem is then to find the β's, called regression weights, or *beta* weights. The answer is relatively simple when the problem entails only two predictors:

$$\beta_1 = \frac{r_{y1} - r_{y2}r_{12}}{1 - r^2_{12}}$$

$$\beta_2 = \frac{r_{y2} - r_{y1}r_{12}}{1 - r^2_{12}}$$

(7-2)

The formulas can be illustrated with the following correlations:

$$r_{y1} = .50 \qquad \beta_1 = \frac{.50 - (.60 \times .30)}{1 - (.30)^2} = .352$$

$$r_{y2} = .60$$

$$r_{12} = .30 \qquad \beta_2 = \frac{.60 - (.50 \times .30)}{1 - (.30)^2} = .494$$

The obtained *beta* weights can be substituted into the multiple regression equation to predict assessment scores. For an individual with standard scores of 1.00 and .50 on tests 1 and 2 respectively, the prediction would be as follows:

$$z'_y = .352 (1.00) + .494 (.50)$$

$$z'_y = .60$$

The prediction is that this person will make a standard score on the assessment of .60.

The *beta* weights can be obtained for any number of predictor tests. However, the procedure for obtaining the weights grows increasingly laborious after more than two predictors are used. The procedures for obtaining *beta* weights for more than two predictors can be found in most advanced texts on statistics (see **2, 4, 7**).

After the *beta* weights are obtained, they in turn can be used to determine the multiple correlation:

$$R^2 = \beta_1 r_{y1} + \beta_2 r_{y2} + \cdots + \beta_p r_{yp}$$

(7-3)

The squared multiple correlation is found by multiplying each predictor-assessment correlation by the *beta* weight for the predictor and summing over the number of predictors being used. The *beta* weights and correlations in the example above can be used to illustrate the computations:

$$R^2 = .352 (.50) + .494 (.60)$$

$$R^2 = .472$$

$$R = .69$$

What the multiple regression equation does is to transform a multivariate comparison to a bivariate comparison. That is, at the start of the problem each person has a number of predictor test scores. The multiple regression equation combines the separate predictor scores into one score (z'_y). The question is then, "How well do the z'_y scores correlate with the actual assessment scores (z_y)?" The answer is given by the coefficient of multiple correlation, Formula (7–3).

The Standard Error of Estimate in Multiple Regression. In Chapter 5 the standard error of estimate was described in the bivariate prediction problem. A similar measure can be derived from a multiple correlation:

$$\sigma_{\text{est}} = \sigma_y \sqrt{1 - R^2} \qquad (7\text{--}4)$$

The only difference between the formula above and that used in the bivariate regression problem is that the multiple correlation, R, is substituted for the simple correlation, r. The standard error of estimate obtained with the multiple correlation has the same properties as that obtained in the bivariate problem. It can be used to set confidence intervals for predicted scores. The standard error of estimate with a multiple correlation of .69 would be:

$$\sigma_{\text{est}} = \sigma_y \sqrt{1 - (.69)^2}$$
$$= .72 \, \sigma_y$$

If predictions are being made of standard scores on the assessment, σ_y equals 1.00; and consequently, the standard error of estimate is .72. If we were predicting either raw or deviation scores whose standard deviation is 2.0, the standard error of estimate would be 1.44.

Sampling Error of the Multiple Correlation. In Chapter 5 we discussed the sampling error problems in using simple correlations. The two most important considerations are: (1) determining whether a particular correlation is significantly different from zero correlation, and (2) determining whether two correlations are significantly different from each other. These two problems also occur in the use of multiple correlation. The first type of problem can be illustrated with two tests that have no predictive validity for a particular assessment: the population values of the correlations between the tests and the assessment are zero. In any particular sample of persons from the population, the obtained correlations would probably not be exactly zero. More to be expected is that the correlations obtained from successive samples would range about zero, with a dispersion dependent on the sample size.

If the multiple correlation formula is applied to the chance coefficients obtained in our hypothetical problem, it will make the most of the chance relationships. It was stated previously that the multiple correlation will never be smaller than the largest predictor-assessment correlation. In nearly all cases, the multiple correlation will be larger than any of the simple correlations between the tests and the assessment, even if by only 1 or 2 points. The multiple correlation tends to "take advantage of chance" to obtain a maximized coefficient. For this reason, special formulas must be used to determine the significance of multiple correlations (see **2**, p. 399; **4**, pp. 276–280). A discussion of these formulas would be too technical for inclusion in this book, but they should be studied when need arises.

The second problem, that of determining the significance of the difference between two multiple correlations, is a very real, practical problem in testing. This chapter began by considering the likelihood that adding tests to a battery will improve the prediction of an assessment. Suppose, for example, that we are using a vocabulary test and a mathematical reasoning test to predict how well students will perform in psychology training. We might then want to add new tests to improve the power of prediction. For this purpose a personality test might be used. Imagine that the multiple correlation with the grades in psychology training is .50 before the personality test is added and .58 after the personality test is added. Before we can consider the practical importance of the apparent gain in prediction, it must be determined whether or not the difference could likely be due to chance. A statistical check should be made to provide some assurance that the new test actually improves the prediction of the assessment.

Because of the tendency for multiple regression analysis to "take advantage of chance," the *beta* weights obtained in a sample will produce a higher multiple correlation in that sample than they will when applied to a new sample of persons. This is the same as saying that the multiple correlation tends to "shrink" when the *beta* weights are applied to a new group of persons. In the example above, the *beta* weights applied to the *same* sample on which they were derived produced a multiple correlation of .69. If the *beta* weights are now applied to a new group of people, the predicted assessment scores will probably not correlate .69 with actual assessment scores. The odds are that using the *beta* weights obtained from the first sample will lead to a lower multiple correlation in the second sample. The shrinkage is small if the first sample is large, say, over 300 persons; but if the *beta* weights are determined originally on as few as 50 persons, the shrinkage is often substantial (see **4**, pp. 185–186). The amount of shrinkage is also related to the number of predictor tests being used. The more tests there are, the more opportunity there is to "take advantage of chance," and consequently, the more shrinkage to be expected. The proper way to determine the predictive efficiency of a set of *beta* weights is to "cross validate." That is, the *beta* weights should be determined on one sample of persons and then tried out on a second sample. The correlation between the predicted scores in the second sample and the actual assessment scores is the best estimate of the predictive efficiency of the battery.

SELECTION OF TESTS FOR A BATTERY

When only one test is to be used in predicting a particular assessment, there is little difficulty in deciding how to choose the test. The test that correlates the most with the assessment would be chosen. When a battery of tests is being formed, the matter of choosing tests is not so simple. The strategy is to select the fewest tests which will give the largest multiple correlation with the assessment. This may make for some apparently unusual choices in some situations. To picture one such situation, consider the following multiple correlation problem for two tests and one assessment:

$$r_{y1} = .00$$

$$r_{y2} = .60 \qquad R = .70$$

$$r_{12} = .50$$

The first thing that strikes the eye is that 1 correlates zero with the assessment. If this test were being considered separately as a predictor of the assessment, it would be of no use. However, the multiple correlation demonstrates that test 1 can be used to improve the prediction that is obtained from test 2 alone. A test which correlates low with the assessment and high with one of the other predictor tests is called a *suppressor* test. That is, it works to suppress, or cancel out, a part of the variance of the second test in such a way as to improve the multivariate prediction.

In the example above the *beta* weights for tests 1 and 2 would be $-.4$ and $.8$ respectively. The regression equation would then be:

$$z'_y = -.4z_1 + .8z_2$$

You can see how in this way test 1 works to suppress, or cancel out, the invalid variance in test 2.

The example of the suppressor test is given to show that it is easy to be fooled about how useful a new test will be until a statistical analysis is undertaken. The complexity of intercorrelations among predictors and the assessment makes it difficult to judge the utility of a particular test without first working out the multiple correlation.

Although the purpose of this chapter is to show the value of multiple measurements, it should be said that multiple regression analysis is not a panacea for the person who works with tests. The usual experience is that the multiple correlation grows only very slowly as the battery of tests increases from three, to four, to five, and so on. A substantial increase in predictive efficiency is often obtained from adding a second test to an initially good predictor, and in many cases a third test will prove valuable. However, in only a few cases has it been found that using more than four or five tests adds significantly to the predictive efficiency of the battery.

The apparent limit to the gain from adding new tests is not an intrinsic characteristic of the prediction problem. It is due to the fact that psychological tests tend to duplicate each other's content so much that it is difficult to find more than four or five truly different kinds of measures. There is always the hope and the possibility that a new type of test will add to the predictive power of existing test batteries.

There is usually a practical limit to the size of a test battery. The question is whether or not the gain in predictive power obtained from using a new test is worth the expense and effort. For example, if a test raises the multiple correlation of a battery from .50 to .55, it can be asked whether this gain is sufficient ground for including the test in the battery. The answer to that would depend on the testing situation. For example, if the expense of training a person in a particular occupation is large, as it would be in most graduate school programs or as it would be in training a pilot in the Air Force, then a gain of 5 points in predictive power could well justify the use of the additional test.

DIFFERENTIAL PREDICTION

Earlier in this chapter it was said that the testing situation may entail a number of assessments to be predicted, as was illustrated with the selection of students for various graduate training programs. Suppose that only one test could be used to select persons for the different graduate schools. The test would then have a separate correlation with the grades in each of the graduate training programs. It might be found that the test is better able to predict the grades of students in psychology than in physics. If the test correlates positively with all of the assessments, even though it correlates higher with some than others, then the higher the individual's score on the test, the more likely he is to succeed in any of the programs. An over-all index of aptitude for graduate school would be of some use but would be little help in making decisions about which students should be allowed to enter particular programs.

Generally we would find a battery of tests, instead of a single test, being used to predict a group of assessments. For example, we might use a vocabulary test, a reading comprehension test, a mathematical reasoning test, and an interest test in a battery. A multiple correlation could be obtained between the test battery and each assessment. With each multiple correlation would be obtained a set of *beta* weights. There would be a different regression equation for each assessment to be predicted, and the *beta* weights would probably not be the same in the prediction of the different assessments. For example, the vocabulary test might correlate highly with grades in the history department but very little with grades in engineering. Then the *beta* weight for vocabulary would be different in the prediction of success in the two programs. A prediction could be made as to the program in which an individual would most likely succeed by trying out his test scores in the regression equations for each assessment. He would then have a predicted score for each program. The student could then be advised that, whereas he probably would not succeed in certain school programs, he probably would make the grade in others.

In the actual use of test batteries to predict multiple assessments, a number of nontest factors must be taken into consideration. If persons were being allocated to different training programs in the Armed Forces, it would be necessary to consider the time and expense which is involved. If the training program is relatively expensive, it would be wise not to accept an individual unless his predicted performance is very high. It is also necessary to consider the number of men needed in different specialties and the number of people who can be trained at any one time. If there is a shortage of, say, airplane mechanics, it would be wise to lower the standards somewhat by "gambling" on persons whose test scores forecast only moderate success. In nearly all situations the individual's own interests and desires are taken into account to at least some extent.

We need differential prediction because different jobs often require different abilities. For example, it may be that high scores in the vocabulary test and the reading comprehension test are essential for a person in journalism, but it might matter little what score the person makes in mathematical reasoning. If we find a person who scores high in the first two tests, he would be a good bet for the journalism department even though he has a very low grade in the mathematical reasoning test. If instead of using differential prediction, the student's test scores are averaged to form one general index of ability, the score in mathematical reasoning might make the average very low. On the basis of the general index of ability, the student might be refused admission to graduate school, without account being taken of the fact that his pattern of abilities makes him suited for one of the programs. Whenever there are a number of assessments in the selection situation, the potential advantage is with differential prediction rather than with the use of only a single test variable.

DISCRIMINATORY ANALYSIS

A handy way to study an individual's scores on a battery of tests is to present the information in the form of a graph, or profile, as shown in Figure 7–4. Figure 7–4 shows the standard scores for two persons on five tests. There are a number of characteristics of profiles that prove helpful in testing (see **1, 5**).

FIGURE 7–4. Test profiles for two persons.

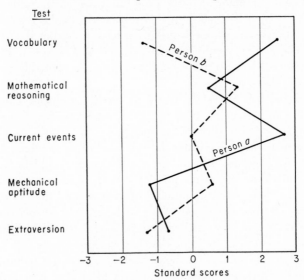

Level. One important feature of a test profile is the *level,* or the extent to which the person does well on the tests as a whole. The level is defined as the mean standard score made on the tests by an individual. From Figure 7–4 we find that person *a* has a mean of .78 and person *b* has a mean of −.01. Then it is said that the level is higher for *a* than for *b*.

The profile level provides direct information about people only if all of the tests correlate positively with the assessment being predicted. If all the tests correlate positively with the assessment, high test scores are "good" in the sense that they portend successful performance. If the profile concerns scores on tests of the ability type only, it is usually the case that all tests correlate positively with the assessment, even if the correlations are very small in some cases. Therefore, the level is usually a meaningful measure when all of the tests concern human abilities. Some cautions must be exercised in interpreting the profile level if some of the tests measure nonability type functions, such as interests, attitudes, and social traits. In Figure 7–4 there is one test of the nonability type, the test for extraversion. Consequently, adding in extraversion scores with the four tests of the ability type would be meaningful only if extraversion were important in the particular assessment being predicted.

If all the tests correlate positively with the assessment, and if we have no information about people except the profile level, we would choose the people with the highest levels. A high profile level means that the person scores generally high on all of the tests, even though he may score higher on some tests than on others.

Scatter. *Scatter* concerns the extent to which an individual does better on some of the tests than on others. The standard deviation of the individual's scores on the separate tests serves as an index of scatter. In Figure 7–4 each person has five standard scores. The scatter for each person is computed by substituting his five standard scores in the standard deviation formula. Computing these indices for the two profiles in Figure 7–4, there is a standard deviation of scores for person *a* of 1.62 and a standard deviation of 1.08 for *b*. This shows that the scatter for *a* is more than that for *b*. An approximate measure of scatter can be obtained by using the range of the person's scores. Person *a* does best on the current events test and worst on the mechanical aptitude test. Subtracting the lowest score from the highest, a range of 4.0 is found for person *a*. In a similar way, a range of scores of 2.8 is found for person *b*. In comparison to other persons with the same profile level, a person with a wide scatter is likely to do relatively well on some jobs and relatively poorly on others. A person who has a very small amount of scatter is likely to do as well, or as poorly, on all of the performances being predicted.

Shape. There is one more important type of information in the profile, which is called the profile *shape*. The shape concerns the ups and downs in ability shown in the profile. The shape is defined as the order of test scores for the individual. Person *a* makes his highest score on the current events test, his next highest score on the vocabulary test, and so on to his lowest score which is made on the mechanical aptitude test. In addition to the differences between persons *a* and *b* in terms of level and scatter, there are differences in profile shape. Person *b* makes his highest score on the mathematical reasoning test and his lowest score on the vocabulary test. The profile shape offers a way of fitting an individual to a particular job. In so far as the individual does better on some tests than others, he can be placed on a job which capitalizes on his strongest points. The use of profiles in this way is an alternative to the multiple regression approach.

The reader should be warned not to take the term shape to mean literally anything about the physical appearance of the profile. The shape refers strictly to the individual's rank-order of performance on the tests.

A naïve individual studying a test profile might mistakenly impute meaning to the "picture" represented by the profile. If the individual scored lower on the even-numbered tests than on the odd-numbered tests, this would give the profile a jagged appearance. This might mistakenly be assumed to represent something about the individual. However, the ordering of tests in the profile is arbitrary. The tests can be reordered to make the profile "look" quite different. However, this will have no effect on shape, as it is defined above, or on level and scatter.

The Standard Error of Difference Scores. Before practical use can be made of profile information, it must be determined whether differences in test scores within the profile are statistically significant. For example, it can be seen from Figure 7–4 that person *a* makes a standard score of 2.5 on the vocabulary test and .5 on the mathematical reasoning test. If it can be shown that this is a real difference, a difference not due to the unreliability of the tests, the difference would be useful in predicting how well person *a* would do on particular jobs.

In Chapter 6 we discussed the reliability of separate tests. Difference scores also have some measurement error, or unreliability. If we gave person *a* the test battery on two separate occasions, we could see if the difference between the scores on the vocabulary test and the mathematical reasoning test would still be 2.0 standard score units. Perhaps the second time the difference score would be 1.5 or 2.5.

The reliability of a set of difference scores [1] can be determined from the separate reliabilities of the tests as follows:

$$r_{\text{dif}} = \frac{r_{11} + r_{22} - 2r_{12}}{2(1 - r_{12})} \qquad (7\text{-}5)$$

where r_{dif} is the reliability of differences between standard scores on tests 1 and 2

r_{11} is the reliability of the first test
r_{22} is the reliability of the second test
r_{12} is the correlation between the two tests

Let the reliability of the first test be .85, the reliability of the second test be .95, and assume that there is a correlation of .65 between the tests. These values can be substituted into the above equation:

$$r_{\text{dif}} = \frac{.85 + .95 - 2(.65)}{2(1 - .65)} = .71$$

You are probably struck by the fact that the reliability of the difference scores is less than that of either of the separate tests. This will usually be the case when the correlation between tests is positive. It can also be seen from inspecting the formula that the reliability of a set of difference scores decreases as the correlation between the tests becomes larger.

[1] The formula assumes that differences are obtained between sets of standard scores.

Thus, if in the illustration above the correlation between the two tests had been .75 instead of .65, the reliability of the difference scores would drop to .60. It would have worked the other way had the correlation between tests been negative. In that case, the difference scores would have been more reliable than the average reliability of the tests.

The reason for the decrease in reliability of difference scores as the correlation between tests grows larger is that as the correlation increases, the difference scores become smaller and smaller. If the correlation between two tests is 1.00, people have the same standard scores on both tests, and consequently, the score differences are all zero. If the correlation were −1.00, the differences would be as large as possible and, consequently, as reliable as possible.

It is unsafe to interpret difference scores unless the individual tests are highly reliable and the correlations among tests are relatively low. In the extreme case where the correlation between two tests is the same as the average of their individual reliabilities, the reliability of difference scores is zero. This would happen if, for example, the respective reliabilities are .70 and .80, and the correlation between tests is .75. Fortunately, such extreme cases are unlikely to occur in the use of tests; but it is sometimes the case that correlations among tests are so high and individual reliabilities are so low as to make difference scores highly unreliable.

Prediction from Test Profiles. Assuming that the cautions regarding the reliability of difference scores have been heeded, the individual's test profile offers a basis for predicting how well he will perform in particular situations. A useful beginning is to compute a *composite profile* for each assessment to be predicted. This would be the profile of mean scores for the persons who perform well. For example, if we study the mean test scores of successful policemen, it might be found that they make above-average scores in vocabulary, high scores in current events, low scores in mathematical reasoning, and so on. The policemen could be compared with a group of successful accountants, who might be found to make high scores in mathematical reasoning, low scores in extraversion, high scores in current events, and so on. For each group, the mean test scores can be plotted as a profile, a composite profile for each job. In Figure 7–5 hypothetical profiles have been drawn for the two groups, and the profiles for two persons, *a* and *b*, have been included to show how the composite profiles are used in making predictions. (Persons *a* and *b* shown in Figure 7–5 are not the same as persons *a* and *b* shown in Figure 7–4.)

A most useful type of information would be the *ideal profile* for each job. This would be found from the mean test scores of *excellent* policemen and *excellent* accountants. Then, if an individual's test profile closely resembles the ideal profile, it is a good bet that he will do relatively well on the particular job. Although we do not have the ideal profile for each job, we do have the composite profile of successful men. In other words we have the profile of *satisfactory* policemen but not necessarily that of *excellent* policemen.

Before people can be classified for different jobs, some way is needed of determining how similar one test profile is to a composite profile. This might be done impressionistically by simply looking at the similarities and

FIGURE 7–5. The test profiles of two persons compared with the composite profiles for policemen and accountants.

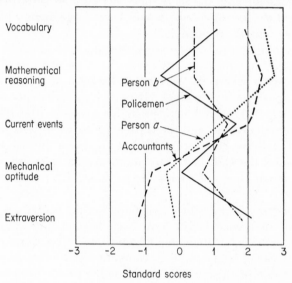

	Policemen	Accountants	Person *a*	Person *b*
Vocabulary	1.1	1.9	2.5	0.5
Mathematical reasoning	−0.5	2.4	2.8	0.5
Current events	1.7	2.0	1.2	1.4
Mechanical aptitude	0.1	−0.8	−0.5	0.7
Extraversion	2.2	−1.2	−0.2	1.8

differences. Looking at Figure 7–5 it can be seen that the profile for person *a* is more similar to the composite profile for accountants than to the composite profile for policemen. The profile for person *b* appears more similar to the profile for policemen than to the profile for account-ants. Although in extreme cases a simple inspection of similarities and differences would suffice to assign people to jobs, it would not be sat-isfactory for less clearcut cases. What is needed is a measure of the similarity between test profiles.

In order to explain a technique for measuring the similarity between profiles, it will be helpful to give a geometric interpretation of test scores. In Figure 7–6 the mean scores are shown for policemen and accountants and for persons *a* and *b* on the mathematical reasoning and extraversion tests only. We could have plotted all of the successful accountants' scores on the graph instead of only their mean scores. Then the accountants would have formed a swarm of dots extending out around their mean location. The plot of a set of mean scores is referred

FIGURE 7–6. Graphic representation of scores on the extraversion and mathematical reasoning tests.

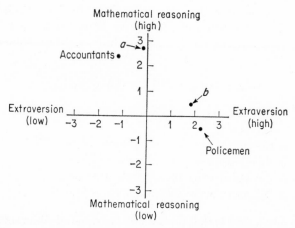

to as a group *centroid*. It is the point about which the scores for the group balance in all directions. Likewise, the mean scores for the policemen define a centroid, one that is different from that for accountants. If each person in the group of accountants had been plotted instead of the group means, it would have shown the density of the group, or the degree to which the group is spread out around the centroid. It might have been found in this way that the accountants are more densely ordered about their centroid or more homogeneous in respect to test scores.

Instead of plotting the scores for only two tests, a three-dimensional model could have been constructed to show the scores for three of the tests. This could be done with a boxlike structure in which balls are hung to represent the scores on three tests. In this way we could obtain a physical representation of the scores made by the two groups and by persons *a* and *b* on the vocabulary, mathematical reasoning, and extraversion tests. The mean group scores would then locate centroids in three dimensions. If each of the persons in the group of successful accountants was plotted instead of only the centroid, there would be a scattering of the persons about the centroid in all directions. The method that will be used to compare test profiles and the statistics that will be developed in respect to the method can be employed with any number of tests. Of course, when the number of tests is more than three, there would be no way of constructing a physical model of the scores; but this will in no way affect the generality of the concepts and mathematical procedures that apply. The mean test scores for a group of persons on five, six, or any number of tests can still be thought of as defining a centroid in that number of dimensions.

The Distance Measure, D. In Figure 7–6 it is apparent that the centroids are different for accountants and policemen. It would be helpful here to have a measure of how far apart they are. The statistic that has proved useful for this purpose is called the D measure. It could be used quite simply to determine the distance of the two groups from each other as follows:

$$D_{ap}^2 = (M_{1a} - M_{1p})^2 + (M_{2a} - M_{2p})^2 \qquad (7\text{–}6)$$

where D_{ap} is the distance between the centroids of accountants, a, and policemen, p

M_{1a} is the mean score of accountants on test 1
M_{1p} is the mean score of policemen on test 1
M_{2a} is the mean score of accountants on test 2
M_{2p} is the mean score of policemen on test 2

What the formula says is that the sum of the squared differences between the means equals the square of the distance between the two centroids.

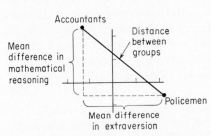

FIGURE 7–7. Graphic representation of mean differences and over-all distance between the scores of accountants and policemen on the extraversion and mathematical reasoning tests.

The D measure is a use of the Pythagorean theorem, which says that for a right triangle the sum of the squares of the sides is equal to the square of the hypotenuse. How this works is illustrated in Figure 7–7. The D measure can be applied to the scores of individuals to show their distance from one another and from the centroids for particular groups. If we want to find the distance of person a from the centroid for accountants, the mean score for accountants on mathematical reasoning is subtracted from the score made by a and squared. This is then added to the squared difference between the score made by person a and the mean for accountants on extraversion. The square root of this quantity is then the distance of person a from the centroid for accountants:

$$D^2 = (2.8 - 2.4)^2 + (-.2 + 1.2)^2$$

$$= (.4)^2 + (1.0)^2$$

$$= .16 + 1.0$$

$$= 1.16$$

$$D = 1.08$$

The first step in making decisions about people with the D statistic is to compute the distance of each person's score profile from the composite profile for each job. The individual would then be assigned to the job whose composite profile is closest to his own profile. This would be very easy to do in the situation in which there are only two jobs to consider and only two tests on which to base the decision. It would only be necessary to find the distance of a person from the two centroids. Considering only the mathematical reasoning and extraversion tests, person a is 4.08 from the centroid for policemen and 1.08 from the centroid for accountants.

There will generally be more than two tests in discriminatory analysis. The D measure can be used with any number of tests by expanding the formula as follows:

$$D_{ab}^2 = (z_{1a} - z_{1b})^2 + (z_{2a} - z_{2b})^2 + \cdots + (z_{pa} - z_{pb})^2 \qquad (7\text{-}7)$$

where D_{ab} is the distance between persons a and b or the distance between the centroids of groups a and b

z_{1a} is the standard score of person a on test 1 or the mean standard score of group a on test 1

z_{1b} is the standard score of person b on test 1 or the mean standard score of group b on test 1

The formula says that the distance between two persons, or the distance between the centroids of two groups, is determined by squaring the differences on the separate tests, summing these, and taking the square root of the sum. In this way it is found that over the five tests person a has a distance of 1.50 from the centroid for accountants and a distance of 4.59 from the centroid for policemen. Using this procedure, person a would be classified as a potential accountant rather than as a policeman. (Some criticisms of this method of classifying people will be given later.)

The D measure could be used to discriminate more than two groups.

For example, in addition to policemen and accountants, there might be composite profiles for successful social workers and for successful plumbers. For each group there will be a centroid. If the centroids are different, the individual can be classified in terms of the centroid which his score combination most nearly approaches. Theoretically it is possible to classify a person on the basis of any number of tests into one of any number of groups. In practical problems the number of groups will usually be limited to only several, and the number of tests will not generally be more than a half dozen.

The Linear Discriminant Function. Although the D measure provides an approximate solution to discriminatory analysis, it has a number of shortcomings. If tests correlate with one another, and substantial correlations are usually expected, the distance between persons on one test will tend to be perpetuated on other tests. Therefore, what appears to be a large distance between persons, or between groups, may be only a reflection of the correlations among tests. For example, if two persons have widely different scores in vocabulary, they are also likely to have widely different scores in similar tests such as reading comprehension and verbal analogies. Even if the two persons had very similar scores in mathematical reasoning and extraversion, the differences due to the three verbal comprehension tests would make the D large, which would give a distorted picture of the actual differences between the two persons.

Another drawback to using the D measure as a means of classifying people is that it does not fully take account of the degree to which different variables differentiate one job from another. For example, it may be that there is a considerable dispersion of mechanical aptitude among successful policemen. This means that mechanical aptitude is not an important variable in choosing policemen. Then if an individual makes a very high or very low mechanical aptitude score, the D statistic will be affected by the difference between the individual's score and the mean score for policemen. The more proper approach is to weigh each test in terms of the degree to which it discriminates one job from another.

Another factor that must be considered in discriminatory analysis is that of obtaining inferential statistics which will tell the probability that persons are correctly classified. The standard error of estimate is the analogous statistic used in correlational analysis. These statistics must consider the relative density, or scatter, of the members of each group about their centroid. In order to overcome the shortcoming of the D measure, more elaborate procedures must be used. The most widely used procedure is the *linear discriminant function* (see **3, 6**). The more complex procedures are modifications of the D statistic rather than basically different approaches. Whereas the D statistic is a useful approximation, the more complete procedures should be sought when need arises (see **6**).

A COMPARISON OF REGRESSION AND DISCRIMINATORY ANALYSIS

Two different ways have been described for dealing with multiple measurements: multiple regression and discriminatory analysis. It has not yet been made explicit how the methods differ. The major difference is that the multiple-regression methods assume that the ideal profile touches only the extremes of the test continua. That is, the multiple-regression methods assume that the "more the better" on each test regardless of the job, or task, being predicted. The reason for this is that the regression methods assume linear relationships. If there is a linear relationship between a predictor and an assessment, then the higher the score made on the predictor, the better the indication that the person will succeed. This means that the ideal score is the highest that can be made on the test. It may be, of course, that the correlation between test and assessment is negative. This would mean that the lower the score made by the individual the better is his chance of succeeding. If there is a linear relationship between each test and the assessment, the ideal profile would touch one end of each test continuum.

When dealing with human abilities, linear relationships are usually found between tests and assessments. However, this is not necessarily the case. For example, it may be that very high "general intelligence" indicates that a person will do poorly in very routine tasks such as those of the truck driver or elevator operator. In the areas of interests, attitudes, and personality characteristics it is more likely that some of the relationships between predictors and assessments will be nonlinear. A curvilinear relationship would be expected between school grades and the amount of anxiety toward school work, as pictured in Figure 7–8.

In Figure 7–8 the hypothesis is that the persons who make the highest grades have a moderate amount of anxiety. Both the persons who

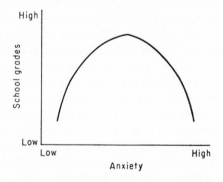

FIGURE 7–8. Hypothetical relationship between amount of anxiety toward school work and grades.

show very high anxiety and those who show very low anxiety make low grades in school. The low anxiety students would make low grades because they are so uninterested in accomplishment that they do not make the necessary effort. The high anxiety students are so worried about failure that they have no attention left for school work. This is an example of the type of nonlinear relationship that could not be used in multiple-regression analysis but could be used in discriminatory analysis. In discriminatory analysis the ideal profile point for the anxiety variable would be in the middle of the test continuum.

Linearity of relationships should be checked by an inspection of the scatter diagrams before a decision is made as to the type of analysis to use. The discriminatory type of analysis is more general and can use the information provided by some types of nonlinear relationships. However, regression analysis is easier for most persons to understand and compute. When the nonability areas of measurements are more effectively developed, it can be expected that methods of discriminatory analysis will come more widely into use.

A second feature which distinguishes the two types of analysis is the nature of the assessment score distribution. Multiple-regression analysis assumes that the assessment scores are continuously distributed, or at least approximately so. Discriminatory analysis assumes that the assessment is a qualitative distinction, a category rather than a continuum: all of the people who are successful in a particular job are considered to be of equal merit.

There are advantages and disadvantages in considering the assessment as a continuously distributed variable rather than as a category. In many situations it makes more sense to assume that there are gradations of ability within the category of success. Such would be the case in school work, salesmanship, athletic ability, and job performance. However, it is not always possible to measure the fine gradations of ability, and sometimes only the crude index of "pass" or "fail" can be used as the assessment. This is particularly so in the personality area, where it makes sense to validate an adjustment inventory against the dichotomized assessment of mental hospital patients versus nonhospital patients. To obtain finer gradations on the assessment would be very difficult. Some variables are inherently categorical rather than continuous. Examples of these are men versus women, sailors versus soldiers, and plumbers versus barbers.

Whenever the purpose of the analysis is to distinguish qualitatively different groups or when only a dichotomized assessment can be obtained, discriminatory rather than multiple-regression analysis should generally be used. If continuous assessments are available and relationships between predictor tests and assessments are reasonably linear, multiple regression should generally be used.

In order to give any rules at all as to when multiple-regression analysis is preferable to discriminatory analysis and vice versa, it has been necessary to oversimplify the problems involved. Primarily it is necessary to consider whether the test battery is used for selection, guidance, or classification. In selection, the purpose is to choose only those people who are likely to succeed in one or more of the positions involved. If regressions between tests and assessments are linear, multiple-regression analysis will provide an estimate of each person's performance in each assessment situation. In this way people can be selected who will likely succeed in at least one position. It is best to think of selection as an *institution-oriented* procedure: the purpose is to choose the most promising persons and to reject those persons who fail to give promise for at least one position.

Classification and guidance are more *person oriented*. The purposes are to place people in positions in which they will do *better* and to advise them to try positions in which they will do *better*. However, even if an individual is given the best placement possible, if he is relatively untalented, he may be only moderately sucessful. Such an individual would probably be rejected in a selection program. In classification and guidance, individuals cannot be rejected: the best placement must be found for each individual regardless of his over-all ability.[2] In guidance and classification, the discriminatory approach has certain advantages over the multiple-regression approach, especially when regressions between tests and assessments are nonlinear. Discriminatory analysis will help put the individual into a position which is shared by other individuals of the same general interests, personality characteristics, and abilities. This is likely to make the individual feel comfortable in his job and comfortable with his work mates.

Obviously, the institution-oriented and person-oriented philosophies and procedures are somewhat at odds with each other. In the long run, it can be expected that there will be a marriage of the two philosophies which will incorporate the concerns of both and provide more comprehensive procedures for making decisions about human beings. This is presently one of the frontiers of measurement methodology.

THE MULTIPLE-CUTOFF METHOD

A third approach to the use of multiple measurements for the selection of personnel is to set cutoff scores on each of the tests. A person is selected for the particular job, school, or position, only if he scores at least as high as the cutting score on all tests. For example, a set of cutoff scores for selecting students for electronics training might be 80 on an intelligence test, 50 in perceptual speed, and 65 in motor dexterity. The actual cutoff points would be determined in such a way as to raise the probability that the selected individuals will succeed. For example, the cutting

---

[2] Rejection occurs in vocational guidance only in the extreme case where an individual is subnormal to the extent that he is advised not to enter school or work at all. In classification, rejection occurs only when an individual is released after an initial training period or when he is assigned to a low-level job not specifically intended for members of the group into which the individual was originally selected.

score for each test might be set so that 75 per cent of the persons scoring at or above the cutting score succeed on the job.

The *selection ratio* determines how high the cutting scores are placed. If there is a large number of applicants and only a relatively small number of these must be selected, the cutting scores can be placed high. On the other hand, if most of the people who apply must be selected, the cutting scores necessarily must be low.

The multiple-cutoff method is particularly valuable when, as is sometimes the case, tests are predictive only on their lower extremes. This tends to be the case for some of the motor, perceptual, and sensory abilities. For example, minimal levels of auditory and visual acuity are essential for a number of jobs. However, beyond the minimum requirement, success on the job does not increase with higher and higher auditory and visual acuity.

Multiple regression is a compensatory model in that a high score on one test can compensate for a low score on another test. This is a sensible model in some situations, such as in college training, where an individual can, to some extent, substitute one ability for another. However, in some situations a high score on one measure cannot compensate for a low score on another measure. For example, in the operation of sound detection devices in submarines, the operator must have a certain level of auditory ability. Otherwise he will fail, regardless of how high he might score in intelligence and other abilities.

The multiple-cutoff method is preferable to the multiple-regression model and discriminatory analysis when the tests are predictive only on their lower extremes. This can be seen by looking at the scatter diagrams comparing test performance with job performance. If the test is predictive only on the lower extreme, the regression will tend to be curvilinear and the points will be more closely packed about the regression line on the lower-score section of the test. An example is shown in Figure 7–9.

The multiple-cutoff method can be used in conjunction with other approaches. It is usually unwise to select an individual for a position or, in vocational guidance, to advise an individual to take a position, if he is very low in any one of the related abilities. Consequently, it is useful to set relatively low cutoff points for each test, and not consider an individual for a position if he is below the cutoff point on any one of them. Then if, in the remaining group, test scores tend to correlate with job success in a linear manner, scores can be combined by multiple regression. The final selection would be made on the basis of the combined scores. If people are being selected for several jobs, the procedure can be repeated for each job. Each job would have its minimum-cutoff scores for weeding out the obviously unfit, and each job would have its multiple-regression equation for the final selection.

FIGURE 7–9. Relationship between test scores and job performance in which a cutting score would be useful for selecting personnel.

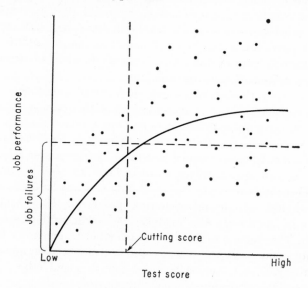

PRACTICAL APPLICATIONS OF TEST BATTERIES

There is a choice in many testing situations as to whether one general test should be used or whether a number of different tests should be administered in a battery. The potential advantage is always with multiple measurements: more information cannot lower prediction. Moreover, there are some circumstances in which it is especially important to measure the individual's differential ability. One such circumstance is vocational guidance. The individual comes for advice; and, regardless of how high or low his over-all ability (profile level), the problem is to find the occupations that are best suited to his pattern of abilities (profile shape). Even the person who makes a very low score on a general intelligence test might have certain aptitudes, such as motor dexterity and mechanical ability, that would suit him for some jobs.

Any circumstance in which the effort is to classify persons after preliminary selection especially requires the use of multiple predictors. The officer training programs in the Armed Services exemplify such situations. First, the potential officers are tested as a prelude to acceptance in the officer training programs. One general measure can be used as a basis for preliminary selection. The general measure would then indicate much of what we have spoken of as level in the test profile. If the individual has a high level, it is certain that he is high in some of the separable abilities. After the course of training, the new officers can then be classified, or in other words, placed on particular jobs. In the Army some might become artillery officers, some members of the intelligence sections, and others might enter communications activities. It would then be important to know the individual's differential ability in order to match his special talents with particular assignments. Whereas the general test is sufficient for the initial selection of men, it is necessary to give a battery of tests for effective classification of the men later.

After discussing the advantages of multiple measurements, it is important to consider why test batteries rather than single tests are not employed more widely in practical work. One reason is that test batteries are more expensive to construct and use than single tests. Another reason is that good test batteries require careful preparation and research, and it is often the case that hastily constructed batteries fail to work well in practice. There is little doubt that well-designed test batteries will eventually come into use in many testing programs. They will pay for themselves by improving the guidance, selection, and classification of individuals. The know-how is already available to construct better test batteries for many uses; and it will come to fruition when administrative officials in schools, the Armed Services, industry, and other institutions supply the funds and resources which are needed.

REFERENCES

1. Cronbach, L. J., and Gleser, G. C. Assessing similarity between profiles. *Psychol. Bull.*, 1953, **50**, 456–473.
2. Guilford, J. P. *Fundamental statistics in psychology and education.* (3rd ed.) New York:McGraw-Hill, 1956.
3. Johnson, P. O. *Statistical methods in research.* Englewood Cliffs, N.J.: Prentice-Hall, 1949.
4. McNemar, Q. *Psychological statistics.* (2nd ed.) New York: Wiley, 1955.
5. Mosier, C. I. Batteries and profiles. In E. F. Lindquist (Ed.), *Educational measurement.* Washington: American Council on Education, 1951.
6. Pickrel, E. W. Classification theory and techniques. *Educ. psychol. Measmt*, 1958, **18**, 37–46.
7. Thorndike, R. L. *Personnel selection: test and measurement techniques.* New York: Wiley, 1949.

CHAPTER 8

Test Construction

So far we have talked about how tests are studied after they are developed, but no attention has been given to test construction. Here we enter into one of the most complex parts of measurement theory, and this introductory text will be able to cover only some of the general principles. The rules for test construction change in terms of the way in which tests are used. For example, if the question is asked, "Should a 'good' predictor test have items that are homogeneous to one another or should they be heterogeneous to one another?" the answer is, "Yes!" We will see how this and other seemingly paradoxical rules work in special testing problems.

The rules for constructing a particular instrument can be clarified at the outset by deciding whether the test is intended to be a predictor or an assessment. Although there are desirable features which should be present in both types of instruments, such as high reliability, there are other points on which the standards are very different. We will begin by discussing the construction of predictor tests, then assessments, and end the chapter with a discussion of some features which they should have in common.

CONSTRUCTION OF PREDICTOR TESTS

As was cautioned earlier, before work is undertaken on a predictor test, some attention should be given to what it is meant to predict, the criterion, or assessment. In particular, studies should be undertaken to ensure that the criterion is at least moderately reliable. If not, the test constructor can perform some "criterion research," as it was alluded to in Chapter 4, to help establish a reliable assessment.

Job Analysis. Although it was said that a predictor test is initially formed from a hypothesis—a hypothesis that a particular kind of item will predict an assessment—the early hunches can usually be improved by studying the assessment situation. That is, if we are composing tests to predict success in the operation of particular machinery, we will want to become acquainted with the job before constructing tests. Among other things, we will want to interview men who presently work at the job, talk with persons who manage the operation, and make notes about the exact duties which the job entails. Among the prominent things to look for are the following:

1. *Physical requirements.* Does the job require considerable physical strength? Does a tall or a short person have an advantage in the work? (Aircraft companies employed midgets during the Second World War to work inside the wings of large airplanes.) Would an older person meet with difficulties?

2. *Sensory and motor skills.* Does the job require particular kinds of muscular coordination? Is acuity of vision, or hearing, or touch vital to the job? Is rapidity of movement a necessary attribute?

3. *Intellectual abilities.* What is the employee required to know? Is it necessary for the employee to study and understand complex instructions? What kinds of decisions does the job require?

4. *Personality requirements.* Using the word "personality" in the broad sense, what type of person gets along well on the job? Is it necessary for the employee to supervise other persons? Does the job require courage and/or calmness? Does the employee work independently or in cooperation with other men?

A job analysis such as this will give some hints as to the kinds of tests which are likely to serve as successful predictors. In some situations, it is not necessary to go through such formal procedures of job analysis before constructing predictor tests. For example, in making up tests to predict school success, it is often assumed that the intellectual abilities will be the most important determinants of success; and tests appropriate to the type of school program can often be constructed without a careful scrutiny of the classroom work. However, when a new assessment is to be predicted, and the test constructor is not well acquainted with the job, a job analysis offers the most logical first step in a testing program.

Type of Test. After surveying the job requirements and making some decisions about the attributes which will be tested, it is necessary to decide what form the tests will take. It may be that some of the attributes will have to be tested on single individuals, whereas some of the other tests can be given to a group of men at one time. Some of the attributes may require performance tests, and mechanical "gadgets" will need to be constructed. Some of the tests may be susceptible to "objective" scoring; judges may be required for the rating of other test results. Such decisions about the nature of tests are determined in a large measure by practical considerations, by the resources available to the testing programs and the amount of time which each subject can spend

CONCLUSION

in taking tests. That is why paper-and-pencil multiple choice tests are used more frequently than any other kind. They are the easiest to construct, administer, and score.

The Item Pool. After a decision has been made to construct a particular type of test, the next step is to compose a large number of test items, an *item pool.* The item is the lowest common denominator of a test, the individual "thing" which is scored. An item may be the time taken to assemble a mechanical puzzle, the blood pressure of a subject, or an arithmetic problem. In each case the item is the indivisible scoring unit.

The kinds of items which are included in the item pool depend on the definition of the *item universe,* which can, at least theoretically, be thought to underlie particular tests. For example, if it is thought that mathematical reasoning problems will predict an assessment well, the item pool is filled with mathematical reasoning items. However, there are different kinds of mathematical reasoning items, and the test constructor sometimes has difficulty in stating explicitly which kinds will be included and which will be ignored.

The more items which are composed for the item pool, the more room there will be to pick and choose among them in constructing a test. As a minimum, the item pool must, of course, have as many items as are planned for the eventual test. If resources permit, the item pool should have three or four times as many items as will be used in the test. It helps to have several persons compose items; otherwise the items might overemphasize the language and types of problems known to one person.

The Review of Items. Before items are tried out empirically, the item pool should be inspected by several sophisticated judges for obvious flaws. The judges should look for the following things:

1. *Unclear statement of problems.* It is possible to phrase an item so poorly that even a person who knows the subject matter thoroughly will mark the wrong alternative. Most of us are better able to find other people's awkward expressions than to note our own mistakes. Therefore, an independent group of judges can usually point out a number of items which should either be thrown away or should be reworded.

2. *Wrong answers.* Test constructors are capable of making errors, and what is stated to be the correct answer for a problem may not be correct at all. It is not uncommon to find tests some of whose items have no correct alternatives. The probability of this happening diminishes with the number of sophisticated individuals who inspect the items.

3. *Inappropriate difficulty.* An inspection of the items will help weed out some of those which are either so easy that everyone will get them correct or so hard that practically no one will get them correct. An empirical tryout of the items will give more exact information about the

difficulty of items, but some initial inspection of the item pool can weed
out extreme deviants.

4. *Inappropriateness to item universe.* Judges should look for items
which appear to be unrelated to the attribute which the test is intended
to measure. For example, if a test of mathematical reasoning is being
constructed, you would not want to have questions which use Latin
words. It would then become partly a test of the individual's knowledge
of Latin. You would probably not want to have problems dealing with
specialized mathematical techniques, such as calculus. The individual's
ability to answer the question would depend on whether or not he had
studied the specialized techniques rather than on his ability to reason
mathematically. In general, the item pool should be kept free of all
abilities and types of information which are not directly related to the
attribute to be measured.

Empirical Tryout of Items. The next step in test construction is to
administer the whole item pool to groups of subjects. If the item pool is
large, say over three hundred items, it may be necessary to give part
of the items to one group and part to another group. If more than one
group is used, the groups should be homogeneous in respect to ability.
It is essential that relatively large numbers of individuals try each item.
If there are fewer than 100 persons, only a limited amount of information
can be obtained from the tryout. In order for the results of the tryout to
be acceptably stable, as many as 300 subjects should be obtained, and
the use of 1,000 subjects is not unusual. The availability of subjects sets
a limit to the methods of test construction which can be used. If only
several dozen subjects are available, which is often the case in composing
tests for particular jobs, an empirical tryout of items will give statistical
results which are more misleading than helpful. However, an empirical
tryout with a few subjects is helpful in improving the test instructions
and administration procedure.

After the empirical tryout of the item pool, a number of statistical
procedures can be used to help construct a test. The purpose of item
analysis is to select from an item pool a minimum number of items
which will give a maximum prediction of a criterion.

MULTITEST ITEM ANALYSIS

In establishing the item pool, it is assumed that the items all measure
the same thing. However, in spite of the best efforts, it may turn out
that there are several different attributes involved in the items. For
example, in a group of mathematical reasoning items, it may be found
that the questions which require considerable arithmetic computation go

together as an attribute and that the items which require little computation and considerable reasoning go together as another attribute.

Factor Analysis. There are statistical procedures which can be used to determine whether or not an item pool contains only one attribute, and if not, how many attributes are involved. The most thorough procedure to use is factor analysis (to be discussed in the next chapter). This and other related procedures deal with the correlations among items. That is, just as it is possible to correlate tests with one another, the separate items within a test can be correlated with one another. If only a "pass" or "fail" score is given to each item, as is usually the case in multiple choice tests, special correlational formulas are required (see **8**, chap. 10; **10**, chap. 6).

An attribute, or factor, is defined by a group of items whose members correlate highly among themselves and correlate very little with the items in other groups. If two items correlate highly, it means that they are measuring much the same thing. In very few testing programs is it feasible to undertake the labors of intercorrelating all of the items in an item pool. If there are 300 items, 44,850 separate correlation coefficients would need to be computed. The subsequent work of analysis would be even more laborious, making for an amount of calculation which would strain even our modern electronic computers.

Approximate Procedures. One approximate procedure is to factor analyze only a part of the total item pool. It is within practicality to factor analyze, say, a group of 50 instead of 300 items. The items which are factor analyzed can either be selected randomly from the total item pool; or, if it is suspected that certain groupings of the items will occur, a number of items can be chosen from each of the suspected groups. A factor analysis will then show how many factors are involved in the subsample of items from the pool. Then, by correlating all the items which were not in the factor analysis with each of the factors, the groupings for the total item pool can be estimated. There are numerous other such approximate procedures which are used to decide how many tests should be constructed from an item pool (see **14**).

Difficulty Levels. If the multitest approach is being used and statistical analyses have been undertaken to specify the item groupings, one more type of information is required before composing tests to measure the factors. It is necessary to determine the difficulty level for each item, which is the per cent of persons who get an item "correct." You will remember that the purpose of item analysis is to maximally predict a criterion. In Chapter 5 the effect of the standard deviation on the correlation coefficient was described: the larger the dispersion, the higher the correlation in general. The difficulty levels of the items in a test determine, in part, the standard deviation of scores on the test. Some illustrations will help to show how this works. If the items are so easy that everyone gets all of the items "correct" (the difficulty level for each item is 100 per cent), everyone will obtain the same score, and the standard deviation will be zero. The standard deviation will also be zero if the items are so hard that no one gets any of the items correct.

If a multiple choice test is being used, guessing will probably influence the item difficulty levels. A certain per cent of the subjects will get an item correct by guessing even if no one really knows the answer. If there are n alternatives for an item, $1/n$ of the subjects would probably get the item correct by guessing alone. Consequently, it is not expected to find items with difficulty levels below $1/n$. The minimum expected difficulty for five alternatives is 20 per cent, for four alternatives 25 per cent, and so on.[1]

The number of alternatives used for each item usually restricts the range of possible scores. With five alternatives, the range is from 20 per cent correct answers to 100 per cent correct answers. Then in a 40-item test the scores could range from about 8 to 40. The problem is to choose items in terms of difficulty levels in such a way as to spread people out widely in the possible score range. The rule is to pick a set of items whose average difficulty level is near the middle of the possible score range. That is, in developing a test with five alternatives for each item, items should be chosen in such a manner that their average difficulty is about 60 per cent. The average difficulty is found by summing the separate difficulty levels and dividing by the number of items. It is not important that the mean difficulty be exactly at the middle of the possible score range, but the standard deviation of test scores will be lowered if the mean difficulty is near either the bottom or top of the possible score range.

In addition to the decision to choose items that have a mean difficulty near the middle of the possible score range, there is a question as to the distribution of difficulties that should be sought. Should all of the items have difficulties close to the middle of the score range, should half of the items be very easy ones and the others very hard items, or should a particular distribution of difficulties be sought? The ideal distribution of difficulties varies in terms of the use which will be made of the test and the intercorrelations of the items. Consequently, no "airtight" rule can be given for all situations.

After an empirical tryout of an item pool, a good general procedure is to choose approximately an equal number of items at each difficulty

[1] Although this rule is generally useful, there are special circumstances in which it is inappropriate. This is particularly so when the item alternatives are carefully designed to contain "misleads."

level in the possible score range.[2] That is, if a 40-item test is being constructed with 5 alternatives for each item, the procedure would be to choose 5 items with difficulties between 20 and 30 per cent, 5 items with difficulties between 30 and 40 per cent, and so on to 5 items with difficulties between 90 and 100 per cent. If in the item pool there are more than the required number of items at particular difficulty levels, there is a question as to which of the items should be included in the test. If the items have been previously studied by factor analysis, those items should be used that correlate most highly with the factor which the test is intended to measure.

The Results of a Multitest Item Analysis. A test should be constructed for each of the major item groupings (factors), or at least for the ones that appear to be useful predictors. Scores on the separate tests can be combined in the ways which were discussed in Chapter 7 to give the best prediction of a particular criterion.

UNITEST ITEM ANALYSIS

It may be decided in a testing program that only one test can be used or, in other words, that it will be permissible to derive only one test from an item pool. This decision may be determined in part by principles of economy, because it is usually more expensive to derive and use more than one test. However, there is some confusion as to what constitutes *one* test. If the scores on 60 items are added up to obtain one score, it is said that *one* test is in use; but if the items are divided into three groups of twenty each, and each of the three groups of items is scored separately, it is said that *three* tests are in use. It is customary to say that there are as many tests being used as there are separate scores for each person, and the number of scores given to each person is not necessarily related to the length or appearance of the test material.

It is unwise to begin the study of an item pool with the assumption that only one test will be developed, because, as was said in the previous section, statistical analyses may indicate that a number of factors underlie the item pool. Although it is usually advantageous to use the multitest approach on the item pool, the most legitimate reason for using the unitest approach instead is that the laborious procedures of statistical

---

[2] It must be kept in mind that the rule is most applicable to general-purpose tests, in which reliable differentiations at all points on the score continuum are equally important. In certain special cases a test is used only to distinguish certain "upper" and "lower" groups, for example to pick out the top 25 per cent. In that case the item difficulties would be massed near the cutting point rather than near the middle of the possible score range. That is, most of the items would be chosen in the 60 to 90 per cent difficulty range. Other procedures of item selection are required for special purposes.

analysis needed to determine the factors in an item pool are not feasible in many testing situations.

Multiple Regression. If the whole item pool has been given an empirical tryout, there is an ideal way to combine the items into a test: namely, to combine all of the items by multiple-regression formulas to predict the criterion. The analysis would first require all of the intercorrelations among the items, plus the correlation of each separate item with the criterion. Then it would be necessary to run a complete multiple-regression analysis, obtaining a *beta* weight for each item. If this ideal method of analysis were undertaken, it would give the best "least squares" prediction of the criterion and would even do a better job than the multitest approach. Unfortunately, such an analysis is totally impractical. Multiple-regression weights are difficult enough to compute with five or six variables; it is out of the question to perform such an analysis for, say, the 300 items in an item pool. Not being able to perform this ideal type of analysis, some approximate approaches are necessary.

Item Difficulties. What was said about item difficulties in respect to the multitest approach holds as well for the unitest approach. The more variance in the total scores the more the test is likely to correlate with the criterion. Therefore, a set of items should be chosen whose mean difficulty is at about the middle of the possible score range. The items should also be scattered along the range of difficulty in general resemblance to the scheme which was previously described.

Item-criterion Correlations. If it is possible to perform the labors of correlating each item in the item pool with the criterion, this information can be combined with a knowledge of difficulty levels to make a more predictive test. The test score is usually obtained as a sum of the item scores, which is the number of correct responses. If the individual items do not correlate with the criterion, the total score will not correlate with the criterion either.

A test will be more predictive if the items which correlate well with the criterion are chosen. The rule is that from the items at each difficulty level select those which correlate highest with the criterion. That is, if the item pool has 20 items with "difficulties" between 30 and 40 per cent, and the test will only be long enough to use five items in that category, the five items should be chosen which have the highest correlations with the criterion.

Interitem Correlations. If it is possible to obtain not only the difficulty levels and the item-criterion correlations, but the intercorrelations of all of the items in the item pool as well, this information can be used to derive a more predictive test. It was said that multiple regression is the ideal method of unitest analysis. You will remember from Chapter 7 that the multiple correlation is highest when the predictor variables (items in this case) correlate high with the criterion and low with one another. Therefore, items should be chosen which not only correlate as much as possible with the criterion and conform to the requirements for difficulty level but which correlate as little as possible with one another. There are a number of item-analysis procedures which take into consideration both item-criterion correlations and interitem correlations (see **3, 6, 7, 10, 12**).

In the multitest method, items are grouped, or placed in factors because they correlate highly with one another. In the unitest method, items should correlate low with one another. In other words, the items within any one of the tests derived by the multitest approach should be homogeneous in respect to one another, and the items within a test obtained by the unitest approach should be heterogeneous in respect to one another. Consequently, the apparent paradox introduced earlier in the chapter is not a paradox after all: different rules apply in accordance with the item-analysis strategy being used.

DECISIONS ABOUT THE CONSTRUCTION OF PREDICTOR TESTS

Having seen some of the formal procedures of analysis which can be used, we should next ask, "What do people usually do in constructing tests?" To begin with, tests are often constructed without any kind of item analysis. People are often able to "dream up" a set of test items, which, when tried out, conforms fairly well to the statistical requirements. The author often requires his students to compose tests for the prediction of school grades. The students have neither the time nor the resources to compose large item pools, undertake empirical tryouts, or perform elaborate statistical analyses. It is surprising to find how many of these tests actually predict the criterion with moderate success and also have distributions of item difficulties which are acceptable.

It is not recommended that formal procedures of test construction be ignored, but it is possible, and often happens, that an intuitively composed test will give satisfactory prediction. However, the item-analysis procedures are not dependent on the success of the individual's intuitive processes, and the item-analysis methods will almost always lead to a higher test-criterion correlation.

If resources are available for performing item analyses, then a decision must be made as to what procedures should be used. A failure to distinguish between the multitest and unitest approaches has caused some confusion about proper methods of analysis. If the additional labors required by the multitest method can be undertaken, that will usually give the most satisfactory results.

In addition to the likelihood of obtaining a higher prediction of the criterion from the multitest approach, the results have a generality beyond the immediate testing problem. The unitest method tends to produce a conglomeration of items which is directly related to only one assessment, or criterion. The multitest method divides items into homogeneous groups, or factors, which can be validated against numerous criteria. Factor analysis is often used when there is no particular criterion to be predicted. Then the effort is to derive general attributes which can, in the course of events, be used to predict many different criteria.

Taking Advantage of Chance. There is an important caution to be noted in the interpretation of the results of any item analysis which selects items in terms of the item-criterion correlations (which is done with some of the unitest methods but not with the multitest methods). If there are many items in the item pool, some of them will correlate highly with the criterion if only by chance. The more individuals used in the empirical tryout, the smaller will be the sampling error of correlation coefficients. As an extreme example, if the number of individuals is no larger than the number of items, it is always possible to find a perfect multiple correlation between the items and any other variable. You can name any other variable that you like, the weights of the subjects, for example, and the perfect multiple correlation can be found. However, the apparent validity would be only a spurious capitalization on sampling errors.

When we select only the few items which correlate highly with the criterion, this "takes advantage of chance." A second empirical tryout will show that the selected items correlate lower with the criterion than was indicated in the first tryout. Consequently, a test derived from the use of item-criterion correlations will work less well in subsequent use than it appears to work on the original tryout group. After obtaining a test from item-criterion correlations, the test scores can be correlated with the criterion scores. We refer to this type of correlation as re-correlation, because the measure of predictive validity is obtained on the same sample of scores used to develop the test. Re-correlations are almost always spuriously large. There have been numerous instances in which a derived test has been re-correlated with the criterion to produce a seemingly handsome validity, only to find in subsequent research that the test has no predictive validity at all.

Cross validation. Re-correlations are so misleading that it is better not to compute them. After the item analysis of the first tryout group, the test obtained should be administered to a second group of individuals. The correlation between the scores made by the second group and the criterion is the predictive validity of the test. The use of a second group in this way is referred to as *cross validation.*

CONSTRUCTION OF ASSESSMENTS

The major concern in this section will be with the construction of classroom examinations. Many of the varied assessments which are made of human performance are not, properly speaking, tests at all. The promotion of a naval officer, the hiring of a chef, the elevation of a business executive to a higher position may entail none of the formal, standardized procedures which we call tests. However, many of the requirements of a good assessment test apply to assessments in general.

The Importance of Tests. Whenever students receive grades for their work, tests have a very large influence on human lives. The grade which a student obtains may determine whether or not he graduates from high school, is given a better position in civil service, or receives a commission in the Armed Forces. The teacher who takes his work seriously finds the fair allotment of grades to be the most arduous, and sometimes painful, part of his job. Every teacher has seen the time when a student's whole life had to be rearranged because of a failing grade.

Tests not only share in the responsibility of allotting grades, they also determine in large measure what is learned. Students are very quick to detect what the teacher emphasizes in examinations, and it is only human for the student to work hardest on the things which are likely to appear on the test. Tests can also affect what the teacher teaches. If standard achievement tests are used, as they are in many school systems, the teacher is often under pressure to have the students do as well as possible. He is then likely to slant his instruction toward the things emphasized on the achievement test, even to the point of nearly rehearsing the actual examination.

Because of the importance of classroom examinations, they merit very careful preparation. It is unfortunate that the work load imposed on many teachers prevents their careful attention to the construction and grading of each test. A classroom examination is "good" if it is both reliable and valid. Anything that can be done to raise the reliability of the examination along the lines discussed in Chapter 6 will make for a better test. Validity of a classroom examination means content representativeness, in other words, that a wide sample of *important* questions has been employed.

Educational Goals. What constitutes important materials can be determined only by the teacher's careful attention to the aims of the course. Part of this decision should be determined by the future courses which the student will take. The first course in calculus must prepare the students for the second course in calculus. Although there is some latitude as to how it is taught, there are certain fundamentals to be covered.

Outside the common core of knowledge that is expected to be imparted in a particular course, the instructor adds his own particular flavor to the subject he teaches. The student "takes the instructor" as well as taking the course. Each teacher has his own pet theories, anecdotes, and his strong and weak points in imparting the course material. To an extent this is very good, because much of education is concerned with learning how other people think. Whatever special directions are given to the subject matter, the instructor should be aware of what he is trying to teach and make course examinations which will reflect his goals.

Outline of Content. Most instructors find it helpful to outline the goals of a course, to write down the important principles that they want to convey. Such an outline is not quite the same as the usual course outline, the latter being more concerned with the order of presenting topics than with the goals of instruction. In this textbook, for example, the goal is to convey several dozen general principles, some of which concern:

1. The logical foundations of psychological measures
2. The distinction between "processes" and individual differences
3. The characteristics of assessments and predictors
4. The nature of statistical prediction
5. The influence of measurement error on predictions

The author bases his own course examinations on a longer list of such issues. These are the things which he thinks will help the student in taking future courses, provide the widest background for using tests, and generally make him more erudite in the subject matter.

The outline should be spelled out in greater detail than the several points listed above, including subheadings under each topic concerning the more particular goals in each section of instruction. Although most instructors agree, at least in principle, that the general points of view are the more important things to convey, the outline will include a knowledge of particular techniques, facts, and even some names and dates. The instructor must decide which details are important for students to learn and, consequently, which of these will find their way into examinations.

A carefully done outline of course goals will not only prove useful in constructing examinations, it will help the instructor in teaching his course. He may note that he has been underemphasizing important points in the outline, or that relatively unimportant topics have occupied too much of the course time. After the outline is constructed, and some changes in it would be expected with the instructor's continued experience with the subject matter, the problem is to translate the outline into a successful examination. At this point we depart from the skills of classroom instruction and move into the specialty of psychological measurement. The instructor who is wise in the ways of teaching and who may outline excellently the class goals may fail miserably in translating the goals into a creditable examination. Similarly, the measurement specialist is often not qualified to make decisions about the importance of various aspects of particular subject matters. A happy blending of skills occurs when the teacher has a firm understanding of the basic principles of testing.

ESSAY VERSUS MULTIPLE CHOICE EXAMINATIONS

As with predictor tests, there is, at least conceivably, a wide choice of forms for a particular assessment, including performance tests, work samples, ratings, and many others. The attention here will be given to paper-and-pencil forms, by far the most popular type of classroom examination.

In the essay examination, the student is presented with a few questions or problems and asked to supply the answers. In the multiple choice form the student is presented with a large number of questions, with a limited number of alternative answers for each. Considering the wide use of both of these forms and the amount of controversy which has been generated over which is "better," their differences and special advantages will be discussed in some detail.

Convenience. The essay examination is comparatively easy to construct but difficult to grade with more than a dozen students. An adequate multiple choice examination is much more difficult to construct, but it can be graded easily even with hundreds of students. There are no forms to be reproduced with the essay examination and no special materials are needed. The questions can be written on the blackboard for all students to see. It is usually necessary to have the multiple choice examination typed and mechanically reproduced, both of which may be a strain on school facilities. In addition, the multiple choice test may require special answer sheets and scoring forms. In general, the more students to be tested either at one time or in the eventual use of the test, the more practical convenience is obtained from the multiple choice form.

Reliability. The multiple choice test is usually more reliable, and substantially more so, than the essay test. The unreliability of the essay examination comes from two main sources: from test scoring and from the sampling of content. Teachers often disagree about the grade for particular papers, and individual teachers often give considerably different marks to the same papers which they regrade after a period of time. Such inconsistencies are dependent on the teacher, with some instructors being much less reliable in their grading. There is more error due to the sampling of content in essay examinations because of the small number of questions which are used. A student's grade can depend considerably on his "luck" in having understood the particular materials on the test. The many items which can be used on a multiple choice test provide an opportunity to spread questions widely over the subject matter.

Representing the Important Content. It is in this category that the strongest arguments have been given for the use of the essay examination. It has been pointed out by many persons that the multiple choice examination often emphasizes the simple facts of a subject matter while providing no evidence about the student's knowledge of more general issues. The multiple choice test has been criticized as being only a measure of memory rather than a measure of understanding. Another argument is that the multiple choice examination reflects none of the student's creative ability.

Proponents of multiple choice examinations point out that regardless of how valid essay examinations might be in theory, the unreliability of essay examinations keeps them at a relatively low level of validity in practice. The criticisms of multiple choice examinations usually concern how bad they can be when improperly constructed and ignore the extent to which *important* materials can be framed in multiple choice form by the ingenious test constructor. There is a considerable amount of research evidence which indicates that *well-constructed* multiple choice examinations can effectively measure many different kinds of course content, even with materials that would not seem appropriate. For example, Tyler (13) found a correlation of .85 between the ability of students to draw generalizations from data and a multiple choice test, the alternatives being better and worse generalizations which could be attributed to the information. Even in the testing of French pronunciation, high correlations were found between samples of speech and a multiple choice test (9). Other studies have shown that multiple choice tests can effectively measure some of the skills in writing and mathematics (2, p. 73).

Rather than try to decide whether multiple choice examinations are generally better than tests of the essay type, or vice versa, it would be more appropriate to see how they can both be made as effective as possible and how they can be used in conjunction with one another. When the course material is mainly factual and technical, or the concepts to be taught are relatively simple, there is a definite advantage for the multiple choice test. Multiple choice tests are generally more applicable at lower than at higher levels of education. Multiple choice tests can be justified in elementary school, and in many of the courses in high school and college. Some of the courses in high school and college which require creative talents and the ability to organize ideas have a more definite need for essay type examinations. In most graduate studies, it is very difficult to place the whole burden of determining grades on multiple choice tests alone.)

COMPOSING ESSAY EXAMINATIONS

The Wording of Questions. Essay questions should range as broadly as possible across the course content. Content representativeness can be increased by having a larger number of questions for which the student is expected to write only a paragraph or two. Very general questions should be avoided, such as "How did Hitler come to power?" "What happened to art in the fifteenth century?" It directs the student more accurately to a particular topic if the essay question spells out the points which are to be discussed, an example being as follows:

Discuss the use of the standard error of estimate with tests under the following headings:

1. The statistical derivation
2. The meaning of the "per cent of variance explained"
3. The effect on the standard error of estimate of changes in the dispersion of assessment scores
4. The assumption of homoscedacticity

Choice of Questions. A widely used procedure with essay examinations is to let the student choose a few from a larger number of questions. Although this is a popular procedure with students, it has definite disadvantages. Because the questions on a test are intended to be a sample of the course content, allowing the student to choose among the questions reduces the value of the test as a sample. Also, this procedure makes it difficult to compare students with one another. It is possible that two students would write on entirely different questions, providing no basis of comparison between them.

Grading. There are several steps which can be taken to remove the largest flaw in essay examinations, the unreliability of grading. The primary way to increase the reliability is to use more than one grader. The student should then be given the average grade. The use of two graders will substantially raise the reliability, and if it is feasible, as many as five instructors can collaborate to make the grades even more reliable. Multiple gradings are usually employed with important graduate school examinations.

If several persons grade the same examinations, each grader should have no knowledge of the grades given by the other graders. In order to discount the personal likes and dislikes of the graders, the students' names should not be placed on the tests. Before giving grades, it helps the instructor to first read through all, or a number, of the tests. A better basis of comparison can be had by grading one question through all of the examinations and then returning to the second question. It is better to list the grades for each question on a separate sheet. If grades are placed on the tests, the first grades which are given might prejudice the instructor toward later questions.

It is very difficult for the instructor to avoid certain biases in the grading of essay examinations. The student who writes well in general has an advantage on most essay questions. If there are too many questions set for the allotted time period, an advantage is given to the person who can express himself rapidly in writing. The student with poor penmanship and spelling is often penalized on examinations that have little to do with basic writing skills. Unless the course material specifically concerns writing skills, the instructor should grade in terms of the content, not in terms of the elegance of presentation.

THE CONSTRUCTION OF MULTIPLE CHOICE EXAMINATIONS

The Item Pool. A collection of items is needed for the classroom test as well as for the construction of a predictor test. It is also helpful to have many more items than will be used in the test. The principles used in the selection of the "best" items for the classroom test are different from those used to compose a predictor test. In composing a predictor test, items are selected in such a way as to maximize the prediction of a criterion. In constructing an assessment test, items are selected in such a way as to maximally represent the performance or, in the case of a classroom examination, the course content.

The outline of content serves as a guide to the collection of items. One way to proceed is to make up a number of items for each of the subheadings in the outline. Instructors usually find it easier to collect items over a period of time to fit the various parts of the outline, rather than compose them all at once. The author establishes an item pool for a course in tests and measurements by writing down items as they occur to him, or after an important issue has been raised in classroom discussion. Over a period of time some hundreds of items have been obtained in this way, with different item pools available for each of the several tests used during the semester.

Choice of Items. Most instructors agree that the general points of view and the ability to use course content are more important than segregated facts and memory for specific details. Although some simple factual items should appear in most tests, many of the items should concern the student's ability to understand issues and reason from one situation to another. Items of that kind are difficult to construct, but carefully composed multiple choice items can measure the student's understanding of complex issues.

The Wording of Questions. Careful attention should be given to the wording of both predictor and assessment test items. There is generally more difficulty in the wording of classroom examinations because the questions are usually more complex. The inexperienced instructor often makes some glaring mistakes in the wording of multiple choice items. There is a considerable body of information on the writing of test items (see **1, 4, 11**). Some of the most important rules will be briefly described.

1. Make all of the alternatives grammatically consistent with the stem (the "question"). For example, with a stem like "The piston ring is," you would not use a plural noun for an alternative, such as "three small gears." Or if the stem ends with the article "a," you should not include alternatives which begin with vowels. There are many other ways in which grammatical inconsistencies can "give away" an item.

2. Do not make the correct alternatives consistently longer or shorter than the incorrect alternatives. In the same vein, do not overspecify the correct alternative, such as using remarks in parentheses and extra detail which will give away the answer. A typical mistake is to be rather casual in the formulation of incorrect alternatives and to highly specify the correct alternatives.

3. Make the incorrect alternatives plausible. Sometimes an individual gets the correct answer because the other alternatives are obviously not related to the subject matter. The rule is that all of the alternatives should be equally appealing to the person who does not know the answer, but only one alternative should make sense to the person who knows the answer. Illustrating this rule with the question, "Which one of the following is one of the psychophysical methods?" we would not employ an incorrect alternative such as "calculus," but a plausible, though incorrect, alternative such as "triadic inconsistencies."

4. Avoid alternatives like "none of the above." It is difficult to frame items in such a way that one of the alternatives is absolutely true in all circumstances. The better logic is to construct alternatives in such a way that one of them is markedly *more* correct than the others. The use of "none of the above" places a double and somewhat confusing burden on the student: he not only must detect the alternative which is most correct, he must decide whether or not it is absolutely correct.

5. Use a random order for the alternatives in each item. This can be done with a table of random numbers to be found in many books on statistics (see **5**). Another approach is to write the alternative positions on separate file cards (if there are five alternatives, the letter *a* would be written on one card, the letter *b* on another and so on to *e*); the cards can then be shuffled and dealt out to allot alternatives to their positions beneath the question. Some instructors arrange the alternatives systematically throughout the test, insuring that the correct alternative ap-

pears an equal number of times at each position. Even this method can give away answers. Randomization of alternatives is the safest procedure.

Review of Items. As in the construction of predictor tests, it is helpful to have several persons, or at least one person, review the items which go into a classroom examination. This may be too laborious for the whole item pool, but someone should at least read and criticize the smaller number of items which are used in the test. All of the points mentioned earlier in respect to the review of predictor test items apply to assessment tests.

Selection of Items for the Test. Whereas elaborate methods of item analysis were recommended for the selection of items for a predictor test, the item pool need only be sampled to obtain the items for an assessment test. If the item pool is representative of the important course content, and this rests on the instructor's judgment, a sample of the items will serve as an adequate test. The author selects the items for his classroom tests by drawing 40 items at random from an item pool. Any random sample of forty will give much the same results that would be obtained from any other random sample and much the same results as if the whole pool were made into a test. The sample of items should be inspected to make sure that they have all been covered in the course work.

Some people feel uneasy in randomly selecting items from the item pool, because they think this method is loose and inexact. But randomness is desirable both from the standpoint of sampling logic and to prevent the test from being slanted toward any particular feature of the content. If the class is told in advance that the items will be randomly drawn from a larger pool, they are more content to apply themselves to the whole subject matter rather than to try to "dope out" what the test will be about. Also, because the instructor will not want to use the same test over and over with new classes, a new test can be constructed by a second random drawing of items.

It is sometimes useful to divide the items in a pool into several categories and randomly select a number of items from each. This can be done if there are definite divisions of the subject matter. However, the score obtained on a completely random selection of items will be very much the same as obtained by using categories.

Item Analysis. Some information can be obtained about the effectiveness of an assessment test by an examination of the scores obtained by students. The classroom instructor seldom has the facilities to administer the whole item pool to a group of students and must rely, instead, on the results from the items in one test. There are several desirable features which should appear in multiple choice examinations. One of these is that the frequencies of choices for the incorrect alternatives should be approximately equal. If practically no one chooses an alternative, it is a "give away" and should be replaced with a more plausible incorrect alternative. If one of the incorrect alternatives is chosen more frequently than the designated "correct" alternative, the instructor may be wrong himself, or the question may be misleading. Even on a classroom examination there is little reason for retaining an item that no one, or almost no one, gets correct. It is more reasonable to retain a few very easy items as a way of giving the average student a feeling of accomplishment.

It is axiomatic that students should receive better grades on an examination after the course of instruction than before the course begins. Similarly the questions which show the biggest change in number of students who get the correct answer from before to after are more particularly concerned with the course content. In large school programs, such as some of those in the Armed Forces, examinations are sometimes constructed on the basis of an improvement in item scores from before to after the course. This logic can be carried too far in that an item might be very difficult both before and after the course not because of inappropriateness, but because of shortcomings of the instruction.

PREPARING TESTS FOR ADMINISTRATION

After items have been selected from an item pool, either in the construction of a predictor or an assessment test, some practical decisions must be made about how the items will be assembled and administered. It must be decided whether or not to order the items in terms of difficulty, placing the easier items at the first of the test and the harder ones toward the end. It is sometimes desirable to order the items in terms of difficulty to prevent students from becoming discouraged because of several difficult items which might appear near the beginning of the test. The items can be ordered in terms of difficulty only if an empirical tryout has been made. Such information is likely to be available for a predictor test but not for the usual classroom examination. What an instructor thinks will be an easy item may prove to be very difficult for the class and vice versa. If difficulty levels have not been obtained from an empirical tryout, it is better to randomly order the items throughout the test and inform the students about it. If each item has been written on a separate file card, the randomization can be performed by shuffling the cards thoroughly and "dealing" them out in the order of their appearance.

Test Instructions. The test instructions bear a considerable burden of accurately directing subjects to the test content. The failure to make test instructions sufficiently clear and detailed is one of the most obvious shortcomings of the inexperienced test constructor. The people who deal extensively with tests realize that some of the subjects will become confused by even the most straightforward instructions. It is not uncommon for subjects to fail to put their names in the designated place. If the subjects are told not to write on the test booklet, some booklets will have numerous marks on them. If the items are at all complicated, such as asking the subjects to pick the two most correct alternatives instead of only one, some of the subjects will inevitably become confused. The ease with which subjects become confused with unusual test items, or marking procedures, often forces the test constructor to abandon an apparently promising new approach.

The rule is to write test instructions as though all of the subjects were of very low intelligence. Test instructions should be written so that the dullest and most confused individual will understand them. To do this, the instructions should be made redundant and all points should be generally overexplained. For example, in a multiple choice test for which only one alternative is to be marked, instructions should be written as follows: "Mark one of the alternatives for each question. Do not mark more than one alternative for each question. Leave none of the questions blank." If special answer sheets are used with the test, at least one, and sometimes several, examples should be given.

Time Limits. If there is a time limit for completing the test, and there usually is, the test constructor must determine in advance how much time should be given. If the attribute being tested is logically concerned with speed, studies should be undertaken to determine the time limit which will produce the largest standard deviation of test scores. This can be done by trying a number of different time limits with separate groups of subjects. The time which works the best can then be made the standard time limit.

There has been a general tendency to make restrictive time limits on tests which are not inherently concerned with speed. Some of the predictor tests, such as numerical computation and perceptual speed, are defined as "speeded" abilities. However, we often find speeded tests of reasoning and vocabulary, where there is little ground for restrictive time limits. There are few classroom examinations where restrictive time limits are justified. Some classroom topics, such as typing and shorthand are naturally concerned with the ability to work quickly. However, there is little reason to believe that speed is necessarily involved in the understanding of physics, history, psychology and most other school topics. When the test is not intended to measure speed, per se, subjects should be given a comfortable time limit. A few students will feel that they do not have an adequate amount of time even if they work an hour after the rest of the students have left. Some time limit is necessary simply as a convenience for the instructor, but most of the students should be able to complete the test without feeling pressured by the time limit.

Auxiliary Materials. Preparations must be made for any special materials which are needed for the test. If a particular kind of pencil is required, an adequate supply must be on hand. If devices such as rulers, drawing equipment, or other instruments are needed, subjects should be informed well in advance of the test. If mathematical problems are part of the test, the subjects should either be told to bring "scratch" paper or it should be provided at the time of testing. Here again, it pays to overexplain the test requirements. If the answer sheet must be marked in pencil, some of the students will come only with a pen. Some pencil points will inevitably break and there must be either extra pencils or a sharpener handy. Trivial as these points seem, the test constructor must either provide for them or the test reliability will be lowered.

SUMMARY

There are two basically different approaches to test construction depending on whether the instrument is intended to be a predictor or an assessment. A predictor test is constructed in terms of statistical strategy, the purpose of which is to squeeze the last ounce of predictive efficiency out of an item pool. Some of the statistical methods which ideally should be applied are too complex and laborious to be used except in special cases. Therefore, there is a hierarchy of preferred procedures, depending on the time and facilities available.

An assessment test is constructed in terms of rational rather than statistical standards. The purpose is to include the important content in an examination. Only by a clear statement of the goals of instruction, or in a nonclassroom situation, the merits of different behaviors, can an assessment test be meaningfully reviewed, discussed, and eventually changed for the better. In the construction of both predictor and assessment tests it is important to write items clearly, standardize the scoring, state the instructions carefully, and systematize the administration procedure.

REFERENCES

1. Bean, K. L. *Construction of educational and personnel tests*. New York: McGraw-Hill, 1953.
2. Cronbach, L. J. *Essentials of psychological testing*. New York: Harper, 1949.
3. Davis, F. B. Item analysis in relation to educational and psychological testing. *Psychol. Bull.*, 1952, **49**, 97–121.
4. Ebel, R. L. Writing the test item. In E. F. Lindquist (Ed.), *Educational measurement*. Washington: American Council on Education, 1951.
5. Edwards, A. L. *Experimental design in psychological research*. New York: Rinehart, 1950.

6. Guilford, J. P. *Psychometric methods.* (2nd ed.) New York: McGraw-Hill, 1954.
7. Horst, A. P. Item selection by means of a maximizing function. *Psychometrika,* 1936, **1**, 229–244.
8. McNemar, Q. *Psychological statistics.* New York: Wiley, 1949.
9. Tharp, J. B. A modern language test. *J. higher Educ.,* 1935, **6**, 103–104.
10. Thorndike, R. L. *Personnel selection: test and measurement techniques.* New York: Wiley, 1949.
11. Thorndike, R. L., and Hagen, E. *Measurement and evaluation in psychology and education.* New York: Wiley, 1955.
12. Toops, H. A. The L-method. *Psychometrika,* 1941, **6**, 249–266.
13. Tyler, R. W. *Constructing achievement tests.* Columbus, Ohio: Ohio State Univer. Press, 1934.
14. Wherry, R. J., and Winer, B. J. A method for factoring large numbers of items. *Psychometrika,* 1953, **18**, 161–179.

CHAPTER 9

The Structure of Human Abilities

The term "general intelligence" has been used with reluctance in previous pages because of two misleading connotations which it bears. The first is that the tests which are used to measure "general intelligence" are not assessments, as the term "intelligence" suggests, but are predictor tests which have gained their meaning from numerous relationships with important human variables. The second misleading connotation is that the word "general" implies that there is only one kind of intelligence rather than separate dimensions of intelligence.

We usually talk as though human abilities are general. We say, "He is a 'smart' person," without bothering to differentiate the ways in which the individual is particularly gifted. Sometimes we do make a distinction, as in saying, "He is very good in mathematical work, but he is not so good in understanding written material."

If intelligence is perfectly general, the person who can do one type of intellectual problem well can do all other kinds of problems well, and the person who does poorly on one type of problem will do poorly on all others. Looking at it in terms of the ability to do school work, if abilities are perfectly general, the child who learns easily to solve arithmetic problems will have the same facility in learning spelling, geography, and other topics. Another possibility is that human abilities are completely "specific," that there are no correlations between different intellectual tasks. Then, if we know that a particular child is very adept at learning arithmetic, this offers no basis at all for predicting how well he will do in spelling or geography. Taking the case further, if abilities were completely unrelated, the child who could add numbers very quickly might be slower than the average child in performing multiplications.

Human abilities are neither completely general nor completely specific. The real story lies between these two extremes. In this chapter, we will discuss the history of this problem, the mathematical procedures of factor analysis, and some of the different abilities which underlie human intellect.

Faculty Psychology. The belief was prevalent in the early nineteenth century that human behavior is determined by a large number of separate capacities, or faculties, as they were called (see **3, 12**). There were proposed faculties of attention, memory, reason, will power, esthetic appreciation, and many others. It was the early belief that each faculty resides in a particular brain location and that "bumps on the head" are prognostic of the strength of particular faculties (see **12,** p. 56). Although the anatomical theories were soon discarded, the belief in a large number of specific human faculties lingered throughout the remainder of the nineteenth century.

Binet and "General Intelligence." Alfred Binet's early efforts to measure intelligence were in line with the faculty psychology of the time. He worked at first with the same kind of sensory and motor tests that were used by Galton and others. Some of these included suggestibility, size of the cranium, tactile discrimination, graphology, and even palmistry. Like the others who were trying to measure human abilities, he found that these simpler functions do not measure intelligence, as we commonly think of it.

Binet abandoned sensory and motor tests in favor of a "molar" conception of intelligence. For practical reasons, Binet thought that it would not be possible to measure all of the simple skills that underlie intelligent behavior; instead, it would be more feasible to study the end products of intellectual functioning. Consequently, his tests emphasized the ability to make sound judgments. He defined intelligence as "the tendency to take and maintain a definite direction; the capacity to make adaptations for the purpose of attaining a desired end; and the power of auto-criticism" (**15,** p. 45).

The Binet-Simon scale provided each child with one score, a *mental age* score (mental age scores were introduced in the 1908 revision). Because each child receives only one score, it must be assumed that intelligence is general, or that only one factor is involved in the test items. If there are, say, two kinds of intelligence involved in the test, the use of only one score is somewhat misleading. Two children could make the same score, not because they are alike in respect to their abilities but because one child is high in one of the factors and low in the other, and vice versa for the other child. The same assumption of the generality of human abilities is involved in all of the general intelligence tests which have followed from Binet's early work.

THE GENERAL FACTOR THEORY

Spearman's G. At the same time that Binet and Simon were working in France on the first practical mental test, a psychologist in England,

Charles Spearman, was working from a different standpoint. Spearman hypothesized a general factor of intelligence, which he called the G factor. The G factor was thought of at that time as being a kind of "mental energy." Unlike Binet, Spearman undertook extensive investigations to determine whether or not there is only one common factor of intelligence (see **14**). In order to do this, he administered batteries of tests to school children, and by statistical analysis of the scores, he tried to show that only one common factor underlies all mental tests. In this work he introduced the techniques of factor analysis to psychology. Earlier, Karl Pearson (**13**) had made some of the fundamental mathematical developments.

Correlation Matrices. If a number of tests have been given to a group of people, each of the tests can be correlated with each of the others, resulting in what is called a correlation matrix. It is with such correlation matrices that factor analysis is undertaken. A hypothetical matrix showing the correlations between four tests is given in Table 9–1. To read the

TABLE 9–1. INTERCORRELATIONS OF FOUR SCHOOL SUBJECTS

	Sp.	Ar.	Rd.	Sc.
Spelling	( )	.50	.68	.44
Arithmetic	.50	( )	.49	.71
Reading	.68	.49	( )	.55
Science	.44	.71	.55	( )

matrix, simply look down a column and across a row to find the intersection of two tests. By looking down the arithmetic column and across to the reading row, a correlation of .49 is found between arithmetic and reading. Note that each correlation appears twice in the matrix. A correlation of .49 is also found by looking down the reading column and stopping at the arithmetic row. The diagonal cells of the matrix have been left blank. These are the correlations of the tests with themselves, which are, technically, all 1.00, but are allowed to assume different values in the actual factor-analytic work.

The Search for G. Spearman's hypothesis can be more completely specified by the statement that mental tests have only one common factor and that all else is due to factors specific to each test. That is, part of the test variance can be accounted for by one common, or general, factor, and otherwise, mental tests have nothing in common. Spearman thought that each test would have some particularity, or some *specificity*, connected with its items. The concept of "variance explained" and the diagrams used to show the overlap of variances (from Chapter 7) can be used here to demonstrate factorial composition of tests. The overlapping variances (squared correlations) for one common factor in three tests can be pictured as in Figure 9–1.

In Figure 9–1 the three tests overlap in only one area, the cross-hatched section, which is labeled *G*. Each test then has a portion of its area which is specific: it does not overlap with the *G* area and it does not overlap with the other tests outside of the *G* area.

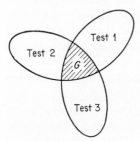

FIGURE 9–1. Variance diagram of one common factor (*G*) in three tests.

Spearman proved that if there is only one common factor in a set of test scores, the columns of coefficients in the correlation matrix will be proportional to one another (14). A hypothetical matrix which fulfills this requirement is given in Table 9–2. The proportionality of the columns in Table 9–2 can be tested by successively dividing the correlations in one column by those in any other, for all except the vacant diagonal cells. Going down columns *A* and *B* in this way, it is seen that the coefficients in *A* are 1.1 times as large as the coefficients in *B* (.67 over .61, .61 over .56, and .55 over .50). The coefficients in any other pair of columns are proportional also.

TABLE 9–2. A HYPOTHETICAL CORRELATION MATRIX SHOWING ONE COMMON
FACTOR IN FIVE TESTS *

	A	B	C	D	E
A	( )	74	67	61	55
B	74	( )	61	56	50
C	67	61	( )	50	45
D	61	56	50	( )	41
E	55	50	45	41	( )

* All decimal points have been removed; consequently, 74 should be understood as a correlation of .74.

Twenty years or more were spent by Spearman and others in England trying to determine whether only one common factor, *G*, underlies all mental tests. The tests used in the first stages mainly concerned simple sensory discrimination, but these were soon abandoned for the more complex functions of the type made popular by Binet. Batteries of tests, usually containing no more than a dozen instruments, were administered, mainly to school children. Correlation matrices were computed and the proportionality of columns was studied. Even if there were only one common factor among all tests, the actual correlation coefficients would not strictly obey the proportionality criterion because of sampling error. Consequently, very laborious studies of the departure from proportionality had to be undertaken, some of these lasting for months.

After much investigation, at first in England and later by American psychologists, it became apparent that one common factor is not sufficient to account for the intercorrelations among mental tests. In a few restricted cases, where the tests were much alike, the proportionality criterion was approximated. When a broad range of tests was used, however, it was apparent that more than one common factor was needed. Spearman won his point, in part, in that one common factor can be shown to explain much, but by no means all, of the overlap between mental tests.

MULTIFACTOR THEORY

Rather than argue over whether one common factor is sufficient to explain intellectual behavior, the question soon shifted to that of how many factors are required to explain the intercorrelations of tests. The original statistical technique for determining a general factor is of little use when in fact more than one factor occurs. Procedures were developed for discovering how many factors are involved in a battery of tests. These statistical procedures are referred to as "multiple-factor analysis." Pearson (13) provided the original solution to the problem. Cyril Burt (5) in England, T. L. Kelley (11) in America, and later L. L. Thurstone (19) in America were prominent figures in the development of factor-analytic techniques.

Cluster Analysis. An approximation to factor analysis can often be made by a simple inspection of the correlation matrix—consider the matrix in Table 9–3 for example. A cluster is defined as a group of tests whose members correlate highly among themselves and correlate relatively low with tests not in the cluster.

TABLE 9–3. A HYPOTHETICAL CORRELATION MATRIX FOR SIX TESTS [*]

	A	B	C	D	E	F
A	( )	01	64	06	72	−13
B	01	( )	−07	42	08	56
C	64	−07	( )	−02	55	−19
D	06	42	−02	( )	11	47
E	72	08	55	11	( )	−04
F	−13	56	−19	47	−04	( )

[*] All decimal points omitted.

One way to begin a cluster analysis is first to locate the highest correlation in the matrix. In this case, it is the correlation of .72 between tests E and A. These two tests can form the nucleus of the first cluster. Any other test that correlates highly with both A and E can also be placed in the cluster. Test C correlates .64 with A and .55 with E, so it can be classified in the cluster. None of the other three tests correlates highly with A, C, and E; therefore, no other tests belong to the first cluster.

If there are substantial correlations among the tests which do not go into the first cluster, this means that one or more additional clusters remain. We then look at the correlations among tests B, D, and F. The three intercorrelations are .42, .47, and .56. There are then two clusters, or in the same sense, two factors, in these six tests. The two clusters can be seen more easily if we rearrange the correlations in Table 9–3 to make the first three rows and columns contain the tests for the first cluster and the last three rows and columns contain the tests for the second cluster. This has been done in Table 9–4. Table 9–4 has been sectioned off to

TABLE 9–4. A REARRANGEMENT OF THE COLUMNS AND ROWS OF TABLE 9–3

	A	E	C	D	B	F
A	( )	72	64	06	01	−13
E	72	( )	55	11	08	−04
C	64	55	( )	−02	−07	−19
D	06	11	−02	( )	42	47
B	01	08	−07	42	( )	56
F	−13	−04	−19	47	56	( )

show more clearly the intercorrelations of the tests within the two clusters and the correlations between the tests in the different clusters. Arranged in this way, it is easy to see that there are two different kinds of abilities involved in the six tests.

If the clusters were generally as clear-cut and as easy to locate as they are in the example above, there would be little need for more formal procedures of analysis. When the number of tests is as large as that contained in present-day factor analyses, often more than fifty, it becomes very difficult to locate clusters. Also, it will almost never be the case that tests will divide themselves neatly into clusters such that each test belongs unequivocally to only one cluster. More often it is difficult to decide whether a test should be placed in one cluster or another, and the tests in one cluster usually have at least moderate correlations with the tests in other clusters.

The Vector Model. A model which is more general than variance diagrams is required to demonstrate how multiple-factor analysis works. Correlations can be portrayed by lines, or vectors, and by the angles between vectors. In Figure 9–2 three correlations have been pictured with vectors. In the vector model, each test is represented by one line. The closer the lines are to one another, the higher the two tests correlate. In the diagram on the left in Figure 9–2, the vectors for tests 1 and 2 are

FIGURE 9–2. Three correlation coefficients represented by pairs of vectors.

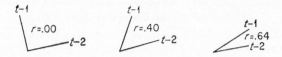

at right angles, that is, 90 degrees apart. This always means a zero correlation between two tests. In the middle diagram, the vectors are less than 90 degrees, and consequently, there is a correlation greater than zero, .40, in this case. The diagram on the right shows an even smaller angle between vectors, portraying a correlation of .64.

The vectors are not all of the same length in the vector model. The length of the test vector depends on the over-all amount of correlation the test has with the others in the matrix, the "communality." The correlation between two tests in the model depends both on how large the angle is between two vectors and the length of the two vectors. A fuller explanation of how this works would take us far beyond the mathematical complexity which can be permitted here (see **7, 16, 19**). However, the meaning of the model can be grasped if it will be kept in mind that long vectors and small angles mean high correlations. The shorter the vectors and the nearer the angle approaches 90 degrees, the less the correlation.

All of the intercorrelations in Table 9–4 can be cast in the form of one vector model, which is shown in Figure 9–3. The vector model demonstrates the two clusters noted earlier. Tests *A*, *C*, and *E* cluster together

FIGURE 9–3. Vector model of the correlation coefficients shown in Table 9–4.

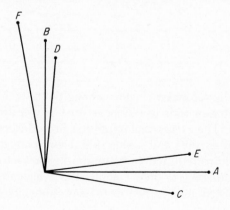

in the space, and similarly, tests *B*, *D*, and *F* are near one another. The tests in one cluster are separated in general about ninety degrees from the tests in the other cluster, showing the low correlations between the tests in the different clusters.

Factor Loadings. What factor analysis does is to place new lines, or vectors, in the vector model. The number of new vectors is generally

FIGURE 9–4. Vector model with factor axes.

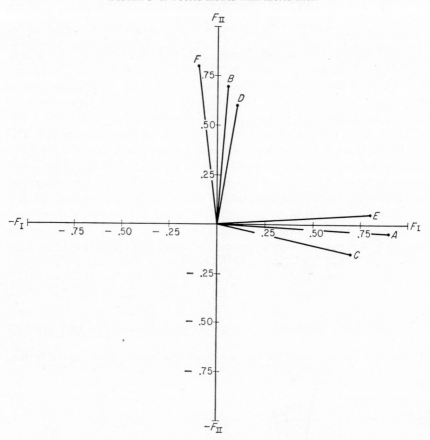

equal to the number of major clusters among the tests. Figure 9–4 shows how a typical factor analysis would locate two new vectors, F_I and F_{II} in the vector model. The factor vectors go out in both directions from the origin, having both a plus and minus side. Describing the mathematical techniques which are required to place the factor vectors in the vector model would again take us into complexities which cannot be treated here. (The interested student can learn more about factor-analytic procedures from **7, 16, 19.**) However, it is not necessary for the reader completely to understand the mathematics of factor analysis to comprehend what the factor vectors mean once they have been located in the vector model.

Each of the factor vectors reads like a yardstick, with the numbers on the scale showing the amount of correlation with the tests. The two factor vectors constitute a coordinate system, much like the axes on a piece of graph paper. The correlations of the tests with the factors are referred to as loadings. Each test has a loading on each of the two factors. Reading from the graph, test A has a correlation, or loading, of .90 on Factor I and a loading of −.05 on Factor II. The full set of factor loadings, called a factor matrix, is given in Table 9–5.

TABLE 9–5. FACTOR MATRIX FOR SIX TESTS

Test	Loading	
	F_I	F_{II}
A	.90	−.05
E	.80	.05
C	.70	−.15
D	.10	.60
B	.05	.70
F	−.10	.80

The Results of a Factor Analysis. A factor analysis can serve to simplify the original battery of test scores and the intercorrelations among the tests. The factor matrix in Table 9–5 shows that there are only two general kinds of abilities involved in the tests instead of six. At this point we do not know what these two underlying abilities are. Let us say that tests A, E, and C are concerned respectively with reading ability, comprehension of written material, and vocabulary. We could then interpret Factor I as having to do with verbal ability, with the understanding of words. Say that tests D, B, and F concern addition, multiplication, and mathematical reasoning respectively. The second factor is concerned with numerical computation, the ability to perform arithmetic operations.

After the factors are interpreted and named, a score can be given to each person on each of the factors. Although a precise determination of such scores requires some complicated calculations (see **16,** chap. 15) a good approximation could be obtained in the present example by simply averaging the individual's scores on the three tests which have high loadings on a factor. That is, if an individual's scores on tests A, E, and C are averaged, this provides a good approximation of the score which he has on Factor I. Similarly, scores on Factor II could be obtained by averaging the scores on tests D, B, and F.

The Complete Model. The simplified example portrayed in Figures 9–3 and 9–4 requires only two dimensions, which is another way of saying that the vectors lie completely on the flat surface of a page. The angles between the vectors might be such that they could not be pictured on a flat surface, and at least a three-dimensional model would be required. In practical work the test vectors will seldom lie on a flat surface, and even three dimensions are often not sufficient for portraying the model. Of course, when the model requires more than three dimensions, there is no physical way of portraying the vectors. However, this does not hinder the mathematical derivation of four, five, and even ten dimensions, or factors, to account for the correlations among tests.

The ultimate aim in performing factor-analytic studies is to reduce the nearly infinite number of tests which can be composed to a smaller number of basic abilities, or factors. This not only achieves a real parsimony in practical work; it helps us to understand the nature of human abilities. Factor analysis is most useful in the early stages of research, when not much is known about an area of investigation. It is a very helpful way of "mapping" the territory before proceeding to a more detailed study of particular attributes.

Correlations among Factors. In Figure 9–4 the two factor vectors are placed 90 degrees apart, which signifies that there is a zero correlation between the two factors. However, in many factor analyses the factor vectors themselves are allowed to correlate, or in other words to assume angles different from 90 degrees. If the correlation between any two factors is allowed to become too large, then the factors begin to lose their value as "different" kinds of abilities. It is not uncommon to find factor solutions in which the correlations between particular factors are as high as .50. Considering that the factors themselves are correlated, this means that factors represent *separable* but not completely *independent* abilities.

Factor analysis can be used in many different kinds of problems, but our primary concern will be with its application to psychological tests. Factor analyses have been made of mechanical abilities, interest tests, and personality tests, as well as of the more intellectual functions. We will look at the factor-analytic results in the domain of tests of the intellectual type in this chapter and later refer to factor-analytic findings that relate to other kinds of human attributes.

FACTORS OF ABILITY

The large amount of factor-analytic work performed during the last fifty years permits us to speak with confidence about at least some of the factors which underlie tests of the ability type. One cardinal finding is that the correlations among human abilities are almost always positive, even if small in some cases. Consequently, it would be rare to find one human ability for which high performance indicates that the individual will do poorly in another type of performance. Because of the tendency for all tests of ability to correlate positively with one another, the factors which have been found also tend to correlate positively with one another. This is a partial confirmation of Spearman's *G*. Spearman was both correct and incorrect: there is a moderate tendency for the individual to do as well or as poorly on nearly all ability tests, but there are also definite clusterings of tests into separable factors.

How Many Factors? Factor analysts have differed not so much in the kinds of factors they have found, but in how many factors they have derived. The number of factors used to explain ability tests is dependent on how finely one wants to attack the problem. One could be content with only the general factor reflected in the tendency for tests to correlate positively with one another. Or, the factor analyst can stop with the several most prominent factors, those which explain most of the test variance. Most of the British factor analysts have been content with exploring only the major factors. At the other extreme, one can continuously search for more and more factors of less and less importance.

An analogy may help in portraying the question of how many factors should be derived. In constructing a topographic map, the cartographer has a choice as to how finely differences in elevation will be shown in the contour lines. If contour lines are used to show differences in elevation of 1,000 feet, a mountain might appear as one smooth peak. If contour lines were used to show differences in elevation of 200 feet, the increased detail might show that there are actually several peaks on the same base. Increasing the fineness of the contours to show differences in elevation of 10 feet would bring out considerably more detail about the terrain. One can imagine a logical extension to the use of contours to reflect inches of elevation, and then every stone would be visible. The cartographer must strike a balance between two opposing standards. The more grossly the contours reflect differences in elevation, the easier the terrain is to survey and to picture as a map. The more finely the contours reflect elevation, the more nearly the map approaches the actual terrain; but, after a point, the map becomes difficult to interpret.

The factor analyst faces much the same problem as the cartographer: he must decide at what point a continued derivation of highly specialized factors no longer adds to the knowledge of human abilities. Most of the work in factor analysis has concentrated on the derivation of new factors rather than on exploring the usefulness of the factors which are derived. Although the major factors have already proved useful as predictor tests, it remains to be seen whether or not some of the factors will add to the predictiveness of test batteries. When more research is done on the meaning and usefulness of factors, we will be in a better position to say which factors are important human attributes and which are merely artifacts of psychological tests.

A Factor-analysis Problem. To illustrate the steps that are required in a factor analysis, the research reported by the Thurstones in 1941 (**20**) will be described. In an earlier analysis of tests given to college students, Thurstone and his colleagues had found nine factors (**17**). The purpose of the second analysis was to see if the same factors would be found in children. Sixty tests were constructed for this purpose—a considerable amount of test construction. Tests which had produced particular factors in previous analyses were included along with new tests, which it was hoped would point to undiscovered factors. In order for important factors to appear, it was necessary for the tests to range as broadly as possible across the ability functions. The tests varied from familiar forms like arithmetic and vocabulary to the solving of picture puzzles and the counting of dots on paper.

Each test was separately standardized on a tryout group of children. Then test forms were reproduced and arrangements were made for the administration of materials. All 60 tests were given to 710 eighth-grade students in the Chicago schools. The tests were given, a half-dozen at a session, over a period of 10 school days.

All intercorrelations were computed for a 63 by 63 matrix. This included intercorrelations of the 60 tests plus the three additional variables of age, sex, and mental age (obtained from previous testing). This required the computation of 1,953 correlation coefficients. Elaborate factor-analysis procedures were then applied to the correlation matrix. In all, it was a very large research venture, as all such substantial factor-analytic studies tend to be.

The Thurstones found seven definable factors in the study of children. Previous research in England and America and research since the Thurstones' study have generally supported the seven factors and added a number of others. The major factors which have been found are described in the following section.

VERBAL FACTORS

(V_c) *Verbal Comprehension.* This factor has been found in many different factor analyses (cf. **4, 6**). It concerns the ability to understand words and written material. Some tests which have high loadings on V_c are vocabulary, sentence completion, and reading comprehension.

Typical items:

1. Which one of the following words means most nearly the same as
   salutation?
     a. offering
     b. greeting
     c. discussion
     d. appeasement
2. Which one of the following words is most nearly the opposite of
   languid?
     a. unemotional
     b. sad
     c. energetic
     d. healthy

(V_f) **Word Fluency.** This is another verbal factor that has been found
in numerous studies (see **4, 6**). It is concerned with the production of
words, in contrast to V_c, which is concerned with the understanding
of words. Any test which requires the subject to produce words rapidly
has some loading on V_f. Although there is a moderate correlation between
V_c and V_f —a correlation of .42 in the study described above (**20**)—the
two abilities are well distinguished. It is possible for an individual to be
able to produce words rapidly with little understanding of the meaning of
words. The factor V_c tends to be prominent when there is a range of difficulty in words. Factor V_f becomes more important when the words are
simple and the concern is with how rapidly the words are produced. The
contrast between V_c and V_f fits in well with the observation that there are
individuals who have difficulty in expressing their own ideas but are
quite good at understanding written material.
   Typical items:

1. Write as many names of foods as you can in the next two minutes.

   _____

   _____

   _____

2. In each of the following rows write three words that mean almost
   the same as the given word.

   small   _____   _____   _____
   helpful   _____   _____   _____
   kind   _____   _____   _____

   (Note that the words here are simple and that the subject is
   required to produce the new terms.)

NUMBER FACTORS

(N) **Numerical Computation.** One very clear numerical factor has been found in different analyses (see 4, 6). It concerns the speed of solving arithmetic problems of all kinds—addition, subtraction, multiplication, and division problems. The factor is not present in all tests that employ numbers but only in those tests where actual computations are required. Some of the perceptual factors and reasoning factors to be discussed employ numbers but have little of the factor N.

Typical items:

$$\begin{array}{cc} 246 & 8754 \\ +943 & -\ 381 \end{array} \qquad 16 \times 22 = \underline{\hspace{2cm}} \qquad 284/4 = \underline{\hspace{2cm}}$$

REASONING FACTORS

Reasoning is a complex domain of attributes. Some of the factors have been found in a number of investigations and others are still in dispute (see 6, 8, 9).

(R_g) **General Reasoning.** The most common, and most commonly found, factor of reasoning is concerned with the ability to invent solutions to problems. Arithmetical reasoning problems are most characteristic of R_g.

Typical items:

1. If two men can build one house in twelve weeks, how many houses can twelve men build in two weeks?
2. How would you get exactly 7 quarts of water from a stream if you had one 5-quart container and one 3-quart container?

(R_d) **Deduction.** This factor is concerned with the drawing of conclusions, as in logical syllogisms. In this type of reasoning there is nothing in particular to be discovered or invented, the ability being concerned with evaluating the implications of an argument (see 8, 9).

Typical items:

1. John is younger than Fred.
   Bill is older than Fred; therefore, Bill is _____ than John.
2. A student has 10 marbles. No one else in his class has 10 marbles. This means that
   a. no one else in the class has marbles.
   b. all of the other students have less than 10 marbles.
   c. some of the students have less than 10 marbles.
   d. some of the students have more than 10 marbles.
   e. only one student has exactly 10 marbles.

(R_e) **Eduction of Relationships.** A third factor of reasoning has appeared often enough to be cited here, but it is not as firmly established as R_g and R_d (see **8, 9**). The factor involves the ability to see the relationship between two things or ideas and to use the relationship to find other things or ideas. The factor is best represented by verbal analogies and design analogies.

Typical item:

> Ship is to sail, as automobile is to
> > *a.* ship
> > *b.* seat
> > *c.* motor
> > *d.* wind
> > *e.* driver

MEMORY FACTORS

The domain of memory factors is complex and only partially explored. A recent factor analysis by Kelley (**10**) has helped considerably to clarify the area.

(M_r) **Rote Memory.** The best-established factor of memory concerns the ability to remember simple associations where meaning is of little or no importance (see **4, 6, 10**).

Typical item:

> The subject is given a list of names, each of which is paired with a number. He is given a minute or so to memorize which number goes with which name. Then he is told to turn the page. The next page contains the list of names without the numbers. The subject is instructed to write the proper numbers next to the names.

Other items which concern M_r are of the same general kind as the one shown above. They would be such as pairing colors with words, initials with last names, and photographs with geometrical forms.

(M_m) **Meaningful Memory.** There is substantial evidence to indicate that there is a factor involved in the retention of meaningful relationships which is separable from *rote memory* (see **10**). Factor M_m appears when the subject is requested to memorize sentences, meaningfully related words, and lines of poetry.

Typical items:

> 1. The subject is asked to read and try to remember a list of sentences like the following:
>   John repaired the wagon by welding the broken axle.
>   The list of sentences is taken away and the subject is then given

the same sentences with one or more of the words deleted from each, like the following:

John repaired the wagon by welding the broken _____.

2. The subject is shown a list of meaningfully related pairs of words such as the following:

dog   bark
shoe   leather
hard   candy
small   box

The list is taken away and the subject is presented with only one member of each pair as follows:

dog   _____
shoe   _____
hard   _____
small   _____

There is evidence for several other memory factors. A number of investigators have reported a *memory span* factor concerning the ability to recall perfectly for immediate reproduction a series of unrelated items (cf. **6, 10**). A typical item would be to read a series of five to a dozen numbers and ask the subject to give the numbers back in their exact order. There is also some evidence for a *visual memory* factor in which the ability to grasp the relationships within a picture or pattern is important (see **6, 10**). A typical item would consist of showing an individual a landscape picture and asking him to remember the details. Then the picture would be taken away, and the subject would be presented questions like "How many sheep were in the picture?" "What was the boy handing to the man?" "Where was the swing located?" The *visual memory* factor might be related to the ability to remember faces, license numbers, and witnessed events.

SPATIAL FACTORS

(S_o) *Spatial Orientation.* This factor concerns the ability to detect accurately the spatial arrangements of objects in respect to one's own body (see **6, 18**). The factor would be necessary in deciphering pictures taken from a maneuvering airplane. If the plane is simultaneously turning and climbing, the landscape looks very different from the normal view that we get. The individual who can accurately detect what maneuver the airplane is going through from looking at only a picture of the landscape from that vantage point is high in *spatial orientation*. The factor appears most prominently when the spatial problems are presented under "speeded" conditions.

(S_v) **Spatial Visualization.** This second spatial factor differs in a subtle manner from S_o. It is present when the subject is required to imagine, or "visualize," how an object would look if its spatial position were changed. Although there is good statistical support for both of these factors, there has been considerable difficulty in understanding the underlying processes (see **6, 9, 18**). *Spatial orientation* seems to require either an actual or imagined adjustment of one's own body. In *spatial visualization* the observer cannot solve the problem by a bodily adjustment; instead, he must conceive of how an object would look if its spatial position were markedly changed. In contrast to *spatial orientation, spatial visualization* is best tested under relatively "unspeeded" conditions.

Typical item:

> The subject is shown a folded piece of paper with a number of holes punched in it. He is asked to choose from a number of alternatives how the paper would look if unfolded.

PERCEPTUAL FACTORS

A number of factors have been found which concern the ability to detect accurately visual patterns and to see relationships within and among patterns. Some of these factors are apparently of only limited importance, such as the ability to judge certain types of illusions. Several of the more important factors will be described.

(P_s) **Perceptual Speed.** This factor is concerned with the rapid recognition of perceptual details and particularly with the similarities and differences between visual patterns (see **9, 18**).

Typical items:

1. The subject is shown a geometrical form and asked to choose from a number of other forms the one that is the same as the first.
2. The subject is told to make a check mark by each pair of letter groupings if they are identical and to make no mark if they are different.

_____	x'#.Iq	X'#.IQ
_____	a&30(k	a&3(oK
_____	_ro-/w	_ro-/w

(Fifty to several hundred pairs would be used, depending on the time allowed.)

(P_c) **Perceptual Closure.** This factor concerns the perception of objects from limited cues (see **9, 18**). The word "closure" means a sudden awareness of an obscure object or relationship. *Perceptual speed* requires only the recognition of a perceptual form. *Perceptual closure* requires the

"putting together" of a perceptual form when only part of it is presented.
(See Figure 9–5.)

There is some evidence for the existence of a *flexibility of closure* factor
in problems which require the subject to detect one perceptual pattern
which is imbedded in a distracting or competing pattern (see **9, 18**). This
factor is found in such items as the hidden-picture games that are printed

FIGURE 9–5. Items pertaining to the *Perceptual Closure* Factor. The configuration in
each frame is projected briefly on a screen. The subject must determine the hidden
word, letter, or number. (Adapted from Thurstone, 18, pp. 13, 21.)

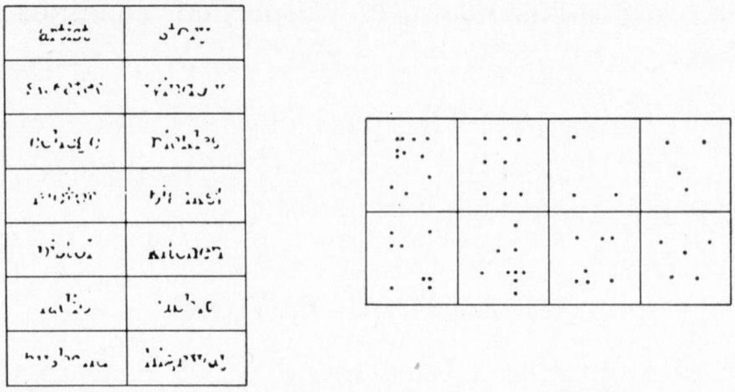

in newspapers and some children's magazines. At first glance, the picture
looks like a normal landscape, but after careful scrutiny, a number of
faces can be found hidden in the trees and rocks. In order to see the
faces, it is necessary to resist or "break down" the perception of the
object in which the faces are imbedded.

SPEED

The question of whether a test should be "speeded" or not has come up
a number of times in previous chapters. Nearly all tests have a time limit
for practical purposes, if for no other reason. In a vocabulary test, for
example, there is no intention of hurrying the subject, and the time limit
is usually liberal enough to satisfy most individuals. Some abilities are
intimately connected with speed, such as typing and shorthand speed; and
also some of the factors which have been discussed, such as *word fluency*
and *perceptual speed*, can only be measured by the use of "speeded" tests.

Considerable interest has been shown over the last fifty years in determining whether or not speed and accuracy are the same in psychological
tests. Although the findings on this topic have not been consistent and the
answer is not the same with all tasks, the general conclusion is that speed
goes along with accuracy to an extent, but that these two attributes are far
from perfectly correlated. A comparison of scores given under "speeded"

and "nonspeeded" conditions shows that at least one and perhaps a number of speed factors can be isolated (see **4, 6**). It is not known at this time just how speed factors interact with the other ability factors.

MULTIFACTOR TEST BATTERIES

From this point on, the book will take a practical slant with the examination of typical tests and measurement methods in use in psychology. No effort will be made to give an exhaustive list of current tests. There are thousands of commercial tests available, and any effort to describe a sizable fraction of these would provide very dull reading. Tests come and go, and better ones will always be forthcoming as our knowledge of testing increases. Rather than make this a catalogue of tests, the book is intended to impart a logic for measurement methods which can be applied to tests in general. A list of test publishers is presented in Appendix 1. The individual who uses tests in professional work will want to obtain test catalogues and in this way keep up with new tests as they are developed.

In the sections to follow, several tests will be described to illustrate the measurement of each type of human attribute. The usual procedure will be first to discuss one of the older tests in each area to provide historical perspective; then, one or several of the leading tests in the area will be discussed.

Judging a Multifactor Battery. Differential aptitude tests can be constructed either rationally or from the results of a factor analysis. Preferably the battery should come from a factor analysis. Otherwise there is no guarantee that the tests will measure different attributes or that the tests will cover a wide range of attributes. If the battery is derived from factor analysis, each of the tests should have high "factorial validity." A test has high "factorial validity" if it correlates highly (has a high loading) with the factor it is intended to measure.

The statistical necessities of efficient differential prediction as described in Chapter 7 apply to all differential aptitude, or multifactor, batteries. Reiterating, each of the subtests should have high individual reliability and should correlate as low as possible with one another. On the practical side, differential aptitude batteries should be judged in terms of the amount of research which has been done on the instrument, the representativeness of the norms, the appropriateness of the battery for different groups of persons, and the time and expense of using the tests.

The Primary Mental Abilities Test (PMA). The *PMA* tests were developed directly out of the factor-analytic work of Thurstone and his colleagues, one phase of which was described previously. This was the first comprehensive multifactor battery and marked a milestone in psychological measurement. The first regular edition appeared in 1941. It was called the Chicago *PMA* Tests for Ages 11 to 17. Three tests were used to represent each of six factors. The following factors were represented: (1) *rote memory,* (2) *verbal comprehension,* (3) *word fluency,* (4) *numerical computation,* (5) *spatial orientation,* and (6) *general reasoning.*

Science Research Associates (*SRA*) later assumed publication of the *PMA* series and issued forms for the 5-to-7, and 7-to-11, as well as for the 11-to-17-year levels. The batteries have been considerably shortened, with only one short test being used to measure each factor. Some of the factors are not represented at one or more of the age levels: for example, the *rote memory* factor is dropped from the 11-to-17-year battery. Figure 9–6 shows typical items which appear on current forms of the *PMA.*

Evaluation of the PMA. In spite of the very important research which preceded the *PMA,* the current tests fall short of the standards of an efficient multifactor battery. The fact that only one short test is used to

FIGURE 9–6. Sample Items from the *SRA* Primary Mental Abilities Tests for Ages 11 to 17. (Reproduction by permission of Thelma G. Thurstone and Science Research Associates.)

Verbal meaning is tested by multiple choice vocabulary items like the following:

Safe: A. secure   B. loyal   C. passive   D. young

The word which means most nearly the same as the first word is to be marked.

Space is tested by items like the following:

(*a*)   (*b*)   (*c*)   (*d*)   (*e*)   (*f*)

Every figure that could be obtained by a rotation of the first figure is to be marked.

Reasoning is tested by items like the following:

a b m c d m e f m g h m | g | | h | | i | | j | | m | | n |

The letters form a series based on a rule. The subject is to discover the rule and mark the next letter in the series.

Number is tested by items like the following:

$$\begin{array}{r} 63 \\ 17 \\ 89 \\ \hline 140 \end{array}$$ | R | | W |

Word fluency is tested by requiring the subject to write as many words beginning with a certain letter as possible during five minutes.

measure each of the factors has two unfortunate consequences. First, to have high factorial validity, it is usually necessary to use several tests. By averaging scores, much of the specificity of each test is canceled and more of the underlying common factor is tapped. Secondly, either averaging the scores on several tests for each factor or making one longer test for each factor raises the reliability.

In some forms of the *SRA PMA*, reliability statistics have been either incorrectly computed or inadequately reported. Split-half reliability estimates have been made without regard to the highly speeded nature of some of the tests. In a restudy of the *PMA* reliability, Anastasi (1, p. 366) found that when properly computed some of the reliabilities fell markedly. For example, the *word fluency* test reliability dropped from a reported .90 to an actual .72, and the *spatial relations* test from .96 to .75. These reliabilities are too low for an adequate multifactor battery.

Compounded with the insufficient reliability of some of the *PMA* subtests, there are moderately high correlations among them. For the seven-to-eleven-year form, intercorrelations were found to range from .41 to .70; and for the five-to-seven-year battery, intercorrelations ranged from .51 to .73. The combination of relatively low reliabilities on some subtests and generally high intercorrelations of subtests considerably weakens the *PMA* as a multifactor battery.

Although the *PMA* test manuals make claims for the specific vocational and educational implications of scores, only a small amount of actual research has been done with the battery. Although norms are given for the battery, very little information has been obtained about the nature of the populations tested. No information is given on sex differences even for the subtests on which significant sex differences are usually found.

The *PMA* tests have not kept up with the increasing knowledge about ability factors. For example, the reasoning test employed in the 11-to-17-year battery, the series completion type of test, has since been found to be a mixture of factors and is not the best test to measure *general reasoning*. Also, a more modern multifactor battery should include several kinds of reasoning tests in line with more recent factor-analytic findings. Subsequent research might show that the *PMA* tests depend excessively on speed. Some of the tests, such as *word fluency*, should be speeded, but it is doubtful that speed will add to the predictiveness of other tests, such as reasoning and *verbal comprehension*.

The Differential Aptitude Tests. The Differential Aptitude Tests (*DAT*) were developed by The Psychological Corporation, principally for use in the vocational and educational guidance of high school students (2). Although the tests were intended for use with students in grades 8 through 12, they have a sufficient range of item difficulty to be used with most adult groups. The tests were not developed directly out of factor-analytic work but were composed in such a way as to incorporate some of the major findings from factor analysis.

The subtests of the *DAT* are as follows (see Figure 9–7 for sample items):

1. *Verbal Reasoning.* The items consist of verbal analogies, in which the reasoning component rather than the difficulty of words is emphasized. The test is more concerned with the reasoning factors than with *verbal comprehension.*

2. *Numerical Ability.* The test covers a wide range of numerical computations. It should be a good measure of the *numerical computation* factor, as it was previously described.

3. *Abstract Reasoning.* This test differs from the *verbal reasoning* test in that all of the problems deal with abstract patterns.

4. *Spatial Relations.* The test items concern the individual's ability to imagine how objects would look if they were rotated in space and to visualize a three-dimensional object from a two-dimensional pattern.

5. *Mechanical Reasoning.* The test items consist of pictures which portray mechanical problems. The subject is asked questions about each picture.

6. *Clerical Speed* and *Accuracy.* The test is modeled closely after the *perceptual speed* factor. The subject is required to find identical sets of numbers and figures.

7. *Language Usage.* This test is more concerned with acquired knowledge, or achievement, than with a specific aptitude. The two parts of the test concern spelling ability and grammatical usage in sentences.

Evaluation of the DAT. Although the *DAT* was not derived directly from factor analysis, the tests represent a collection of reasonably independent measures which range broadly over those factors most directly related to school achievement. The tests were constructed primarily for

FIGURE 9–7. Sample items from the Differential Aptitude Tests. (Reproduced by permission of The Psychological Corporation.)

Verbal Reasoning

. . . . . is to one as second is to. . . . .

| 1. middle | 2. queen | 3. rain | 4. first |
| A. two | B. fire | C. object | D. hill |

. . . . . is to night as breakfast is to. . . . .

| 1. flow | 2. gentle | 3. supper | 4. door |
| A. include | B. morning | C. enjoy | D. corner |

Pick out words which will fill the blanks so that the sentences will be true and sensible. For the first blank, pick out one of the numbered words. For the second blank, pick out one of the lettered words.

FIGURE 9–7.—*Continued*

Abstract Reasoning

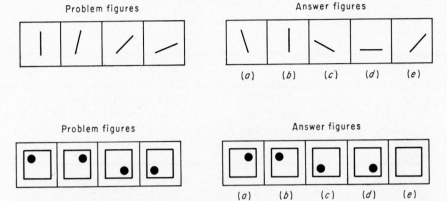

Each row consists of four figures that are called Problem Figures and five called Answer Figures. The four Problem Figures make a series. You are to find which one of the Answer Figures would be the next, or fifth one, in the series.

Space Relations

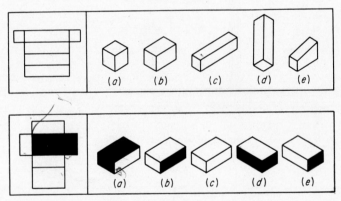

The test consists of forty patterns which can be folded into figures. For each pattern, five figures are shown. You are to decide which of these figures can be made from the pattern shown.

Numerical Ability

Add 13			Subtract 30		
12	A	14	20	A	15
—	B	25	—	B	26
	C	16		C	16
	D	59		D	8
	E	none of these		E	none of these

Choose the correct answer.

Figure 9–7.—*Continued*

Mechanical Reasoning

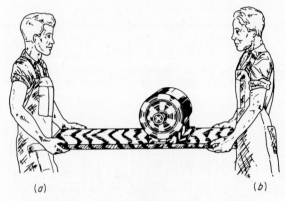

Which man has the heavier load? (If equal, mark C.)

(*a*)   (*b*)

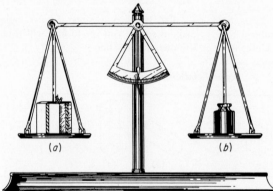

Which weighs more? (If equal, mark C.)

(*a*)   (*b*)

Language Usage Part I: *Spelling*

man
gurl
catt
dog

Indicate whether or not each word is spelled correctly.

Language Usage Part II: *Sentences*

Ain't we / going to the / office / next week / at all.

A   B   C   D   E

The test consists of a series of sentences, each divided into five parts, lettered A, B, C, D, and E. You are to look at each and decide which of the lettered parts have errors in grammar, punctuation, or spelling.

FIGURE 9–7.—*Continued*

Clerical speed and accuracy

TEST ITEMS		SAMPLE OF ANSWER SHEET

V. <u>AB</u> AC AD AE AF	V AC AE AF **AB** AD
W. aA aB BA Ba <u>Bb</u>	W BA Ba **Bb** aA aB
X. A7 7A B7 <u>7B</u> AB	X **7B** B7 AB 7A A7
Y. Aa Ba <u>bA</u> BA bB	Y Aa **bA** bB Ba BA
Z. 3A 3B <u>33</u> B3 BB	Z BB 3B B3 3A **33**

Each test item consists of five letter and number combinations. You are to look at the one combination that is underlined and find the same combination on the answer sheet. (The examples above are all correctly done.)

school programs, and it is doubtful that they would meet with the same level of success in other testing situations. The correlations between the tests vary considerably, going from .06 to as high as .67. The intercorrelations run about .50 on the average. Although it is desirable to have lower correlations, they are not so high as to prevent the battery from functioning as a measure of differential aptitudes.

The reliabilities of the tests are generally high, ranging from .85 to .93 for all except the mechanical comprehension test. The reliability for men on the mechanical comprehension test is sufficiently high, with a mean coefficient of .85, but the reliability for women is only .71.

TABLE 9–6. MEDIAN CORRELATIONS OF DIFFERENTIAL APTITUDE TEST SCORES WITH SCHOOL GRADES *

(Adapted from G. K. Bennett, et al., 2)

Test	English	Math.	Science	Soc. stud., history	Languages	Typing	Shorthand
Verbal Reasoning (VR)	50	39	54	50	30	19	44
Numerical Ability (NA)	48	50	51	48	42	32	27
Abstract Reasoning (AR)	36	35	44	35	25	27	24
Space Relations (SR)	27	32	36	26	15	16	16
Mechanical Reasoning (MR)	24	22	38	24	17	14	14
Clerical Speed and Accuracy (CSA)	24	19	26	26	23	26	14
Spelling (Spell.)	44	29	36	36	31	26	55
Sentences (Sent.)	52	36	48	46	40	30	49

* Decimal points omitted.

A particular point in favor of the *DAT* is the large amount of research that went into the standardization and validation of the instrument. The norms are based on the testing of 47,000 students in grades 8 to 12 scattered widely over the United States. Because sizable sex differences were found on some of the tests, separate norms are given for boys and girls.

Thousands of correlations between *DAT* scores and various criteria have been computed. Some correlations between test scores and class grades are shown in Table 9–6. A follow-up study was undertaken of students two years after completing high school. The results are shown in

TABLE 9–7. PERCENTILE EQUIVALENTS OF AVERAGE SCORES ON THE DAT FOR MEN IN VARIOUS EDUCATIONAL AND OCCUPATIONAL GROUPS
(Adapted from G. K. Bennett, et al., 2)

Group		Percentiles							
	No.	VR	NA	AR	SR	MR	CSA	Spell.	Sent.
Degree-seeking students:									
Premedical	24	88	86	81	72	77	77	90	90
Science (biology, chemistry, and math.)	25	81	85	60	67	68	74	81	72
Engineering (includes architectural)	70	80	86	80	81	82	67	68	74
Liberal arts (includes prelaw)	68	79	75	78	61	64	75	78	81
Business administration	64	72	73	61	63	60	71	67	68
Education (includes physical education)	25	68	66	58	57	48	68	67	66
Various: predental, agricultural, etc.	30	64	67	74	60	73	59	55	64
Non-degree students in two-year schools:									
Business, technical, fine arts, etc.	43	63	62	71	72	68	60	54	61
Employed:									
Salesmen	23	56	53	53	52	57	44	50	49
Clerks: general office work	55	45	42	52	44	41	41	52	53
Mechanical, electrical, and building trades	66	34	41	46	49	56	44	28	29
Various skilled: butcher, baker, etc.	26	47	37	43	41	49	51	52	45
Various unskilled: truck driver, laborer, etc.	85	35	30	36	42	49	37	35	36
Military service	129	46	42	46	51	50	49	46	41
Unclassified:									
No consistent work or school record	58	53	48	51	54	54	46	47	52

Table 9–7. In Table 9–7, scores for the total group are broken down in terms of subsequent occupation or college specialty. Some of the groups in Table 9–7 are represented by only several dozen individuals, and consequently, the results should be considered tentative. However, there is an apparent tendency for occupations to be represented not only by differences in performance level but by "shape" characteristics as well. More research of this kind will provide the *DAT* and other similar test batteries with a firmer basis for vocational counseling. The *DAT* is a model of careful test design, practicality, thoroughness of research, and frankness of reporting.

Other Differential Aptitude Batteries. A number of other batteries are available. Some of these will be listed and briefly described.

General Aptitude Test Battery (GATB). This is a very broad battery of 15 tests constructed by the U.S. Employment Service. More attention would be given to the battery here, but unfortunately the tests are available only to state employment services. The tests were developed directly from factor-analytic studies, and, in most cases, scores from more than one test are used for each factor. The following attributes are measured: (*G*) called "general intelligence," (*V*) verbal aptitude, (*N*) numerical aptitude, (*S*) spatial aptitude, (*P*) form perception, (*Q*) clerical perception, (*A*) aiming, (*T*) motor, (*F*) finger dexterity, and (*M*) manual dexterity.

Flanagan Aptitude Classification Tests (FACT). The battery consists of 14 relatively independent tests ranged broadly across the ability functions. The battery is published by Science Research Associates. Weightings are given for the prediction of 30 occupational groupings. Almost no evidence is presented to support the claims of validity.

Guilford-Zimmerman Aptitude Survey. The tests in this series are an important effort to represent a large share of the known factors of human abilities. The tests are constructed on the basis of factor analyses undertaken in the Air Force. Each test is intended to have high factorial validity for one of the known factors. The present battery includes tests for the following factors: *verbal comprehension, general reasoning, numerical computation, perceptual speed, spatial orientation, spatial visualization,* and mechanical knowledge (not an aptitude factor). Tests are being prepared to represent more factors.

An insufficient amount of research has been done with the battery to know how well it will work. The evidence so far suggests, as would be expected, that using only one test does not provide an adequate measure of each factor. The battery is still in an experimental stage.

The Status of Multifactor Batteries. Whereas there has been a considerable amount of research done to find new factors of human ability, relatively little research has been done to develop test batteries for practical use. This is due in part to the tendency for measurement specialists to be more interested in the theoretical aspects of the problem than in the more mundane practical aspects. Another reason is that test batteries can often be sold for considerable profit, and it is tempting to place tests on the market before their actual worth has been determined.

REFERENCES

1. Anastasi, Anne. *Psychological testing*. New York: Macmillan, 1954.
2. Bennett, G. K., Seashore, H. G., and Wesman, A. G. *Differential Aptitude Tests: Manual*. (2nd ed.) New York: Psychol. Corp., 1952.
3. Boring, E. G. *A history of experimental psychology*. (Rev. ed.) New York: Appleton-Century-Crofts, 1950.
4. Burt, C. The structure of mind: a review of the results of factor analysis. *Brit. J. educ. Psychol.*, 1949, 19, 100–111; 176–199.
5. Burt, C. *The factors of mind*. London: Univer. London Press, 1940.
6. French, J. W. The description of aptitude and achievement tests in terms of rotated factors. *Psychometr. Monogr.*, 1951, No. 5.
7. Fruchter, B. *Introduction to factor analysis*. Princeton, N.J.: Van Nostrand, 1954.
8. Green, R. F., et al. A factor-analytic study of reasoning abilities. *Psychometrika*, 1953, 18, 135–160.
9. Guilford, J. P. The structure of intellect. *Psychol. Bull.*, 1956, 53, 267–293.
10. Kelley, H. P. *A factor analysis of memory ability*. Princeton, N.J.: Educ. Testing Serv., 1954.
11. Kelley, T. L. *Crossroads in the mind of man: a study of differentiable mental abilities*. Stanford, Calif.: Stanford Univer. Press, 1928.
12. Murphy, G. *An historical introduction to modern psychology*. (Rev. ed.) New York: Harcourt, Brace, 1949.
13. Pearson, K. On lines and planes of closest fit to systems of points in space. *Phil. Mag.*, Ser. 6, 1901, 2, 559–572.
14. Spearman, C. "General intelligence" objectively determined and measured. *Amer. J. Psychol.*, 1904, 15, 201–293.
15. Terman, L. M. *The measurement of intelligence*. Boston: Houghton Mifflin, 1916.
16. Thomson, Sir Godfrey. *The factorial analysis of human ability*. London: Univer. London Press, 1951.
17. Thurstone, L. L. Primary mental abilities. *Psychometr. Monogr.*, 1938, No. 1.
18. Thurstone, L. L. A factorial study of perception. *Psychometr. Monogr.*, 1944, No. 4.
19. Thurstone, L. L. *Multiple factor analysis*. Chicago: Univer. Chicago Press, 1947.
20. Thurstone, L. L., and Thurstone, T. Factorial studies of intelligence. *Psychometr. Monogr.*, 1941, No. 2.

CHAPTER 10

General Intelligence Tests

The text discussion is far enough along to permit a more direct explanation of what "general intelligence" tests measure. In Chapter 9 it was shown that the domain of intellectual abilities is not entirely "general," that a number of separable factors can be shown to underlie tests of human ability. The tests which will be discussed in this chapter are general instruments in that the individual receives only one score. The one score is an over-all, or general, measure of his ability to perform the different kinds of material in the test.

What the General Intelligence Tests Measure. Having gone to some lengths to show that the concept of "general intelligence" is somewhat misleading, at this point let us consider the arguments supporting the practical use of general measures. The general intelligence tests take advantage of the fact that the separable factors of intellect are themselves correlated. In addition, not all of the factors are intimately related to intelligence as it is popularly conceived. Factors such as *verbal comprehension* and *general reasoning* are more commonly thought of as constituting intelligent behavior than are factors like *spatial orientation* and *perceptual speed*. Therefore, the general intelligence tests have tended to incorporate material largely from the factors which more nearly fit the popular conception of intelligence. The use of one score represents primarily the adding together of only several factors rather than the many that can be found in diverse tests.

The content of most general intelligence tests is predominantly related to the *verbal comprehension* factor, the *numerical computation* factor, and various mixtures of the reasoning factors. The remaining material in these tests tends to be scattered thinly over the memory, spatial, and perceptual factors. Most of the intelligence tests correlate highly with one another, coefficients as high as .80 being commonly found between some of them. However, the correlations are in most cases far enough from perfect to show that the tests measure partially different things, or factors. Factor-analytic studies have been made of some of the major tests, and these findings will be discussed in the pages ahead.

Some psychologists argue for the use of general measures because they have not given up the concept of general intelligence. They remain suspicious of factor-analytic findings and maintain a "holistic" view of intelligence. Their viewpoint is that the individual's "effective intelligence" comes from a pattern or combination of underlying factors that is difficult to predict from scores on the separate factors. There is some support for this viewpoint, particularly in relation to school work. It is possible for individuals to solve the same problem successfully yet use different approaches. For example, one individual may rely heavily on his spatial ability to help solve geometrical problems. Another person may solve the same problems more abstractly by relying on his reasoning ability.

Another argument for the holistic conception of intelligence is that the grades in different school courses tend to correlate highly with one another. This is perhaps partially the fault of teachers, who tend to form over-all impressions of students; but it also indicates that to an extent the underlying factors are somewhat interchangeable in real-life situations. Regardless of the theoretical merit of the holistic viewpoint, the kinds of tests which have traditionally been used as measures of general intelligence are composed of a number of different factors.

Another argument for the use of general intelligence tests arises from the defects in many multifactor, or differential aptitude, batteries. It was previously said that an efficient differential aptitude battery must have highly reliable subtests which correlate low or only moderately with one another. Otherwise, the battery will manifest only statistically insignificant differential scores, and it would be as well to add the tests together to form one dependable measure. This is a telling argument against some of the less carefully constructed multifactor batteries. However, as more research is done on the construction of multifactor batteries, the general intelligence tests will probably assume less importance as measurement devices.

INDIVIDUAL VERSUS GROUP TESTS

Tests can be given to each individual separately, or a group of individuals can be tested at one time. Although this is a consideration for tests of all kinds, it is a particularly important issue in the use of general intelligence tests. The multifactor batteries are almost always group tests. There is considerable competition between individual and group tests of general intelligence. Numerous articles have appeared in the psychological literature arguing whether group or individual tests should be used with particular age groups.

Individual Tests. The first practical general intelligence test, the Binet-Simon scale (9), was administered individually. This was necessary because the subjects were young children. The individual test requires a highly experienced examiner. The examiner is in essence a part of the standardized testing procedure, and he must standardize his own treatment of the child to conform to established methods. It is not necessarily the examiner's job to get the "best" score from the subject but to obtain a score which is the same as would be found by other expert examiners. If one examiner is more or less friendly and encouraging than another, this will inevitably lower the test reliability.

Many of the items on individual tests cannot be scored unambiguously as right or wrong. Instead there may be a number of acceptable responses, and different scores are often required to indicate the degree of correctness. The better-established individual tests go to considerable effort to specify just what will be considered a correct response and how much credit should be given for a response. The examiner must follow the established scoring procedures meticulously and not permit his subjective judgment of a child to influence the test results. Any idiosyncracies in scoring will make the test less reliable.

Group Tests. As was discussed previously, the first practical group tests of general intelligence were developed for the Armed Forces during the First World War. Here again necessity was the mother of invention: the number of men to be tested required a quick and economical measurement device, and the individual test was unsuited for that purpose.

Most group tests are sufficiently self-explanatory so that the test examiner need have little or no specialized knowledge of testing procedures. The test forms are simply passed out to subjects; either they are allowed to work at their chosen rate or the examiner directs the subjects when to start and stop.

Comparison of Individual and Group Tests. Although the following rules are not precisely correct for all group and individual tests, the rules are sufficiently general to offer a reasonable basis for choosing between the two kinds of tests in most situations.

1. *Individual tests are required with young children.* Starting at the earliest age, there are no group tests that can be used with infants. Each infant must be examined separately, and any effort at standardization of procedures is difficult. With preschool children and children in the early grades of grammar school, it is usually necessary to use individual tests. Young children either cannot read at all or they lack the reading ability to take the self-explanatory group forms. As an additional factor, young children are highly distractable, and it is all that the expert examiner can do to keep one child working at the test materials. Young children are often not motivated to do well on tests, and it is only through the examiner's careful, but standardized, encouragement that a meaningful measure can be obtained.

2. *Group tests are generally more desirable in testing "normal" adults.*
The well-standardized group tests prove to be as good predictors as the
individual tests when working with most teen-age and adult groups.
Although the evidence is clear that individual tests are better predictors
for young children and that group tests do as well with adolescents or
older, it is not certain which kind of test is generally more valid with the
in-between age group.

Adolescents and older persons are usually motivated and attentive
enough to manifest a meaningful score on a group test. Also, they are
less embarrassed by the group testing situation than they would be in the
face-to-face individual testing situation.

Because group tests tend to be equally valid as individual tests when
administered to adults, group tests are much to be preferred in practical
work. Group tests are much less expensive and time consuming. It takes
no more time to administer and score 100 group tests than it does to
administer and score 1 individual test.

3. *Individual tests are often useful in clinical settings.* The clinical psychologist can often learn considerably more from the individual test than
the subject's score would indicate. The child who appears dull in the
classroom may be only hard of hearing. Another child may do poorly in
school work because he wants to do poorly, giving wrong answers when
he knows what is correct. The older adult may appear to be "demented"
because he is discouraged and withdrawn. These things probably would
not be found in group testing situations, but an experienced clinician can
often use the individual testing situation to diagnose why an individual
is performing poorly.

4. *Group tests are usually easier to construct than individual tests.* For
the person who plans to construct a predictor test, an individual test
should not be undertaken unless measurement specialists are available
and it is planned to spend considerable time and money in test construction. The difficulties in constructing test materials, standardizing the test,
and particularly the setting of instructions for administration and scoring,
make the development of an individual test a time-consuming, expensive
job. Training test examiners for the individual tests creates additional
expense.

VERBAL VERSUS PERFORMANCE TESTS

There has been some confusion as to the difference between "verbal"
tests and "performance" tests and the distinction is itself somewhat misleading. The following outline of verbal components in tests is offered as
a basis for discussing test content:

Verbal requirements
 1. Understand spoken language

2. Understand written language
3. Speak language
4. Write language
5. *Verbal comprehension* factor

There are many different combinations of the above verbal requirements in particular tests. A test may require the first four items in the list, but deal with language at so simple a level that very little ability in *verbal comprehension* is required to obtain a high score. It is possible to make up a test in which almost none of the five aspects is required. This can be done by giving the test instructions in pantomime and using test materials that require neither written nor spoken responses. It is also possible to compose a test in which none of the first four aspects is present and the fifth aspect, *verbal comprehension,* is a cardinal requirement. If the test requires the child to manipulate abstract symbols or to deal with pictures, this will tap, in part, the *verbal comprehension* factor. Each test should be examined in terms of its combination of verbal requirements rather than simply classified as "verbal" or "nonverbal."

Another distinction can be made between tests in terms of the way in which responses are made:

Nature of response

1. *Symbolic response.* The subject indicates the correct answer either through the use of language or by marking one of a number of choices. The symbolic response might be made in respect to objects rather than printed materials, although this is usually not done.
2. *Manipulative response (performance).* The subject is required to handle objects in such a way as to complete a specified product. The product may be anything from a completely finished piece of machinery to the arrangement of a set of blocks.

Some items are not clearly differentiated in terms of the two kinds of responses. For example, in maze tracing, the child is required to coordinate the pencil and move to the goal—the response is as symbolic as it is manipulative.

It has been the custom to call instruments "performance" tests if they deemphasize language requirements, employ three-dimensional materials, and require manipulative responses. Because of these components, the "performance" tests usually measure motor coordination, speed, and perceptual and spatial factors. Instruments are usually referred to as "verbal" tests if they are printed forms, emphasize *verbal comprehension,* and require symbolic responses. Because of the ease with which certain kinds of test materials can be placed on printed forms, the "verbal" tests tend to measure the *verbal comprehension, numerical computation,* and the reasoning factors. There is no clear-cut separation between the factors found in "verbal" and "performance" tests, but there is a tendency for different factors to arise in the two kinds of materials.

THE BINET TEST AND ITS FOLLOWERS

The 1905 Binet-Simon test (see **33**) consisted of the following 30 items:

1. Follow a lighted match with head and eyes.
2. Grasp a cube placed on the palm.
3. Grasp a cube held in line of vision.
4. Make a choice between pieces of wood and chocolate.
5. Unwrap chocolate from paper.
6. Execute simple orders.
7. Touch head, nose, ear, cap, key, and string.
8. Point to objects which experimenter names in picture.
9. Name objects pointed out in a picture.
10. Judge which of two lines is the longer.
11. Repeat immediately three digits read by examiner.
12. Judge which of two weights is heavier.
13. Solve problems that embody novel, ambiguous, or contradictory solutions.
14. Define house, horse, fork, and mamma.
15. Repeat sentence of 15 words after a single hearing.
16. Describe differences between: paper and cardboard; fly and butterfly; wood and glass.
17. Memorize 13 pictures of familiar objects.
18. Memorize immediately two designs.
19. Memorize immediately lists of digits.
20. State the similarities between: blood and wild poppies; fly, butterfly, and flea; newspaper, label, and picture.
21. Judge differences in length of lines.
22. Rank order weights of 3, 6, 9, 12, and 15 grams.
23. Determine which weight the examiner removes from No. 22.
24. Make rhymes.
25. Complete sentence from which one word has been deleted.
26. Construct sentence which contains the words Paris, gutter, and fortune.
27. Describe the best action to take in 25 real-life situations.
28. Tell what time it would be if the hour hand and minute hand were interchanged at 3:57 and at 5:40.
29. Make a drawing of how the holes in a folded piece of paper would look if the paper were unfolded.
30. Describe what is different between liking and respecting, and between being sad and being bored.

The list of questions was tried on about fifty children and provisional norms were established (see 33). It was found that the first five items could be passed by idiots and normal two-year-olds. Most three-year-olds could go no further than about the ninth item. Most five-year-olds could go no further than about the fourteenth item.

After considerable use of the 1905 scale, a revision was published in 1908 (see 33). Items in the earlier scale which did not seem to work well were eliminated and new ones were added. The outstanding feature of the 1908 revision was the grouping of items by age. A group of items was chosen to represent each age level so that about half the children at the age level could answer the items correctly. The level at which the child missed not more than one of the items was called his *basal age*. To the basal age was added one year for each five items he answered correctly at higher age levels. The basal age plus the years' credit for items answered at higher levels constituted the child's *mental age*. The mental age arrived at in this way was but a crude approximation of the child's intellectual standing. The number of tests at different age levels varied from three to eight, and this was not taken into account when figuring the mental age. No credit was given for fractional "years" on the scale, the mental ages being restricted to whole numbers. As a more general criticism, the selection of items and the determination of age levels were based on a rather small amount of standardization research.

American Adaptations of the Binet-Simon Scales. During the first decade of this century the Binet-Simon scales became very popular in America. Instruments of this kind were needed in the care of the feebleminded, in educational research, and in the understanding of juvenile delinquency. Goddard (19) made an early adaptation of the scales, principally translating them into English and making minor revisions. Later Kuhlmann (26) revised the scales and made an effort to extend the test downward to the age of three months.

The Terman Revision of the Binet-Simon Scales. The first extensive revision of the Binet-Simon scales was undertaken by Terman and his colleagues at Stanford University. The new scale, published in 1916, was referred to as the Revised Stanford-Binet (46). The revision was so extensive as to constitute essentially a new test. Over one-third of the items in the revision were new and a number of items remaining from the original form were altered and moved to different age levels.

For the first time, considerable empirical work went into the standardization of the Binet type scales. The test was standardized on approximately 1,000 children and 400 adults. An effort was made to select a sample of persons that would approximately represent the population of the United States. Although the standardization sample left much to be desired by modern standards, the effort to obtain a representative group of people set a milestone in psychological measurement.

In the 1916 revision, careful attention was given to the writing of instructions for test administration and scoring. The *IQ* type of scoring was employed for the first time in the Binet series of tests. Because of the careful work that went into the revision, the test became the standard clinical instrument for measuring intelligence. It was probably used more frequently than any other test during the twenty years after it was published.

The 1937 Revision. The second revision of the Stanford-Binet (47) was a ten-year undertaking. Instead of developing only one form, two equivalent forms, Form *L* and Form *M*, were produced. They are so different from the 30 items with which Binet began the series that it is only out of courtesy to Binet that his name is linked to the 1937 tests.

Each of the new tests was longer than the 1916 test; different kinds of test items were used, and an even more strenuous effort at standardization was made. A large number of items was tried out on groups of children and adults. In all, about 1,500 persons were used in the empirical tryout of items. The principal criterion for selecting items was that they each have a "steep age gradient." That is, an item is desirable for the six-year level if few of the five-year-olds get the item correct, most of the seven-year-olds get it correct, and about half of the six-year-olds get the item correct. In order to find sets of items for the different age levels, a considerable amount of testing and statistical analysis was undertaken.

After the selection of items and the provisional construction of Form *M* and Form *L*, the forms were administered to a carefully selected sample of the United States population. The sample included 3,184 white, native-born persons from the ages of 1½ to 18 years. An equal number of boys and girls was tested at each age level. The sample was drawn from 17 communities in 11 widely separated states. An effort was made to distribute the subjects in each age level equitably across the socioeconomic levels. Although the sample was not entirely representative of the United States population, there has never been a more strenuous effort to create a well-standardized test.

The results obtained from the large sampling of responses to Form *L* and Form *M* were again item analyzed. The items in each form were rearranged in such a manner that the mean *IQ* at each age level is very close to 100 and the mean *IQ* for boys and girls is nearly identical. An effort was also made to obtain equal standard deviations for the *IQ*s at each age level. However, the researchers were not entirely successful in equating standard deviations.

The Stanford-Binet test is still used as widely or more widely than any other clinical instrument. There are hundreds of articles in the psychological literature on the use of the test, on developments in testing procedure, and on reliability and validity.

Administration of the Stanford-Binet. The test materials (see Figure 10–1) include a box of performance items (beads, toys, pictures, etc.), test blanks on which the child's responses are recorded, and a manual of instructions (**47**). As was mentioned previously, the administration of an

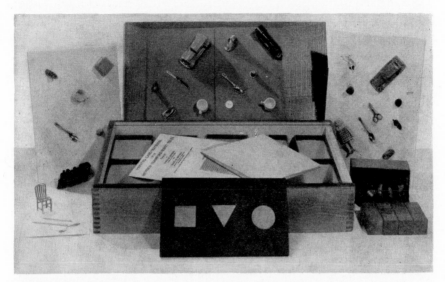

FIGURE 10–1. Some of the test materials used with the Stanford-Binet. (Courtesy of Houghton Mifflin Company.)

individual test of this kind requires a highly trained examiner, and no faith should be placed in the scores obtained by an amateur tester. The test can usually be given in a period of fifty to seventy-five minutes.

No individual is administered all of the items. Instead, the individual is started slightly lower in the age scale than he is expected to reach. For

TABLE 10–1. COMPUTATION OF IQ FOR A CHILD OF SEVEN YEARS AND SIX MONTHS (six items at each of the age levels)

Test-year level	Number of items passed	Months' credit per item	Years' credit
VII	6		
VIII	6 (*basal age*)		8
IX	4	2	⅔
X	2	2	⅓
XI	0 (*maximal age*)		
			Total: 9 years

Mental age = 9.0   Chronological age = 7.5 $IQ = \left(\dfrac{9.0}{7.5}\right) 100 = 120$

example, a typical procedure would be to start a seven-year-old off on the five-year-level questions. The child is then taken up through the age levels as far as he can go. The highest level at which he gets all of the items correct is called the *basal age*. The level at which the subject gets none of the items correct is called the *maximal age*. The subject's mental age equals his basal age plus specific extra credits for items correct above the basal age. The *IQ* is then obtained by dividing mental age by chronological age and multiplying the result by 100 (see Table 10–1).

The Content of the Stanford-Binet. The present test still bears many of the earmarks of the original Binet emphasis on cultural artifacts: words, objects, and knowledge of the cultural environment. A knowledge of words and their usage plays a predominant part in the scale, particularly at the upper levels. Although a number of items of the performance type are used at the earlier ages (see Figure 10–1), these are also primarily concerned with the child's recognition and use of common everyday objects. Memory items are found throughout the scale, particularly in the immediate recall of digit series. A few items concerning perceptual and spatial abilities are found at different age levels. Many of the items concern one or more kinds of reasoning ability. To illustrate the nature of the scale, the items at four different age levels are described as follows:

Two-year level

1. *Three-hole form board.* The child is shown a form board containing a cut-out square, circle, and triangle. The pieces are removed and the child is asked to put them in their places. The child receives credit if all three objects are put in place.
2. *Identifying objects by name.* The child is shown six toy objects (button, spoon, etc.) and is asked to identify them. Credit is received for correctly naming four of the six objects.
3. *Identifying parts of body.* The child is shown a large paper doll and is asked to point to parts of the body. ("Show me the dolly's hair," etc.). Credit is received for correctly pointing out three of the parts.
4. *Block building.* A box of blocks is placed before the child. The examiner builds a tower of four blocks and asks the child to do the same. Credit is received if the child makes a tower of at least four blocks.
5. *Picture vocabulary.* The child is shown 18 cards containing pictures of common objects. With each picture he is asked, "What is this?" Credit is given if the child names at least two of the objects.
6. *Word combinations.* The examiner notes the spontaneous speech of the child during the test. Credit is given if the child uses at least a two-word combination such as "see kitty."

Six-year level

1. *Vocabulary.* The child is asked the meaning of words from a graded list of 45 terms. Credit is given for five correct definitions. (The same list of words is used throughout all higher age levels.)
2. *Copying a bead chain from memory.* The examiner makes a chain of seven beads using alternately a square and then a round bead. The child is asked to make a bead chain like the examiner's. Credit is given if all beads are placed correctly.
3. *Mutilated pictures.* The child is shown five pictures in which an object has a missing part, e.g., a wagon with only three wheels, and asked to say what is missing in each. Credit is given for getting as many as four of the problems correct.
4. *Number concepts.* Twelve blocks are put in front of the child. He is asked to give different numbers of the blocks to the examiner. Credit is given for selecting three correct numbers of blocks out of four trials.
5. *Pictorial likenesses and differences.* The child is shown six cards with a number of figures on each. On each card one figure is different in some way from the others. The child is asked to point to the figure which is different. Credit is given for five correct responses out of six.
6. *Maze tracing.* The child is shown three designs each of which shows two ways for a person to get home. One route is longer than the other. The child is asked to trace the shorter route. Credit is given for two correct responses out of three.

Ten-year level

1. *Vocabulary.* The child is asked to define words from the standard list. Credit is given for 11 or more correct definitions.
2. *Picture absurdities,* II. A picture is shown in which an individual is acting in an illogical manner. The child is asked, "What is foolish about that picture?" Credit is given if the child can explain what is illogical.
3. *Reading and report.* The child is asked to read a selection of material. He is then asked to recall as much as possible of what he read. Credit is obtained if there are not more than two errors in reading and at least ten events are recalled.
4. *Finding reasons,* I. The child is asked to explain why two social rules are necessary, e.g., "Give two reasons why children should not be too noisy in school." Credit is given for supplying two reasons.
5. *Word naming.* The child is asked to name as many words as he can in two minutes. Credit is given for 28 words or more.

6. *Repeating six digits.* Six digits such as 4, 8, 2, 1, 6, 3 are read at one-second intervals. The child is asked to repeat the digits in their exact order. Credit is given if one or more complete series out of three are recalled correctly.

Average adult level

1. *Vocabulary.* The subject is asked for definitions of words in the standard list. Credit is given if 20 or more are defined.

2. *Codes.* The subject is shown a short sentence and a coded version of the sentence. The code consists of interchanging certain letters of the alphabet. The subject is asked to figure out the code and then write the word "hurry" in the code. Next, another similar item is given. Credit is allowed if 1½ of the two codes are mastered.

3. *Differences between abstract words.* The subject is asked to distinguish between three pairs of associated words, e.g., *poverty* and *misery.* Credit is given if two or more of the distinctions are correct.

4. *Arithmetical reasoning.* The subject is asked to solve three problems; e.g., "If two pencils cost 5 cents, how many pencils can you buy for 50 cents?" Credit is given for two or more correct solutions.

5. *Proverbs,* I. The subject is asked to explain the meaning of three proverbs, e.g., "A burnt child dreads the fire." Credit is given for two or more correct interpretations.

6. *Ingenuity.* Three problems are given. An example is, a boy is sent to the river to get exactly three pints of water, and he has only a 7-pint container and a 4-pint container. How can he measure the water? Credit is given if two problems are solved.

7. *Memory for sentences,* V. The subject is asked to recall a sentence after one hearing. Credit is given if at least one of two sentences is exactly recalled.

8. *Reconciliation of opposites.* The subject is asked in what way pairs of opposing terms are alike, e.g., *sick* and *well.* Credit is given for three correct answers out of six.

ANALYSIS OF THE STANFORD-BINET

With each of the major tests and measurement methods which are described in the remainder of the book, a critical analysis will be given. The comments which are made should not be relied upon solely as the basis for selecting tests for specific purposes. When tests are being obtained, the relevant research literature should be studied (see Chapter 18). Each critical analysis will provide an opportunity to utilize the principles and methodology of measurement which were presented in the first half of the book. In criticizing particular measurement methods, a careful distinction should be made between how well an instrument measures up to ideals and how well it works in comparison with other procedures. In many places we will see that a measure which is crude in terms of ideal methods turns out to be much better than the even cruder procedures which might otherwise be used.

What Does the Stanford-Binet Measure? One obvious feature of the Stanford-Binet is that it is not *a* test in the sense in which the term is customarily used. Because different persons take different items in terms of their age, scores are not directly comparable from age to age. Some types of items are used over a wide age range, particularly the memory for digits and vocabulary. Other types of items appear in only one or several age levels, such as maze tracing, form board, and the interpretation of proverbs.

One of the primary criteria for the selection of items was the correlation of items with chronological age.[1] This seems to be a reasonable procedure in that whatever "intelligence" connotes to people it is thought to grow as the child grows. It is, however, by no means safe to assume that *anything* that increases with age is necessarily an index of intelligence. Children of twelve years not only have larger vocabularies than eleven-year-olds, their feet are longer also. No one would consider using the length of a person's foot as a measure of intelligence. The constructors of the scale used not only "age differentiation" to select items, they used their intuitions as well. As Binet had done, they selected items which *looked* as though they related to intelligence, as it is popularly conceived, and then weeded out items which failed to show the required statistical characteristics.

The Factor Structure of the Stanford-Binet. Looking more precisely at what the Stanford-Binet measures, different investigators have found the test to embody at least several factors. This is so in spite of the effort to select items which correlate highly with one another. McNemar (**29**) reported the results of 14 factor analyses of the Stanford-Binet items. He found that a first factor at each age level accounts for from 35 to 50 per cent of the item variance. It was his interpretation that the first factor is much the same at different age levels. A second factor was found to explain from 5 to 11 per cent of the item variance, and a third factor was found to account for from 4 to 7 per cent of the item variance. Taking these results at face value, they seem to give supporting evidence for the existence of one major factor in the Stanford-Binet. Several points, however, need to be examined before this conclusion is reached. If only one factor were found in the items, this would not mean that "intelligence" is

[1] Equally important was the correlation of each item with total score on the test.

general but only that the items in the Stanford-Binet had been chosen in such a manner as to represent only the common ground of human abilities (McNemar had not tried to show otherwise by his analyses).

McNemar performed his analyses in such a way as to make the most of the common ground in the items. He showed that a general factor can account for much of the item variance. If one tries, however, to search for factors in the Stanford-Binet rather than minimize them, it can be shown that a number of factors are present. A thorough factor analysis of the items would need to include an extensive array of the kinds of tests which have led to the discovery of known factors. Also, McNemar's conclusion that the first factor obtained from the analyses is the same for different age levels is open to question.

Jones (24) offers a different interpretation of the factor structure of Stanford-Binet items. He performed separate factor analyses of the items for children at the ages of 7, 9, 11, and 13 years. Each analysis employed 100 boys and 100 girls. Jones made an effort to find the complete factor structure of the items. Like McNemar, he used only the Stanford-Binet items in the analyses, without the inclusion of reference tests of known

FIGURE 10–2. Names and relative influence of factors reported at several age levels. (From L. V. Jones, 24, p. 315.)

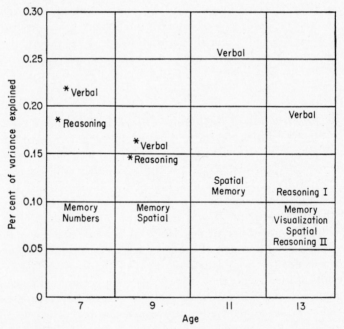

* Factors differing in item content from Verbal and Reasoning factors at ages eleven and thirteen years.

factor composition. He found a number of separable but correlated factors at each age level. His results are summarized in Figure 10–2.

Factor analyses of items usually give less clear-cut results than factor analyses of whole tests. Jones's factors, therefore, are not clearly interpretable. Aside from the difficulty of interpreting all of the factors clearly, his analyses strongly indicate that the factor structure is not the same at all age levels. For example, although what appear to be reasoning factors occur at ages 7, 9, and 13, nothing of the kind was found in the 11-year age group. The verbal factors which predominate at the four age levels are less important at some ages than others.

The answer then to whether the Stanford-Binet embodies only one and the same factor at different age levels is both yes and no. Much of the item variance can be accounted for by one factor. The one major factor, however, is not quite the same at different age levels, which makes the interpretation of *IQ* scores somewhat difficult. When an effort is made to isolate the indicators of more than one factor as Jones did, it is apparent that the traces of a number of other factors can be found.

The Scoring System. The Stanford-Binet is one of the few careful attempts at the construction of an *age scale*. Although numerous other tests employ the mental age and the *IQ*, few of them meet the statistical requirements. A successful age scale should have a mean *IQ* of 100 and equal standard deviations of *IQ*s at different age levels for some defined population of persons. In order for the standard deviations of *IQ* scores to remain constant, it is necessary for the standard deviation of mental age scores to increase by regular amounts from one age level to the next. This is an almost impossible thing to accomplish in test construction. The standard deviation of *IQ* scores on Form *L* varies from 20.6 at age 2½ to 12.5 at age 6 years. Special correction tables (**29**) had to be constructed to make *IQ* scores comparable at different age levels.

The great difficulty that is met in achieving the required statistical properties of an age scale makes it doubtful that an age scale is worth the trouble. The *IQ* concept bears the unwarranted surplus connotations that the general intelligence tests *assess* intelligence and that a ratio scale is available for its measurement. An equally logical and much simpler procedure is to use standard scores instead of *IQ* units. The mental age concept has been clung to by clinicians and school workers because of its practical meaning and the ease with which it can be explained to laymen.

The Testing of Adults. On both subjective and empirical grounds there is reason to believe that the Stanford-Binet is a better test for children than adults. One reason for this is that the concept of general intelligence is more meaningful with children than adults. This point will be discussed later in the chapter. The Stanford-Binet does not have a high enough "ceiling" to measure the ability of superior adults. That is, the range of difficulty at the adult level is not sufficient to tap the ability of highly gifted individuals. Because no persons over eighteen years of age were included in the standardization sample, the norms for adults are suspect. In addition, there is a logical difficulty in using the *IQ* concept with adults. Because the mental age for an individual stops growing in the late teens, it no longer makes sense to obtain the *IQ* by dividing mental age by chronological age. If this were done, the *IQ*s of adults would constantly drop. What actually occurs in using the test is that for any individual who is sixteen years or over, the chronological age is considered to be fifteen years. This results, however, in a number of complicated corrections that must be made to obtain the *IQ* (**47**). Even worse than the statistical difficulties in assigning *IQ*s to adults, the *IQ* is a meaningless measure with adults. For example, if a twenty-year-old person has an *IQ* of 150, this does not mean that he has the intelligence of an average thirty-year-old.

Reliability. Very careful research was undertaken to determine the reliability of the Stanford-Binet *IQ* at different age levels (**29**). An equivalent-form reliability estimate was made separately for each age. Correlations were found between the scores obtained on Form *L* and Form *M* administered to the same subjects within one week's time. In general, the findings show that the Stanford-Binet is a highly reliable scale, with most of the reliability coefficients equal to or greater than .90. Scores tend to be more reliable for persons in their teens than they do for young children. The studies also show that low scores are somewhat more reliable than high scores in each age range. In other words, a bit more faith can be placed in the precision of a very low score than in a very high score.

Predictive Efficiency of the Stanford-Binet. The test has shown itself to be a good predictor of different criteria, particularly of school grades. In general, the findings have been that Stanford-Binet *IQ*s correlate in the neighborhood of .70 with grammar school grades, .60 with high school grades, and .50 with college grades (**3, 42**). (The decline in validity is probably due to the progressively decreasing dispersion of intellectual ability.) The following correlations were found between Form *L IQ* and high school achievement test scores (**10**). The number of students ranges from 78 to 200.

Reading comprehension	.73	Spelling	.46
Reading speed	.43	History	.59
English usage	.59	Geometry	.48
Literature acquaintance	.60	Biology	.54

Clinical Utility. Presumably, a test like the Stanford-Binet should be judged, in the long run, by the success with which it predicts different criteria. However, many of the uses to which this and other general intelligence tests are put are so subtle as to make direct empirical validation difficult. For example, the test might be used to decide what type of psychotherapy should be used with a disturbed child. Because of the difficulty in measuring therapeutic success and the difficulty in deciding the importance of "intelligence" for the outcome, it is hard to determine how well the test works in the situation. In many situations only the clinical impression of how well the test performs a particular job can at present be used as an indication of "validity." Judging from the wide acceptance of the test in clinical settings, it is apparent that the Stanford-Binet is judged to be as valuable or more valuable than any other test for use with children.

THE WECHSLER INTELLIGENCE SCALES

David Wechsler, working at the Bellevue Psychiatric Hospital in New York, developed an individual test which was intended to differ from the Stanford-Binet in the following respects:

1. The test items were to be more appropriate for adults, and representative norms for adults were to be obtained.

2. Age levels were to be discarded in favor of a number of subtests which all subjects would take.

3. Separate sets of verbal and performance tests were to be constructed, allowing for both a verbal and performance *IQ*.

4. The *IQ* was to be determined by a transformation of standard scores rather than through the use of mental age scores.

5. The test would be constructed to fit clinical conceptions of "intelligence" rather than in terms of "age differentiation."

The Wechsler-Bellevue. The first test in Wechsler's series was presented in 1939 (see **52**). Like the Stanford-Binet, the logic for the test is mainly based on the somewhat misleading concept of "general intelligence" and on rational rather than empirical validity. Like his predecessors in the measurement of general intelligence, Wechsler begins with a definition: "Intelligence is the aggregate or global capacity of the individual to act purposefully, to think rationally and to deal effectively with his environment" (**52**, p. 3). Wechsler (**52**), as late as 1944, held to the belief that one common factor underlies intellectual functions and cited Spearman's work as support for the belief. Very few persons would share that belief today.

The subtests for the Wechsler-Bellevue were selected by combing the test literature for tests that had worked well in practice. After some preliminary research, 12 of the tests were selected for special study and administered to over a thousand subjects. One of the tests, Cube Analysis (see **52**), proved to be difficult to explain to subjects and large sex differences were found. The other 11 tests were found to have desirable ranges of difficulty and practicality of administration. Brief descriptions of the 11 subtests in the Wechsler-Bellevue are as follows:

Verbal Scale

1. *General Information.* The subject is asked 25 questions concerning a wide variety of facts. The questions are not intended to tap academic training or specialized branches of knowledge. They are meant to cover the kinds of information that any alert individual can learn from his cultural contacts.

2. *General Comprehension.* The test contains 10 items concerning why certain social rules are necessary and how everyday problems are solved.

3. *Arithmetical Reasoning.* Ten problems of the kind that would be typically encountered in elementary school arithmetic are given. Both speed and correctness of response are scored.

4. *Digit Span.* This is the familiar memory for digits which also appears at different levels of the Stanford-Binet. From three to nine digits are read to the subject, and he is asked to repeat them in their exact order. In the second part of the test, the subject is asked to repeat the digit series backwards.

5. *Similarities.* The subject is asked to tell what is similar about 12 pairs of terms. This subtest is also very similar to material found on the Stanford-Binet.

6. *Vocabulary.* The subject is asked the meanings of 42 words. Although in the original plan of the Wechsler-Bellevue the vocabulary test was included only as an alternate, it has worked so well in practice that it is usually given as a regular part of the verbal scale.

Performance Scale

7. *Picture Completion.* The subject is shown 15 incomplete pictures and asked to describe the missing part in each. This is also very much like material found on the Stanford-Binet.

8. *Picture Arrangement.* The subject is handed a set of pictures and asked to arrange them in an order that tells a story. Six sets of pictures are given. Both speed and accuracy are scored.

9. *Object Assembly.* The subject is asked to put together three jigsaw puzzles. Each puzzle pictures some part of the human body. Both speed and accuracy are scored.

10. *Block Design.* The subject is shown a set of small blocks. Surfaces of the blocks are painted white, red, and red-and-white. The subject is presented with a picture of a design and asked to

reproduce it with the blocks. Seven designs are given in turn. Both speed and accuracy are scored.

11. *Digit Symbol.* This is an adaptation of the familiar coding test. The subject is given a sheet of paper on which nine symbols are paired with nine numbers. Farther down on the page a jumbled list of the numbers is given and the subject is asked to write in the matching symbols.

Administration and Scoring of the Wechsler-Bellevue. Like most individually administered general intelligence tests, only an expert examiner should be trusted to give the Wechsler-Bellevue. The test is somewhat easier to administer than the Stanford-Binet. The subject is given each of the subtests in turn. The individual's raw score for a subtest indicates how many items he answered correctly and/or how quickly the task was completed. Tables are available (52) for converting raw scores on each subtest to transformed standard scores. The transformed standard scores have a standard deviation of 3 and a mean of 10. The means and standard deviations were obtained from a normative sample of 1,751 persons between the ages of seven to seventy years.

Three separate *IQ*s can be found from the tests. The six verbal tests are added together to form one *IQ* score. Similarly, the five performance tests can be added to give another *IQ*. Then, the two subscales can be combined to form one over-all *IQ*. The *IQ*s are simply transformed standard scores. In this case, the transformation at each age level was done in such a way as to have the usual mean *IQ* of 100 and a standard deviation close to that of the Stanford-Binet.[2] Because it was found that raw scores tend to gradually decline in going from people of twenty-five to seventy years of age, the *IQ* is determined about the mean raw score for each age group.

Analysis of the Wechsler. *The Norms.* All of the subjects in the standardization sample were obtained from the State of New York, the majority coming from New York City. The 1,751 persons used in the normative sample were selected from 3,500 cases in such a way as to represent the occupational distribution of white citizens in the United States. There were considerably more men than women in the sample. Although the effort to obtain a representative sample was more systematic than that for many other available tests, the derived norms are likely to be somewhat misleading when applied to the country as a whole.

It is an open question whether the *IQ* should be determined about the mean of each age group as is done on the Wechsler-Bellevue or about an over-all mean. The *IQ* as determined from the Wechsler-Bellevue has the

[2] Because the standard deviation of Wechsler-Bellevue *IQ*s is slightly smaller than that of the Stanford-Binet, *IQ*s obtained from the two tests are not directly comparable.

advantage of not "penalizing" persons of middle age and over. (The relationship between age and intelligence will be discussed in the latter part of this chapter.) In the absence of definite evidence showing that "general ability" as well as test scores decline, the safest procedure is to center scores about the mean at each age level.

The Test Content. It is obvious from an inspection of the subtests that much of the material is similar to other tests and particularly to the Stanford-Binet. Studies of unselected adolescent and adult groups have generally found correlations of .80 (36, 51, 52) and higher between the Wechsler-Bellevue and the Stanford-Binet. The similarity, however, in content of the two tests, does not distract from the purpose of the Wechsler-Bellevue. It was Wechsler's intention to select a more proper range of difficulty in adult items, not necessarily to invent entirely new kinds of test materials.

Davis (14) factor analyzed the 11 Wechsler-Bellevue subtests along with reference tests for some of the known factors of human ability. He used a sample of 202 eighth-grade pupils in the analysis. Davis found evidence of a number of factors in the subtests: verbal comprehension, visualization, numerical facility, mechanical knowledge, general reasoning, perceptual speed, and eduction of conceptual relations. The conclusion to be reached from this and other factor-analytic studies (1, 5) is that the Wechsler-Bellevue is factorially complex, apparently more so than the Stanford-Binet.

It is an open question whether Wechsler did right in prominently including materials of the performance type on the Wechsler-Bellevue. This is an argument that could be solved straightforwardly if the worth of the test were entirely determined by how well it predicts stated criteria. In general, peformance tests tend to be somewhat less reliable than verbal tests, correlate less among themselves, and are generally poorer predictors of available criteria (mainly, school grades). As a wider range of prediction problems is studied, it may be found that there are assessments which can be better predicted by the performance tests than by the verbal tests.

Reliability. The evidence is that the total test *IQ* has a reliability comparable to that of the Stanford-Binet, in general being about .90. As is always the case, the individual subtests are less reliable. In a group of normal adults, retest reliability coefficients for the subtests ranged from .62 to .88 (15). Thus, although the total test *IQ* is highly reliable, marked fluctuations are to be expected in some of the subtest scores.

Profile Analysis. It has been a common clinical practice to use the subtests of the Wechsler-Bellevue in profile analysis to detect different clinical disorders. The underlying assumption is that different types of pathology manifest themselves in different score patterns. Wechsler hypothesized

(**52,** p. 150), for example, that the following variations in subtest scores characterize the schizophrenic patient:

Object Assembly much below Block Design

Very low score on Similarities with high Vocabulary and Information

Sum of scores on Picture Arrangement plus Comprehension less than sum of scores on Information plus Block Design

Other profile patterns have been hypothesized for brain-damage cases and a number of other clinical types.

Profile analysis is undertaken with the Wechsler-Bellevue in the situation in which it is least warranted—insufficient reliability for the individual subtest and moderate to high correlations among the subtests. Summaries of the relevant research (**36, 51**) show that profile analysis efforts with the subtests have met with essentially negative results. Studies of the relationship between test profiles and other human attributes should be based on the results of well-standardized multifactor batteries, not on the subtests within general intelligence tests.

Predictive Efficiency. Basing his test as he did on a rational approach to the measurement of intelligence, Wechsler (**52**) reports only a few specific correlations with performance criteria, and these are based on small numbers of cases. Other studies report correlations in the .40s and .50s between Full Scale *IQ* and freshman college grades (**3, 42**). The separate Verbal Scale *IQ* had higher correlations than Full Scale *IQ* with grades; the Performance Scale proved to be a much poorer predictor of freshman grades.

THE WECHSLER ADULT INTELLIGENCE SCALE (WAIS)

To meet the criticisms which were made of the Wechsler-Bellevue, a revision of the test, *WAIS,* was published in 1955 (**54**). All the original subtests were retained but many new items were substituted for less satisfactory old ones. The instructions for administering and scoring the test have been revised. An effort was made to obtain a wider range of item difficulty in each subtest, which should provide more adequate testing of persons at both extremes of the ability range. The norms for the *WAIS* are much more representative of the United States population than were those for the Wechsler-Bellevue. A carefully balanced sample of 1,700 persons was tested in 24 communities spread across the country. The sample resembles closely the United States population in terms of urban and rural, men and women, geographic region, and occupation. The test manual (**54**) is more frank, clear, and complete than was that for the Wechsler-Bellevue. Although it will be some time before the ultimate worth of the test can be determined, the indication is that the *WAIS* will be a better test than the Wechsler-Bellevue.

THE WECHSLER INTELLIGENCE SCALE FOR CHILDREN (WISC)

Although the Wechsler-Bellevue provides norms for children down to the age of ten years, it is primarily an adult test. A separate test, the *WISC* (**53**), was constructed specifically for children, aged five to fifteen years. The general organization of the test is much like the parent form:

Verbal Scale	Performance Scale
1. General Information	6. Picture Completion
2. General Comprehension	7. Picture Arrangement
3. Arithmetic	8. Block Design
4. Similarities	9. Object Assembly
5. Vocabulary	10. Coding (or Mazes)
Alternate: Digit Span	

The subtests are similar in most cases to those in the Wechsler-Bellevue. The tests, however, are easier and the materials are more directly related to the child's world. Digit Span can be used as an alternate to one of the five verbal tests. The examiner has the choice of using either Coding or Mazes as a tenth test.

Deviation IQs are obtained for each separate age level. Tables (**53**) are supplied for the conversion of raw scores to *IQ*s for every four-month interval from 5 to 15 years. The conversion formula was determined in such a way that the mean *IQ* for each age level in the standardization sample is 100 and the standard deviation is 15. The manual (**53**) gives the percentage of children that fall at different *IQ* levels, with a verbal description of what particular scores mean. (See Table 10–2.)

TABLE 10–2. CLASSIFICATION OF IQs ON THE WISC
(Adapted from Wechsler, **53**, p. 16)

Description	IQ ranges	Per cent of children
Very superior	130 and above	2.2
Superior	120–129	6.7
Bright	110–119	16.1
Average	90–109	50.0
Dull normal	80–89	16.1
Borderline	70–79	6.7
Mental defective	69 and below	2.2

The *WISC* is a much more carefully standardized test than the Wechsler-Bellevue. Particular care went into the gathering of norms. One hundred boys and 100 girls were tested at each age level, giving a total of 2,200 children in the standardization sample. A strenuous effort was made to choose a representative cross section of white children in the United States. The sample was drawn from 85 communities in 11 states. The distribution of subjects closely resembled the country at large in terms of urban-rural proportion, geographical area, and parental occupation. The *WISC* standardization sample is as representative as that used in any current general intelligence test.

Analysis of the WISC. Because no alternate form of the test is available, it was necessary to use split-half reliability estimates (**53**). The reliability was carefully studied at age levels 7½, 10½, and 13½ years. The Full Scale reliabilities at these age levels were found to be .92, .95, and .94 respectively. For the Verbal Scale, the reliabilities were found to be .88, .96, and .96 respectively. As is usually the case, the reliabilities were slightly lower for the Performance Scale: .86, .89, and .90. In general these coefficients represent good reliabilities for the three *IQ* scores. Here again the lesson is learned that high reliability of composite scores does not mean that subtest reliabilities are all high. Although most of the subtest reliabilities are in the .60s, .70s, and .80s, some go as low as .50. This should be a warning to anyone who tries to consider profile differences among the subtest scores. It is safe enough to compare verbal *IQ* with performance *IQ*, and this should have diagnostic meaning for the child who suffers a language handicap, but no finer inspection of the differences among subtests can be trusted.

Several studies found correlations between the Stanford-Binet and the *WISC* ranging from the .60s to the .90s. Correlations with the Stanford-Binet are lower with the *WISC* Performance Scale than with the Verbal Scale. The test is too new to know what predictive validity it will have for different performance criteria. Few criteria are available for children except school grades. Considering the appearance of the test materials, the reliability, and the correlations with other tests, it is to be expected that the test will show about the same predictive efficiency for school grades as that afforded by the Stanford-Binet. Although the test is currently receiving generally good response from clinical settings, it takes a considerable amount of experience with a new instrument to know whether or not it has clinical value and practicality of use.

GROUP TESTS OF GENERAL INTELLIGENCE

Like the individual tests of general intelligence, the group tests are usually composed of *verbal comprehension, numerical computation,* and various mixtures of the reasoning factors. Although the tests differ from one another in appearance and sometimes in their factor composition, they tend to correlate highly with one another. At the teen-age and adult levels the group tests correlate highly with the individual tests, such as the Wechsler-Bellevue. We see the interesting result that people who started off in seemingly different directions to compose intelligence tests ended up with rather similar measures. Where the group tests differ from one another is in their practical advantages. Some are longer and thus more reliable than others. Some have obtained norms in a careful and representative manner; others have only scant or misleading information on norms. Some have either higher or lower "ceilings," making them more useful with one or the other extreme of ability. Considerable research has been done with some of the tests, and only "face validity" can be claimed for others.

The Binet and Wechsler scales dominate the field of individual tests of general intelligence. Among group measures neither one nor several tests have dominated the field. The tests, therefore, which will be discussed here are only examples of the measures available.

Group Tests for Young Children. The youngest ages at which it has proved feasible to use group tests are the five- and six-year levels. Only small groups of approximately a dozen children can be tested in this way, and even then the examiner must exercise considerable skill to obtain the necessary cooperation and attention. Tests at this age level cannot employ written language and the child cannot be expected to write his own responses. Test instructions must be given orally and supported by illustrations and gestures.

One of the most widely used tests for young children is the Pintner-Cunningham Primary Test (34), which has been in use for over twenty years. The test is available in three equivalent forms, A, B, and C. Each form is composed of seven subtests which are added together to obtain one score. (Illustrative items are shown in Fig. 10–3.)

Equivalent form reliabilities are found to be generally high for groups of kindergarten and first-grade children (34), ranging from .83 to .89. Correlations between the Pintner-Cunningham and the Stanford-Binet are usually about .80 (34). In a group of 260 first-grade children, the Pintner-Cunningham correlated .63 with scores on a reading test. Other group tests which are suitable for use with young children are the Kuhlmann-Anderson Intelligence Tests (27) and the Otis Alpha (31).

Group Tests for the Elementary School Level. As children progress through the elementary school levels, more and more written material can be employed in tests. In the first several grades it is still necessary to rely heavily on oral instructions and pictorial test materials. One of the oldest tests available for the elementary school range is the National Intelligence Test (22). The test was developed soon after the First World War in the wake of the successful use of group tests with Armed Forces personnel.

FIGURE 10–3. **Illustrative items from Form A of the Pintner-Cunningham Primary Test. (Reproduced by permission of World Book Company.)**

Test 1. Mark the things that mother uses when she sews her apron

Test 2. Mark the prettiest girl

Test 3. Mark the two things that belong together

Test 7. Look at how each picture is drawn; make another one like
it in the dots

The test comes in two similar parts, Scale *A* and Scale *B*. Each scale has four verbal and one numerical subtest. A total score is obtained by adding the subtests together. Equivalent forms have been constructed for each scale. The test relies heavily on *verbal comprehension*, utilizing such subtests as verbal analogies, opposites, and sentence completion. The test was used for many years as a standard instrument; but because it has not been revised in a long time, it is now generally being replaced by more recently developed tests. Other tests which are used with elementary school children are the Kuhlmann-Anderson Intelligence Tests (27), the Otis Beta (32), Lorge-Thorndike Intelligence Tests (Houghton Mifflin Company), Henmon-Nelson Tests of Mental Ability (Houghton Mifflin Company), and the California Test of Mental Maturity (45).

Group Tests for High School Students and Average Adults. General intelligence tests for teen-agers and above tend to rely heavily on *verbal comprehension* and general information, with only small inclusion of other factors. Some of the tests are designed primarily to predict future achievement in school. These are usually weighted heavily with questions on general information and look much like achievement examinations. Other tests are designed primarily to test *aptitude*—not what the individual knows but his ability to learn. The two kinds of tests, however, tend to correlate highly. As was previously mentioned, tests of intelligence, or aptitude, tend to rely heavily on the individual's knowledge of the culture about him; thus, they are not very different from tests of acquired knowledge. There are exceptions: persons who score considerably lower on tests of information than on intelligence tests; and for these persons, the difference in scores on the two kinds of tests is of diagnostic importance.

One of the oldest group tests for teen-agers and average adults is the Army Alpha, which did so much to popularize group tests after the First World War. Civilian adaptations and revisions of the test (**55**) are still in use. The Pintner, Otis, and Kuhlmann-Anderson series, mentioned in respect to the testing of younger children, have forms with high enough "ceiling" for the testing of average adults.

One of the leading tests for this age level is the Terman-McNemar Test of Mental Ability (**48**). It has seven subtests, all of which are predominantly concerned with *verbal comprehension*. (See Figure 10–4 for illustrative items.) Norms were carefully determined on a sample of persons from 200 communities in 37 states. Conversion tables are used to express scores in terms of percentiles, mental ages, and deviation *IQs*.

Another test that is available for use at this age level is the Army General Classification Test (*AGCT*), which was used in the first years of the Second World War. The test is now available for civilian use (**59**). The test includes an equal proportion of verbal, numerical, and spatial items. The effort to include at least several factors in an intelligence test is a departure from the usual emphasis on *verbal comprehension* alone.

Group Tests for College Students and Superior Adults. Tests in this category, like those in the next lower level, either emphasize aptitude or general information. As the higher levels of education and ability are reached, the creation of an adequate measuring device becomes more of a challenge to the test constructor. Generally it is much easier to compose adequate tests for idiots than for geniuses, and the difficulty usually mounts when going from the lowest to the highest extreme. General classification tests have been modestly successful in predicting college grades, with correlations in the .50s not uncommon. It has been a particularly annoying thorn in the side of professional test builders that they

FIGURE 10–4. Sample items from the Terman-McNemar Test of Mental Ability. (Reproduced by permission of World Book Company.)

Test 1. *Information*

Mark the word that makes the sentence TRUE.
  Our first President was—
  1. Adams   2. Washington   3. Lincoln   4. Jefferson   5. Monroe

Test 2. *Synonyms*

Mark the word which has the SAME or most nearly the same meaning as the first word.
  Correct   1. Neat   2. Fair   3. Right   4. Poor   5. Good

Test 3. *Logical Selection*

Mark the word which tells what the thing ALWAYS has or ALWAYS involves.
  A cat always has—
  1. Kittens   2. Spots   3. Milk   4. Mouse   5. Hair

Test 4. *Classification*

In each line below, four of the words belong together. Pick out the ONE WORD which does not belong with the others.
  1. Dog   2. Cat   3. Horse   4. Chicken   5. Cow

Test 5. *Analogies*

Hat is to head as shoe is to—
  1. Arm   2. Leg   3. Foot   4. Fit   5. Glove

Test 6. *Opposites*

Choose the word which is OPPOSITE, or most nearly opposite, in meaning to the beginning word of each line.
  North   1. Hot   2. East   3. West   4. Down   5. South

Test 7. *Best Answer*

Read the statement and mark the answer which you think is best.
  We should not put a burning match in the wastebasket because:
  1. Matches cost money.   2. We might need a match later.
  3. It might go out.   4. It might start a fire.

---

have generally met with only small success in predicting the more creative side of human behavior as it is manifested in graduate school and beyond.

Among the most widely used tests at this level are those which are designed specifically for the selection of college freshmen. One of the best known of these is the American Council on Education Psychological Examination for College Freshmen (*ACE*) (**56, 57**), which was used for many years but has now been discontinued. A new form of the test was constructed each year for use with college applicants. Three of the six subtests combine to form a linguistic score (L), and the other three form a quantitative score (Q). The L subtests consist of Verbal Analogies, Completion, and Same-Opposite. The Q tests consist of Arithmetical Reasoning, Number Series, and Figure Analogies. Scores on parts Q and L were usually added together, and the composite used in the selection of students. The *ACE* has high reliability, with usual retest coefficients of around .90 (**58**). Other tests which are similar in purpose and solidity of construction to the *ACE* are the College Board Tests (**60**), the College Qualification Tests (The Psychological Corporation), and the Ohio State University Psychological Test, Form 21 (Ohio College Association).

The Miller Analogies Test (**30**) is an interesting effort to predict success in graduate school and in high-level professional work. The test consists of 100 verbal analogies ranging widely in difficulty. The analogies are cleverly constructed in such a way as to measure both *verbal comprehension* and reasoning ability. The major advantage of the test is that it has a high enough "ceiling" to distinguish among persons who would make much the same score on the usual intelligence test. Split-half reliabilities for the test are generally found to be over .90. The Miller Analogies Test has been used frequently to predict grades in graduate school. The predictive efficiency of the test varies widely in terms of the school and the academic specialty being studied. Validity coefficients tend to be about .50 on the average. Another test which is both well constructed and capable of differentiating at high levels of ability is the *CAVD* (**49**).

Achievement test scores in college and course grades are generally as valid as the intelligence tests for predicting graduate school and professional performance (some of the achievement tests which can be used for this purpose will be mentioned in Chapter 12). A combination of the three kinds of measures by multiple regression usually makes for more efficient prediction.

GENERAL INTELLIGENCE TESTS FOR INFANTS AND PRESCHOOL CHILDREN

A separate section has been reserved here for the discussion of infant and preschool tests because of the special problems that are involved. One of the pioneers in the testing of infants is Arnold Gesell. For over 20 years he and his colleagues have performed longitudinal studies of child development. A group of 107 infants was systematically observed at 4, 6, and 8 weeks and at every 4-week interval to 56 weeks. The children were studied again at 18 months and at the ages of 2, 3, 4, 5, and 6 years. On the basis of these observations the Gesell Developmental Schedules (**16**) were prepared. They are intended to measure the following attributes:

1. *Motor behavior.* How well the child can hold his balance, coordinate, stand, walk, and manipulate objects.

2. *Adaptive behavior.* How well the child can solve the problems of his small world: obtain objects, remove obstacles, solve puzzles, and react to stimuli.
3. *Language behavior.* How well the child can communicate, using the word in its broadest meaning, including the use of gestures and primitive words, to the later development of real language.
4. *Personal-social behavior.* How well the child learns habits of personal care such as toilet-training, dressing, and feeding himself. At a later age consideration is given to how the child manages himself in social situations and in play activity.

During the first year of life, when the Gesell scales would supposedly have their unique value, most of the observations have to be made about motor behavior. The 4-week old infant cannot, of course, talk or follow oral instructions of any kind. The most that can be done at the infant stage is to watch the child's spontaneous movements and note how he reacts to various stimuli. At 1.4 months the average child can coordinate his eyes on an object held before him. At 3 months he will make reaching movements for an object. At 5.5 months he will react differently to strangers than to his parents. (See Figure 10–5 for illustrative test mate-

FIGURE 10–5. Test materials used with the Gesell Developmental Schedules. (Courtesy of The Psychological Corporation.)

rials.) Other tests for infants are the Cattell Infant Intelligence Scale
(11), the California First-Year Mental Scale (7), and the Northwestern
Infant Intelligence Tests (18).

Analysis of Infant Tests. Tests for infants are difficult to standardize,
administer, and score. They are, of course, all individual measures. Infant
tests are less reliable than tests for older children. The reliability is considerably lower during the first six months than afterward. Several studies
of different tests have found reliabilities around .65 for testing during the
first six months (6, 11). After 6 months the reliabilities move up to
respectable figures in the .80 to .90 range (6, 11). Except for the first
weeks and months, the infant tests do measure something consistently.
The question is, what do they measure? A real difficulty in validating
infant scales is that there are almost no criteria available until the child
enters school. A customary procedure has been to correlate infant tests
with scores made several years later on more established intelligence tests
like the Stanford-Binet. Studies (8) have shown that infant tests given at
the age of one year or less correlate about zero with intelligence tests
given 5, 10, and 15 years later to the same persons. It is obvious that
infant tests do not measure intelligence as it is customarily measured in
older children. The key to this dilemma seems to be that the infant scales
primarily measure motor and sensory ability, and the research on reliability shows that there is some consistency in the development of these
attributes. It is quite likely that the infant tests would predict motor and
sensory skills later in life, but interestingly enough, almost nothing has
been done to test this hypothesis.

Preschool Tests. Between the ages of 2 and 5 the developing intellectual
processes become accessible to psychological tests. After the child develops speech, can manipulate objects, and becomes acquainted with the
world about him, he can be tested with some of the materials that are
customarily used in intelligence tests. However, many of the difficulties
in test standardization and administration still remain. The test materials
must be largely pictorial or consist of performance problems.

The difficulty in testing infants is that they usually do little one way or
the other to indicate the status of their intellectual abilities. Children
between the ages of 2 and 5 do too much. They are so active and distractable that it is difficult to carry on any formal testing procedures.
Many children in this age group are shy with strangers and will give little
if any cooperation to the examiner. They are often not highly motivated to
impress the examiner or themselves with how well they can perform.
Consequently, the test must be posed as an interesting game to the child,
and much depends on the examiner's skill.

One of the most prominent tests for young children is the Minnesota
Preschool Scale (20, 21). There are two equivalent forms, each with

Figure 10–6. Test materials used in the Minnesota Preschool Scale. (Reproduced by permission of Educational Test Bureau, Minneapolis.)

26 items. Some of the items are as follows (see Figure 10–6 for an illustration of some of the testing materials):

1. Pointing to parts of the body on a doll
2. Telling what a picture is about
3. Naming colors
4. Digit span
5. Naming objects from memory
6. Vocabulary
7. Copying simple geometrical designs
8. Block building
9. Jigsaw puzzle
10. Indicating missing part in pictures

Many of the items are similar to those at the lower age levels of the Stanford-Binet. The instrument is largely a power test with no emphasis on speed, and the items are little concerned with motor skills. Tests at this age level which depend on speed and motor skills are probably poorer measures.

The Minnesota scale was standardized on a group of 900 children ranging in age from 1½ to 6 years. Equivalent-form reliabilities of the total scale vary from .80 to .94 (**20, 21**). There are some reasons to believe that the Minnesota scale is not an entirely adequate measure below the age of 3. Although scores for children above 3 tend to correlate highly with Stanford-Binet scores obtained later, the correlation for children below the age of 3 is only .21 (**21**). Also, clinical experience indicates that some of the test materials are not sufficiently interesting to hold the attention of children below the age of 3. Two other preschool tests are the Intelligence Test for Young Children (**50**), and the Merrill Palmer Scale (**44**).

PERFORMANCE AND "CULTURE FAIR" TESTS

The customary measures of intelligence have been criticized for their emphasis on *verbal comprehension*. With a test like the Stanford-Binet, there is no way, for example, of measuring the ability of the deaf child. The child must be able to hear the examiner's instructions and respond to what is said. The child who has a speech difficulty is also at a disadvantage. He will have difficulty in responding even if he knows the answers. The child who is new to this country and its language may be classified as feeble-minded by the Stanford-Binet yet have above average ability when examined in his native language.

Performance Tests. Tests of the performance type were developed to circumvent the traditional emphasis on *verbal comprehension*. In a performance test the subject does not necessarily have to read, write, speak, or understand spoken language (the instructions can be given in pantomime). One of the most widely used tests of this type is the Pintner-Paterson Performance Scale (**35**). The scale contains 15 items, but the 10 of these which are considered the best are used in most practical work. Brief descriptions of the 10 items are as follows:

1. *Mare and Foal.* A picture is presented showing a mare and a foal in a country setting. Some cut-out pieces are removed from the picture. The subject must place the pieces in their proper places.
2. *Seguin Form Board.* A wooden board is presented with 10 cut-out geometrical forms. The subject is asked to place the forms in their proper places.
3. *Five-figure Form Board.* Similar to the Seguin Form Board but more difficult because each geometrical form is divided into several parts.
4. *Two-figure Form Board.* Another form board which proves more difficult for most subjects than the Five-figure Form Board.
5. *Casuist Form Board.* This form board also uses geometrical designs which are divided into several pieces. It is made difficult because of the close similarity between some parts of the cut-out geometrical forms.
6. *Manikin.* A wooden figure of a man is assembled from cut-out arms, legs, head, and body (see Figure 10–7).
7. *Feature Profile.* Wooden pieces are used to assemble the profile of a human face (see Figure 10–8).

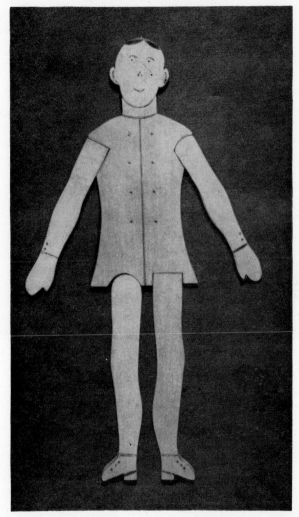

FIGURE 10–7. Manikin Test. (From Pintner-Paterson Performance Scale; courtesy of C. H. Stoelting Company.)

8. *Ship Test.* A jigsaw puzzle of a ship is put together (see Figure 10–9).

9. *Healy Picture Completion,* I. Cut-out sections are removed from a picture of children playing. The subject is asked to place the cut-out sections in their proper places.

10. *Knox Cube Test.* A test of immediate memory involving four wooden cubes. The examiner taps the cubes in a sequence and asks the subject to do likewise.

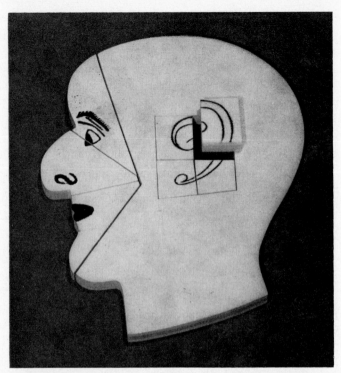

FIGURE 10–8. Knox-Kempf Feature Profile Test: Pintner-Paterson Modification. (Courtesy of C. H. Stoelting Company.)

FIGURE 10–9. Ship Picture Form Board. (From Pintner-Paterson Performance Scale; courtesy of C. H. Stoelting Company.)

Credit is given on the items for both speed and accuracy. Many of the performance tests are so easy for the average person that only through the "speeding" of performance is any dispersion of scores obtained. The emphasis on speed is probably a weakness of the Pintner-Paterson and other similar performance tests. Speed of response is conditioned by age, subculture, and personality. Although the point is not settled, it is doubtful that a heavy emphasis on speed in general intelligence tests leads to good measures.

The Pintner-Paterson is composed almost entirely of jigsaw puzzles in one form or another. The test standardization and the obtaining of norms are crude in comparison to tests like the Stanford-Binet. The reliability of the test is considerably lower than that for most "verbal" tests. Correlations between the Pintner-Paterson and traditional intelligence tests are usually low. Other performance scales are the Arthur Point Scale (4) and the performance scales on the Wechsler tests. Both of these performance scales are generally more satisfactory instruments than the Pintner-Paterson.

Analysis of Performance Tests. The seemingly good idea of constructing performance measures of general ability has not borne fruit. The tests tend to be too much alike and more in the nature of incidental games than measures of important functions. In general the scales have lower reliability and less validity for the available criteria than do the traditional "verbal" tests. There is little reason to believe that performance tests are "better" to use with children in general. The remaining use for these measures is in testing the individual with a language handicap of some kind. If there is a marked difference in performance by such persons between performance tests and "verbal" tests, it is an important diagnostic clue. Fewer research funds and much less energy have gone into the construction of performance scales than into "verbal" intelligence tests. Perhaps a more strenuous research effort would produce more useful performance tests.

"Culture Fair" Tests. Objections have been made not only to the emphasis on language in traditional intelligence tests but to the inclusions of cultural artifacts of all kinds. For example, the Zuñi Indian child or a child reared in the Tennessee mountains might have difficulty in identifying a locomotive, interpreting a picture about sea life, or answering questions about how city people live. The advent of radio, television, and other arms of the mass media of communication has tended to provide all people with a common set of cultural symbols and information. However, the opportunity to absorb cultural information is a matter of degree. Everyone is to some extent isolated in a subculture of his family, friends, religion, and geographical environment. Living in some subcultures rather than others makes a difference in the ability to score well on traditional

intelligence tests. The person in the crossroads of our culture, the urban, highly "Americanized" individual, is given the most advantage.

In order to have measures which are "culture free" or "culture fair," tests have been composed which not only make very little use of language but are little dependent on the symbols and information of the culture. The items on such tests are generally composed of geometrical designs, simple pictures, and abstract symbols. One of the better-known tests of this kind is the Progressive Matrices Test developed in England by Raven (37). The test consists of 60 designs, or matrices, each of which has a cut-out section. The subject is shown six to eight alternative cut-out pieces and asked to indicate which should be placed in the matrix (see Figure 10–10 for illustrations of the items). Raven has collected extensive standardization data on the test in England. Rimoldi (38) obtained rather similar norms on children in Argentina, suggesting that the test is, to an extent, "culture fair." High correlations have been found between the Progressive Matrices and "verbal" tests. A factor-analytic study (39) shows that the test measures some components of the reasoning factors, most likely emphasizing *eduction of relationships,* plus elements of the spatial factors in some items. The Progressive Matrices gives promise of being an important instrument for testing persons with a language handicap and for cross-cultural comparisons. Other "culture fair" tests are the Semantic Test of Intelligence (41), the Culture-free Test of Intelligence (12), and the Leiter International Performance Scale (28).

The "culture fair" tests have not been studied sufficiently to estimate their eventual worth. The critical question is whether the type of tests being used can measure the broad functions which underlie human abilities. The performance tests have overspecialized in the measurement of speed, spatial factors, and motor skills. The "culture fair" tests have apparently been able to tap a broader range of functions, particularly some of the reasoning abilities. However, it is questionable whether a test which deemphasizes *verbal comprehension* will be ultimately the most valid. Traditional "verbal" measures are still better predictors of the available criteria. It may be that as performance in real-life situations beyond school is studied more fully the "culture fair" type of test will come into its own.

It would seem that an even more valid test could be developed if some way were known for measuring *aptitude* for *verbal comprehension* as distinct from the status of *verbal comprehension* at a particular time. The only way that is presently available for testing *verbal comprehension* is through vocabulary tests and measures of reading skill. It is doubtful that an individual would appear "intelligent" or be able to accomplish intellectual goals if he could not eventually, through training and wider acquaintance with the culture, come to master the language and its usage.

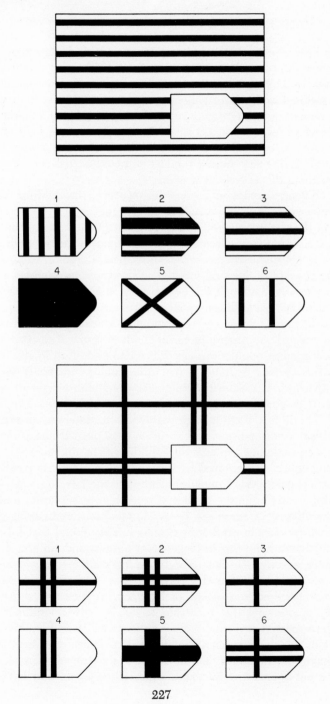

THE NATURE OF "GENERAL INTELLIGENCE"

It has been shown that in spite of the separable factors that underlie tests of human ability there is a common ground among ability functions that can be reliably and usefully measured. The "verbal" intelligence tests, both individual and group, generally correlate highly enough with one another for us to speak of their common characteristics. If a marked difference in test scores is found between two kinds of people with one of the tests, the difference would most likely be reflected in the others. The wide use of intelligence tests during the last half-century has shown a number of things about the underlying process:

1. Intelligence cannot at present be measured in children below the age of two years and not very well below the age of five or six years. Earlier in the chapter the difficulties of constructing tests for infants and preschool children were discussed. Perhaps the next decade will show an improvement in the early measurement of general ability.

2. The concept of "general intelligence" is more meaningful with children than adults. Although the evidence on this point is somewhat conflicting, it seems that abilities are more "general" in children. Comparative factor analyses of children and adults tend to show that there is more of a tendency toward one general factor in children. Some of the factors which are found in adult populations are difficult to find at all in children. This may be due in part to the fact that different test materials have to be used with children than with adults. However, the weight of the argument is that abilities are more "general" in children. The factorial diversity of abilities in adults is probably due to different life experiences and different kinds of school and vocational training. It makes more sense to use general intelligence tests with children than adults.

3. Intelligence as measured by current "verbal" tests is partly due to heredity and partly due to environment. The most telling arguments for this position come from the studies of resemblance between family members in intelligence. Conrad and Jones (13) administered intelligence tests to over 200 families in rural New England. They found that for children above the age of five years intelligence of parents and children correlates .49. Numerous other studies have found correlations very close to .50. Conrad and Jones also found a correlation of .49 between siblings (between brothers, between sisters, or between brothers and sisters). Roberts (40) pointed out that a correlation of .50 between siblings is what would be expected from multifactor inheritance. It is possible that the correlations which have been found between family members could be due to environment rather than heredity. Family members tend to share the same environment, talk about topics in common, and have similar

kinds of schooling. Environment may explain part of the resemblance, but studies of twins (see **2**) make it apparent that this is not a complete explanation. Correlations between the intelligence test scores of fraternal twins (dizygotic) are usually higher than between siblings, usually ranging from .50 to .70. Correlations between identical twins (monozygotic) are usually around .90—almost as high as the reliability of the tests! Fraternal twins can have very different genetic structures, but the genetic structures of identical twins are exactly alike. This leaves little doubt that at least a portion, and apparently a sizable portion, of intelligence is due to inheritance.

4. After the age of about six years, the individual's intelligence tends to remain stable in respect to his age group. That is, the superior people at

FIGURE 10–11. Effect of age at initial testing and test-retest interval on prediction of later Stanford-Binet *IQ* from earlier test. (Adapted from Honzik, McFarlane, and Allen, 23.)

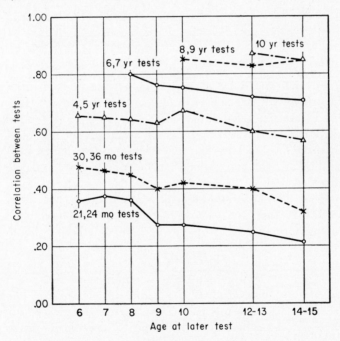

one age level tend to be the superior people at other age levels (see Figure 10–11 for evidence on this point). The relationship is far from perfect, and isolated individuals may show drastic changes over a period of years.

5. From the test results obtained at one period in time, intelligence increases with the age of the persons tested up to the late teens. The intelligence level gradually decreases throughout adulthood and old age (see

Figure 10–12). This has been erroneously interpreted to mean that each person's intelligence grows and then declines. This is not at all what Figure 10–12 shows. It shows the scores of different persons of different ages tested at about the same time. There are a number of different ways of explaining the trend in addition to the one that older people decline in intelligence. The older people probably had less schooling, were reared

FIGURE 10–12. Age changes in full-scale standard scores on the Wechsler-Bellevue Intelligence Scale. (Adapted from D. Wechsler, 52, p. 29.)

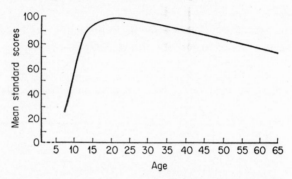

in different times and different environments, and reacted differently to psychological tests (particularly to highly "speeded" tests). It will be a long time before the growth and decline of intelligence for individuals will be determined. Nevertheless, it is important to note that older people generally make lower scores than their younger contemporaries. Whether the same finding will be obtained ten or twenty years from now is an interesting speculation.

6. There are definite group differences in intelligence test scores. Lower scores on the average are made by people of low socioeconomic status, people living in rural areas, people living in the Southern or Southwestern part of the United States, immigrants from southern Europe, and Indians and Negroes. The interpretation of differences of this kind places a large strain on the logical foundation of intelligence tests. As was discussed previously in this chapter, the traditional measures of intelligence are constructed in such a way as to favor certain groups. The question is whether or not the subgroups which tend to make lower scores would make high scores if afforded the advantages of the wider culture. There is some evidence to show that they would. It was found (25) that Southern Negro children who migrate to New York make higher scores the longer they are in the city environment. Another point that should be considered is that even though some subgroups score lower on the average than others, at least some high-scoring individuals can be found in each. The whole question of ethnic and socioeconomic differences is highly

charged with emotion in both professional and lay circles and is a point about which much more information needs to be obtained.

7. Many different kinds of attainment involve intelligence as measured by traditional "verbal" instruments. In particular, intelligence is one of the major factors in successful school work. Numerous correlations of .50 and above between particular tests and school grades were cited in this chapter. Intelligence test scores differentiate occupational groups (see Table 10–3). However, it should be noted that there is considerable over-

TABLE 10–3. AGCT STANDARD SCORES OF OCCUPATIONAL GROUPS
IN THE SECOND WORLD WAR
(Adapted from N. Stewart, **43**)

Occupational groups	Percentile				
	10	25	50	75	90
Accountant	114	121	129	136	143
Teacher	110	117	124	132	140
Lawyer	112	118	124	132	141
Bookkeeper, general	108	114	122	129	138
Chief clerk	107	114	122	131	141
Draftsman	99	109	120	127	137
Postal clerk	100	109	119	126	136
Clerk, general	97	108	117	125	133
Radio repairman	97	108	117	125	136
Salesman	94	107	115	125	133
Store manager	91	104	115	124	133
Toolmaker	92	101	112	123	129
Stock clerk	85	99	110	120	127
Machinist	86	99	110	120	127
Policeman	86	96	109	118	128
Electrician	83	96	109	118	124
Meatcutter	80	94	108	117	126
Sheet metalworker	82	95	107	117	126
Machine operator	77	89	103	114	123
Automobile mechanic	75	89	102	114	122
Carpenter, general	73	86	101	113	123
Baker	69	83	99	113	123
Truck driver, heavy	71	83	98	111	120
Cook	67	79	96	111	120
Laborer	65	76	93	108	119
Barber	66	79	93	109	120
Miner	67	75	87	103	119
Farm worker	61	70	86	103	115
Lumberjack	60	70	85	100	116

lap between most groups. Comparing the extremes in Table 10–3, the top 10 per cent of lumberjacks score higher than the lower 10 per cent of accountants. Scores on intelligence tests are predictive of success on many but not all jobs (see Table 10–4). The fact that the correlations between test scores and job success are near zero in some cases does not necessarily mean that intelligence is not important for the job. The dispersion of intellectual ability usually is narrowed considerably in most jobs

TABLE 10–4. MEDIAN VALIDITY COEFFICIENTS OF INTELLIGENCE TESTS
FOR VARIOUS OCCUPATIONAL GROUPS IN THE PREDICTION OF JOB PROFICIENCY
(Adapted from E. E. Ghiselli and C. W. Brown, **17**, p. 577)

Occupational group	Median validity coefficient	Number of validity coefficients
Clerical workers	.35	85
Supervisors	.40	9
Salesmen	.33	4
Sales clerks	−.09	18
Protective service	.25	6
Skilled workers	.55	6
Semiskilled workers	.20	45
Unskilled workers	.08	13

by the individual's gravitating toward a job at which he can work comfortably and by the selection procedures that are used in industrial settings. Also, it is important to note that the variability of intelligence test scores is higher for lower-level than for higher-level jobs. This indicates that, as would be expected, intelligence is a more important determiner of success in high-level occupations. The individual's ability to succeed is determined by his intelligence and by a host of other things as well: abilities not measured by intelligence tests, interests, personality traits, and just plain luck.

REFERENCES

1. Alderdice, E. T., and Butler, A. J. An analysis of the performance of mental defectives on the Revised Stanford-Binet and the Wechsler-Bellevue Intelligence Scale. *Amer. J. ment. Defic.*, 1952, **56**, 609–614.
2. Anastasi, Anne, and Foley, J. P., Jr. *Differential psychology.* (Rev. ed.) New York: Macmillan, 1949.
3. Anderson, E. E., et al. Wilson College studies in psychology: I. A comparison of the Wechsler-Bellevue, Revised Stanford-Binet and American Council on Education tests at the college level. *J. Psychol.*, 1942, **14**, 317–326.
4. Arthur, G. A. *Point Scale of Performance Tests. Revised Form II. Manual for Administering and Scoring the Tests.* New York: Psychol. Corp., 1947.

5. Balinsky, B. An analysis of the mental factors of various age groups from nine to sixty. *Genet. Psychol. Monogr.*, 1941, **23**, 191–234.
6. Bayley, N. Mental growth during the first three years. *Genet. Psychol. Monogr.*, 1933, **14**, 1–93.
7. Bayley, N. The California First-Year Mental Scale. *Univer. Calif. Syllabus Series*, 1933, No. 243.
8. Bayley, N. Consistency and variability in the growth of intelligence from birth to eighteen years. *J. genet. Psychol.*, 1949, **75**, 165–196.
9. Binet, A., and Simon, T. Méthodes nouvelles pour le diagnostic du niveau intellectuel des anormaux. *Année psychol.*, 1905, **11**, 191–244.
10. Bond, E. A. Tenth grade abilities and achievements. *Teach. Coll. Contr. Educ.*, 1940, No. 813.
11. Cattell, P. *The measurement of intelligence of infants and young children.* New York: Psychol. Corp., 1947.
12. Cattell, R., and Cattell, A. *Handbook for the Individual or Group Culture-free Intelligence Test: Scale 3.* Champaign, Ill.: Inst. Pers. Ability Testing, 1950.
13. Conrad, H. S., and Jones, H. E. A second study of familial resemblance in intelligence: environmental and genetic implications of parent-child and sibling correlations in the total sample. *39th Yearbook, Nat. Soc. Stud. Educ.*, 1940, Part 2, 97–141.
14. Davis, P. C. A factor analysis of the Wechsler-Bellevue Intelligence Scale, Form I, in a matrix with reference variables. *Amer. Psychol.*, 1952, **1**, 296–297.
15. Derner, G. F., Aborn, M., and Canter, A. H. The reliability of the Wechsler-Bellevue subtests and scales. *J. consult. Psychol.*, 1950, **14**, 172–179.
16. Gesell, A., et al. *Gesell Developmental Schedules.* New York: Psychol. Corp., 1949.
17. Ghiselli, E. E., and Brown, C. W. The effectiveness of intelligence tests in the selection of workers. *J. appl. Psychol.*, 1948, **32**, 575–580.
18. Gilliland, A. R. *Northwestern Intelligence Tests. Test A, for Infants 4–12 Weeks Old.* Boston: Houghton Mifflin, 1949.
19. Goddard, H. H. A revision of the Binet Scale. *Train. Sch.*, 1911, **8**, 56–62.
20. Goodenough, F., and Van Wagenen, M. J. *Minnesota Preschool Scale. Form A and B.* (Rev. ed.) Minneapolis: Educ. Test Bureau, 1940.
21. Goodenough, F., and Maurer, K. *The mental growth of children from two to fourteen years: a study of the predictive value of the Minnesota preschool scales.* Minneapolis: Univer. Minn. Press, 1942.
22. Hagerty, M. E., et al. *National Intelligence Tests: Manual of Direction.* Yonkers, N.Y.: World, 1923.
23. Honzik, M., McFarlane, J., and Allen, L. The stability of mental test performance between two and eighteen years. *J. exp. Educ.*, 1948, **17**, 309–324.
24. Jones, L. V. A factor analysis of the Stanford-Binet at four age levels. *Psychometrika*, 1949, **14**, 299–331.
25. Klineberg, O. *Negro intelligence and selective migration.* New York: Columbia Univer. Press, 1935.
26. Kuhlmann, F. A revision of the Binet-Simon system for measuring the intelligence of children. *J. Psycho-Aesthenics, Monogr. Suppl.*, 1912, **1**, 1–41.

27. Kuhlmann, F., and Anderson, R. G. *Kuhlmann-Anderson Intelligence Tests Handbook*. (6th ed.) Princeton, N.J.: Personnel Press, 1952.
28. Leiter, R. G. *Part II of the Manual for the 1948 Revision of the Leiter International Performance Scale*. Washington: Psychol. Service Center Press, 1952. (Test now published by Stoelting.)
29. McNemar, Q. *The revision of the Stanford-Binet Scale: an analysis of the standardization data*. Boston: Houghton Mifflin, 1942.
30. Miller, W. S. *Manual for the Miller Analogies Test, Form G*. New York: Psychol. Corp., 1947.
31. Otis, A. S. *Otis Quick-Scoring Mental Ability Tests: Manual of Directions for Alpha Test*. Yonkers, N.Y.: World, 1939.
32. Otis, A. S. *Otis Quick-Scoring Mental Ability Tests: Manual of Directions for Beta Test*. Yonkers, N.Y.: World, 1939.
33. Peterson, J. *Early conceptions and tests of intelligence*. Yonkers, N.Y.: World, 1926.
34. Pintner, R., Cunningham, B., and Durost, W. *Pintner-Cunningham Primary Test: Manual of Directions*. Yonkers, N.Y.: World, 1946.
35. Pintner, R., and Paterson, D. *A Scale of Performance Tests*. New York: Appleton-Century-Crofts, 1917.
36. Rabin, A. I., and Guertin, W. H. Research with the Wechsler-Bellevue test 1945–1950. *Psychol. Bull.*, 1951, **48**, 211–248.
37. Raven, J. C. *Guide to using progressive matrices (1947), sets A, Ab, B*. London: Lewis, 1951.
38. Rimoldi, H. J. A. A note on Raven's progressive matrices test. *Educ. psychol. Measmt*, 1948, **8**, 347–352.
39. Rimoldi, H. J. A. Study of some factors related to intelligence. *Psychometrika*, 1948, **13**, 27–46.
40. Roberts, J. A. F. Resemblances in intelligence between sibs selected from a complete sample of an urban population. *Proc. int. genet. Congr.*, 1941, **7**, 252.
41. Rulon, P. J. A Semantic Test of Intelligence. *Proc , 1952 Invit. Conf. Testing Problems, Educ. Testing Serv.*, 84–92.
42. Sartain, A. Q. A comparison of the New Revised Stanford-Binet, the Bellevue Scale, and certain group tests of intelligence. *J. soc. Psychol.*, 1946, **23**, 237–239.
43. Stewart, N. A.G.C.T. scores of army personnel grouped by occupations. *Occupations*, 1947, **26**, 5–41.
44. Stutsman, R. *Mental measurement of preschool children*. Yonkers, N.Y.: World, 1931.
45. Sullivan, E., et al. *California Test of Mental Maturity: Manuals for Pre-Primary, Primary, Elementary, Intermediate and Advanced Batteries*. Los Angeles: Calif. Test Bureau, 1951.
46. Terman, L. M. *The measurement of intelligence*. Boston: Houghton Mifflin, 1916.
47. Terman, L. M., and Merrill, M. A. *Measuring Intelligence: A Guide to the Administration of the New Revised Stanford-Binet Tests of Intelligence*. Boston: Houghton Mifflin, 1937.
48. Terman, L. M., and McNemar, Q. *Terman-McNemar Test of Mental Ability: Manual of Directions*. Yonkers, N.Y.: World, 1949.
49. Thorndike, E. L., et al. Four new forms of the I.E.R. intelligence scale for use on the college and higher levels. *Sch. and Soc.*, 1935, **42**, 271–272.

50. Valentine, C. W. *Intelligence tests for young children.* London: Methuen, 1945.
51. Watson, R. I. *The clinical method in psychology.* New York: Harper, 1951.
52. Wechsler, D. *The measurement of adult intelligence.* (3rd ed.) Baltimore: Williams and Wilkins, 1944.
53. Wechsler, D. *Wechsler Intelligence Scale for Children: Manual.* New York: Psychol. Corp., 1949.
54. Wechsler, D. *Manual for the Wechsler Adult Intelligence Scale.* New York: Psychol. Corp., 1955.
55. Wells, F. L. *Modified Alpha Examination, Form 9: Manual of Directions.* New York: Psychol. Corp., 1951.
56. *American Council on Education Psychological Examination for College Freshmen: 1949 Norms.* Princeton, N.J.: Educ. Testing Serv., 1949.
57. *American Council on Education Psychological Examination for College Freshmen, 1952 Edition (Manual of Instructions, 1950).* Princeton, N.J.: Educ. Testing Serv., 1952.
58. *American Council on Education Psychological Examination—High School Edition: Manual of Directions, including Tables o,̊ Equivalent Scores and Percentile Ranks.* Princeton, N.J.: Educ. Testing Serv., (n.d.).
59. *Army General Classification Test (First Civilian Edition): Examiner Manual.* Chicago: Science Research, 1947.
60. *College Board Tests, 1953–4: How to Take Tests; Sample Questions.* New York: College Entrance Examination Board, 1953.

CHAPTER 11

Special Abilities

There are many human attributes to measure other than the kinds of abilities which were discussed in the previous two chapters. There we talked about the components of intelligence or intellectual ability. These are usually thought of as the "higher processes," the most prized of abilities. However, individual differences are as easily found, and sometimes as important to study, in sensory, motor, mechanical, and artistic abilities.

In order to understand fully an individual's potentialities and liabilities, much must be learned about him in addition to his intellectual capabilities. Two persons could make the same score on a general intelligence test and yet be very different in other important ways. Similarly, for all of the factors which were described in Chapter 9, two persons could have exactly the same profile of scores and differ importantly in terms of other abilities. One person might be underweight and frail, the other an excellent physical specimen. This would make quite a difference if they were both being considered for jobs as arctic explorers, test pilots, or steeple jacks. One person might have a flair for mechanical work, whereas the other could have little ability. This would be important to know if they were both considering careers as mechanical engineers. There are many, many other ways in which the two persons could differ importantly—in auditory acuity, depth perception, finger coordination, musical ability, sense of balance, athletic ability, resistance to disease, and so on.

It would be futile to try to list even a sizable fraction of the special abilities that are touched on in psychological work. Instead, a number of abilities will be described which are important concerns in school placement, vocational counseling, and personnel selection.

SENSORY TESTS

The first tests in psychology, those of Galton and his immediate followers, were largely measures of sensory ability: the fineness of sensory thresholds, reaction time, and sensory acuity. The early investigators became discouraged with these measures because they failed to predict school grades, teachers' ratings of intelligence, and other criteria of intellectual accomplishment. However, sensory tests have come back in the last several decades as important measures in their own right. Attention will be given here to some components of vision and audition, omitting the interesting individual differences to be found among the remainder of the "five senses": touch, smell, and taste. Indeed, the range of individual differences extends to numerous other senses that are seldom listed. There are internal senses like thirst, sensitivity to movement of the limbs, and awareness of specific organic tensions.

VISION

The popular practice of talking about "good" and "poor" eyesight does considerable injustice to the complexity of visual functions. There are a number of separable and only partially related kinds of "good" vision. A primary distinction must be made between near acuity and far acuity. Near acuity concerns how well the individual can discern visual forms within 1 or 2 feet of his eyes. Far acuity concerns how well the individual can discern visual forms placed 20 or more feet away. A third component of "good" vision is depth perception, the ability to judge the proximity of objects to one another. Another component is the ability to distinguish colors. Although it is commonplace to think of "color blindness" as a unitary characteristic, there are different kinds of color blindness. Also, the ability to distinguish colors is partly a matter of degree rather than an all-or-none attribute.

Wall Charts. The most familiar measure of visual ability is the ordinary wall chart, which nearly everyone has encountered in applying for a driver's license or taking a physical examination. The Snellen Chart is used extensively for this purpose. It consists of rows of letters, each lower row containing smaller letters than the one above it. The chart is placed 20 feet from the subject. If he can read the row of letters that the average man can, he is said to have 20/20 vision. If he can read the row of letters that the average person can read at only 15 feet from the chart, he is said to have 20/15 vision. Similarly, if he needs to stand 20 feet from the chart to read the row that the average person can read from 40 feet, he is said to have 20/40 vision.

Although the Snellen Chart is an adequate device for detecting gross deficiencies in visual acuity, it has a number of disadvantages. Like all of the wall charts, it tests only far acuity. A school child could have excellent far acuity and still have crippling visual defects of other kinds. Some alphabetical letters are easier to distinguish than others, and this is not taken into account when using the Snellen Chart. Also, the rows of letters are easy to remember, and the test can often be "faked" by the person who has some prior knowledge of the chart. The amount of light on wall charts should be carefully controlled, but in much practical work this is given little consideration. When controlled conditions are obtained, the reliabilities of the Snellen and other wall charts are satisfactorily high. One study (51) reports a reliability coefficient of .88 for the Snellen Chart.

Color Vision. One of the oldest tests for color vision is the Holmgren Woolens. The subject is given different colors of yarn and asked to sort the ones that are alike. It is a crude test which serves only to distinguish persons who are very deficient in color vision. A more systematic measure can be obtained with the Ishihara color plates.[1] The plates are composed of small patches of color. The person who has good color vision can see a number on the plate. The color-deficient person either does not see the number or sees a different number. More recent color vision tests are the Farnsworth Dichotomous Test for Color Blindness (15), the Farnsworth-Munsell 100 Hue Test (16), and the Illuminant-Stable Color Vision Test (19). In order to keep color vision tests adequately standardized they must be used in the same illumination and protected from fading or soilage.

Multiple-component Tests of Vision. In recent years devices have been constructed which test a number of different aspects of vision. The three best-known instruments are the Ortho-Rater (Bausch and Lomb), the Sight-Screener (American Optical Company), and the Telebinocular (Keystone View Company). Each of these instruments tests near vision, far vision, depth perception, color discrimination, and control of the eye muscles. In general, the multiple-component instruments are a considerable advance over the older, single-component tests.

AUDITION

The sense of hearing is also composed of a number of different functions. Only auditory acuity will be treated here, the ability to detect faint sounds. Auditory acuity is itself complex: the person who can hear well at one tone level may be near deaf at higher or lower frequencies. Because of their relevance to musical aptitude, some of the other auditory functions will be considered in a later section.

The older tests of auditory acuity employed sound sources like whispered speech or the ticking of a clock. In the whispered speech test, the examiner stands some distance from the subject and whispers a number of words. The subject tries to say what each word is in turn. The examiner walks farther and farther from the subject to determine the distance at which the whispered words can be heard. Although tests of this kind are

---

[1] Obtainable from C. H. Stoelting Company.

adequate for detecting gross losses of hearing, they have a number of defects. It is difficult to standardize both the loudness and clarity of whispered speech. One examiner will inevitably whisper a bit louder and/or clearer than another in spite of the best efforts at standardization. Such tests measure auditory acuity within a narrow range of the tone, or frequency, continuum. The person who can hear whispered speech well might not be able to hear sound at a different frequency, such as the sound of a ticking clock. The difference in the acoustical properties of testing rooms and the problem of ruling out extraneous noises add to the difficulty of standardizing this type of test.

FIGURE 11–1. Audiogram of a child with severe high-tone deafness. (Adapted from L. A. Watson and T. Tolan, 48.)

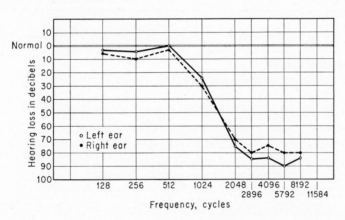

A number of instruments have been developed for measuring auditory acuity at different points on the frequency continuum. These are called pure-tone *audiometers* (see **11, 48**). Earphones are used to test one ear at a time. The standard procedure is to gradually raise the sound intensity until the subject indicates that he can hear the tone. Then, starting with a sound that the subject can hear well, the intensity is lowered to a point where it can no longer be heard. (You will remember this as one of the psychophysical methods for determining *thresholds*, the *method of limits*.) The procedure is repeated at different frequency levels. The resulting data can be plotted as a profile of auditory acuity (see Figure 11–1).

Pure-tone audiometers are now available for group testing. Earphones are given to all of the subjects. Standard answer sheets are used for the subjects to indicate whether or not they hear the tone at different intensities. It is not possible to determine the individual's auditory acuity as finely in the group testing situation. The individual who shows a marked loss in any frequency range on the group test should, if possible, be given the individual test to determine more accurately the nature of his hearing deficiency.

PRACTICAL USES FOR SENSORY TESTS

The individual with a visual or hearing defect is at a definite disadvantage in many performance situations. Particularly, the young school child is handicapped. It is sometimes found that poor vision or hearing is responsible for apparent dullness. The child who cannot see the blackboard or hear the teacher will learn very little regardless of his latent capacity for learning. Reading difficulties can often be traced to visual defects. In order to speak correctly the child must imitate the speech of others. He cannot imitate what he cannot hear. To do well on most psychological tests, the child must be able to hear the instructions and to read the test content. As is common practice in many school programs, children should be systematically tested at different age levels for auditory and visual ability.

Even the sophisticated adult is often unaware that he has a visual or auditory defect. It often happens that individuals who wear *glasses* for the first time are surprised that the world "looks that way." Persons with poor far acuity often take it for granted that everyone sees objects more than 50 feet away as "big blurs." Consequently, the individual cannot be relied upon to detect his own sensory difficulty and seek help. He is likely to blame his inability to perform well on "dumbness" rather than on a visual or hearing loss.

Sensory ability is necessary for many different occupations. The classic example is the baseball umpire's dependence on "good eyesight." Color discrimination is paramount to the interior decorator, the tailor, and the artist. A moderate level of auditory acuity is necessary for most jobs, particularly if it is required to talk with others or to follow spoken instructions. However, there are few jobs in which high-level sensory ability is the primary attribute. Even jobs that would seem to depend heavily on sensory acuity usually require only average ability. A typical example is that of a *sonar* operator, who uses a sound echoing device to detect hostile submarines. It was found that up to a certain point auditory acuity is a "must" for the job; but above the level of average hearing, auditory acuity is not a predictor of good and poor sonar operators.

Sensory disabilities are often prominently involved in adjustment problems. It is not uncommon for the person who is partially cut off from his environment because of a sensory disability to become withdrawn, depressed, and resentful. Sensory tests can be used to detect difficulties in audition and vision. Correction or compensation for the sensory disability often leads to an improvement in the individual's personal relations.

MOTOR DEXTERITY

It has long been recognized that the person who works well with his "head" does not necessarily work well with his hands. Accomplishments like shaping a fine piece of pottery, hitting a home run, and operating complex machinery, have little to do with intelligence or with formal school training.

Among the oldest motor tests are the peg boards, designed to measure arm, hand, and finger dexterity. A typical example is the Stromberg Dexterity Test (46; see Figure 11–2). The first part of the test requires the

FIGURE 11–2. Stromberg Dexterity Test. (Courtesy of The Psychological Corporation.)

subject to place 60 cylindrical blocks into holes as fast as he can. In the second part, the blocks are removed, turned over, and put back in the holes. Another widely used test is the Crawford Small Parts Dexterity Test (10; see Figure 11–3). In the first part of the test, the subject uses tweezers to place pins in holes and then places a small collar over each pin. In the second part, small screws are put in place with a screwdriver.

Some tests are designed specifically to test how well the individual can work with tools and small mechanical parts. A typical test of this kind is the Bennett Hand-tool Dexterity Test (4; see Figure 11–4). The test requires the subject to remove and replace nuts and bolts as quickly as possible.

More complex tests involving hand, arm, and leg coordination have been designed for particular jobs. One of the best known of these is the

FIGURE 11–3. Crawford Small Parts Dexterity Test. (Courtesy of The Psychological Corporation.)

Complex Coordination Test (**36**) used for the selection of pilots by the Air Force (see Figure 11–5). The test is a partial replica of an airplane cockpit, complete with stick and rudder. Lights on a control panel simulate the maneuvers of an airplane. The subject must use stick and rudder to match the stimulus lights, the counterpart in the test of coordinating stick and rudder as required by the situation in an airplane.

Analysis of Motor Tests. Most tests of motor dexterity are highly dependent on speed. Consequently, they prove to be better predictors of jobs in which speed rather than quality is important. There are many jobs in which speed is only a minor consideration. The person who can saw a board quickly does not necessarily have the craftsmanship of the skilled cabinetmaker.

Motor dexterity tests have acceptably high reliabilities, usually over .80 and sometimes over .90. An important characteristic of motor tests is that they tend to correlate very little with one another. Slightly different manipulations of the same material often have little in common. For example, the two parts of the Crawford Small Parts Dexterity Test correlate on the average less than .50 (**10**). A correlation of only .57 was found between the two parts of the Stromberg Dexterity Test (**46**). Correlations

FIGURE 11–4. Bennett Hand-tool Dexterity Test. (Courtesy of The Psychological Corporation.)

between different motor tests prove to be even smaller. Factor-analytic studies of motor dexterity tests have generally found few broad common factors. Tests in this area are characterized by high specificity.

Because of the small overlap between motor dexterity tests, there are no general measures of motor ability such as the general intelligence tests supply for intellectual functions. Motor tests are then of relatively little use in vocational counseling. They are most legitimately used in industrial selection where the job is simple, requires a definite set of motor skills, and is highly dependent on speed. Among jobs of this kind are those in production line work, sewing machine operation, and packaging.

Motor dexterity tests show at best only moderate predictive validity for most situations in which they are used (see Tables 11–1, 11–3, 11–4, and 11–5). However, if they are used in conjunction with other ability tests, they often add a small, but important, increment to the over-all validity of the battery. Motor tests tend to be more valid when they are made to resemble the actual machine or instrument which is featured on

Figure 11–5. Complex Coordination Test. (Courtesy of the U.S. Air Force.)

the job. Tests designed in this way are called *job miniatures*. If the job is that of lathe operator in a machine shop, the best motor test would employ a miniature lathe with the same kinds of dials, handles, and controls that appear on the real lathe. During the Second World War, the Army Air Force used a variety of motor tests for the selection of pilot trainees. The Complex Coordination Test, which resembles most closely what the pilot actually does, generally proved to be one of the most valid instruments.

MECHANICAL APTITUDE

Mechanical ability is popularly thought of as concerning the making and fixing of things as distinct from clerical, sales, administrative, and professional abilities. In general, we speak of mechanical ability in relation to *trades* and various levels of skilled work. There is no fine dividing line between mechanical occupations and those that are not mechanical. Some occupations that most of us would classify as mechanical are plumber, carpenter, automobile mechanic, and boat builder.

There is no one type of test function which underlies mechanical work to the same extent that the general intelligence tests relate to school work. In order satisfactorily to predict a particular mechanical job, a range of different kinds of tests must be used in a battery. Different combinations of tests are usually needed for different jobs. Some of the kinds of tests that have proved useful in the prediction of mechanical work and in vocational guidance are described in the following sections.

Intellectual Ability. Because an individual is involved in making and fixing things, it does not mean that intelligence is an unimportant attribute. When it is possible to do so, either a battery of the major intellectual factors, or, at least a general intelligence test, should be tried as a predictor. The spatial and perceptual factors are very useful in predicting many mechanical jobs. Some tests embodying these functions will be considered in the subsequent discussion. However, it is important also to consider the verbal, numerical, and reasoning factors as well in the prediction of mechanical work. Because the "verbal" intelligence tests are mainly composed of these factors, a good general intelligence test is often one of the best predictors of job success (see Tables 11–1, 11–2, 11–3, 11–4, and 11–5).

TABLE 11–1. CORRELATIONS OF ABILITY TEST SCORES WITH MEASURES OF JOB PERFORMANCE
(Adapted from E. E. Ghiselli, [20])

Test	Type of job				
	Clerical	Protective service	Skilled trade	Semi-skilled	Unskilled
General intelligence	.36	.28	.45	.20	.16
Arithmetic	.42	−.12	...	.15	
Number comparison	.28	.25	...	.15	.15
Spatial relations	.06	...	.45	.30	.27
Mechanical principles	...	...	.45	.25	
Finger dexterity	.22	.20	.21	.30	.05

General intelligence tests tend to be more predictive of how well the individual does in job training than how well he performs subsequently on the job. This is probably because the training phase requires more abstract ability. In many cases the training program involves classroom-like procedures, reading of materials, and the learning of machine operations. These are the kinds of things that intelligence tests predict best. Predictor tests usually correlate higher with performance in training than with later job performance because, as a rule, performance is more reliably measured in the former than in the latter. Progress in training is usually graded more carefully. There is more of an opportunity to observe the worker, and, in many cases, tests are used to assess progress in training.

TABLE 11–2. MINIMUM MENTAL AGES FOR SEVERAL JOBS
(From A. S. Beckman, 3)

Mental age, years	Boys	Girls
5	Dishwasher	Sewer (simple patterns) Vegetable parer
6	Mixer of cement Freight handler	Mangle operator Crocheter (open mesh)
7	Painter (rough work) Shoe repairer (simple tasks)	Cross stitcher Hand-iron operator
8	Haircutting and shaving Gardener	Scarf-loom operator Dressmaker (not including pattern work)
9	Foot-power printing-press operator Mattress and pillow maker	Fancy-basket maker Cook (simpler dishes)
10	Sign painter Painter (shellacking and varnishing)	Sweater-machine operator Launderer
11	Storekeeper Greenhouse attendant	Librarian's assistant Power sealer in cannery

The general intelligence tests tend to be more predictive of success in high-skill rather than low-skill jobs. That is, validities are usually higher for such jobs as electrical technicians and complex machine operators than they are for jobs like truck drivers and furniture movers. The difference in validity is probably due to the increased importance of abstract ability in more highly skilled work. In selecting people for unskilled work, the problem is to set up minimum standards of intelligence rather than to seek persons of high intelligence (see Table 11–2).

Spatial and Perceptual Tests. A wide variety of mechanical work requires the spatial and perceptual factors which were described in Chapter 9. The automobile mechanic needs *spatial orientation* in his work. In a typical job situation he is lying under the automobile and must remove a nut from the engine above him. The nut is slanted at a 45-degree angle, and he must remove it with a wrench that has two joints. The mechanic must orient himself spatially to the complex of angles and movements in order to do such work. In draftsmanship, it is necessary to portray three-dimensional objects on two-dimensional pieces of paper. In some drawings the objects must be shown in tilted positions or partially disassembled. It takes spatial ability, either *spatial orientation* or *visualization*, to work as a draftsman and at many other jobs.

FIGURE 11–6. Sample items from the Revised Minnesota Paper Form Board. For each item, the subject must choose the figure which would result if the pieces in the first section were assembled. (Courtesy of The Psychological Corporation.)

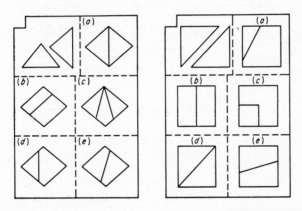

One of the best known spatial tests for mechanical aptitude is the Minnesota Paper Form Board Test (33, 39). It is a useful predictor of grades in shop courses, supervisors' ratings of workmanship, objective production records, and many other measures of mechanical performance (see Figure 11–6).

Perceptual ability is required in a variety of jobs. The *perceptual speed* factor has been used most often as a predictor, but it is likely that the other perceptual factors will eventually find their place in vocational guidance and job selection. The individual who sits by a fast-moving conveyor belt and looks for flaws in manufactured products uses perceptual ability. Any job in which it is necessary to detect aspects of a visual scene requires perceptual ability to some extent.

Examples of perceptual tests can be found in some of the multifactor batteries which were discussed in Chapter 9. Some tests designed specifically for industrial selection will be described in the section on clerical aptitude. (See Tables 11–1, 11–3, 11–4, and 11–5 for typical validities.)

TABLE 11-3. AVERAGE VALIDITY COEFFICIENTS OF VARIOUS APTITUDE TESTS FOR THE TRADES AND CRAFTS

(From Ghiselli and Brown, 21, p. 232)

Type of test	Mechanical repairmen		Electrical workers		Structural workers		Processing workers		Complex machine operators		Machining workers		Average, all trades and crafts	
	Training	Proficiency	Training	Proficiency	Training	Proficiency	Training	Proficiency	Training	Proficiency	Training	Proficiency	Training	Proficiency
Intellectual:														
Intelligence	.38	.04	.43	.47	.29	.09	.35	.24	.34	.28	.30	.08	.35	.20
Immediate memory ...	.30	...	.31	...	.13	.13	.31	.15	...	.30	.12	−.02	.23	.17
Substitution	...	...	...	...	.31	...	...	...	...	.26	.27	.21	.29	.24
Arithmetic	.40	.19	.45	.07	.30	.15	.35	...	...	.29	.33	.20	.37	.18
Number comparison ..	...	...	...	...	−.04	.08	.24	...	...	.14	.02	...	.07	.11
Name comparison	...	...	...	...	−.01	.08	.14	.20	.20	.22	−.02	...	.08	.17
Cancellation	...	...	...	...	...	...	...	...	...	...	.28	...		
Spatial and perceptual:														
Tracing	.21	...	.24	.15	...	.30	.17	.24	.22	.19	.21	.06	.21	.19
Location	.24	...	.24	.23	.23	.23	.24	.21	.28	.25	.24	.04	.25	.22
Pursuit	.17	...	.12	.32	...	...	...	.17	...	.33	...	.01	.15	.21
Spatial relations	.34	.19	.33	.33	.28	.31	.35	.16	.36	.30	.33	.11	.33	.23
Speed of perception ..	.40	...	.43	...	.29	.35	.34	.19	...	...	.35	...	.36	.27
Mechanical principles .	.37	.29	.40	...	.31	...	.40	...	...	.40	.33	.57	.36	.42
Motor:														
Tapping	−.01	...	...	.19	.20	.18	−.01	...	...	.19	.05	.08	.06	.16
Dotting	.20	...	...	...	.13	.20	.02	...	...	.11	.14	.06	.12	.12
Finger dexterity	.19	.16	.15	.18	.24	.30	.22	.30	.11	.14	.24	.08	.19	.19
Hand dexterity	.17	.12	...	...	...	...	...	...	...	...	...	.29	.03	...
Arm dexterity	.08	...	...	...	...	...	...	.32	...	...	−.03	.11	.03	.22

248

TABLE 11–4. AVERAGE VALIDITY COEFFICIENTS OF VARIOUS APTITUDE TESTS FOR INDUSTRIAL OCCUPATIONS

(From Ghiselli and Brown, 21, p. 234)

Type of test	Machine tenders		Assemblers		Inspectors		Packers and wrappers		Gross manual		Average, all manipulative and observational	
	Training	Proficiency	Training	Proficiency	Training	Proficiency	Training	Proficiency	Training	Proficiency	Training	Proficiency
Intellectual:												
Intelligence	...	.16	.02	.22	.19	.35	.22	.13	−.03	.26	.10	.22
Immediate memory	...	.17	...	.06	...	.14	...	.24	...	...	...	.13
Substitution	...	.19	...	.12	...	−.01	...	.16	...	...	...	.12
Arithmetic	...	.15	.39	.09	...	.18	.43	.14	...	...	.41	.14
Number comparison	...	.20	...	.15	...	−.02	...	.13	...	...	...	.12
Name comparison	...	.17	...	.10	...	.17	...	.20	...	...	...	.16
Cancellation	...	.25	...	.36	...	...	...	.24	...	...	...	.28
Spatial and perceptual:												
Tracing	...	.16	.16	.18	...	.20	...	.12	...	...	...	.17
Location	...	.11	.29	.19	.19	.18	...	.16	...	...	.24	.16
Pursuit	...	.15	.28	.15	.09	.09	...	.16	...	...	.19	.14
Spatial relations	...	.11	.24	.15	.27	.24	.22	.13	...	...	.24	.16
Speed of perception	...	...	.26	.27	.22	...	...	...	...	...	.24	...
Mechanical principles	...	...	...	.56	...	.42	...	...	...	...	...	.49
Motor:												
Tapping	...	.12	.16	.14	.10	.06	...	.14	...	...	.13	.12
Dotting	...	.15	.22	.15	...	.06	...	.13	...	.15	...	.12
Finger dexterity	...	.15	.44	.25	.00	.14	...	.08	...	...	.22	.15
Hand dexterity	...	.23	.50	.14	...	−.02	...	.15	...	...	...	.13
Arm dexterity	...	.15	.54	.24	...	.00	...	.24	...	.43	...	.21

TABLE 11–5. AVERAGE VALIDITY COEFFICIENTS OF VARIOUS APTITUDE TESTS
FOR PROTECTIVE OCCUPATIONS, SERVICE OCCUPATIONS,
AND VEHICLE OPERATORS

(From Ghiselli and Brown, 21, p. 229)

Type of test	Protective occupations		Service occupations		Vehicle operators	
	Training	Proficiency	Training	Proficiency	Training	Proficiency
Intellectual:						
Intelligence	.46	.26	.50	.07	.18	.14
Immediate memory	.28	.26				
Arithmetic	.30	.08	.59	−.11	.14	.04
Number comparison	...	.25	...	.14		
Name comparison	...	.36	...	−.17		
Cancellation	...	...	...	−.27		
Spatial and perceptual:						
Location	...	...	...	...	...	.18
Spatial relations	.33	.04	.42	...	.21	
Speed of perception	.30	...	...	...	.08	
Mechanical principles	.41	.20	...	...	.36	.21
Motor:						
Tapping	...	...	...	...	...	.32
Dotting	...	...	...	...	...	.28
Finger dexterity	.19					
Hand dexterity	...	...	...	−.09		
Arm dexterity	...	...	...	−.01		
Simple reaction time	...	...	...	...	...	.27
Complex reaction	...	...	...	...	...	.35

Motor Dexterity. The kinds of motor tests which were discussed earlier
in the chapter are often featured in mechanical aptitude batteries. Motor
tests were placed in a separate section because they are involved in a
number of aptitudes other than mechanical aptitude, athletic aptitudes,
for example (see Tables 11–1, 11–3, 11–4, and 11–5 for typical validities).

Mechanical Comprehension. Among the most successful tests of
mechanical aptitude are those designed to measure the mastery of
mechanical principles, or the ability to reason with mechanical problems.
In a typical problem, a truck driver is rushing medical supplies to a fire-
damaged town. He discovers that his truck is about an inch too tall to
clear a bridge leading to the town. What should the truck driver do? The
answer is to let some air out of the tires. As another example, a motorist
must remove a boulder which blocks the road. He finds a long, stout
pole to do the job. He must then decide whether to use the pole as a pry

or a lever. He can construct a lever by balancing the pole on a rock placed between the boulder and himself (the lever exerts more force than a pry). After deciding to use the lever action with the rock as a balancer (a *fulcrum*), he must then decide where to place the balancer (rock) and how to best exert his strength against the pole. As a third example, a hoist is being built to lift tree trunks into the bed of a truck. A system of gears and chains is set up to transfer the power from an electric motor to the hoist. It must be decided how large the different gears should be to give the desired power to the hoist.

FIGURE 11–7. Sample items from the Bennett Mechanical Comprehension Test, Form AA. (Courtesy of The Psychological Corporation.)

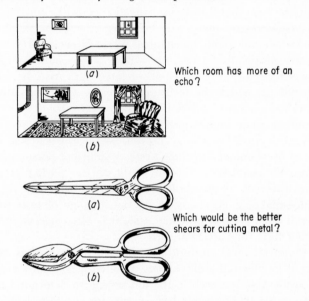

The three problems above are typical of those found in mechanical comprehension tests. Tests of this kind tend to range over several ability factors. Because of the paucity of factor-analytic studies of mechanical comprehension tests, it is not always possible to say just what a particular test measures. Some of them emphasize the spatial factors, which are prominently involved in many tests of mechanical aptitude. Other functions which appear in some mechanical comprehension tests are *numerical computation*, various aspects of the reasoning factors, and familiarity with tools and machinery. Examples of mechanical comprehension tests are the Bennett Mechanical Comprehension Test (5, 6) (see Figure 11–7), the Mechanical Reasoning Test of the *DAT* (discussed in Chapter 9), and the *SRA* Mechanical Aptitude Test (40).

Mechanical Information. One of the most useful measures for the selection of skilled and semiskilled workers is a test of information, or knowledge, about tools and machinery. For example, a set of questions like the following would be useful in the selection of automobile mechanics:

1. What is a torque converter?
2. What is a ratchet?
3. Where is the "needle valve" in an automobile?
4. What source of power is used to run the generator in most automobiles?
5. How do you recognize "pre-ignition"?

Information tests can be constructed either to measure general knowledge of mechanical work or to measure knowledge of one particular job. It is usually the case that a test constructed specifically for one job, such as for television repair men, will be more predictive than a test of knowledge in general about mechanical work. However, the test which is constructed specifically for one job is likely to be useful only for selecting personnel for that job or for closely related jobs. Also, because of the specific knowledge which the instrument measures, it is usually of little use in vocational guidance, where it is usually necessary to measure broad functions rather than highly specialized information. A more general measure of mechanical knowledge is often useful in vocational guidance.

Analysis of Mechanical Aptitude Tests. A sufficient personnel-selection program usually requires a careful study of the particular industrial setting. The diversity of psychological functions which is required by different jobs makes it necessary to try out a range of tests to find the ones that will work well in practice. Also, it is often necessary to invent and construct tests for particular jobs.

Few of the mechanical aptitude tests have been studied as extensively as the tests of intellectual ability. Consequently, it is usually necessary to perform considerable research in the job setting to determine the utility of particular tests. In few cases have norms for the tests been obtained on a sufficiently representative sample to use them as dependable guides. It is generally more meaningful to obtain local norms for particular personnel selection or school programs.

Mechanical aptitude tests are fairly easy to standardize and make reliable. Reliabilities in many cases approach those of the better general classification tests. Mechanical aptitude tests have modest validity for many different jobs, the amount varying considerably with the job. The seemingly small validities for some jobs should be regarded from a number of standpoints. Primarily there is the possibility that formal abilities such as those measured in psychological tests have little to do with job success. Another possibility is that the criterion of job success, the assessment, is unreliable and consequently cannot be predicted. If the assessment is determined only from the sketchy impressions of foremen and managers, it is seldom very reliable. It is meaningful in this instance to make the correction for attenuation as discussed in Chapter 6, correcting for the unreliability of the assessment. Because of the unreliability inherent in most job assessments, mechanical aptitude tests are often considerably more valid than apparent from the correlation coefficients (this was discussed more fully in Chapter 6). The third point to consider is that the modest to low individual validities should not obscure the fact that a combination of several tests in a battery will often produce reasonably good predictive efficiency.

CLERICAL AND STENOGRAPHIC APTITUDES

Clerical Aptitude. Clerical aptitude, as it will be discussed here, concerns the office clerk, the individual who deals with files, ledgers, accounts, and correspondence. The term clerk is much more general than this particular usage, referring variously to grocery clerk, department store clerk, and even court clerk. *Perceptual speed* tests have a special importance in the prediction of clerical performance. *Perceptual speed* is involved in chores like proofreading letters, searching for particular accounts in a long list, and alphabetizing names.

A typical test which emphasizes *perceptual speed* is the Minnesota Clerical Test (1). The test is divided into two separately timed parts, Number Comparison and Name Comparison (see Figure 11–8). Retest

FIGURE 11–8. Sample items from the Minnesota Clerical Test. (Courtesy of The Psychological Corporation.)

66273894	———————	66273984
527384578	———————	527384578
New York World	———————	New York World
Cargill Grain Co.	———————	Cargil Grain Co.

If the two names or numbers of a pair are exactly alike, make a check mark on the line between them.

reliabilities range from .85 to .91. Extensive validation research shows correlations ranging up to .60 between the Minnesota Clerical Test and business school and job performance criteria. Other *perceptual speed* tests for clerical aptitude are the Clerical Speed and Accuracy Test of the *DAT*, the Clerical Perception Test on the *GATB*, and parts of the General Clerical Test (50).

Perceptual speed is a necessary component of many clerical jobs, but other functions should be tested as well. *Verbal comprehension* is a desirable attribute, especially a knowledge of spelling and grammar.

Clerical work often involves routine arithmetical operations, and therefore, a *numerical computation* test is likely to be a useful selection instrument. If the clerical job requires the use of accounting machines or other equipment, some of the motor dexterity tests may be of use. The *DAT* tests not only *perceptual speed* but a variety of verbal and arithmetic abilities; hence, it probably would serve well in the selection of office clerks. The General Clerical Test (**50**) is a short battery designed to cover the major functions required in clerical work. Scores on nine subtests are combined to form clerical, numerical, and verbal scores.

Stenographic Ability. The selection of stenographers is best made on the basis of specific job requirements. Typing and shorthand ability are the major requirements in most stenographic jobs. Therefore, proficiency tests in these skills offer a sound basis for the selection of stenographers (for typical tests, see **7, 8, 47**). Here as in many other testing problems, the needs of a selection program are not always the same as those of the vocational guidance situation. In vocational guidance, before the individual has had an opportunity to test himself in specialized training or on the job, some prediction must be made as to how well he will perform. Although an insufficient amount of research has been done on the aptitude for stenographic work to allow us to speak with certainty, the most promising attributes seem to be the motor skills involved in typing, measures of *verbal comprehension* and language usage, and interest in stenographic work.

ARTISTIC APTITUDES

The nature of art and artistic ability have been matters of interest to psychologists for well over a hundred years, dating back to and before Fechner. In spite of this long interest, the measurement of artistic ability lags behind the testing of other ability functions. This is due in part to practical considerations. There has always been a more urgent need for intellectual and vocational tests than for tests of artistic ability. Research on classifying men in the Armed Forces, testing children in school, and selecting men in industry, has won financial support because of the immediate gains to be expected. Although the study of artistic ability offers some practical advantages, it never has promised a sufficient commercial market to attract large numbers of psychologists.

Another reason that tests of artistic ability lag behind is the intrinsic complexity of the functions to be measured. In this area, it is very difficult to distinguish aptitude from achievement. The accomplished musician or painter can be judged by what he currently does. But it is difficult to find the underlying aptitudes that give one child an advantage over another in reaching eventual artistic accomplishment.

Good art is largely a matter of time and place. Chinese music sounds cacophonous to us, and no doubt much of our music seems strange to the Chinese. Some primitive music centers almost entirely on the drum and other percussion instruments. Complex rhythmic patterns used are too elusive for the "civilized" ear. We would miss the esthetic appreciation that the primitive has for his music as much as he would be baffled by the symphony orchestra. The delicate sensitivities of a Japanese poem are lost on an Occidental audience. We might cite many other examples to show that art is a matter of values. Different people have different values, and values change over the ages.

Different abilities are involved in the production of art and in the appreciation of art. The music critic may not be a musician at all; the art historian may have never painted. Different abilities are required in the production of different kinds of art work.

The measurement of artistic aptitude evolves into several components. For producing works of art there are probably some underlying abilities that cut across different times and different cultures. In graphic art work, the ability to make line drawings, to combine colors, and to achieve properties of "balance" are required in most paintings. In musical ability there are the basic sensory skills of tonal memory, sense of pitch, and recognition of rhythms, which to some extent cut across different kinds of musical production.

Another attribute which can be tested is the appreciation of art forms. Appreciation is dependent on the values in a particular culture and on the individual's knowledge and acceptance of those values. Finally, tests can be made of how well the individual can produce particular art forms; such achievement is dependent both on his initial aptitude and the training that he has had.

MUSICAL APTITUDE

Seashore Measures. One of the oldest and most widely used musical tests is the Seashore Measures of Musical Talents (42). The test stimuli are reproduced on phonograph records, which can be used for the testing of moderate-sized groups of subjects. The battery includes the following subtests:

1. *Pitch discrimination.* The subject is asked whether the second of two tones is higher or lower than the first. The items are made progressively more difficult by decreasing the difference in pitch between the pairs of tones.
2. *Loudness discrimination.* The subject judges which of two tones is louder.
3. *Time discrimination.* One tone is presented for a longer period of time than another. The subject judges which of the two tones is longer.

4. *Rhythm judgment.* The subject judges whether two rhythmic patterns are the same or different.
5. *Timbre judgment.* The subject judges whether or not two tones are of the same musical quality.
6. *Tonal memory.* Two series of notes are played. In the second series one of the notes is altered. The subject judges which of the notes is different.

Scores on the subtests correlate near zero on the average with intelligence tests (17). The subtest scores are partly independent, with median intercorrelations ranging from .48 to .25 for different samples (17). Split-half reliability estimates for the subtests range from .62 to .88. Rhythm and timbre are the least reliable. If, as is often done, the six subtests are added to form one general measure, high reliability can be expected for the test. Except for large differences in scores, the subtests are not sufficiently reliable for considering differential aptitudes within the test.

Scores on the Seashore test are affected very little by age. Similar norms are found for grammar school, high school, and adult populations. Although the research results are somewhat contradictory (17, 41, 44), it seems that scores are affected only slightly by musical training. These two findings taken together suggest that the Seashore subtests measure some basic aptitudinal functions which are possibly inherited. The larger question is whether the aptitudinal functions involved in the tests are of any importance in predicting musical accomplishment.

An insufficient amount of research has been done with the Seashore test to speak with firmness about its predictive utility. Modest to small correlations have been found with grades in music classes and with teachers' ratings of musical ability (12, 24, 31, 38). The test differentiates moderately well between students who complete specialized musical training and those who drop out. It is reasonable to think that at the level of specialized music training most of the persons with poor ability in the Seashore type of measures will have already been eliminated.

A number of persons have argued that the Seashore measures are not very similar to the skills that are involved in the actual production of music. The Seashore subtests measure certain types of sensory discrimination which might be necessary for musical ability but not sufficient. Where the Seashore test would have its most important value is in helping parents decide whether their children would be likely to profit from extensive musical training. This would save considerable money and would keep the neighbors from having to hear little Susan grind away for years at an instrument she will never master. At present the Seashore test is difficult to administer below the age of ten, and the predictive validity of the test at younger ages is not known.

Wing Test. The Wing Standardized Tests of Musical Intelligence (**49**) were designed to stay as close as possible to the skills involved in musical production and appreciation. Like the Seashore test, the Wing test uses phonograph recordings. The following seven functions are tested:

1. *Chord analysis.* Judging the number of notes in a chord.
2. *Pitch change.* Judging the direction of change of notes in a repeated chord.
3. *Memory.* Judging which note is changed in a repeated melodic phrase.
4. *Rhythmic accent.* Judging which performance of a musical phrase has the better rhythmic pattern.
5. *Harmony.* Judging which of two harmonies is better for a particular melody.
6. *Intensity.* Judging which of two pieces has the more appropriate pattern of dynamics, or emphasis.
7. *Phrasing.* Judging which of two versions has the more appropriate phrasing.

The first three subtests measure complex sensory abilities. The other four concern the esthetic value of different compositions. The subtest scores are added to form one general measure of musical aptitude.

The Wing test has received favorable response from teachers of music, who feel that the test covers many of the skills that are important in musical training. Little is known about how well the test can predict available criteria. The author (**49**) reports correlations of .60 and above between the test and teachers' ratings of musical ability in three small groups. It is possible that the Wing test will prove to be a better differentiator of musical talent at higher levels of ability than the Seashore. The Wing test might then be useful in the guidance and selection of students who want to go on from some initial musical training to more advanced training.

There are a number of other tests based on phonographically recorded tones and musical phrases. The Drake Musical Memory Test (**13, 14**) emphasizes the memory component, which appears in only one subtest of the Seashore and Wing batteries. The Drake memory test is different in that the items concern short musical melodies instead of groups of tones. The subject must determine whether two melodies are the same, and if not, whether the change has been made in the key, the timing, or in specific notes. The Kwalwasser-Dykema Music Tests (**30**) comprise a battery of 10 subtests. Six of the subtests are similar to those on the Seashore. The subtests cover much the same ground as the Seashore plus the ability to read musical notation and some components of musical appreciation.

Analysis of Musical Aptitude Tests. Not enough research has been done to say how well the current tests work. A particular problem is the dearth of adequate criteria of musical accomplishment. School grades in the history, techniques, and general knowledge of music are the most reliable indices. But these are not the same as artistry in musical production. Judgment of the actual mastery of musical instruments must necessarily be based on the impressions of teachers and other persons, and impressions of this kind usually have only modest reliability. Even if there are some difficulties in validating the instruments, much more research should be done to determine how well they work.

The tests which were discussed in the previous sections are all, strictly speaking, tests of appreciation. That is, the subject is not required actually to play an instrument but only to listen and judge what he hears. However, some of the complex judgments involved seem to underlie the skills that are needed in musical production. It is likely that other types of tests could be used in conjunction with the conventional measures to obtain a better estimate of musical ability. Motor skills are involved in playing most musical instruments, the piano being an outstanding example. Motor tests might be profitably used in the prediction of musical accomplishment. Although intelligence tests correlate very little with the available musical tests, this does not mean that they would be of no use in predicting musical accomplishment. It would be expected that intelligence and, more generally, the factors which underlie differential aptitude tests would be useful in the prediction of course grades in musical curricula and in special music schools.

It is likely that an individual's interest in musical work will be as predictive of later success as tests of the ability type. Two such interest tests are the Farnsworth Scales (18) and the Seashore-Hevner Tests for Attitude toward Music (43). The small amount of research that has been done indicates some promise for tests of musical interest.

GRAPHIC ART

McAdory Test. The field of graphic art testing has been dominated by a particular type of item, in which a "masterpiece" is compared with one or more altered versions of the same work. One of the oldest tests of this kind is the McAdory Art Test (34), which came out in 1929. The test contains pictures of 72 art works covering a wide variety of contemporary art forms, ranging from pictures of furniture and automobiles to works of art in museums. Four versions of each art work are given; these differ in shape, arrangement, shading, and use of color. The subject is required to rank-order the four versions in terms of his preferences.

Items for the McAdory test were selected in terms of the judgments of experts, including teachers, critics, and artists. Items were retained only if at least 64 per cent of the judges agreed on the ranking of the four versions of each picture. A primary weakness of the test is its dependence on contemporary art values. For example, it is likely that the preferences for furniture, automobile design, and even paintings have changed since the test was constructed.

FIGURE 11–9. Illustrative items from Meier Art Judgment Test. (Reproduced by permission of Norman C. Meier.)

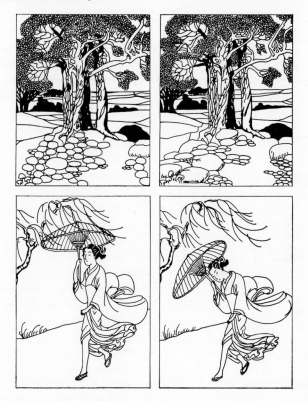

Meier Test. The Meier Art Judgment Test (35) is by far the most widely used test of art appreciation. It also uses the altered-version type of item. The test differs from the McAdory in that only one alternative version is given for each original art work, and the items concern relatively timeless art masterpieces. The items are all in black and white. The altered version of each masterpiece is meant to destroy the esthetic organization. In a typical altered version, one figure is moved to the side in such a way as to change the balance of the painting (see Figure 11–9).

The initial selection of items was made on the basis of expert judgments. Items on which there was high agreement among 25 experts were retained. The items were further pared down in terms of internal consistency statistics. Only those items showing a high correlation with the total score were placed in the final form.

Split-half reliabilities for the Meier test range from .70 to .84 in relatively homogeneous groups of subjects. Scores correlate only negligibly with traditional measures of intelligence. Only a small amount of research has been done to determine how well the test predicts available criteria. It has been shown that the test differentiates art students from non-art students and different art students in terms of the amount of training that they have had. A correlation of .46 was found with the grades of 50 art students (**27**). Correlations ranging from .40 to .69 were found with ratings of creative art talent (**9, 37**).

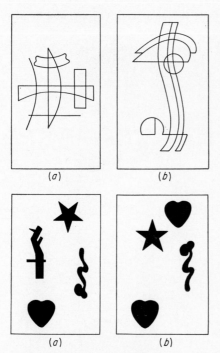

(*a*)   (*b*)

(*a*)   (*b*)

Figure 11–10. Illustrative items from Graves Design Judgment Test. (Courtesy of The Psychological Corporation.)

Graves Test. To remove the test as much as possible from traditional and contemporary art values, the Graves Design Judgment Test (**22, 23**) consists entirely of abstract designs (see Figure 11–10). Each test item consists of either two or three versions of the same basic design. The altered version or versions were constructed to violate accepted esthetic principles. The judgments of art teachers and art students were used to select the best 90 items from an original list of 150. Split-half reliability estimates range from .81 to .93. Although the Graves test gives promise of being a useful measure, only a small amount of empirical work has been done with the instrument.

Worksample Tests. A number of tests were designed to test how well individuals can actually produce graphic art works.

Typical of these is the Horn Art Aptitude Inventory (**25, 26**), which includes the following subtests (see Figure 11–11):

1. *Scribble exercise.* Making outline drawings of 20 simple objects
2. *Doodle exercise.* Making abstract compositions out of simple geometrical forms

3. *Imagery.* Working from a given set of lines to a completed composition

Other tests which are largely concerned with the production of art works are the Knauber Art Ability Test (29) and the Lewerenz Tests in Fundamental Abilities of Visual Art (32).

FIGURE 11–11. Sample item from the Imagery Test of the Horn Art Aptitude Inventory. The subject is shown only the lines in rectangle *A* from which he is to make a drawing. Examples of completed drawings are shown in *B* and *C*. (From C. Horn, 25; reproduced by permission of the American Psychological Association.)

The worksample tests must rely on the judgments of graders. Product scales are used, in which a particular drawing is compared to a standard set. Sample drawings are available for each score level. The grader gives a score in accordance with the apparent nearness in quality of the subject's drawings to the product scale examples. In spite of the apparent subjectivity of the scoring system, moderately high reliabilities are reported for tests of the worksample type (25, 26, 28, 29). Current evidence indicates that the worksample tests predict course grades as well as the appreciation tests and do a better job of predicting teachers' ratings of creative ability (2, 26).

Analysis of Graphic Art Tests. The difficulties of defining and measuring musical aptitude are magnified in the measurement of graphic art aptitude. Since the graphic arts are more dependent on fashion, criteria of accomplishment are weaker; hence the underlying aptitudes are more difficult to determine. Unlike the sensory discrimination functions in musical aptitude, the current measures of graphic art aptitude appear to depend heavily on training. Consequently they are of less use in the early guidance of prospective art students, where all tests of art aptitude would seem to have their most promising use.

Current tests are biased toward certain cultural groups. For example, it was found (45) that much lower scores on the McAdory test are made by Navajo Indian children than by children in New York City, in spite of the fact that the Navajo culture has a highly developed art form of its own. The available tests appear in most cases to be clever and well designed, but the paucity of research which characterizes the testing of artistic abilities leaves many questions about how well the tests work in practice. Perhaps future factor-analytic studies of graphic art tests will lead to a better knowledge of the underlying functions and how they can best be measured.

REFERENCES

1. Andrew, D. M., and Paterson, D. G. *Minnesota Clerical Test: Manual.* New York: Psychol. Corp., 1946.
2. Barrett, H. O. An examination of certain standardized art tests to determine their relation to classroom achievement and to intelligence. *J. educ. Res.,* 1949, **42**, 398–400.
3. Beckman, A. S. Minimum intelligence levels for several occupations. *Personnel J.,* 1930, **9**, 309–313.
4. Bennett, G. K. *Hand-tool Dexterity Test: Manual.* New York: Psychol. Corp., 1947.
5. Bennett, G. K. *Test of Mechanical Comprehension, Form AA: Manual.* New York: Psychol. Corp., 1948.
6. Bennett, G. K. *Test of Mechanical Comprehension, Form BB: Manual.* New York: Psychol. Corp., 1951.
7. Bisbee, E. U. *Commercial Education Survey Tests: Junior and Senior Shorthand.* Bloomington, Ill.: Public School, 1933.
8. Blackstone, E. G., and McLaughlin, M. W. *Blackstone Stenographic Proficiency Tests: Stenographic Test.* Yonkers, N.Y.: World, 1932.
9. Carroll, H. A. What do the Meier-Seashore and the McAdory Art Tests measure? *J. educ. Res.,* 1933, **26**, 661–665.
10. Crawford, J. E., and Crawford, D. M. *Small Parts Dexterity Test: Manual.* New York: Psychol. Corp., 1949.
11. Davis, H. (Ed.) *Hearing and deafness.* New York: Murray Hill Books, 1947.
12. Drake, R. M. The validity and reliability of tests of musical talent. *J. appl. Psychol.,* 1933, **17**, 447–458.
13. Drake, R. M. *Musical Memory Test: Manual.* Bloomington, Ill.: Public School, 1934.

14. Drake, R. M. Factor analysis of music tests. *Psychol. Bull.*, 1939, **36**, 608–609.
15. Farnsworth, D. *The Farnsworth Dichotomous Test for Color Blindness: Manual.* New York: Psychol. Corp., 1947.
16. Farnsworth, D. *The Farnsworth-Munsell 100 Hue Test for the Examination of Color Discrimination: Manual.* Baltimore: Munsell Color Co., 1949.
17. Farnsworth, P. R. An historical, critical, and experimental study of the Seashore-Kwalwasser test battery. *Genet. Psychol. Monogr.*, 1931, **9**, 291–393.
18. Farnsworth, P. R. Rating Scales for Musical Interests. *J. Psychol.*, 1949, **28**, 245–253.
19. Freeman, E., and Zaccaria, M. A. An Illuminant-Stable Color-vision Test, II. *J. opt. Soc. Amer.*, 1948, **38**, 971–976.
20. Ghiselli, E. E. The validity of commonly employed occupational tests. *Univer. of Calif. Publ. Psychol.*, 1949, **5**, 253–287.
21. Ghiselli, E. E., and Brown, C. *Personnel and industrial psychology.* (2nd ed.) New York: McGraw-Hill, 1955.
22. Graves, M. *Design Judgment Test: Manual.* New York: Psychol. Corp., 1948.
23. Graves, M. *The art of color and design.* (2nd ed.) New York: McGraw-Hill, 1951.
24. Highsmith, J. A. Selecting musical talent. *J. appl. Psychol.*, 1929, **13**, 486–493.
25. Horn, C. C. *Horn Art Aptitude Inventory: Preliminary Form, 1944 Revision, Manual.* Rochester, N.Y.: Rochester Inst. Technology, Office Educ. Res., 1944.
26. Horn, C. C., and Smith, L. F. The Horn art aptitude inventory. *J. appl. Psychol.*, 1945, **29**, 350–355.
27. Kinter, M. *The measurement of artistic abilities.* New York: Psychol. Corp., 1933.
28. Knauber, Alma J. Construction and standardization of the Knauber art tests. *Education*, 1935, **56**, 165–170.
29. Knauber, Alma J. *Knauber Art Ability Test: Examiner's Manual.* Cincinnati, Ohio: Author, 1935. (Distributed by Psychol. Corp.)
30. Kwalwasser, J., and Dykema, P. W. *Kwalwasser-Dykema Music Tests: Manual of Directions.* New York: Carl Fischer, 1930. (Also distributed by Stoelting.)
31. Larson, R. C. Studies on Seashore's measures of musical talent. *Univer. Iowa Stud., Aims Progr. Res.*, 1930, No. 6, 83.
32. Lewerenz, A. S. *Tests in Fundamental Abilities of Visual Art: Manual of Directions.* Los Angeles: Calif. Test Bureau, 1927.
33. Likert, R., and Quasha, W. H. *Revised Minnesota Paper Form Board Test: Manual.* New York: Psychol. Corp., 1948.
34. McAdory, M. *The McAdory Art Test: Manual.* New York: Teachers College, Bur. Publ., 1929.
35. Meier, N. C. *The Meier Art Tests. I. Art Judgment: Examiner's Manual.* Iowa City, Iowa: Univer. Iowa, Bur. Educ. Res. Service, 1942.
36. Melton, A. W. (Ed.) *Apparatus Tests. AAF Aviation Psychology Program Research Reports, Rep. No. 4.* Washington: GPO, 1947.
37. Morrow, R. S. An analysis of the relations among tests of musical, artistic and mechanical abilities. *J. Psychol.*, 1938, **5**, 253–263.

38. Mursell, J. W. What about music tests? *Music Educ. J.*, 1937, **24**, 16–18.
39. Paterson, D. G., et al. *Minnesota Mechanical Ability Tests.* Minneapolis: Univer. Minn. Press, 1930.
40. Richardson, Bellows, Henry, and Company, Inc. *SRA Mechanical Aptitudes: Manual.* Chicago: Science Research, 1950.
41. Seashore, C. E. *Psychology of music.* New York: McGraw-Hill, 1938.
42. Seashore, C. E., Lewis, D., and Saetveit, J. G. *Manual of Instructions and Interpretations for the Seashore Measures of Musical Talents.* (1939 revision) Camden, N.J.: RCA Victor Div. Radio Corp. Amer., 1942. (Now published and distributed by Psychol. Corp.)
43. Seashore, R. H., and Hevner, K. A time-saving device for the construction of attitude scales. *J. soc. Psychol.*, 1933, **4**, 366–372.
44. Stanton, H. M. Measurement of musical talent. *Univer. Iowa Stud. Psychol. Music*, 1935, **2**, 140.
45. Steggerda, M. The McAdory Art Test applied to Navajo Indian children. *J. comp. Psychol.*, 1936, **22**, 283–285.
46. Stromberg, E. L. *Stromberg Dexterity Test: Preliminary Manual.* New York: Psychol. Corp., 1951.
47. Thurstone, L. L. *Examination in Clerical Work: Form A, Thurstone Employment Tests.* Yonkers, N.Y.: World, 1922.
48. Watson, L. A., and Tolan, T. *Hearing tests and hearing instruments.* Baltimore: Williams and Wilkins, 1949.
49. Wing, H. Tests of musical ability and appreciation: an investigation into the measurement, distribution, and development of musical capacity. *Brit. J. Psychol., Monogr. Suppl.*, 1948, **8**, No. 27.
50. *Psychological Corporation General Clerical Test: Manual.* New York: Psychol. Corp., 1950.
51. Studies in visual acuity. PRS Report 742, *Personnel Res. Sect., AGO*, 1948, 161.

CHAPTER 12

Achievement Tests

The achievement test is a natural outgrowth of the teacher's own class-room examination. Now achievement tests are used more broadly to assess levels of skill in numerous endeavors in addition to school work—in military, industrial, and particularly in government civil service work. Most of the instruments discussed in this chapter are commercial tests which can be purchased and used in a wide variety of training programs.

In terms of the effort spent in test construction and the number of tests that are used, achievement tests overshadow all other psychological measures. They also have an immediate importance not shared by any other type of test. Achievement tests are helpful in assigning school grades, in planning school curricula, in remedial training, and in vocational guidance. Achievement tests are of sufficient importance to merit the work of hundreds of specialists, and the tests are used in such quantities as to make the development of a new instrument a sizable commercial venture. Numerous books (see 1, 2, 13, 17) are devoted either wholly or in part to the development and use of achievement tests.

Aptitude and Achievement. Achievement tests are meant to measure accomplishment, as distinct from aptitude tests and intelligence tests, which are intended to measure the capacity for accomplishment. In some situations it is meaningful to distinguish aptitude and accomplishment even though it is difficult to measure them separately.

Achievement tests necessarily measure an interaction of more basic aptitudes with the learning that takes place in specific training situations. As a group, children who do well in school work must have at least moderately high aptitude for such training, combined with personality traits and interests which lead them to accomplishment. However, it is not necessarily true that children who do poor work in school are lacking in aptitude. Some of them may be suffering from physical difficulties such as poor vision, from disrupted personalities, and from economically impoverished or unwholesome family environments. Children of this kind sometimes show marked improvement in school progress after their physical and personal problems have been dealt with.

Validity of Achievement Tests. The achievement test is a primary example of an assessment as described in Chapter 4. The purpose of an achievement test is to measure an individual's accomplishment either in a specific unit of instruction or in a more general course of training. The achievement test might be a good predictor of later school grades or professional accomplishment, but this is not its primary purpose. Although it is hoped that achievement at one stage of training will be predictive of later success, it would be unfair to judge achievement tests on this basis alone. If predictions of behavior were the standard for achievement tests, it would be very difficult to decide which later behaviors to predict and even more difficult to measure them. For example, what future behavior should be predicted by course grades in ancient history? The individual might master the course content quite well yet take no further courses in history nor enter an occupation for which knowledge of ancient history is an obvious prerequisite.

The achievement test is valid if it faithfully represents the important behaviors in a performance situation. This is referred to by some people as "circular validity" or "intrinsic validity." It was said previously that the validity of achievement tests and assessments generally is dependent on content representativeness. Validity in this sense means that the achievement test should concern a broad sample of the information and problems that are thought to be important in a course of training.

Construction of Achievement Tests. The primary steps in constructing an achievement test are those which were outlined in Chapter 8 in the section entitled "Construction of Assessments." Preparatory to the construction of the test, an outline should be made of the skills which the particular training course is intended to teach. Because of the funds and personnel that are available for constructing most large-scale achievement tests, the outline can usually be spelled out in more detail than is possible in the individual teacher-made course examination. The outline should be carefully compared with the texts, drills, and lecture content of the training course. If the achievement test is to be used widely in different schools, the outline should be discussed with numerous teachers. Some of the major headings in an outline of reading skills are as follows:

1. *Perception of written material.* The child must first be able to see the individual letters and words before he can read adequately. It is also necessary for the child to have a proper balance of eye muscles and to coordinate eye movements in reading.

2. *Vocabulary.* The next essential is for the child to have a knowledge of the words that appear in written material at his level of schooling.

3. *Reading speed.* Although, within limits, reading speed is not as important as the understanding of what is read, the very slow reader is handicapped in his school work.

4. *Retention.* Before any further understanding is possible, the child must be able to remember some of the factual content of what he reads.

5. *Critical reaction.* At the highest level of reading accomplishment, the child should be able to synthesize what he reads with past knowledge, analyze the implications of what is read, and react critically to the material.

6. *Auxiliary skills.* These include a familiarity with tables of contents, the meaning of footnotes and references, acquaintance with library filing systems, and a familiarity with dictionaries and reference sources.

Each major heading in the outline should be filled out in much more detail than the example above (see **5**, chap. 7; **15**, pp. 272–273 for more complete outlines of reading skills).

After the outline is completed, the next step is to compose test items for each part of the outline. Considerable material has been written on the composition of achievement test items (see **2**; **15**, chap. 4; **17**). Some of the principal points to consider were outlined in Chapter 8. After a large collection of items (an item pool) has been made, a number of judges should be used to estimate the clarity, relevance, importance, and representativeness of the items for the particular achievement area. In Chapter 8, we described some methods of item analysis which are useful in selecting those items from an item pool which will produce a better achievement test.

The Content of Achievement Tests. Because nearly all standard achievement tests are "objective" examinations which employ some variant of the multiple choice type of item, they have been criticized as measuring only the memory for simple factual details. Most teachers agree that the memory for details is not the important thing to be gained from a unit of instruction. Here in this book, for example, the reader will soon forget the names of many of the tests, the specific formulas, and the numerous statistical results which are cited. But it is hoped that the total impact of the book will be such as to provide the reader with a set of principles, a logical scheme, and a way of thinking about human measurement which will not fade with time.

The content of multiple choice tests was discussed in Chapter 8, the viewpoint expressed there being that objective tests often do focus on simple factual details but that this need not be the case. There is considerable empirical evidence and practical experience to show that carefully constructed multiple choice tests can adequately measure the understanding of complex principles, the ability to draw conclusions, and the ability to make inferences from one set of facts to another. The standardized achievement tests often embody more *important* content than the teacher's own multiple choice examinations. This is because there are more funds, facilities, and expert services available for the construction of standardized achievement tests. Because the standardized achievement tests successfully use multiple choice items, teachers should not assume that all examinations should be of that kind. The poorly constructed multiple choice test is often less effective than an essay examination. Specific examples will be shown later in the chapter of how achievement tests can adequately measure the high-level understanding of different subject matters.

Achievement Test Scores. The most popular scoring procedure is the straight multiple choice form in which the question, or *stem,* is supplied with anywhere from two to more than a dozen alternatives, one of which is designated the "correct" response. A number of variants of the multiple choice form are useful in special circumstances. One of these is the matching type of item, in which each of a number of names, for example, is matched with one of a number of accomplishments or events. A typical item is as follows:

Columbus	_____	*a.* invented the compass
Balboa	_____	*b.* sailed around the world
Magellan	_____	*c.* discovered Australia
		d. discovered America
		e. invented the steamship
		f. discovered the Pacific Ocean

The matching question usually has more names or terms than the three in the example above. An important rule is that there should be considerably more events or definitions than persons or terms. Otherwise, "guessing" plays an important part in the responses. The matching question is most useful when there are many names, definitions, and specific facts to be tested. In such cases, it provides a handy way of condensing a number of separate questions into one large item.

Another variant of the multiple choice type of item is to require the subject to rank the alternatives from most to least correct. In many tests, the "correct" alternative is not completely correct and the "incorrect" alternatives are not equally incorrect. It is reasonable then to think that more information could be obtained from each question by having all of the alternatives ranked. Although there is something to say for this procedure, it offers a number of drawbacks. Principally, it is difficult to construct alternatives for an item in such a manner that they can be logically ordered from most to least correct. In many questions, the alternatives are either true or false, and there is little basis for choosing among the false alternatives. Also, items of this kind take much more time to administer, and, consequently, the range of items that can be used is severely restricted if, say, only an hour is available for the test. In addition, such items are difficult and time consuming to score.

Another variant of the multiple choice item is to have the subject mark all of the alternatives which he is sure are incorrect. Like the rank-ordering of alternatives this should logically provide more information about the subject's knowledge than the straight multiple choice item. The subject's score consists of the number of incorrect alternatives marked as incorrect. The major problem with this type of item is that it introduces personality factors to an unknown extent. Some people are more willing to take chances than others and consequently to gamble on more of the incorrect alternatives. Such predispositions will influence test scores, making them partly measures of personality characteristics, which should logically not enter into achievement tests.

Although it is important to continue exploring new types of test items, the weight of the argument is in favor of the straight multiple choice form for most purposes. In most cases, it allows the presentation of more items in a shorter time, is the easiest type of item for subjects to understand, and is easier to construct and score. It is usually found that more complex scoring systems give results which correlate very highly with the straight multiple choice form.

Achievement Test Norms. Because the purpose of most achievement tests is to compare either a pupil or a unit of instruction with more general educational standards, it is important to have truly representative norms. The norms available for many of the standard achievement tests are generally superior to those used with other kinds of tests. In many ways, the task of obtaining norms is simpler with achievement tests than with predictor tests. The normative population to be used with predictor tests is sometimes difficult to define. The normative populations for achievement tests are more easily specified, e.g., all of the sixth-grade students in the United States. Also, because the normative population is contained in specific training programs, subjects are more available for testing, and procedures of sampling can be more effectively applied.

The question often arises as to whether national norms or more local norms should be employed with achievement tests. This depends on how the tests are used. If, for example, achievement test scores are being used to select students for advanced classes in a particular city, it would be wiser to use local norms. If the purpose is to compare the amounts and kinds of training in different schools across the country, national norms should be used.

Classifications of Achievement Tests. There are a number of different ways of classifying achievement tests in terms of their uses. A primary distinction is made between tests designed to measure one subject only, such as the knowledge of geography, and batteries designed to cover a broad range of subject matters, which might include a geography subtest along with subtests for literature, history, mathematics, and other subjects. They will be referred to respectively as *unisubject* and *multisubject* achievement tests. The distinction is a matter of degree because some of the unisubject tests, particularly those for language and mathematical skills, divide the subject matter into a number of separately tested parts.

A distinction is often made between *survey* achievement tests and *diagnostic* tests. The survey tests are meant to measure *how much* a person knows. The diagnostic tests are meant to tell *why* a person is or is not achieving adequately. Survey tests are the typical kind used to measure the mastery of different subject matters. Diagnostic tests are used primarily in guidance and remedial work to offer clues as to why children are doing poorly in certain subject matters. The distinction between survey and diagnostic tests is also a matter of degree. There is an unfortunate tendency for people to refer to all unisubject tests that measure a number of components as diagnostic tests. Examples of more truly diagnostic tests will be discussed in the coming sections.

USES FOR ACHIEVEMENT TESTS

Assignment of Grades. Teacher-made tests are used more often than standardized achievement tests for the assignment of course grades in elementary school, high school, and college. The advantage for the teacher-made test is that it is tailored to the particular unit of instruction. It is also the teacher's responsibility to decide what grades should be given. The use of achievement tests for the assignment of grades would, in many cases, be unfair because of the differences in content of courses bearing the same name. In order to keep a semblance of order in the recording of school progress, it is essential that courses with similar names have at least a core of knowledge in common. For example, if an individual receives a passing grade in *plane geometry*, it is expected that he has a familiarity with certain facts and concepts. However, it is reasonable to expect the instructor to emphasize certain topics more than others and to include material that another instructor might not discuss. Therefore, the standardized achievement test used for the assignment of school grades might penalize particular students to some extent.

Standardized achievement tests are more often used to assign course grades in special school programs, in government, military, and industrial training. For example, achievement tests are frequently used in assigning grades to participants in technical training schools in the Armed Forces. It is sensible to use achievement tests to assign grades in special school programs for a number of reasons. The course content is usually more standardized than that in, say, most colleges. For example, in a course on the "maintenance of small arms" there are rather definite rules to be taught. It is expected that all instructors will teach very much the same information, and it is not uncommon for all instructors to use a standard teaching syllabus to insure uniformity of instruction. The course content of many special training programs remains relatively fixed over moderate periods of time. Therefore, a standard achievement test may be usable for the assignment of course grades over a period of several years or more with only minor revisions in test content. In many special training programs, the instructor is not sufficiently trained in pedagogic techniques to assign course grades effectively. Although the instructor may be a very good salesman, infantry sergeant, or machinist and also may be a good teacher, he may have little knowledge of testing procedures and the grading of students. Consequently, it is more meaningful to assign grades on the basis of achievement test scores.

Classification of Individuals. Achievement tests are used more frequently to test the individual's mastery of a whole range of subject matter than to grade his performance in an individual unit of instruction. Multisubject achievement tests are often administered to graduating grammar school students preparatory to entering high school. Although the student may have good marks in individual courses, it is still uncertain what his total educational experience has been. He may have forgotten large amounts of the subject matter, or the particular school may have underemphasized certain subject matters which are necessary in high school. Students who do poorly on parts of the achievement test, in grammar, for example, can then be classified into a group needing special preparatory instruction during the freshman year of high school.

Achievement tests are often used to classify students into special courses or curricula within grammar school, high school, or college. There is a growing trend toward tailoring instruction to the individual. A widely used procedure is to assign students to one of several sections on the basis of over-all progress shown either by previous course grades or by achievement tests. An even more logical method of classification, if resources permit, is to gear the instruction not only to the student's over-all level of achievement but to his own strong and weak points as well. One of the multisubject achievement tests is useful for that purpose.

Counseling and Remedial Training. Achievement tests are useful to the school psychologist and the clinical psychologist in understanding the school difficulties of particular children. The practice in some schools of promoting children from one grade to the next even if they do very poorly often permits the child with little aptitude for school work to get far over his head in difficult subject matters. This will frustrate him as well as lower the morale of teachers and students. Achievement tests can be used to indicate the generally low level of such a student's school progress, and this in turn can suggest placement of the student in a training program more suited to his ability.

The diagnostic achievement tests are designed primarily to help in the counseling and remedial training of students who show a difficulty in mastering certain school topics, and particularly to help understand the underlying reasons for reading difficulties. If it is found, for example, that the child understands what he reads but that he reads very slowly, specific remedial training can be undertaken to increase reading speed.

The cause of truancy or poor conduct in the classroom is often indicated by achievement tests. Such disruptive behavior is sometimes related to a low level of achievement. The student takes out his frustration on the teacher and his classmates. A very high score on an achievement test can also be indicative of a student's difficulties in conduct. The very bright student is often bored by the relatively low level of the curriculum and turns to misbehavior or truancy.

Vocational Guidance. Achievement tests in combination with course grades are useful in helping the student to choose future programs of school work or vocational training. They are particularly useful in helping students to decide whether or not to go on from high school to college, and if so, which kind of college training to undertake. If, for example, the student is considering premedical training in college, he should show achievement in biology, science, and have a generally high level of accomplishment. There are exceptions of course—the student who does poorly in high school but goes on to high accomplishment in college. But the achievement test scores at least indicate the amount of improvement the student will need to show in order to reach minimum standards for subsequent schooling.

Two students with the same over-all level of accomplishment at the end of high school may have different strong and weak points in particular subjects. The measurement of such differential achievement with multi-subject tests provides a basis for deciding about careers and future training.

Achievement tests used in vocational guidance must be evaluated as predictors, not as assessments. Test scores are used essentially to forecast how well an individual is likely to perform later. Using achievement tests in vocational guidance is relatively safe when the question concerns going on from high school to college or from college to graduate work. For example, the individual who performs poorly in the language arts in college is not likely to meet with success in the graduate school specialties of journalism and English. It is less safe to use achievement test scores to advise students to go into vocations such as sales work, carpentry, and forestry. If the predictive validity of the achievement test is not known for the vocations in question, the vocational guidance is as good or as bad as the counselor's judgment.

Measuring the Effectiveness of Instructional Techniques. The primary reason that many teachers are unfriendly to standardized achievement tests is that they are viewed as tests of teaching ability. For example, if it is found that the students in a particular school do poorly on the biology section of an achievement test in comparison to the scores made by students in neighboring schools, it suggests that the biology teacher is not doing a good job. There are three major variables contributing to the grades that students make on an achievement test: the initial aptitude of the students, the effectiveness of the training program, and the nature of the test. These three factors should be carefully considered before blame or praise is placed on the teacher alone.

The teacher cannot bring students to high achievement if they are lacking in initial aptitude. Large differences are found in the achievement test scores of children in different schools, varying with geographic region, ethnic background, and socioeconomic status.

It is unfair to use achievement test results to measure the effectiveness of teachers if the test itself is poorly constructed. If the test is poorly standardized or if the content is generally trivial, it is not the teacher's fault that students do poorly.

If the achievement test is well constructed and if account is taken of the over-all level of achievement for a group, the teacher cannot entirely escape the blame for a low level of achievement in a particular subject matter. The low level of achievement may be due in part to crowded classrooms, lack of proper equipment, and to a poorly run school, but it cannot be denied that the teacher's individual effectiveness is also prominently involved.

The practice of using achievement tests to measure the effectiveness of instruction is disturbing to some teachers. They argue that the achievement test puts a "strait jacket" on instructional methods, forcing the teacher to tailor the instruction to the kinds of material in the achievement test. This may discourage the teacher from experimenting with new methods of instruction and with new aspects of the subject matter. It is not unheard of for a teacher to coach students on materials so similar to those in the achievement test that the effectiveness of the measuring instrument is ruined.

Aside from the use of achievement tests to measure the effectiveness of teachers, achievement tests have a real purpose in measuring the effectiveness of different kinds of instruction. For example, the question might arise as to whether or not a film series would help in the instruction of geography. If students who have the film series do better on an achievement test than those who participated in a straight lecture course, this offers one type of evidence in favor of the films. Achievement tests are helpful in determining the effectiveness of many such variants of teaching methods.

Achievement tests are useful in the organization of school curricula. Decisions have to be made about the level at which students can master particular subject matters and the best sequence for presenting different courses. It might be desirable to offer a course in French earlier in training than had previously been the practice. If the students who take the course at an earlier age do about as well on an achievement test or not much worse than the students who take the course later, this suggests that the course could be given earlier in training.

Selection of Individuals. Although the primary purpose of achievement tests is to assess current performance, they are also useful as predictors of future behavior. Achievement tests can be used to select college students, office workers, insurance salesmen, and many others. When achievement tests are used in this way, they stand on new logical grounds. They are then predictors and are as good or as bad as their correlations with measures of future school or vocational success. The achievement test that is a well-constructed instrument for the assessment of performance in a training program may be no good at all as a predictor of future success in particular vocations.

Achievement tests are best for predicting success in vocations which entail activities similar to those in the training programs for which the tests were originally designed. For example, an achievement test of mathematical skills developed for high school students will more likely be better as a predictor of success in college mathematics courses than it will be as a predictor of success in politics. Because most achievement tests concern school subject matter, they are most useful for predicting success in future educational efforts. Achievement test scores of graduating high school students are generally as effective if not more effective than intelligence tests for predicting college grades. When the two kinds of tests are combined with high school grades, good predictive efficiency is usually obtained.

Achievement tests are used prominently in the selection of persons for specific jobs and professions, particularly in the civil service program. A typical predictor battery is that for stenographers, in which the tests consist of achievement in typing, shorthand, and other skills pertinent to office work. Achievement tests have been used in this way to select individuals for a wide variety of jobs.

SURVEY ACHIEVEMENT TESTS

Standard achievement tests are available for many different subject matters, and there are usually competing forms from which to choose. The following sections will consider several examples in each major area of achievement testing. The person who is interested in acquiring achievement tests for particular purposes should consult the reference sources cited in Chapter 18 and should obtain catalogues from the major test publishers listed in Appendix 1.

The multisubject survey tests are generally favored over the separate unisubject tests. That is, rather than choose separately constructed tests for geography, history, biology, and the other subject matters, it is generally better to use a multisubject battery in which the subtests have all been constructed and standardized alike. Some ambiguity in comparing students on different unisubject tests often comes from the different test construction methods used by different commercial firms. An even greater advantage of the multisubject battery is that the norms are usually obtained for all tests on the same subjects.

There are several exceptions to the preference for multisubject batteries over unisubject tests. Several subject matters are sufficiently complicated within themselves to require extensive individual treatment. This is so of mathematics and reading. Each of these is a unisubject domain in name only. There are various functions that need to be tested in each. In order to test the extensive skills within each of these general subject-matter areas, it is necessary to use such a variety of test materials as to make it impractical in most cases to administer them along with tests for geography, biology, and other subject matters. Another instance in which the unisubject test is preferred over the multisubject batteries is in the testing of special skills such as handwriting and musical accomplishment. The testing of these skills usually requires novel testing methods and scoring procedures which are sufficiently different from the typical multiple choice test to require separate treatment.

Survey Reading Tests. Reading is by far the most important skill to be tested in school children. The first several grades are devoted largely to teaching the child how to read. From that point on, school work is almost synonymous with the comprehension of written material. If a child is having difficulty in reading and understanding what is read, it is important to find it out as soon as possible so that remedial instruction can be undertaken. If a school had its choice of only several tests that could be used in a testing program, it would be wise to use, along with one of the better intelligence tests, a comprehensive test of reading skills.

The distinction between diagnostic and survey tests is particularly tenuous in the measurement of reading skills. Almost all of the reading tests measure a number of related functions and, as such, offer some help in diagnosing reading difficulties. The reading tests cited in the coming section entitled "diagnostic tests" are placed there rather than here because they are more specifically designed to offer clues about underlying reasons for reading difficulties.

A typical survey test of reading is the Gates Basic Reading Tests (3). Separate sections are used to measure ability in: (*a*) reading to appreciate general significance; (*b*) reading to predict outcomes of given events; (*c*) reading to understand precise directions; and (*d*) reading to note details. Illustrative items are shown in Figure 12–1. Age and grade norms are available for grades 3½ through 8. All of the parts are timed, the amount of time varying with the grade up to 40 minutes in all. Subtest

FIGURE 12–1. Sample items from the Gates Basic Reading Test, grades 3½ through 8, 1957 edition. (Reproduced by permission of the Bureau of Publications, Teachers College, Columbia University.)

Type GS. Reading to Appreciate General Significance

Smart as horses are, they do not always know what is good for them. They sometimes want to gallop at top speed, but a good rider will never let them do it. A horse running at his top speed is out of control, just as a high-powered car would be. Unless a horse has been trained as a race horse, top-speed running puts great strain on his delicate legs.

Draw a line under the word that tells what kind of running is bad for a horse.

slow   top-speed   easy   controlled   moderate

Type ND. Reading to Note Details

Next morning she awoke and found herself in a beautiful room. The walls were covered with silken curtains. There were two mirrors made of pure silver. The bed was made of ivory. The coverings were made of silk and velvet. By her bed lay a dress and a pair of slippers. The dress was made of silk. The slippers were covered with diamonds.

Where did the girl find herself?

barn   room   garden   store

What were the mirrors made of?

silver   gold   pearl   silk

What were on the slippers?

rubies   pearls   opals   diamonds

reliabilities range from .80 to .96 for different grades. Although separate scores can be obtained from the four subtests, it is better to average them as an over-all measure of reading ability. The correlations among the four subtests are too high to permit the use of profile difference scores. Except for large differences in subtest scores, score differences would be largely due to chance.

Two other widely used survey reading tests are the Nelson-Denny Reading Test: Vocabulary and Paragraph (**12**); and the Cooperative English Test (**19**). Many of the multisubject batteries also include reading subtests.

Survey Batteries for Elementary School. The multisubject batteries find their widest use in the testing of elementary school children. Achievement tests have a special importance there because so much of the child's education lies ahead of him, and it is important to learn his strong and weak points as early as possible. Because of the greater uniformity of subject matter in elementary school, it is easier to compose a comprehensive battery of achievement tests for this level than for higher levels of education.

FIGURE 12–2. Sample items from Metropolitan Achievement Tests, Advanced Battery. (Reproduced by permission of World Book Company.)

Vocabulary

She *replies* means she—1. complains   2. depends   3. fills   4. answers

Arithmetic fundamentals

What per cent of 24 is 9?   _____

Arithmetic problems

Ned bought one-half dozen roses for $1.68. At that price, what did one rose cost?   _____

English: Part II Punctuation and Capitalization

Put in the capital letters and commas, periods, and other punctuation marks that have been left out.

Does Carl want the candy or the fruit he prefers candy but he likes fruit too.

Literature

Friday was a faithful servant of—

1. Tarzan   2. Huckleberry Finn   3. Robinson Crusoe   4. Robin Hood

Social Studies: History and Civics

Western Europe became interested in exploration because—

1. the feudal system disappeared.   2. many schools were opened.
3. of a desire for new trade routes.   4. the Church favored it.

Science

In the lungs, the blood gains a supply of—

1. argon   2. nitrogen   3. carbon dioxide   4. oxygen

A typical series of achievement tests for the elementary level is the Metropolitan Achievement Tests (9). The series includes four separate batteries ranging from Primary I Battery for the first grade to the Advanced Battery for grades 7 and 8. The Primary I Battery includes three reading tests and one numerical test. Each of the three advanced batteries contains ten subtests: reading, vocabulary, arithmetic fundamentals, arithmetic problems, history, geography, English, literature, science, and spelling. The forms are intended to be power tests (see Figure 12–2 for illustrative items). A battery can be given in from one to four hours. Either four or five equivalent forms are available for each battery. Split-half reliabilities for the subtests range from .80 to .97 for different batteries. Two other widely used multisubject batteries are the Stanford Achievement Tests (**10**) and the California Achievement Tests (**16**).

High School Achievement Tests. Comprehensive achievement test batteries for high school are more difficult to construct than are those for elementary school. Whereas all students tend to study many of the same topics in elementary school, they often diverge widely in their elective topics in high school. Also, the curriculum spreads out to numerous topics such as mental hygiene and civics, which are usually not offered in elementary school. Consequently, the available achievement test batteries tend to capitalize on the core subject matters that underlie high school training, particularly literature, mathematics, general science, and some aspects of social science. The scores that a student makes on high school achievement batteries should be considered in the light of the special course of study which he has undertaken and the grades made in particular units of instruction.

A typical high school achievement battery is the Cooperative General Achievement Tests (**20**). The three subtests concern broad knowledge of the social sciences, mathematics, and natural science. Each subtest is divided into two parts, the first part being concerned with a knowledge

FIGURE 12–3. Sample items from the Cooperative General Achievement Tests. (Reproduced by permission of the Educational Testing Service.)

Social Studies: Terms and Concepts

Most children in the United States attend schools that are supported primarily by—
    1. contributions from churches.
    2. the federal government.
    3. private endowments.
    4. local and state taxation.
    5. tuition paid by pupils.

A reciprocal trade tariff is one in which—
    1. both political parties compromise.
    2. the rates are low.
    3. exclusion of foreign goods is sought.
    4. all sections of the nation benefit nearly equally.
    5. two nations modify their rates on each other's goods.

A typical daily newspaper derives the largest part of its income from—
    1. subscriptions and newspaper sales.
    2. advertising by commercial establishments.
    3. payment for space by news-gathering agencies.
    4. want ads.
    5. donations by political parties, labor unions, etc.

EXAMPLE. STATEMENT: "We need to save time in getting there, so we'd better go by plane."

PROPOSED ASSUMPTIONS:

1. Going by plane will take less time than going by some other means of transportation. (It is assumed in the statement that greater speed of a plane over other means of transportation will enable the group to get to their destination in less time.) ....

2. It is possible to make plane connections to our destination. (This is necessarily assumed in the statement, since, in order to save time by plane, it must be possible to go by plane.) ....

3. Travel by plane is more convenient than travel by train. (This assumption is not made in the statement—the statement has to do with saving time, and says nothing about convenience or about any other specific mode of travel.) ....

EXAMPLE. Some holidays are rainy. All rainy days are boring. Therefore—

1. No clear days are boring. (The conclusion does not follow, as you cannot tell from these statements whether or not clear days are boring and some may be.) ....

2. Some holidays are boring. (The conclusion necessarily follows from the statements, since, according to them, the rainy holidays must be boring.) ....

3. Some holidays are not boring. (The conclusion does not follow from the statements even though you may know that some holidays are very pleasant.) ....

EXAMPLE. Should all young men go to college?

1. Yes; college provides an opportunity for them to learn school songs and cheers. (This would be a silly reason for spending years of one's life in college.)

2. No; a large per cent of young men do not have enough ability or interest to derive any benefit from college training. (If this is true, as the directions require us to assume, it is a weighty argument against all young men going to college.)

3. No; excessive studying permanently warps an individual's personality. (This argument, although of great general importance when accepted as true, is not directly related to the question, because attendance at college does not necessarily require excessive studying.) ....

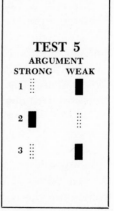

TEST 2
ASSUMPTION
MADE   NOT MADE

TEST 3
CONCLUSION
FOL-LOWS   DOES NOT FOLLOW

TEST 5
ARGUMENT
STRONG   WEAK

* The explanations in parentheses do not appear in the items of the test proper.

of terms and concepts and the second part with comprehension and interpretation (see Figure 12–3 for illustrative items). Other high school achievement batteries are the Iowa Tests of Educational Development (11), The Essential High School Content Battery (8), and the California Achievement Tests (16).

Achievement Tests for Higher Education. Considerable ingenuity in test construction is required to measure the products of college training, graduate study, and professional work. Students can take such different sets of courses that there is little overlap in training. Therefore, achievement tests for higher education are best aimed at particular lines of specialization, such as engineering. It is more hazardous to employ survey batteries that are meant to compare all students in their general college progress. A systematic battery for the diverse courses that students can take would be a very large-scale instrument. Instead of having only one subtest for "science" it would be necessary to have separate subtests for physics, chemistry, and biology. Other related subjects which can be lumped together at lower levels of training should be tested separately at the higher education level.

One of the most widely used achievement test batteries for the college level is the Graduate Record Examination (Educational Testing Service). The battery includes tests of verbal and mathematical ability and subject-matter tests for physics, chemistry, biology, social studies, literature, and fine arts. The separate tests are sufficiently long and well standardized to provide reliable scores. The battery is usually administered at the end of college training. It has proved useful in guidance of college students, selection of graduate students, and research on college curricula.

In addition to their use for the measurement of progress in college programs, achievement tests can be used to test some of the over-all results of higher education. Instruments of this kind are usually referred to as tests of critical thinking. A typical example is the Watson-Glaser Critical Thinking Appraisal (18). The five parts of the test are concerned with the ability to recognize assumptions, make inferences, deduce consequences, interpret statements, and evaluate arguments (see Figure 12–4 for illustrative items). All of the materials are presented as multiple choice items. The test illustrates the measurement of complex thought processes with objective items.

DIAGNOSTIC ACHIEVEMENT TESTS

As was said previously, whether or not an achievement test is "diagnostic" is a matter of degree. Some achievement tests make particular efforts to measure the constituent skills involved in a subject-matter area, and these more rightly earn the name of diagnostic tests.

Diagnostic Reading Tests. Diagnostic tests have assumed their most important place in the measurement of reading skills. This is because reading is a very important part of school achievement and because the attributes which underlie reading skill are complex. A typical diagnostic reading measure is the Iowa Silent Reading Tests (**6, 7**). The series includes an elementary battery for grades 4 to 8 and an advanced battery for high school and college. The advanced battery includes the following subtests:

Test 1. Rate of reading and comprehension of prose

Test 2. Directed reading of prose to answer particular factual questions

Test 3. Poetry comprehension

Test 4. Vocabulary in different content areas

Test 5. Sentence meaning

Test 6. Paragraph comprehension

Test 7. Location of information using an index

Another approach to the measurement of reading skills is through the use of standard oral passages. The child is asked to read aloud a series of graded passages. The Standardized Oral Reading Paragraphs is a form which has been widely used (**4**). While the pupil reads each passage, the examiner uses a standard code to indicate the number and kinds of mistakes which are made. The examiner looks for mistakes like the following:

1. Mispronounced words

2. Mispronounced vowels

3. Repetitions: reading the same word or phrase over before going on

4. Omissions: leaving out a word or phrase

5. Substitutions: saying a different word from that in the passage

6. Insertions: adding words

7. Reversals, such as saying "no" when the word is "on"

In addition to the noting of various kinds of mistakes, the examiner has an opportunity to observe the child while reading. This often provides some clues about reading difficulties, such as stuttering, extreme shyness, and visual or auditory defects.

Diagnostic Tests of Mathematical Skills. Mathematics is second to reading as an area in which diagnostic tests are most needed. A widely used battery is the Compass Diagnostic Tests in Arithmetic (**14**), comprising a series of group tests suitable for grades 2 through 8. Addition, subtraction, multiplication, and division are broken into a number of underlying skills, and each is tested separately. The test might show, for example, that a particular child habitually misplaces the decimal point in long division, has difficulty in carrying figures from one column of addition to another, and fails to line up properly the steps in multiplication.

Appraisal of Diagnostic Achievement Tests. There is undoubtedly a great need for diagnostic tests to help understand particular weaknesses in school achievement. In order to have an adequate diagnostic test it is essential, among other things, to obtain reliable score profiles. The measurement of differential achievement is the object of the diagnostic battery. Unfortunately many of the diagnostic batteries employ subtests which have low reliabilities and high correlations with one another. Consequently, score differences within the batteries are unreliable. In order to have the broad coverage of skills that is necessary for diagnostic purposes and in order to make each subtest long enough to be individually reliable, a thorough diagnostic test must necessarily be a long, time-consuming measure to apply.

REFERENCES

1. Adkins, D., et al. *Construction and analysis of achievement tests.* Washington: GPO, 1947.
2. Bean, K. L. *Construction of educational and personnel tests.* New York: McGraw-Hill, 1953.
3. Gates, A. I. *Gates Basic Reading Tests: Manual of Directions.* New York: Teachers College, Bur. Publ., 1943.
4. Gray, W. S. *Standardized Oral Reading Paragraphs: Manual.* Bloomington, Ill.: Public School, 1915.
5. Greene, E. B. *Measurements of human behavior.* (Rev. ed.) New York: Odyssey, 1952.
6. Greene, H. A., et al. *Iowa Silent Reading Tests. New Edition* (Rev.) *Advanced Test: Manual of Directions.* Yonkers, N.Y.: World, 1943.
7. Greene, H. A., and Kelley, V. H. *Iowa Silent Reading Tests. New Edition* (Rev.) *Elementary Test: Manual of Directions.* Yonkers, N.Y.: World, 1943.
8. Harry, D. P., and Durost, W. N. *Essential High School Content Battery: Manual of Directions.* Yonkers, N.Y.: World, 1951.
9. Hildreth, G., et al. *Metropolitan Achievement Tests: Manual for Interpretation.* Yonkers, N.Y.: World, 1948.
10. Kelley, T. L., et al. *Stanford Achievement Test: Manuals for Primary, Elementary, Intermediate, and Advanced Batteries.* Yonkers, N.Y.: World, 1953.
11. Lindquist, E. F. *Iowa Tests of Educational Development: General Manual.* Chicago: Science Research, 1948.
12. Nelson, M. J., and Denny, E. C. *Nelson-Denny Reading Test: Vocabulary and Paragraph.* Boston: Houghton Mifflin, 1938.
13. Ross, C. C. *Measurement in today's schools.* (3rd ed.) Englewood Cliffs, N.J.: Prentice-Hall, 1954.
14. Ruch, G. M., et al. *Compass Diagnostic Tests in Arithmetic: Manual.* Chicago: Scott, Foresman, 1925.
15. Thorndike, R. L., and Hagen, E. *Measurement and evaluation in psychology and education.* New York: Wiley, 1955.

16. Tiegs, E. W., et al. *California Achievement Tests: Manual of Directions for Primary, Elementary, Intermediate, and Advanced Batteries.* Los Angeles: Calif. Test Bureau, 1951.

17. Travers, R. M. *How to make achievement tests.* New York: Odyssey, 1950.

18. Watson, G., and Glaser, E. *Watson-Glaser Critical Thinking Appraisal: Manual.* Yonkers, N.Y.: World, 1952.

19. *Cooperative English Test: Manual.* Princeton, N.J.: Coop. Test Div., Educ. Testing Serv., 1953.

20. *Cooperative General Achievement Tests: Manual of Directions.* Princeton, N.J.: Coop. Test Div., Educ. Testing Serv., 1954.

CHAPTER 13

Opinions, Attitudes, and Interests

Democracies stir and change in reaction to what the people think and feel. Politicians avidly inspect the current opinion poll results to learn the public sentiment toward arms reduction, farm subsidies, and tax policies. Commercial concerns spend millions to learn the kinds of household goods which are desired by the average housewife. Teen-age whims make and break entertainers in rapid succession. Prejudice of one group toward another presents a barrier to the democratic ideal and a hundred years of rancor and protest result. What the individual wants to do in life determines in good measure the vocation he enters. As a partial consequence, the nation finds itself with a shortage of teachers, nurses, and engineers and a surplus of farmers, lawyers, and actors. In these and many other ways, opinions, attitudes, and interests are important factors in everyday living.

Opinions, attitudes, and interests are prominent influences in the individual's social adjustment. If the husband likes Beethoven and the wife prefers Sinatra, if one is a Republican and the other a Democrat, if one is prejudiced against Negroes and the other is not, disagreement and hostility are hard to avoid. The individual's family and friends have their own attitudes and opinions, and the choice between conformity and conflict is difficult to make. Personalities can disrupt when interests do not match abilities or when strong attitudes conflict with one another.

The four previous chapters were primarily concerned with human ability, with how much a person knows or how well he can solve problems. This and the following chapters will be primarily concerned with personal reactions, or what are variously called social traits, noncognitive attributes, and habitual performance. These human characteristics are often included in the more general term "personality," but it is helpful to distinguish attitudes, opinions, and interests from the kinds of personality attributes which will be discussed in later chapters.

The devices which are used to study attitudes, opinions, and interests are often referred to as "tests," but they are not tests in the same sense as a vocabulary test or a mechanical comprehension test. In an aptitude test the subject cannot control his score, except to cheat or to make a low score on purpose. The most socially approved behavior is to make the highest score possible, and the individual's ability limits the score which is made. This is not at all the case with most measures of attitudes, opinions, and interests. The measurement devices are more properly referred to as questionnaires or inventories. They are standard procedures for obtaining information from the individual about himself. Most of them are dependent on the individual's knowledge of himself and his willingness to tell what he knows.

The individual knows many things about himself which would be difficult to learn in any way other than asking him directly. However, the individual is not always an accurate observer of his own behavior nor a willing reporter. This is particularly the case when the questions concern potentially embarrassing issues such as sexual adequacy, honesty, and personal courage. Depth psychology has taught us that the individual often hides unpleasant things from himself through the mechanisms of projection, repression, and rationalization. Even if the individual is aware of personal deficiencies, he is likely to hide this information from others. Emotionally laden issues predominate in the personality inventories and cause the subject to "fake" responses rather than give accurate answers. Inventories for opinions, attitudes, and interests are sometimes affected by the individual's need to give socially acceptable responses but not nearly so much so as are the personality inventories. (The problem of "faking" will be discussed at greater length in the next chapter.)

Relationships Among Opinions, Attitudes, and Interests. There are no sharp dividing lines among the three types of instruments to be discussed in this chapter. They are all inventories dependent on the individual's reporting of what he thinks and feels. However, it is necessary to distinguish them as well as possible, because they are constructed and used somewhat differently.

It is easiest to begin by distinguishing interests from opinions and attitudes. Interest inventories are meant to measure what the individual does and does not like to do. A typical interest item is, "Do you like to work out of doors?" to which the subject answers either "yes" or "no." Although interest inventories can be constructed for activities of all kinds, they are primarily concerned with activities that distinguish jobs and professions from one another.

Opinions and attitudes concern how the individual reacts to the people, institutions, and ideas in the world about him. The term "opinions" is used more often to refer to judgments and knowledge, whereas the term "attitudes" is more connotative of feelings and preferences. Opinions are usually more verifiable than attitudes. That is, the opinion "There are more

Protestants than Catholics in the United States" is open to direct inquiry and verification. Using the term "opinion" in the stricter sense to refer to verifiable statements, it is possible to determine whether or not an individual's opinion is true or false. An example of an attitudinal statement is, "I dislike capital punishment." This is a statement of feeling, and it does not make sense to inquire whether it is true or false.

Although it is possible to distinguish opinions and attitudes with extreme examples, the two are usually mixed to some extent in most questionnaire studies. For example, the statement "Negroes have lower intelligence than white people" is open to study and as such is an opinion; but it also relates to how an individual feels about Negroes and is consequently an attitudinal statement as well. Our feelings about most persons and ideas usually influence our judgments to some extent. Because of the overlap between the two kinds of reactions, the term "opinions" is often used to refer to both feelings and judgments, or the term "attitudes" is often used to cover the two.

Aside from the psychological functions that are involved in studies of opinions and attitudes, the terms are usually employed to refer to different kinds of studies. The term "opinions" has become associated with the opinion poll, which involves the sampling of responses from a large and broad cross section of the population. The questions are usually very simple, such as, "Will you vote for Jones or for Smith?" and in most cases require only a "yes" or "no" answer. If two or more questions are employed, they are either unconnected or not connected in a logical manner so that they add together to form a total score. Respondents are interviewed on the street while they wait for the bus, or the housewife answers the questions while warming the baby's bottle.

Attitude-measurement devices are more like laboratory instruments. They often involve complex rating methods, and it is usually necessary to employ a dozen or more items. Consequently, attitude scales are seldom administered in mass to thousands of people, but are more often employed to study particular groups of people. Whereas the separate items in an opinion poll do not necessarily add up to a more general measure, this is the essence of the attitude-measurement techniques. The purpose in the study of attitudes is to locate the individual on a continuum, or *scale*, which ranges from very unfavorable to very favorable in respect to the object being rated.

OPINION POLLS

Opinion polling, like most other things, appears quite simple to the individual who makes his living doing something else. On the surface it seems that all that is necessary is to ask some questions of a large number of persons. In fact, the adequate measurement of opinions is an exacting business; and unless the polling is undertaken with considerable care, the results may be very misleading. Considering the number of ways in which opinion polls can go astray, it is surprising that the polling results have been as accurate as they have during the last thirty years.

The opinion poll is an outgrowth of the "straw vote," whose purpose is to sample voting sentiment before an election. One of the earliest recorded "straw votes" was that of the *Harrisburg Pennsylvanian* in 1824. Reporters went out to inquire whether the citizens in the surrounding region would vote for Henry Clay, Andrew Jackson, John Quincy Adams, or William H. Crawford for President. The straw vote grew steadily as an aspect of journalism and gradually extended to topics other than voting behavior. By the early 1930s a number of magazines, particularly *Literary Digest* and *Woman's Home Companion,* were involved in extensive polling activities.

A now famous mishap focused public interest on opinion polls and pointed out the need for more systematic methods. The *Literary Digest* made a very bad estimate of the voting sentiment in the 1936 presidential election (see 1, chap. 10). The magazine predicted a Landon victory with 370 electoral votes, but Roosevelt won 523 of a possible 531 votes. This calamitous mistake drove the magazine out of business.

A look at how the *Digest* poll operated will point up some lessons about opinion polling. The poll was conducted entirely by mail, with 10 million ballots being sent out for the 1936 election, of which less than 2½ million were returned. The voters who reply in this way are usually a select group, overweighted with persons from the upper-income and upper-educational levels. People who reply to mail questionnaires usually have a more direct interest in the election than do those who fail to reply. In this case it was the upper-income individuals who were protesting against Roosevelt.

Worse than the dependence on mail-in ballots, the *Digest* used very poor sampling procedures. The mailing list was obtained from telephone directories and automobile registrations. The people in 1936 who had telephones and automobiles were, as a group, much higher on the socioeconomic scale than those who did not. At that time the lower socioeconomic group voted heavily Democratic and the higher socioeconomic group voted heavily Republican. The *Digest* predicted that Roosevelt would get only 40.9 per cent of the popular vote, whereas he actually got 60.2 per cent.

The *Literary Digest* fiasco taught pollers a lesson that they will never forget. A careful look at the *Digest* polling results for the years before 1936 would have shown the unrepresentativeness of the results. In the election predictions for the years of 1916, 1920, 1924, and 1928, the polls showed average plurality errors of 20, 21, 12, and 12 per cent respectively (1, p. 180).

The first systematic polling organization in this country began in 1935, when George Gallup formed the American Institute of Public Opinion. Knowing the nature of the *Digest* sample, he was able to predict very closely the amount by which their results would be in error before the ballots were even mailed out. Gallup's organization and others have grown in strength since that time. Other leading polling agencies are the *Fortune* Survey (Elmo Roper), the Crossley Poll, the National Opinion Research Center, and the Office of Public Opinion Research (Princeton University).

During the last twenty years the polling agencies have grown in size and influence and have branched out into many areas besides the prediction of elections. Polling activities increased sharply during the Second World War as a means of keeping a constant ear on public opinion. This provided the government with a considerable amount of information about the sentiment for joining the war, reaction to price controls, faith in our allies, and many other pertinent issues.

TABLE 13–1. PREDICTIONS OF VOTING PERCENTAGES FOR WINNING CANDIDATES COMPARED WITH THE NATIONAL VOTE

(Adapted from Albig, 1, p. 212)

Poll	Election				
	1936 * (Roosevelt)	1940 * (Roosevelt)	1944 † (Roosevelt)	1948 † (Truman)	1952 ‡ (Eisenhower)
Literary Digest	40.9	...	...	...	...
Fortune (Roper)	61.7	55.2	53.6	41.5	57.0
American Institute of Public Opinion (Gallup)	53.8	52.0	51.5	47.3	54.0
Crossley Poll	53.8	52.9	52.0	47.3	52.8
National vote	60.2	54.7	53.8	52.3	55.3

* Percentages of total vote including that for minor candidates.
† Percentages of two-party vote only.
‡ Percentages of two-party vote with proportional division of "undecided" votes.

Market research is the major activity of polling agencies today. Commercial firms spend millions of dollars to learn what the public thinks about new products and what type of person is most likely to buy an article. Special polls such as Hooper, Nielsen, and Trendex report the audience reaction to radio and TV programs, and the results have a tremendous influence on the pattern of entertainment in America. Opinion polling has also become a new type of journalism. Polls are conducted solely to stir the public interest, using questions like, "Should the wife or the husband manage the family finances?" and "Would you vote for a woman President?" Poll results now appear regularly in hundreds of American newspapers. The election predictions have remained the showcase of opinion polling, and the predictions have increased in accuracy (see Table 13–1 for some election predictions).

Population Sampling for Opinion Polls. The most accurate way to determine public opinion is to ask questions of every individual in the population. A complete census of this kind is extremely laborious and expensive. The 1940 United States government census cost $50,000,000, and more recent census studies were even more expensive. Consequently, it is necessary to deal with samples of the population as a way of estimating how the total public reacts to an issue.

The results of an opinion poll based on a sample of the population are useful only to the extent that they closely resemble the results that would be obtained from the whole population in question. This will be the case when the sampling is *precise* and *accurate,* in the senses in which the terms will be used here. A sampling procedure is accurate if it is unbiased; i.e., if the sample is not overbalanced with persons of one kind or another. If 20 per cent of the individuals in the nation hold an opinion, the results of an accurate sampling procedure will, as the number of individuals polled grows larger and larger, approach the 20 per cent figure. An example of a biased, or inaccurate, sampling procedure was given on the previous pages in respect to the 1936 election predictions by the *Literary Digest.* If they had gathered larger and larger numbers of persons from telephone directories and automobile registrations, they would still have ended up with the wrong prediction.

The precision of a sample is determined directly by the number of persons sampled. If the sampling procedure is accurate, the true population results will be approximated more and more closely as the number of individuals in the sample is increased. Statistical formulas can be used to determine the likelihood that the population results will differ from the sample results by particular amounts (the formulas are discussed in Appendix 6). For example, if in an unbiased (accurate) sample of 1,000 persons, 55 per cent say that they would vote for candidate A, the odds are less than 1 in 1,000 that fewer than 50 per cent of the entire population would, if polled, say that they would vote for A. If we could estimate things in our daily life, such as whether or not it will rain tomorrow, with odds of only 1 in 1,000 of being wrong, we would feel very comfortable in making decisions.

The cost of polling tends to go up arithmetically with the number sampled. That is, if it costs $2,000 to poll 400 people, it will cost about $4,000 to poll 800 people. The precision of the sample increases in proportion to the square root of the number of persons polled. That is, it takes a sample of 1,600 persons to double the precision of a 400-person sample. There is a point of diminishing returns, where the increasing precision becomes unimportant in comparison to the increasing cost. This is why most large-scale polls use samples that generally range between 3,000 and 5,000 persons. With sample sizes this large, the effect of imprecision alone is not likely to make the results different by more than a percentage point or two from the actual population values.

The erroneous results sometimes obtained in opinion polls are seldom due to lack of precision (sample size). *Literary Digest* in the election of 1936 received over 2 million straw votes. Precision is a necessary starting point for an adequate sample, and except for a few studies which are conducted on less than 100 persons, most polling results have high precision. But even if the sample is highly precise, the sample may be biased and provide misleading results.

Sampling Techniques. Sampling procedures were discussed briefly in Chapter 3 in regard to the gathering of testing norms. Here the subject will be treated in more detail because of the direct importance of sampling techniques for opinion polls (see 20 for a thorough discussion of sampling methods). The population to be sampled in opinion polls may be, as the term is popularly intended, the entire adult United States citizenry, or it may be limited to the population of a certain state or locality. Sometimes the population being sampled consists of all the members of a particular group, such as all of the members of a particular labor union, or all of the Catholics in the United States.

The most obvious and in many ways the ideal method of sampling is to draw a number of persons completely at random from the population. If, for example, a sample of 1,000 persons from a labor union is being studied, the individuals could be randomly chosen from union rolls. (Tables of random numbers which can be found in many statistics books are useful for this purpose.) *Random sampling* is a completely accurate, or unbiased, procedure.

If there are obvious subgroups in the population such as plumbers, carpenters, and machinists, there is a way of improving the random sample. This can be done by ensuring that the subgroups appear in the sample in proportion to their numbers in the population. That is, if 20 per cent of the union members are plumbers, it should be ensured that 20 per cent of the sample is composed of plumbers. Each of the subgroups —plumbers, carpenters, and so on—is referred to as a *stratum*. Ideally the proper number of persons should be chosen randomly within the stratum. That is, in the example above, the specified number of plumbers could be randomly drawn from lists of plumbers only. A sample obtained in this way is called a *stratified-random* sample.

The random and the stratified-random are the most accurate types of sampling available for general use. However, they are too expensive to undertake in many situations, particularly in national polling. A satisfactory approximation can be obtained by an *area sample*. In this case, dwellings are sampled instead of persons. A city can be laid out into a large number of square areas. A number of the areas can be drawn at random, and a number of addresses can be randomly chosen within each area. Opinion pollers can then contact as many designated persons as can be found and will answer the questions. The area sample is ideal for measuring the opinions of the individuals in one city. If the sample is to represent a regional or national population, there is the additional chore of choosing representative towns, cities, and rural areas to study.

Even the area sample is too difficult to obtain in many studies, particularly in the weekly polls on current issues. It is necessary to resort instead to what is called a *quota sample*. The quota sample makes no effort to select people randomly. Instead, persons are deliberately chosen because of their individual characteristics. The effort in the quota sample is to construct a miniature of the entire population in terms of known demographic characteristics. The characteristics which are most often controlled are geographic region, race, urban-rural, age, sex, and income. The individual interviewer, located in, say, Memphis, Tennessee, is told the number of people that he should poll in each of the above categories. He must, for example, ensure that about 10 per cent of his sample is Negro and the remainder white, that 30 per cent of the subjects are from rural districts, that half are above forty years of age, and so on for the other demographic characteristics. Little effort is made to balance out the cross categorizations of persons, so as to ensure that half of the urban subjects are women, and so on for more complex combinations. Some of the categorizations depend on the interviewer's judgment to an extent. Even though the distributions of demographic characteristics for the individual interviewer may only roughly match the percentages of such persons in the United States population, these inconsistencies tend to average out as the results are combined for many different interviewers.

Spot-check Samples. In many studies it is desirable to get an indication of national opinion without going to the time and expense of a large-scale national poll. Sometimes used for this purpose are small local samples, which are selected in such a way as to share approximately the same demographic characteristics as the total population except for the restriction on geographic region. Cantril (4, chap. 12) reports a series of studies in which the results from small local samples are compared with national polls. For example, in one study the local sample consisted of 264 persons all of whom were obtained within 40 miles of Princeton University. The interviewers were instructed to choose persons in the upper-, middle-, and lower-income brackets in the ratios 1:4:5. No systematic effort was made to balance other demographic characteristics. The same questions that were asked of the local sample were incorporated in a large-scale national poll. Very similar results were obtained from the local sample and the national poll (see Table 13–2 for illustrative results from one of the questions). However, as Cantril warns, the representativeness of results from small local samples depends very much on the questions which are asked. If the questions are related to distinctly local issues and feelings, the results are likely to be quite misleading. Such would be the case if opinions about segregation are sampled in Mississippi only or if opinions about international affairs are sampled from persons in Wisconsin only.

TABLE 13–2. COMPARISON OF THE RESULTS OBTAINED FROM AN OPINION QUESTION ADMINISTERED TO A SMALL LOCAL SAMPLE AND TO A LARGE NATIONAL SAMPLE

(Adapted from Cantril, 4, p. 158)

Question: If President Roosevelt made a radio talk explaining that it would be necessary to ration gasoline to reduce everybody's driving by as much as one-third from what is being driven now in order to save rubber, would you be willing to see this done?

Small New Jersey sample, per cent		National poll, per cent	
Yes	88	Yes	87
No	8	No	8
Qualified		Qualified	
answer	4	answer	1
No opinion	0	No opinion	4

Opinion Panels. One of the larger expenses in opinion polling is the gathering of a new sample of persons for each questionnaire which is used. A practice which has developed in recent years is that of forming a *panel,* a representative sample of persons who are periodically interviewed or mailed questionnaires. There are some distinct practical advantages to using a panel and also some likely risks. Once the panel is formed, the gathering of opinions is much less expensive than if new subjects have to be obtained for each study. Because the panel will be used over and over, it is not unduly expensive to obtain a more representative (accurate) sample than is generally possible otherwise. Although it is difficult to handle opinion studies by mail the first time individuals participate, the members of a panel soon learn enough about the use of questionnaires so that studies can be handled entirely by mail.

There is a great saving in the use of this method over the use of many personal interviewers.

The principal danger in using a panel is that the continued experience with questionnaires is likely to change people's viewpoints or at least change what they say about their viewpoints. This is more likely to happen when the majority of the questions are on closely related topics, and particularly when the questions concern the knowledge of issues. For example, if a series of studies is made on popular opinions about health, the panel members are likely to think more about health problems than formerly, read material relating to health issues, and be more aware of health information in the mass media of communications. Consequently, the panel members will tend to become more knowledgeable than the average person and perhaps also will change their feelings about many of the issues. Although the panel may have originally been a representative sample of persons, the group can become unrepresentative through the very act of participating in a series of studies.

Not a great deal is known at the present time about how panels change over time. The practical advantages of using a panel merit more research on this problem. It is safer to use a panel when successive questionnaires concern relatively unrelated topics. Also, it is good to retire periodically some of the panel members and sample new persons to replace them. In this way there is a gradual turnover in panel membership and, consequently, less likelihood of building up an unrepresentative sample of respondents.

PRINCIPLES OF OPINION POLLING

Even if the requirements of an accurate and precise sample are met, there are still many ways in which opinion polls can go wrong. Careful attention must be paid to the wording of questions, the way in which opinions are obtained, and the biases of the interviewer.

Interviewer Bias. The interviewer is supposedly an impartial recorder of opinions who should have no influence on the responses which are obtained. A series of studies (see **4**, chap. 8) shows that this is far from the case. It has been found that interviewers who hold a particular opinion themselves tend to find more members of the general public with the same opinion. In one study the following question was asked of interviewers (**4**, p. 108):

"Which of these two things do you think is more important for the United States to try to do—

    To keep out of war ourselves, or

    To help England win, even at the risk of getting into war ourselves?"

After the interviewers' own opinions were obtained, the interviewers asked the same question of a national sample. Comparisons were then made of the results obtained by interviewers favoring keeping out of the war and favoring helping England. The results are shown in Table 13–3.

TABLE 13–3. COMPARISON OF INTERVIEWERS' AND RESPONDENTS' OPINIONS ON THE SAME QUESTION

(Adapted from Cantril, 4, p. 109)

Interviewer favored	Opinions of respondents reported by interviewer	Per cent
Helping England	Favored helping England	60
	Favored keeping out	40
Keeping out	Favored helping England	44
	Favored keeping out	56

There is a striking difference in the responses obtained by the two groups of interviewers, showing that interviewers themselves affect the responses obtained from the public. A breakdown of the differences in terms of size of city showed that the largest bias occurred in small towns and in rural areas. No difference between the two groups of interviewers occurred in cities with over 100,000 persons. Because interviewers in small towns often know many of the inhabitants, it is likely that they tend to pick respondents who hold opinions similar to their own. Another possibility is that the townspeople know the interviewer and his general opinions and that they give similar opinions in order to please the interviewer. Interviewers with different opinions on unions, political candidates, and other topics tend to get different responses in polling.

Whatever the subtle factors working in the relationship between the interviewer's opinions and the responses which he obtains, this form of bias should be controlled as much as possible. Knowing that bias of this kind occurs more strongly in small towns, it is wise to use an outsider to sample opinions rather than a local interviewer. Also, interviewers should be trained to discount their own opinions in the sampling and interviewing of subjects in so far as that is possible. One interesting control is that used by Gallup in the polling of election sentiment. He employs half Republican and half Democratic interviewers to help balance out the effect of the interviewers' own opinions.

The type of person the interviewer is can bias responses as much as the opinions which he holds. This occurs most prominently when the interviewer is of a different race or ethnic group than that of the respondent. Cantril (4, pp. 114–115) reports a study in which Negro and white interviewers asked the same questions of Negro respondents. The results are shown in Table 13–4. The results show that strikingly different opinions are obtained by the two kinds of interviewers. In this case it is reasonable to think that the Negro interviewers were obtaining more frank opinions. It would be expected that large differences in responses like those shown in Table 13–4 would occur only on questions relating to race or ethnic relations.

TABLE 13–4. RESPONSES OBTAINED FROM NEGRO RESPONDENTS BY WHITE AND NEGRO INTERVIEWERS

(Adapted from Cantril, 4, p. 116)

Question	Negro interviewers reported, per cent		White interviewers reported, per cent	
Would Negroes be treated better or worse here if the Japanese conquered the U.S.A.?	Better	9	Better	2
	Same	32	Same	20
	Worse	25	Worse	45
	No opinion	34	No opinion	33
Would Negroes be treated better or worse here if the Nazis conquered the U.S.A.?	Better	3	Better	1
	Same	22	Same	15
	Worse	45	Worse	60
	No opinion	30	No opinion	24
Do you think it is more important to concentrate on beating the Axis, or to make democracy work better here at home?	Beat Axis	39	Beat Axis	62
	Make democracy work	35	Make democracy work	26
	No opinion	26	No opinion	12

Interview Bias. In addition to the bias which is caused by the interviewer, the interview situation itself can distort responses. The interview is a social situation where at least the interviewer is present to hear the respondent's opinions. When interviews are conducted on the street, there may be one or several friends of the respondent who hear the responses. People tend to express more socially acceptable opinions when they are in the presence of other individuals than when the opinion questionnaire is filled out in privacy. Cantril (4, chap. 5) reports a comparison of the results obtained from a secret response with those from an interview. One sample of subjects was asked the questions in the usual interview situation. A matched sample filled out the questionnaire by themselves in their own homes. Results from one question are shown in Table 13–5. The most socially acceptable response at the time was to favor helping England as much as possible, and consequently, the majority of the respondents gave that opinion in the interview situation. When respondents were allowed the privacy of their own homes, they were more inclined to express a less socially acceptable opinion. Interview bias is more likely to occur when there is strong social pressure about an issue. In the example above, the government, most arms of the mass media of communications, as well as many organizations were backing aid for England.

TABLE 13–5. COMPARISON OF RESULTS OBTAINED FROM AN INTERVIEW AND FROM A SECRET RESPONSE TO AN OPINION QUESTION

(Adapted from Cantril, 4, p. 79)

Question: Do you think that the English will try to get us to do most of the fighting for them in this war, or do you think they will do their fair share of the fighting?

	Will do their fair share of the fighting, per cent	Will try to get us to do their fighting, per cent	Don't know, per cent
Interview	57	25	18
Secret response	42	42	16
Difference	15	17	2

No-opinion Respondents. One of the difficulties that besets the opinion poller is that of interpreting the results from respondents who refuse to answer questions, have no opinion, or who say they have not made up their minds. When a sizable number of the respondents, say, over 20 per cent, express no opinion, it makes the over-all results somewhat questionable. The customary procedure is to divide the no-opinion response proportionally to the responses of those persons who do express an opinion. For example, if in an election poll, 45 per cent of the people say they will vote for candidate A, 40 per cent say they will vote for candidate B, and the remaining 15 per cent say that they have not made up their minds, the 15 per cent would be divided proportionally. This would give an estimated vote of 52.9 per cent for A and 47.1 per cent for B. In spite of the arguments that have been made against the proportional division of no-opinion respondents, the method has often worked well in practice.

Wording of Questions. There are usually a number of different ways to ask a question, and the responses will often be affected by the wording which is chosen. The first rule in opinion polling is to use the simplest terms possible. Otherwise, a large segment of the public will not understand the question.

Prestige names and concepts should be avoided in questions unless they are pertinent to the issues. Table 13–6 compares the results which were obtained from asking a question using Roosevelt's name with the same question asked without identifying the issue with Roosevelt (**4**, p. 39). Emotionally toned words such as Communist, radical, and fascist will also affect responses.

TABLE 13–6. COMPARISON OF THE RESPONSES TO AN OPINION QUESTION USING ROOSEVELT'S NAME AND WITHOUT HIS NAME

(Adapted from Cantril, **4**, p. 40)

Question, Form A: It has been said recently that in order to keep the Germans out of North and South America we must prevent them from capturing islands off the west coast of Africa. Do you think that we should try to keep the Germans out of the islands off the west coast of Africa?

Question, Form B: President Roosevelt said recently that in order to keep the Germans out of North and South America we must prevent them from capturing the islands off the west coast of Africa. Do you think that we should try to keep the Germans out of the islands off the west coast of Africa?

	With Roosevelt's name, per cent	Without Roosevelt's name, per cent
Yes	56	50
No	24	21
No opinion	20	29

Care must be taken not to word a question in such a way that several different interpretations are possible. Respondents (**4**, p. 6) were asked the question "If the German Army overthrew Hitler and then offered to stop the war and discuss peace terms with the Allies, would you favor or oppose accepting the offer of the German Army?" A further inquiry into how people interpreted the question showed that the meaning varied widely for different individuals. Some persons even thought they were being asked whether or not they were in favor of Hitler being overthrown.

Summary of Principles. The previous sections have discussed only the most prominent ways in which opinion polls can go wrong (for more detailed discussions, see **1** and **4**). The intention here is not to cast doubt on all opinion polling. Much of the research has been of a high quality, and the results have proved valid on many occasions. The lesson to be learned is that the opinion poll should be conducted by experts, and that little faith should be placed in haphazard polling attempts. Although much is now known about different kinds of biases that enter into opinion polls and ways to correct them, there will always be unknown sources of bias to distort particular results. Only by repeated studies with different interview techniques, sampling procedures, and wording of questions, can exact measures of public opinion be obtained.

CHARACTERISTICS OF OPINIONS

The results of an opinion poll provide only a surface indication of people's thoughts. Much more needs to be known about opinions: how they develop, their stability, the intensity with which they are held, and their relationship to overt behavior. The practical and directly profitable task of measuring opinions has received the widest attention by polling agencies. Only during the last twenty years have inquiries been undertaken into the psychological background of opinions.

Reliability. Opinion questions are open to measurement error just as all test items are. If the respondent is asked the same question on two occasions, he might give different answers. This may reflect a real change in opinion or only an element of chance in the way in which he responds. If the respondent knows little about the issue or has no firm conviction, his response might be little more than a mental coin flip. Unreliability can come from interviewers who interpret responses differently, accidentally record a "yes" when the respondent says "no," or mix up the answers to different questions. Statistical errors in recording and analyzing the data can add additional unreliability.

Because each question in an opinion poll is usually analyzed separately, rather than added with others as is done on most tests, the reliability of the results is dependent on the separate questions. Only a small amount of research has been done on the reliability of opinion questions. The available data indicates fair to good reliability for different questions, with per cents of agreement often above 80 for repeated interviews with the same questions (see 4, chap. 7).

The unreliability in opinion questions tends to reduce the difference between response categories. That is, if a question is to be answered either yes or no, whatever unreliability is present will bring the over-all percentages of yes's and of no's closer to the 50 per cent mark. If a question were completely unreliable, the expectation is that exactly 50 per cent of the answers would fall in each of the two categories. In the same way, any unreliability in opinion questions will reduce the difference between the responses of any two groups, such as in a comparison of labor and management opinions. Consequently, it can be expected that the raw results from an opinion poll are conservative estimates of the differences between response alternatives and between the responses by different groups of people.

Stability. Even though an opinion might be reliably measured at one point in time, it may change over a short period of time. This seems to have occurred in the 1948 Presidential contest between Truman and Dewey. The voting sentiment apparently shifted to Truman in the last few weeks before the election. Partly because the polling agencies did not sample opinion during the period immediately before the election, they mispredicted and lost considerable public confidence for several years thereafter.

Large shifts in opinion are more likely to occur on issues which are being discussed widely in the mass media of communications. Opinions are also more likely to change when the individual has no first-hand experience with the issue and must rely on secondary sources of information. Opinions generally change more easily on issues which do not affect the individual in an immediate personal way. One critical incident can often have a marked effect on public opinion, such as the Japanese attack on Pearl Harbor. Public opinion often changes markedly when a highly respected person advocates a particular viewpoint.

Knowledge of Issues. Two individuals who give the same response to an opinion question may do so with very different amounts of knowledge about the issues. An individual may agree that it would be a good idea for the government to build and operate a dam on the Snake River but have no idea where the Snake River is or have any conception of the consequences of the government action. In many cases, an individual's opinion may be based on incorrect information rather than lack of information. Whenever the polling question is at all complicated, it is useful to give a short information quiz about the issues along with the usual polling questions. It is sometimes found in this way that the more informed people have different opinions from the uninformed people, which leads in turn to suggestions as to how certain segments of the public can be educated about an issue. If the opinion poll results are being used in an advisory way to help in forming the policy of an institution, more faith can usually be placed in the sagacity of the opinions of people who know something about the issues.

Strength of Conviction. Another dimension of opinions is the strength with which viewpoints are held. One person may say "yes" to the question "Should we help rearm Germany" and feel very strongly about it, very sure that it is the proper thing to do. Another individual may also answer "yes" but do so with considerable indecision and lack of sureness. Respondents are often asked to rate the strength of their conviction after responding to a polling question. One procedure is to ask the individual to endorse one of several statements which best describes the strength of his conviction, such as the following (see 4, p. 57):

I am not at all strongly convinced on this matter.
I guess it is the best thing to do.
I am absolutely convinced this is what ought to be done.

It is important to know the strength of a respondent's conviction for several reasons. When the strength of conviction is low, the individual is more open to outside influence and more likely to change his viewpoint. People who hold beliefs strongly usually exert more influence in social groups and in civic affairs than individuals whose beliefs are less strong. A hard-core minority of people who strongly hold an opinion can often win over the less certain larger group.

Validity. The validity of opinion polls depends on the way in which the results are used. Many studies intend only to gauge the public sentiment, to discover what people say about issues. The opinion poll is then valid if it is free from major sources of bias like those mentioned previously in this chapter. Sometimes the results of opinion polls are used to predict how individuals will behave later. Election polls intend to predict how individuals will vote, and most market research studies intend to predict what individuals will buy. In these cases, the predictive validity of opinion poll results can be measured in terms of how well they actually forecast future behavior. Experience has shown that the carefully executed opinion poll can often predict future behavior with a high degree of accuracy.

The predictive validity of opinion polls depends very much on the issues involved. If there are strong social pressures to hold one viewpoint or preference over others, the results of an opinion poll may serve as a poor predictor of how people will actually behave. A case in point is the story, probably apocryphal, concerning the study of preferences for new automobiles conducted at the end of the Second World War. Most people said that they favored utilitarian, economical, low horsepower, inexpensive, unadorned automobiles. Being suspicious of the results, the polling agency undertook another poll in which each person was asked, "What type of automobile does the average person want?" The dominant picture obtained in the second poll was of a chrome-plated, leather-upholstered, high horsepower, many-gadgeted palace on wheels. The results obtained from the initial study would, as time has shown, have served very badly in forecasting the type of automobile that people would actually purchase during the following decade. This also illustrates the need to use a variety of questions concerning an issue rather than to place complete faith in one question only.

ATTITUDE SCALES

Attitudes are *predispositions to react negatively or positively in some degree toward an object, institution, or class of persons.* What negative and positive reactions are depends in part on the particular culture. However, it is rather universal to consider certain actions as negative and positive, or as evidence of likes and dislikes. A negative attitude toward another person is manifested in wanting to see bodily harm done to the individual, wanting to be removed from his presence, wishing that he would suffer a financial loss, wanting him to lose positions of prominence, and so on. The negativeness and positiveness of attitudes are intuitive concepts which are difficult to define concretely.

There are many ways in which a person can react negatively or positively, ranging from a refusal to buy merchandise from a Jewish businessman to joining the Ku Klux Klan. Verbal reactions are the most widely studied attitudinal reactions. People are asked either to agree or disagree with statements like, "The government should stop letting Italians enter this country" and "We should do everything possible to make Italian immigrants feel at home in this country," or some more complex method of rating is used. Verbal reactions are studied more than other kinds of behavior because of the ease with which they can be handled in research investigations. It is much simpler to have subjects react to a list of statements in a questionnaire than to observe how individuals behave in their daily lives. Although interesting new types of data might be found by studying how people actually behave, the enormous labor and expense which are entailed have permitted only a few investigations of this kind. All of the instruments which will be discussed in this section concern what people say about their feelings.

The object in the measurement of attitudes is to locate each person at some point on a continuum, or *scale*, which ranges from "strong negative attitude" through "neutral" to "strong positive attitude." On the surface this seems like a relatively simple problem. Why not simply ask the individual how he feels about an object or class of persons? This could be done by having the individual rate, say, Negroes on a continuum ranging from "dislike very much" to "like very much." Single ratings of over-all reactions are sometimes used in attitude studies, and although they are useful for making gross comparisons of people, they offer a number of drawbacks.

If an individual is asked to give his over-all reaction on a single continuum, this does not provide a reliable indication of the intensity of his reaction. The reliability of single-rating scales is usually too low to provide a good estimate of attitudes. A more reliable location of the individual on an attitude continuum can be obtained by combining the scores made on a number of items.

Another reason why devices other than the single rating scale must be used is that over-all expressions of likes and dislikes are often dominated by stereotyped reactions which do not represent true feelings. People will rate that they are either neutral or favorable toward Negroes, yet they might also endorse more specific statements like, "I would not like to have

my children in an 'integrated' school," and "Negroes are more likely to
commit crimes than are white people."

An attitude scale is derived from a collection of statements all of which
concern different degrees of positive and negative reaction to the object
or person being studied. First it must be determined whether or not the
statements concern only one attitude. It is possible that there are two or
even several attitudes involved in the items, each of which should form
a separate scale rather than be mingled in one. A statement such as "This
city should help provide housing for migrant Southern Negroes" might be
included in a scale to measure attitudes toward Negroes. It might prove
to be as much or more an attitude toward the use of civic funds to com-
pete with private industry.

After obtaining a group of items which concern only one attitude, a
method of administering and scoring the items must be determined so
that people will be located as precisely as possible along the underlying
continuum, or scale. These are the principal steps that are involved in
attitude scaling. Some of the major techniques for obtaining attitude
scales will be discussed in the following sections.

Thurstone Method of Scale Construction. One of the earliest and still
most widely used methods of generating attitude scales was developed
by Thurstone (see **19**) and his colleagues. The outstanding feature of the
method is the use of judges to determine the points on the attitude continuum. The first step in constructing the scale is to gather several hundred statements which seem to express various degrees of negative and
positive attitudes toward the class of persons or objects being studied.
One way of obtaining statements is to have a group of people write about
their attitudes toward the particular person or object. Other statements
can be obtained from popular literature on the issue. The experimenters
can usually add numerous statements from their own experiences.

Each statement is reproduced on a separate slip of paper. Several hundred persons are then chosen as judges. Each judge is handed the entire
collection of statements and asked to rate them on an 11-point continuum
ranging from "extremely favorable," through "neutral," to "extremely
unfavorable." It is important to note that the judges do not rate the extent
to which they agree with each of the statements; they judge the intensity
of each statement.

The next step in constructing a scale of the Thurstone type is to compute indices of variability for each item. If all of the judges place a statement in the eighth, ninth, and tenth piles, this represents good agreement about the intensity of the item. If the placements are scattered all
up and down the 11 piles, this indicates that the statement is either
ambiguous or perhaps belongs to some other attitudinal factor. The standard deviation of the placements of an item by the judges would serve as

an adequate measure of variability. The index which is actually used is one-half the distance between the 25th and 75th percentile of the judges' ratings. Only those statements are retained for the attitude scale that have relatively low interjudge variability.

The final step in constructing scales of the Thurstone type is to select from the remaining statements a group that spreads evenly over the intensity range. For this purpose the median intensity score is determined for each item. If half the judges place a statement at or above the seventh pile and half place it at or below the seventh pile, the median intensity score is 7. As is usually the case, the median lies at some point between two piles, and consequently medians are expressed to one decimal place, like 7.4 and 9.3. (The arithmetic mean would serve much the same purpose here as the median.) The scale position for each item is then considered to be the median intensity judgment. The final scale consists of the twenty or so items which spread most evenly over the intensity range. Ideally, the items should have median intensity judgments respectively of 0, 0.5, 1.0, 1.5, and so on to the top of the scale.

The final attitude scale is composed by randomly ordering the statements on a printed form. The subject is instructed to mark those statements with which he agrees. The score is the median intensity of the statements which are marked. If one person agrees with statements that have intensity indices of 9.5, 10.0, and 10.5, his score would be 10. In a perfect scale the individual would mark only one statement or several statements with similar intensity scores. However, in practical work with the scales, subjects vary somewhat from this expectation. It would not be uncommon to find a person who agrees with statements that have intensities of 10, 9, 8.5, and then agrees with one of 5 also.

The scale of the Thurstone type is an economical, common-sense type of instrument which has been used widely during the last twenty-five years. Special scales have been constructed for attitudes toward war, Negroes, censorship, patriotism, capital punishment, Chinese, and numerous others. Some of the items on the Scale for Measuring Attitudes toward the Church (19) are shown in Table 13–7.

The use of judges to estimate the intensity of attitudes is both a strong and weak point of the Thurstone scale. It is an advantage in that the scale positions have a rational meaning that would be difficult to obtain by any other method. If the judges are in good agreement that a respondent who marks a particular statement has a positive or negative attitude to a certain degree, this tells us something directly about the respondent. The use of judges is particularly helpful in locating the neutral point on the attitude scale. Attitudes are inherently bipolar, ranging in opposite directions from a hypothetical neutral point. In campaigns to change particular attitudes, it is very important to locate individuals in respect to the neutral point. It is much easier to bring a positive change in an individual whose attitude is slightly positive rather than slightly negative. Sometimes it is more important to know precisely which side of the neutral point the individual is on rather than to know the exact distance from the neutral point in either direction.

TABLE 13–7. ILLUSTRATIVE ITEMS AND SCALE VALUES FOR A THURSTONE TYPE MEASURE OF ATTITUDES TOWARD THE CHURCH

(Adapted from Thurstone and Chave, 19, pp. 60–63)

Scale value	Item
.2	I believe the church is the greatest institution in America today.
1.0	I believe that the church has grown up with the primary purpose of perpetuating the spirit and teachings of Jesus and deserves loyal support.
2.2	I like to go to church, for I get something worthwhile to think about and it keeps my mind filled with right thoughts.
3.1	I do not understand the dogmas or creeds of the church but I find the church helps me to be more honest and creditable.
4.0	When I go to church I enjoy a fine ritual service with good music.
5.1	I like the ceremonies of my church but do not miss them much when I stay away.
6.1	I feel the need for religion but do not find what I want in any one church.
7.2	I believe that churches are too much divided by factions and denominations to be a strong force for righteousness.
8.2	The paternal and benevolent attitude of the church is quite distasteful to me.
9.1	My experience is that the church is hopelessly out of date.
10.7	I think the organized church is an enemy of science and truth.

The Thurstone method of scaling assumes that intensity judgments are independent of the judges' own attitudes. It is conceivable that this is the case, that, say, two individuals who have different attitudes toward Negroes agree on the intensity of statements about Negroes. If judgments of intensity are not independent of attitudes, the scale positions are very much a function of the judges who are chosen. This would change all of the scale positions and would shift the neutral point as well. What would be scored a positive attitude on a scale obtained from one group of judges might be scored as a negative attitude on a scale obtained from a different group of judges.

A number of studies (6, 8, 9) report comparisons of scales obtained from different kinds of judges. Hinckley (8) employed a group of Southern white students who were prejudiced against Negroes to rate the intensity of 114 statements. The scale positions obtained were compared with those for a group of Northern white students who were favorable toward Negroes. The two scales correlate .98, showing a very close agreement in the two relative orderings of the items. This and other studies show that at least the relative position of statements on the scale can often be determined without considering the attitudes of the judges themselves. However, the studies show that there are often significant differences in the absolute intensity of statements when judged by groups that hold different attitudes. (It must be remembered that the correlation coefficient is a measure of covariation, not a measure of agreement.) A prejudiced group and a nonprejudiced group may agree that one statement is more positive than another, but they may differ in their judgments of *how* positive the statements are. When the scale values are dependent in part on the particular group of judges which is used, the neutral point on the scale cannot be determined precisely.

A potentially weak point in scales of the Thurstone type is the absence of any direct procedure for determining whether or not there is only one attitude involved in the statements. Statements that relate prominently to attitudes other than the one being studied would probably have high interjudge variability and would be removed from the scale for that reason. However, this is not a precise method for purifying the scale. As is sometimes done, a scale of the Thurstone type can be purified of extraneous factors by retaining only those items that show a substantial degree of homogeneity with the scale as a whole (see 19 for the procedure which is used).

Likert Method of Scale Construction. The Likert method (see 11) also starts with the collection of a large number of positive and negative statements about an object, institution, or class of persons. Unlike the Thurstone approach, judges are not employed in the Likert method. Instead, the scale is derived by item-analysis techniques. The collection of items is administered to a group of subjects. Each item is rated on a five-point continuum ranging from "strongly approve" to "strongly disapprove." Then each item is correlated with total score, which shows the extent to which the item measures the same general underlying attitude as the total set of items. Items which have low correlations with total score are either unreliable or measure some extraneous attitude factor. Only those items which have high correlations with total score are retained for the attitude scale. The Likert scaling procedure helps ensure that the final scale concerns only one general attitude and that individuals can be located with at least moderate precision at different points on the scale.

Comparing the Likert and Thurstone methods, the Likert approach is more empirical because it deals directly with respondents' scores rather than employing judges. The Likert method more directly determines whether or not only one attitude is involved in the original collection of

items, and the scale which is derived measures the most general attitudinal factor which is present. The use of a five-point scale for each item
provides more information than the simple dichotomy of "agree" or "disagree." The only place in which the Thurstone method might be superior
is in the direct meaningfulness of scale scores. No absolute meaning can
be given to the points on the Likert scale. The scores are relative to the
group from which the scale is constructed. It would be helpful to gather
more general norms, to at least be able to say that an individual is above
or below average by so much, but large-scale norms are seldom obtained.
However, as was pointed out above, the meaning of scores on the Thurstone scale is sometimes dependent on the judges who are used.

On the final scale of the Likert type, the subject marks each statement
in one of the categories of strongly agree (SA), agree (A), undecided
(U), disagree (D), and strongly disagree (SD). If the subject marks
"strongly agree" on a positive statement, a score of 5 is given, "agree," is
given a score of 4, and so on to a score of 1 for "strongly disagree." The
scoring system is reversed for negative items. A "strongly agree" mark is
given a score of 1 and so on to 5 for a "strongly disagree" response. The
individual's final score is obtained by summing the item scores. Illustrative items from one of the scales are shown in Table 13–8.

TABLE 13–8. ILLUSTRATIVE ITEMS FROM A LIKERT TYPE SCALE FOR THE
MEASUREMENT OF CIVILIAN MORALE DURING THE DEPRESSION
(Adapted from Rundquist and Sletto, 12)

The future looks very black.	SA	A	U	D	SD
Times are getting better.	SA	A	U	D	SD
No one cares much what happens to you.	SA	A	U	D	SD
Real friends are as easy to find as ever.	SA	A	U	D	SD
It is difficult to think clearly these days.	SA	A	U	D	SD
There is really no point in living.	SA	A	U	D	SD
It is great to be living in these exciting times.	SA	A	U	D	SD
Most people can be trusted.	SA	A	U	D	SD

The Bogardus Social-distance Scale. As early as 1925, Bogardus (2, 3)
developed a technique for measuring attitudes toward different national
groups. Rather than being a scaling procedure, such as the Thurstone
and Likert methods, the Bogardus instrument is identified by a novel type
of item. The items concern the desired social distance from a particular
national group. The following categories of social distance are usually
employed in the scales:

1. To close kinship by marriage
2. To my club as personal chums
3. To my street as neighbors

4. To employment in my occupation
5. To citizenship in my country
6. As visitors only in my country
7. Would exclude from my country

The scale can be used for any national group simply by placing the name, such as English or Russians, at the head of the social-distance categories. The respondent marks those categories which suit his feelings about the particular national group.

No formal procedures are used to ensure that the Bogardus categories constitute a scale in terms of the requirements given earlier. However, respondents use the categories as though they are points on a scale. Very few inconsistent responses are found, e.g., a willingness to accept a Russian to close kinship by marriage but an unwillingness to have a Russian as a neighbor.

Very little research has been done to determine correlations between responses on the social-distance scale and those on more conventional attitude scales such as the Thurstone and Likert instruments. Social distance is both an interesting and a complex concept. A respondent may express a desire for social distance from a national group such as Norwegians not because he dislikes the class of people but because they are unfamiliar. A person might dislike the English personally but be willing to accept them in close relationships because of the general prestige that the English have with most of the people in this country.

The social-distance scale, as measured by categories like those above, fails to measure extreme negative attitudes. There are various degrees of dislike beyond wanting to have no social contact with a group. Investigators have often found it necessary to employ several conventional attitude items along with the social-distance categories to tap extreme negative feelings. This is illustrated in the following scale developed by Crespi (5) for measuring attitudes toward "conscientious objectors":

1. I would treat a conscientious objector no differently than I would any other person, even so far as having him become a close relative in marriage.
2. I would accept conscientious objectors only in so far as having them for friends.
3. I would accept conscientious objectors only so far as having them for speaking acquaintances.
4. I don't want anything to do with conscientious objectors.
5. I feel that conscientious objectors should be imprisoned.
6. I feel that conscientious objectors should be shot as traitors.

It was necessary to add statements 5 and 6 to get at strong negative feelings.

The Bogardus scale is much easier to construct than the Thurstone or the Likert instruments. It applies only to classes of people: it could not be used, for example, to measure attitudes toward labor unions. The same categories or a slight variant of them can be applied to whatever group is being studied. One of the interesting properties of the social-distance scale is that it concerns actions rather than more general feelings about people. Although the research evidence on this point is very small, the Bogardus social-distance scale might perform better than conventional attitude measures in predicting how two groups of people will behave when brought together.

The Guttman Method of Scale Construction. An interesting new approach to attitude scaling is the procedure developed by Guttman (see 7, 14) in connection with studies of the morale of the American soldier during the Second World War. The objective of the method is to test

FIGURE 13–1. Response pattern for nine persons on nine items for a perfect Guttman Scale. A mark of 1 means that the person agrees with the statement, and a mark of 0 means that he does not agree with the statement.

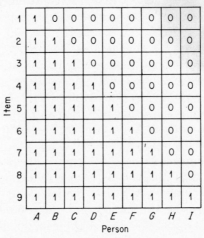

directly whether a collection of items can be scaled on one attitude continuum. The criterion of scalability is that if an individual endorses a more extreme item he should endorse all less extreme items also. The scaling criterion is applied to the scores obtained from a tryout group of respondents. If a single scale underlies all of the items, the items can be arranged to form a triangular pattern like that in Figure 13–1.

Figure 13–1 greatly simplifies the Guttman scale in order to illustrate the principle that is at work. Usually there are both many more items and many more people being studied. Also, Figure 13–1 is composed in such a manner that only one person has each of the different response patterns. Item 1 is the most extreme attitude, let us say extremely negative in this case. Only person *A* agrees with item 1, and as is true in a perfect scale, person *A* agrees with the second most intense statement, 2, the third most intense, 3, and so on to the least intense, but still negative item 9. Person *B* holds the second most intensely negative attitude, and so he endorses item 2 and all of those beneath it in the intensity hierarchy. Person *I* holds the least intensely negative attitude, agreeing to only the least intensely negative item, 9.

The response pattern found in the perfect Guttman scale is exactly what is obtained if people are rank-ordered on a physical continuum. Suppose, for example, that we ask people questions about their height, and assume that they know how tall they are. The person who answers "yes" to the question "Are you above 6½ feet tall?" will answer "yes" to "Are you above 6 feet tall?" and "yes" to all questions about heights down to zero. The person who answers "no" to the question "Are you above 6½ feet tall?" but does answer "yes" to the question "Are you above 6 feet tall?" will answer "yes" to questions about all lower heights. Similarly with persons of all heights, by knowing the most extreme statement that a person endorses, his other responses can be predicted perfectly.

In the example above, we started by knowing that only one scale, height, was involved. The purpose of the Guttman procedure is to test whether or not a collection of attitude statements will exhibit the characteristic pattern. It is an elegant notion; and if a set of items can be found which will fit this pattern, it is convincing evidence of scalability.

Unfortunately there are some important practical drawbacks to the use of the Guttman scaling procedure. The principal one is that almost no collection of statements will meet the strict lawfulness of the scalability criterion. The criterion insists that each separate item be almost completely reliable; but in practical work individual items are notoriously heavy with measurement error. Suggestions have been made for the use of approximately scalable collections of items, but even an approximation of scalability in the Guttman sense is rare to find. One solution to the problem is to search around through the items to find a set which will approximately meet the criterion of scalability. This takes considerable advantage of chance, and it will be expected that in many cases the scaling will not hold up when the items are administered to new groups of subjects.

In the few cases in which the Guttman criterion of scalability has been approximately met, the items prove to be so closely related in content as to constitute near rewordings of the same statement (see 14). There is little reason to believe that collections of statements such as are handled by the Likert procedure will scale in the Guttman sense.

Although the procedures of scaling identified with Guttman are not suitable for most practical work, the concept of what constitutes a unidimensional scale is appealing and deserves more attention. The important thing to note about this concept of scalability is that it is defined entirely in terms of rank-ordering of persons and items. The basic data with which the method begins is the set of qualitative responses (categories), either "agree" or "disagree" on each item, given by the respondents. The example concerning the heights of people illustrates how qualitative responses can define a rank-ordering of people on an underlying scale. Most of the procedures for deriving and validating tests and attitude measurement devices assume that interval scales underlie the responses. This is so because they employ means, standard deviations, correlations, and other statistics which make sense only when an interval scale is assumed for the measures being studied.

Fewer assumptions about psychological data would need to be made if statistical methods that assumed only rank-order scales could be used. The great difficulty is that when the interval scale is abandoned in favor of rank-order and categories, most of the powerful statistical methods such as multiple correlation and factor analysis must be abandoned also. This is squarely the problem that is encountered in using the Guttman criterion of scalability. When the criterion is not met perfectly, and it is highly unlikely that it ever will be, there is little that can be done statistically to determine the number and kinds of scales which underlie the responses. What is needed is a method for analyzing the responses to a diverse collection of attitudinal statements which will determine the number and kinds of rank-order scales which are present in the data. No adequate solutions to this problem have yet been developed. Until they are, Guttman's concept of scalability and the procedures it entails are not likely to be of much practical importance in the construction of attitude scales.

Factored Scales. One of the most direct approaches to determining the number and kinds of scales involved in a collection of items is to factor analyze responses. All of the conventional methods of factor analysis can be used on attitude items in the same way that they are applied to other sets of psychological measures. Desirably, the items should be rated on a continuum, using, say, five or more points, rather than to obtain only an "agree" or "disagree" response. After the collection of items is administered to a group of respondents, preferably with at least several hundred persons included, all intercorrelations among the items are obtained. The intercorrelations are then factor analyzed. Each of the major factors constitutes a separate attitude scale. The items which relate most prominently to a factor can be used to construct the scale.

As was stated above, the use of factor analysis to derive attitude scales assumes that interval scales underlie the responses. This is an assumption

that is quite generally made in statistical work with psychological measures. The tests and attitude scales which have been derived in this way
work well in practice. Factor analysis would have been used more broadly
in the derivation of attitude scales were it not for the statistical labors that
are involved. Now that high-speed computational equipment is becoming
more available, large-scale factor analysis of attitude items will probably
become more common.

Methods of attitude scaling like Thurstone's and Likert's have been
successful without factor analysis largely because they have dealt with
collections of statements which are dominated by one large attitudinal
factor. Although both methods tend to eliminate items that belong to
small extraneous factors, neither method will work well if applied to
collections of items in which several prominent factors are present. Factor
analysis is more necessary in deriving scales in rather subtle attitude
domains, like attitudes of employees toward working conditions in a
particular factory and attitudes of people toward government spending.
In terms of employee attitudes, it is likely that a factor would be found
of over-all negative and positive attitude toward the work; but it would
be expected also to find separable factors relating to different aspects of
the work, such as danger of working conditions, adequacy of tools and
equipment, and pleasantness of surroundings.

The Interview. A not uncommon criticism of attitude scales is that they
restrict the individual's reactions to a relatively narrow range of content
and prevent the individual from expressing his own attitudes in his own
words. If the attitude items have all been constructed in the narrow confines of the psychological laboratory without recourse to what people
actually think and feel, it is possible that few pertinent statements will
enter the final instrument.

Some people prefer an open interview situation to the use of attitude
scales. The respondent is asked a series of "open end" questions like,
"What do you think about school 'integration'?" The respondent is then
allowed to say whatever comes to mind, perhaps with some prodding if
he gets too far off the track. The responses are either written down
verbatim or pertinent parts of the responses are noted.

The advantage of the interview is that it permits a direct inquiry into
attitudes without assuming in advance what specific questions and alternative answers should be used. The responses will not only teach the
investigator something about the issues which loom most largely in the
public mind but will also provide some suggestions as to why people
feel as they do.

There are several difficulties in using the interview to study attitudes.
In the face-to-face interview situation there is usually more pressure to
give socially acceptable responses, particularly those which the respond-

ent thinks will please the interviewer, than is the case in the anonymous response to an attitude scale. In many studies, the interviewer must exercise his own judgment to determine how the respondent feels about an issue or why the respondent answers as he does. The subjectivity which this entails introduces unreliability into the results of the study. The major difficulty with the open interview is that it is very hard to find any systematic way of scoring and summarizing the answers that are given. The results of the study are often highly dependent on the experimenter's intuition as to what the dominant trends in the data are.

A procedure which is used in many investigations is to conduct interviews preparatory to developing more standardized measures of attitudes. Fifty to a hundred persons varying in age and socioeconomic status are interviewed about their attitudes. This provides a rich source of attitudinal statements as well as suggestions about the methods of measurement which will be most effective in subsequent studies.

CHARACTERISTICS OF ATTITUDES

Reliability. Well-constructed attitude scales are usually as reliable as most aptitude tests are. As is true for all kinds of measures, the reliability is directly dependent on the number of items in the scale and the amount of correlation among the items. When short scales are employed containing no more than five or so items, the scores will often not be sufficiently reliable to make predictions about individual respondents. However, even a short and relatively unreliable scale will serve to differentiate the attitudes of whole groups of persons, such as to differentiate the attitudes of employees and management about labor unions.

Validity. Earlier in this chapter it was said that nearly all of the measures of attitudes depend on verbal reactions rather than on observations of behavior. If an attitude scale is to be considered an assessment of expressed feelings, it should have content representativeness. Efforts to achieve content representativeness are made in most of the scaling procedures by starting with a broad collection of the things that people say about an issue. It was recommended to use some open interviews before constructing the scale, to help ensure content representativeness for the items.

Many of the currently available attitude scales do a sufficiently good job of sampling verbal reactions to be considered reasonably valid measures of expressed attitudes. The problem in validating attitude scales is that scores are often given a wide significance beyond verbal reactions.

If the scores on attitude scales are used to predict how individuals will behave in their daily lives, there is no substitute for empirical studies to determine predictive validity. There are vast practical difficulties involved in doing this. It is difficult to decide what specific predictions should follow from attitude scales. Three employees who show the same amount of negative attitude toward a company may do very different things in respect to their expressed attitudes. One might make a speech in a union meeting about grievances toward the company, another might do shoddy work on purpose, and the third employee might do nothing except complain to his wife about the unfairness of the company.

Some confidence in the use of an attitude scale is obtained if it can be shown to relate prominently to at least some other kinds of relevant behavior. For example, Telford (18) compared the average scores on a scale measuring attitude toward the church with reports of church attendance (a low score indicates positive attitude):

Frequency of church attendance	Average score on attitude scale
Regularly	1.91
Frequently	2.48
Occasionally	3.50
Seldom	4.95
Never	6.75

Sims and Patrick (13) applied a scale of the Thurstone type for measuring attitudes toward Negroes to different groups of college students, with the following results (a high score indicates a positive attitude):

	Average score
Northern students	6.7
Northern students living in the South	5.9
Southern students	5.0

Depth of Attitudes. Psychoanalysis and other forms of depth psychology have taught us that what the individual says about his attitudes may be quite different from attitudes which he expresses in other ways. The individual may either consciously cover up socially unacceptable attitudes, or he may even fool himself and be unaware that there is a conflict between what he says and what he does. Some investigators place little faith in attitude scales, claiming that they measure only superficial attitudes and not "real" attitudes. The difficulty is that there are no accepted procedures for measuring "real" or "deep" attitudes. Projective devices have sometimes been employed for this purpose. A typical procedure for studying prejudice is to show the respondent a picture of a Negro talking to a white person. The respondent is asked to guess what they are talking about. If, for example, the respondent says that the white man is demanding back some money which the Negro stole, this could, without too much strain on the imagination, be considered evidence of a negative attitude on the part of the respondent. Procedures of this kind are interesting and might eventually lead to new tools for the measurement of attitudes. However, the projective devices which are presently available depend heavily on the subjective judgment of the interviewer, and there are numerous questions about the validity of the instruments. They are more suited to laboratory studies of small groups of people than they are to general use with diverse segments of the general population. (The projective techniques will be discussed in detail in Chapter 15.)

It should not be assumed that expressed attitudes are less important than other kinds of negative and positive reactions. What people say publicly is often more influential in determining the course of events than whatever they may "really" feel. Expressed attitudes are often derived from conflicts within the individual. A person may have learned in his early years that all foreigners are to be distrusted. Later experience and education could instill in him an attitude of humanitarianism and concern for people of all nations. The two attitudes sit side by side in the individual, both of them genuine feelings. If the individual publicly espouses the doctrine that we should do everything possible to help the downtrodden throughout the world, this does not necessarily mean that the expressed attitude is false or unimportant.

It is necessary for clinical psychologists and psychiatrists to delve within the individual to learn the masking of one attitude with another and the conflicting feelings which lead to personal disturbance. However, for the sake of measuring public attitudes, it is usually more important to learn the feelings that people will express and stand on publicly. These both reflect and determine the public image, the common viewpoint that a group or a nation holds as a basis for action.

The Meaning of Attitudes to the Individual. Two people may show much the same response on an attitude scale and differ importantly in other ways. One variable to consider is the relative abstractness versus concreteness of the attitudinal reaction. Some attitudes are abstract in the sense that they are formed with only a small amount of contact with the object, person, or institution concerned. Other attitudes are formed from considerable first-hand experience. As an example of an abstract reaction, up to ten or so years ago Turks were given markedly unfavorable ratings on attitude scales. This was so in spite of the fact that few of the respondents had any first-hand experience with Turks. This was evidently a historical holdover from the days when the then warlike Turks were in conflict with the Christian world. It is not uncommon to hear young children voicing the prejudices of their parents toward race and religion. Such attitudes are largely second hand, based on little concrete experience.

Sometimes only very slight cues are used for the formation of attitudes. For example, rank your preferences for the following groups of people, rating the most preferred group 1 and the least preferred 4:

Sylvanians   _____
Alusians   _____
Blugdugians   _____
Polurasians   _____

The majority of the people will rate the Blugdugians as the least preferred group—this is so in spite of the fact that these are all imaginary groups of people. The Blugdugians are rated low because of the unmelodious sound of their name.

There is a real danger that some of the attitude studies measure only incidental abstract aspects of the issues. This is particularly likely in measuring attitudes toward institutions and associations, such as General Motors, the Americans for Democratic Action, and Harvard University. Something can be learned about the concreteness of attitudes by employing a standard list of questions concerning the respondents' knowledge and experience with the issue. Although there is no proof of it, the expectation is that highly abstract attitudes change more readily than ones based on considerable concrete experience.

Another important characteristic of an attitude is the strength with which it is held. Some people feel more strongly about an issue than other people do. A common practice in the study of attitudes is to employ a strength of feeling question along with each attitude statement. That is, after the respondent registers his relative agreement or disagreement with a statement like, "All public schools should be 'integrated' as soon as possible," he is asked to rate the strength of his feeling in one of the categories "very strongly," "fairly strongly," or "don't care much one way or the other." Strength of feeling corresponds closely with the negative or positive intensity of the attitude. People who express either strong negative or strong positive attitudes usually say that they feel strongly about the issue. People who hold nearly neutral attitudes tend to say they "don't care much one way or the other." Although it is conceivable that a person could feel strongly about a neutral attitude, this is seldom found. There is some evidence to indicate that intensely negative attitudes are held more strongly than intensely positive attitudes.

INTEREST INVENTORIES

Interests were defined earlier in the chapter as stated preferences for activities. As the word "stated" emphasizes, interest inventories depend on the individual's honest and accurate reporting of what he likes to do. At the outset some justification needs to be given for using interest inventories. The common-sense approach to learning about interests would be simply to ask the individual what occupations he prefers. If the individual already knows that he wants to be a physician, sea captain, or fireman, it would be a waste of time to have him record his preferences on a printed form. The purpose in administering tests is to gain some new information about people.

There is a considerable amount of evidence to show that stated preferences for occupations are unrealistic. This is particularly so among adolescents and young adults, with whom interest inventories are most needed. Young people are usually quite unaware of the specific activities which are entailed in different occupations. The individual's stated preferences for occupations are often prompted by glamorized stereotypes. The physician is remembered as the heroic figure who performs the miraculous operation while the gallery looks down in silent awe. The sea captain is seen holding steadfast to the helm against the stormy onslaught of the sea. The mental picture of the fireman has him descending the ladder with the rescued maiden on his shoulder. All of these images are of course very unrealistic. Few physicians do surgery at all. They must spend many hours in unheroic activities such as reading medical texts, writing reports, and calming the fears of anxious patients. The sea captain has scant opportunity to steer the ship because of the modern electronic gadgetry which automatically navigates. The captain is usually a sea-going businessman, ambassador to passengers and clients, who must be concerned with such matters as bookkeeping, personnel management, and correspondence. No one considers what the fireman does in the larger portion of his time—tending equipment, collecting funds for charities, and helping rescue cats from inaccessible perches.

The purpose of the interest inventory is to ask the individual about his preferences for a wide range of relatively specific activities such as mending a clock, preparing written reports, and talking to groups of people. From these a diagnosis is made of the occupations which most closely match the interests of the individual. A fundamental assumption in the use of interest inventories is that people in different occupations have at least partially different interests. Otherwise there would be no way in which interest tests could be used successfully to advise people to consider one occupation rather than another.

The Strong Interest Inventory. One of the earliest and still most widely used measures of interests is the Vocational Interest Blank (*VIB*) developed by E. K. Strong (**17**). Separate forms are available for men and women. The *VIB* employs 400 questions about relatively specific activities. On most of the items the subject indicates his preferences by marking one of the three categories "like," "indifferent," "dislike." Some illustrative items from the men's form are as follows:

Buying merchandise for a store   L   I   D
Adjusting a carburetor   L   I   D
Interviewing men for a job   L   I   D

Responses to the *VIB* can be scored in terms of 45 occupations on the men's forms and 25 occupations on the women's forms. A separate scoring key is available for each occupation. The scoring keys were developed from the responses to the *VIB* made by successful persons in each of the occupational groups. Each scoring key is composed in such a way as to differentiate the people in a particular profession from people in general. This procedure for developing scoring keys is referred to as *criterion keying*. Each scoring key consists of a set of weights to be applied to the item responses. The weights range from $+4$ to -4. A positive weight means that people in the profession, in accounting, say, mark "like" to the item more frequently than do people in general. A negative weight means that accountants mark the "like" category less frequently than people in general. The larger the difference between the profession and people in general, the larger is the weight. If an item does not differentiate a profession from people in general, it receives a zero weight. A considerable amount of research work was required to obtain the occupational keys, and scoring keys for new occupations are gradually being developed.

The responses of an individual are scored on either some or all of the professions. The scores can be converted to standard scores, percentiles, or to a grading system ranging from A to C. The resulting profile of scores is used to interpret the individual's interests. People usually express high interest in a number of related professions such as mathematician, engineer, and chemist.

The Kuder Interest Inventory. The Kuder Preference Record (**10**) and the Strong *VIB* are the two most widely used interest inventories. The two inventories present an interesting contrast in procedures of test development. Instead of using the "like," "indifferent," "dislike" response categories like those on the *VIB*, the Kuder inventory presents items in triads. The subject picks from three activities the one that he likes most and the one that he likes least. Two illustrative item triads are as follows:

Visit an art gallery   _____
Browse in a library   _____
Visit a museum   _____

Collect autographs   _____
Collect coins   _____
Collect butterflies   _____

Instead of scoring the form in terms of numerous separate occupations, scores are given in 10 general areas: outdoor, mechanical, computational, scientific, persuasive, artistic, literary, musical, social service, and clerical. The 10 categories were derived by item-analysis procedures, much the same as factor analysis would obtain. Unlike the *VIB*, the 10 interest areas on the Kuder inventory were not related in any direct way with the responses of people in specific occupations. The interpretation of an interest profile from the Kuder inventory is largely dependent on the judgment of the counselor as to the interests that are involved in different occupations.

Although the Strong and the Kuder inventories started out on different tracks, recent developments have brought them closer together. A number of broad interest areas have been developed for the Strong *VIB* by factor-analytic studies. Scores on these can be obtained in addition to those for specific occupations. Research done since the Kuder inventory was published shows that the original logical method of analyzing interests leads to good predictions for certain occupations and poor predictions for others. Efforts are now being made to obtain equations for predicting how closely an individual's interests on the Kuder inventory match those of people in different occupations. However, this work is not far enough along to provide the same empirical evidence for interpreting responses as is furnished by the *VIB*.

Interests and Accomplishment. Because a person is interested in certain activities, such as those relating to engineering, it does not necessarily mean that he has the capacity for accomplishment in that field. The relationship between interests and ability is particularly tenuous in children and young adolescents. The child who professes an interest in athletic activities, for example, may have little athletic ability, and similarly for artistic and scientific pursuits. However, there is an increasing congruence between interests and ability as the individual matures. It is very difficult for a person to maintain an interest in activities in which he constantly performs poorly. As the child matures, his interests gradually shift to the things that he can do at least relatively well.

Stability of Interests. Without some stability over time, scores on interest inventories would be of little use in advising people on vocational choices. Interests are notoriously unstable in children and adolescents. They begin to stabilize in the late teens and remain remarkably stable throughout adulthood. Strong (16) found retest correlations in the .70s and .80s over intervals as long as twenty-two years. This is both a credit to the *VIB* and strong evidence that interests are relatively enduring characteristics of human adults.

Interest Inventories in Vocational Guidance. Interest inventories are second only to intelligence tests as aids to vocational guidance. Interests are, at least theoretically, very important to consider in choosing occupations. If an individual really likes a particular type of work, he can often succeed in spite of only a moderate amount of aptitude. No matter how much initial aptitude a person has, he can fail in a line of work through inattention and lack of effort.

In vocational guidance, interest inventories are used for two related purposes: to predict satisfaction in the work and to predict successful performance. The criterion keying on the Strong inventory provides some supporting evidence that interest tests can predict future satisfaction on the job. Another type of evidence is that follow-up studies of individuals who completed the *VIB* in college show a strong tendency for people to enter occupations similar to their expressed interests. Both these pieces of evidence also tend to support the hypothesis that interests are predictive, at least to some extent, of job performance. Strong (15, 17) has gathered more direct evidence to show that interest scores are predictive of performance in some occupations. For example, there is a relationship between the amount of interest shown on the key for insurance agents and the amount of insurance which agents sell.

Even though interests are, at least theoretically, very important to consider in choosing occupations, it does not necessarily follow that the available instruments are maximally effective measures of interests. As is true in most areas of testing, a great deal more research with interest inventories is needed.

It is unfortunate that interest tests cannot be used as successfully in the selection of people for particular jobs as they can in vocational guidance. It has been shown repeatedly that people can fake interest tests to a marked extent. If people are told to mark the Kuder or the Strong inventory as a successful engineer or physician would, they will obtain profiles similar to the profession in question.

People usually give honest responses in a vocational guidance situation. They are there for information and advice, and there is little to gain by faking an interest inventory one way or the other. If, as is usually the case, the vocational guidance facility is not connected with personnel-selection programs, there is no way in which test scores can lower the individual's chances of getting a particular job. When an individual applies for a particular job, he is seldom as desirous of learning about himself as he is of obtaining the position. If the individual is applying for a job as an electrician, he knows that it behooves him to answer "yes" to an interest item like, "Do you like to repair electrical motors?" The small amount of success that interest inventories meet in personnel-selection programs should not mar the important place they have in vocational guidance.

REFERENCES

1. Albig, W. *Modern public opinion.* New York: McGraw-Hill, 1956.
2. Bogardus, E. Measuring social distance. *J. appl. Sociol.,* 1925, **9,** 299–308.
3. Bogardus, E. A Social Distance Scale. *Sociol. and soc. Res.,* 1933, **17,** 265–271.
4. Cantril, H. *Gauging public opinion.* Princeton, N.J.: Princeton Univer. Press, 1944.
5. Crespi, L. P. Attitudes toward conscientious objectors and some of their psychological correlates. *J. Psychol.,* 1944, **18,** 81–117.
6. Ferguson, L. W. The influence of individual attitudes on construction of an attitude scale. *J. soc. Psychol.,* 1935, **6,** 115–117.
7. Guttman, L. The Cornell technique for scale and intensity analysis. *Educ. psychol. Measmt,* 1947, **7,** 247–279.
8. Hinckley, E. D. The influence of individual opinion on construction of an attitude scale. *J. soc. Psychol.,* 1932, **3,** 283–296.
9. Hovland, C. I., and Sherif, M. Judgmental phenomena and scales of attitude measurement: item displacement in Thurstone scales. *J. abnorm. soc. Psychol.,* 1952, **47,** 822–832.
10. Kuder, G. F. *Kuder Preference Record—Vocational Manual.* Chicago: Science Research, 1953.
11. Likert, R. A. A technique for the measurement of attitudes. *Arch. Psychol.,* 1932, No. 140.
12. Rundquist, E. A., and Sletto, R. F. *Personality in the depression.* Minneapolis: Univer. of Minnesota Press, 1936.
13. Sims, V. M., and Patrick, J. R. Attitudes toward the Negro of northern and southern college students. *J. soc. Psychol.,* 1936, **7,** 192–204.
14. Stouffer, S. A., et al. *Studies in social psychology in World War II.* Vol. 4. *Measurement and prediction.* Princeton, N.J.: Princeton Univer. Press, 1950.
15. Strong, E. K. Interest scores while in college of occupations engaged in 20 years later. *Educ. psychol. Measmt,* 1951, **11,** 335–348.
16. Strong, E. K. Permanence of interest scores over 22 years. *J. appl. Psychol.,* 1951, **35,** 89–91.
17. Strong, E. K. *Vocational Interest Blank for Men: Manual.* Stanford University, Calif.: Stanford Univer. Press, 1951.
18. Telford, C. W. An experimental study of some factors influencing the social attitudes of college students. *J. soc. Psychol.,* 1934, **5,** 421–428.
19. Thurstone, L. L., and Chave, E. J. *The measurement of attitude.* Chicago: Univer. Chicago Press, 1929.
20. Yates, F. *Sampling methods for censuses and surveys.* New York: Hafner, 1949.

CHAPTER 14

Inventories for Self-description

This and the succeeding two chapters are concerned with measures of personality. There are almost as many definitions of personality as there are methods to measure personality. The term personality is popularly used to indicate social charm. A person is said to have *a lot* of personality, meaning that he possesses all of the social graces.

Personality is often defined negatively as the nonability or noncognitive functions. Any measurement device that is not clearly either an aptitude or achievement test is often classified as a personality test. It is unsatisfactory to define things in this way. For example, it would be of little help to a Martian to be told only that a dog is something that is neither a cat nor a cow.

It proves very difficult to give concise definitions of personality, mainly because there are many kinds of human attributes which could be so labeled. A typical definition is "personality is the total functioning individual interacting with his environment." This definition certainly lacks little in terms of inclusiveness, but it provides no starting point for the measurement of personality characteristics. The best starting point for a discussion of personality measurement is to distinguish some of the different kinds of personal characteristics which can be studied. In the preceding chapter the human attributes of opinions, attitudes, and interests were defined and treated separately from the kinds of attributes which will be treated here and in the succeeding two chapters.

The following three kinds of attributes are most often discussed under the term personality:

1. *Social traits.* The characteristic behavior of an individual in respect to other people. Typical traits are honesty, gregariousness, shyness, dominance, talkativeness, and humor. Social traits are often referred to as the surface layer of personality, the way that the individual appears in society. Inventories which seek to measure social traits are said to concern the normal personality.

2. *Maladjustment.* This covers a broad range of disorders including hypertension, lack of emotional control, intense fears, disruption of

321

thought processes, and depression, among others. Although the definition of maladjustment depends in part on the values in a particular culture, a person is usually said to be maladjusted if his own behavior is severely disturbing to himself and/or the people around him. When a person becomes highly distraught or his behavior is odd or dangerous, he is classified as mentally ill.

3. *Dynamics.* A difficult to define collection of the underlying individual processes which produce different states of adjustment and different kinds of social traits. Dynamics involves such things as drives, the Oedipus complex, amount of ego strength, body image, dream symbolism —none of which can be observed directly but must be complexly inferred from the individual's behavior.

The instruments which will be discussed in this chapter are primarily concerned with social traits and maladjustment. Although they relate to some extent to dynamics, the projective tests to be discussed in the next chapter are the primary instruments in the realm of dynamics.

A careful distinction should be made between inventories for self-description and other kinds of paper-and-pencil personality tests. The instruments which will be discussed in this chapter are all standard procedures for having the individual say what he is like. Typical items are "Do you lead the discussion when talking to others?" "Do you enjoy competition?" "Are you attractive to the other sex?" There are other kinds of personality inventories which are not concerned with self-description. An example is a measure of suggestibility, or "acquiescence," in which the subject is presented a series of highly ambiguous statements and is asked to indicate whether he agrees or disagrees with each (supposedly the person who tends to agree in this situation is more "acquiescent"). Some inventories which are not directly concerned with self-description will be discussed in the next two chapters.

Dozens of personality inventories are currently available; hundreds have seen general use during the last forty years, and thousands have been employed for particular research and selection problems. Consequently, the inventories which will be discussed in this chapter are examples chosen only to represent different kinds of testing problems.

MALADJUSTMENT

Self-report is one of the basic tools in the diagnosis of illness. The physician asks, "Where does it hurt?" "How is your appetite?" The patient volunteers information like, "I don't sleep so well," and "I am all out of pep." The self-report technique carried over into psychiatry and clinical psychology. The questions are different but the method is the same. The psychiatrist asks the patient whether he has nightmares or feels uncomfortable in a crowd; he inquires how the patient gets along with parents and friends. Over the years it became apparent that certain questions are more successful than others in detecting maladjustment. These have become almost standard questions for all interviews, used along with questions that have particular relevance to a case. It is an easy jump from a list of standard questions to a test: all that is necessary is to write the questions down and have the subject indicate his agreement or disagreement with each. This is exactly how the first personality inventories were developed.

The first self-description inventory that achieved prominence was Woodworth's Personal Data Sheet (19). The inventory was developed as a means of weeding out emotionally unstable persons from the United States Army. A standard, time-saving procedure was needed because of the shortage of trained interviewers. The inventory contains 116 questions concerning "neurotic" tendencies, ten of which are as follows:

Are you troubled with dreams about your work?

Do you often have the feeling of suffocating?

Have you ever had fits of dizziness?

Did you ever have convulsions?

Did you have a happy childhood?

Have you ever seen a vision?

Did you ever have a strong desire to commit suicide?

Can you stand the sight of blood?

Are you troubled by the idea that people are watching you on the street?

Does it make you uneasy to sit in a small room with the door shut?

The questions were obtained from a search of the psychiatric literature and from conferences with psychiatrists. A neurotic tendency score is obtained for each person by adding the number of "neurotic" responses.

A small amount of research was undertaken to standardize the Personal Data Sheet. Items were eliminated if more than 25 per cent of normal individuals gave the "neurotic" response. Comparisons were made between the responses given by unselected draftees and those given by a small group of declared neurotic soldiers. Woodworth recognized that the validity of the Personal Data Sheet depends on the diagnostic value of the questions which are asked and on the honest reporting of the subject. The inventory can easily be faked by anyone who chooses to do so.

The Personal Data Sheet was not considered to be a test in the strict sense of the word. Persons who gave more than 30 or 40 "neurotic" responses were brought in for detailed psychiatric interviews. Although little direct evidence for validity was obtained, people who worked with the Personal Data Sheet during the First World War were generally satisfied with the inventory as an aid to psychiatric screening. After the First World War an interest developed in the construction of tests of all kinds, personality inventories included. Most of the inventories were modeled directly after the Personal Data Sheet, to the extent of using many of the same items.

Bell Adjustment Inventory. A recognized weakness of the Personal Data Sheet is that it provides only one over-all index of adjustment versus maladjustment, providing no information about the kind of maladjustment. The Bell inventory (2) seeks to measure adjustment in the four areas of home adjustment, health adjustment, social adjustment, emotional adjustment, plus a score for total adjustment. The Bell inventory was not only one of the first instruments to measure differential adjustment, it was one of the first to be constructed in terms of item-analysis statistics. Bell had originally hypothesized 10 adjustment areas. Items were either selected from previous inventories or composed to measure each of the 10 areas. The items were administered to groups of students. Items were retained in each adjustment area only if they correlated with the total score in that area. Only 4 of the 10 hypothesized areas hung together well enough to be included in the final form. Ensuring that items in each adjustment area are homogeneous does not mean that they are necessarily valid for any purpose, but it does give some assurance that the items tend to measure the same underlying trait.

The Bell Adjustment Inventory has been used widely during the last twenty years as an aid in the counseling of high school and college students. The inventory is administered routinely in many schools to freshmen students. Those who have low scores in one or several of the adjustment areas are brought in for interviews to see if counseling and other help are required.

Minnesota Multiphasic Personality Inventory (MMPI). The *MMPI* (13, 14) represents the apex of research and detailed test construction in the area of adjustment inventories. Research on the instrument has gone on for twenty years now, and hundreds of journal articles have been devoted to its construction, refinement, and use. The *MMPI* is intended to measure the relative presence or absence of the nine forms of mental illness listed below. Two related items are shown for each type of mental illness. A plus sign means that persons who have the illness are likely to agree with the item; a negative sign means that they are likely to disagree.

Hypochondriasis (Hs). Overconcern with body functions and imagined illness.

Related items:

I do not tire quickly. (−)

The top of my head sometimes feels tender. (+)

Depression (*D*). This is used in the conventional sense to imply strong feelings of "blueness," despondence, and worthlessness.

Related items:

I am easily awakened by noise. (+)

Everything is turning out just as the prophets of the Bible said it would. (+)

Hysteria (*Hy*). The development of physical disorders such as blindness, paralysis, and vomiting as an escape from emotional problems.

Related items:

I am likely not to speak to people until they speak to me. (+)

I get mad easily and then get over it soon. (+)

Psychopathic deviate (*Pd*). An individual who lacks "conscience," who has little regard for the feelings of others, and who gets into trouble frequently.

Related items:

My family does not like the work I have chosen. (+)

What others think of me does not bother me. (+)

Paranoia (*Pa*). Extreme suspiciousness to the point of imagining elaborate plots.

Related items:

I am sure I am being talked about. (+)

Someone has control over my mind. (+)

Psychasthenia (*Pt*). Strong fears and compulsions.

Related items:

I easily become impatient with people. (+)

I wish I could be as happy as others seem to be. (+)

Schizophrenia (*Sc*). Bizarre thoughts and actions, out of communication with the world.

Related items:

I have never been in love with anyone. (+)

I loved my mother. (−)

Hypomania (*Ma*). Overactivity, inability to concentrate on one thing for more than a moment.

Related items:

I don't blame anyone for trying to grab everything he can get in this world. (+)

When I get bored I like to stir up some excitement. (+)

Masculinity-femininity (*Mf*). The relative balance of male versus female interests.

Related items:

I like movie love scenes. (*F*)

I used to keep a diary. (*F*)

There are several noteworthy features of the *MMPI* which set it above most inventories which are used to detect maladjustment. Face validity was not a concern in the construction of the instrument as it is too often with other inventories. The scales used to measure the nine kinds of mental illness were developed on an empirical basis by criterion keying. A large group of items was administered initially to several hundred normal persons and to groups of mental hospital patients whose symptoms matched one of the nine kinds of mental illness. Item analyses were undertaken to find the scoring key for each illness scale which would best differentiate the patients of one type from normals and from other types of patients.

The criterion-keying procedure used on the *MMPI* is much like that used to develop the Strong interest scales. Criterion keying is advantageous in that it promotes the predictive validity of an instrument, and it places little dependence on the insight and frankness of the respondent.

In addition to the nine mental illness scales available on the *MMPI*, four so-called "validity scores" are used. These provide some information about the test-taking attitude of the subject and the relative honesty with which his responses are made. The "validity scores" are as follows:

The Question Score(P). This consists of the number of items marked in the "cannot say" category. The interpretation is that if a person has a high question score, the scale scores for the different kinds of illness appear lower than they should be. If a person has as many as 130 "cannot say" responses, the individual's test record is assumed to be invalid.

The Lie Score(L). This scale consists of 15 items concerning socially desirable actions which few people could truthfully endorse; e.g., "I like everyone I know." The assumption is that an individual who endorses numerous items of this kind is falsifying the inventory.

The Validity Score(F). This consists of 64 items which are endorsed infrequently by normal subjects. They concern a hodgepodge of symptoms which are not likely to occur in any one mental illness. The interpretation is that a person who endorses a number of these items is careless or does not understand the test instructions.

The Correction Score(K). This consists of 30 items which were found to differentiate clinical patients whose scale scores appeared normal from persons who were actually normal. The responses to these items can be used to correct the illness scores for particular persons.

It should not be assumed that "validity scores" like those on the *MMPI* are a panacea in the use of personality inventories. There is not enough evidence yet to support the contention that the "validity scores" actually measure what they are purported to measure. The question, lie, and "validity" scores may indicate that a respondent gives misleading responses, but nothing can be done except to throw away the test record.

The correction score (K) offers a more positive approach, but not enough research has been done to say how well it works.

The results of the *MMPI* can be plotted as a profile showing scores on the nine illness scales and those on the four "validity" scales (see Figure 14–1 for illustrative profiles). It is seldom found that a person scores

FIGURE 14–1. *MMPI* profiles for a normal adult (_ _ _) and for a "typical psychotic" (___). (Adapted from Gough, 11, pp. 554 and 563; reproduced by permission of The Ronald Press Company.)

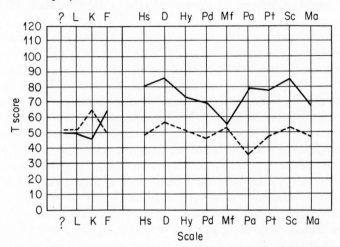

high (the maladjusted direction) on only one of the scales. Typically, the maladjustment spreads across several of the scales. Some of the scales correlate substantially with the others, which is to be expected because mental illness seldom occurs as one specific pattern of traits. It is usually the case that the patient has a mixture of different kinds of mental illness.

In order to interpret the *MMPI* profile, complex pattern scoring methods have been devised (14). Even with these it is necessary to have an experienced clinical psychologist to interpret the results. As is true of many clinical methods, a complex lore has developed about the meaning of different kinds of *MMPI* profiles, much of which has only slight grounding in empirical fact.

Much stands or falls on the eventual validity of the *MMPI*. Never before (and perhaps never again) has so much careful research gone into the empirical derivation of a self-description inventory to measure different kinds of maladjustment. The success of this venture will have a strong effect on the future course of personality measurement. The present evidence indicates that the *MMPI* is better than any comparable maladjustment inventory but not nearly as effective as was hoped for initially.

SOCIAL TRAITS

The difference between measures of maladjustment and social traits is more a matter of degree than a hard and fast distinction. Some of the inventories which are primarily concerned with social traits also contain one or more scales concerning different kinds of maladjustment. The extremes of most social traits border on maladjustment. For example, shyness, until it becomes extreme, can be a manifestation of normal behavior.

Allport Ascendance-Submission Reaction Study. One of the earliest self-description inventories and one that is still very much with us is the ascendance-submission (A-S) inventory developed by the Allports (1). Its purpose is to measure the tendency of a person either to lead and dominate his friends and associates or to be led and dominated by them. Each item describes a situation in which the respondent can show either dominance or submission to some degree. An illustrative item is as follows:

Someone tries to push ahead of you in line. You have been waiting for some time, and can't wait much longer. Suppose the intruder is the same sex as yourself, do you usually:

Remonstrate with the intruder   _____

Call the attention of the man at the
    ticket window   _____

"Look daggers" at the intruder or make
    clearly audible comments   _____

Decide not to wait and go away   _____

Do nothing   _____

Scoring weights for the A-S inventory items were determined in such a way as to differentiate persons who were rated high in dominance, by themselves and by associates, from those who were rated low in dominance. The A-S inventory has been used extensively during the last twenty years, and the research findings show that, on occasion, it can serve as a useful and valid measure.

Bernreuter Personality Inventory. Bernreuter's inventory (3) first appeared in 1932 and has been in wide use since that time. His purpose was to combine in one inventory the information which could be obtained from a number of other inventories. He used items which appeared in current tests of that day and composed scoring keys for the four scales of "neuroticism," "self-sufficiency," "introversion," and "dominance." The only evidence of validity offered by Bernreuter is that the scales on the inventory correlate highly with the parent inventories from which the items were drawn.

One of the difficulties exemplified by the Bernreuter Personality Inventory is that of obtaining independent measures of different traits. If, as on the Bernreuter inventory, there are four scales, it is expected that the four scores concern at least partially different traits. This is far from the case on the Bernreuter and on many other personality inventories. Introversion and neuroticism scores on the Bernreuter correlate .95, meaning that they are almost totally identical.

Beginning in the 1930s and continuing to this time, factor analysis and similar procedures have been used extensively to construct differential personality inventories. Flanagan's (9) factor analysis of the Bernreuter scales set the stage for much such work to follow. He found that two factors account for nearly all of the variance in the four scales which Bernreuter employs. He called these two factors "self-confidence" and "sociability." Bernreuter added scoring keys for Flanagan's two factors, which are used in addition to the other four scales. Six names do not constitute six traits. When the inventory is used, only the two scales developed by Flanagan should be scored.

Multifactor Batteries. An extensive effort has been under way to chart the major factors arising from self-description inventories. The hope is to find a limited number of traits that account for the scores obtained from diverse inventories. A series of studies by Guilford and his associates laid the groundwork in this field. He first collected 35 statements which were purported by different authorities to be primary aspects of introversion-extraversion. These were made into an inventory and administered to groups of subjects. A factor analysis of the items produced five factors instead of the single continuum along which introversion-extraversion is commonly judged. Successive factor analyses were performed on new sets of items until 13 factors were found in all. The 10 most prominent factors appear in the Guilford-Zimmerman Temperament Survey (12). The factor names and descriptions are as follows:

G, *General Activity.* High energy, quickness of action, liking for speed, and efficiency

R, *Restraint.* Deliberate, serious-minded, persistent

A, *Ascendance.* Leadership, initiative, persuasiveness

S, *Sociability.* Having many friends, and liking social activities

E, *Emotional Stability.* Composure, cheerfulness, evenness of moods

O, *Objectivity.* Freedom from suspiciousness, from hypersensitivity, and from getting into trouble

F, *Friendliness.* Respect for others, acceptance of domination, toleration of hostility

T, *Thoughtfulness.* Reflective, meditative, observing of self and others

    P, *Personal relations.* Tolerance of people, faith in social institutions, freedom from faultfinding and from self-pity

    M, *Masculinity.* Interest in masculine activities, hardboiled, not easily disgusted, versus (for femininity) romantic and emotionally expressive

Two other widely used multifactor inventories are The Sixteen Personality Factor Questionnaire (5) developed by Cattell and the Thurstone Temperament Schedule (18).

    Special Areas. In terms of numbers, most of the personality inventories are constructed for particular research or selection problems rather than for commercial distribution. These range from instruments to detect brain damage to inventories for the selection of sales clerks. There has been a boom in the construction of inventories for industrial selection. In some organizations, everyone from the janitor to the company president must make his marks on a self-description inventory. Much of the work which is done on industrial inventories is not reported on in professional journals or in other readily available sources. The reason for this is that such specialized inventories are not of interest to many people, and also there is a desire in many cases to prevent competing commercial concerns from adopting the same or similar inventories.

    A typical inventory developed for a special research problem is that of Burgess and Cottrell (4) used to measure marital happiness. Five of the inventory items are as follows (multiple choice alternatives are supplied for each item):

    Do you kiss your husband (wife) every day?

    Do you ever wish you had not married?

    What things annoy and dissatisfy you most about your marriage?

    If you had your life to live over, do you think you would marry the same person?

    Do husband and wife engage in outside interests together?

The inventory was administered to married couples to measure their level of marital adjustment. The responses were used as a criterion to determine the predictive validity of background data as a forecaster of marriage happiness.

EVALUATION OF SELF-DESCRIPTION INVENTORIES

    The inventories discussed so far in this chapter have been passed over lightly. Little attention has been given to the reliability, norms, validity, and uses for particular instruments. The reason for this is that a detailed discussion of separate inventories would not be worth the space it would take. It is not unduly critical to say that self-description inventories have mainly produced disappointing results (see **7, 8, 10, 17**). The remainder of the chapter will consider some of the reasons why self-description inventories meet with difficulty.

Reliability. Self-description inventories are usually less reliable than tests of aptitude, achievement, interests, and attitude. There are numerous exceptions to this rule, but self-description inventories tend to have lower reliability than most other psychological measures. Reliability coefficients for the better-established self-description inventories usually range between .75 and .85. Well-established aptitude and achievement tests usually have reliability coefficients between .85 and .95. The reliability of self-description inventories is usually not so low as to render them unusable, but the amount of measurement error which is often present is enough to materially impair the validity.

As is true in all tests, the reliability of self-description inventories can usually be raised by increasing the number of items. Some inventories employ large numbers of items in order to make the results reliable. Individual items on self-description inventories are usually less reliable than aptitude and achievement items. It is not uncommon to find, for example, that a 20-item vocabulary or mathematics test has a reliability over .85. It is usually necessary to have twice that many items in a self-description inventory to reach the .85 level of reliability, if that level can be reached at all.

Validity. One of the major observations to make about self-description inventories is that in many cases almost no effort is made to investigate validity. Many of the inventories are founded on "face validity." The inventory items are often so directly related to the trait being measured— e.g., "Do you often feel depressed?"—that it is an easy step to *assume* that inventories measure what they seem to measure. Face validity is not only insufficient evidence of validity, it can actually be a harmful quality in an inventory. The more transparent the items and the more they look like the characteristic to be measured, the more they are open to distortion by the respondent.

Another approach to the determination of validity has been to correlate one self-description inventory with others. This is not necessarily an indication of validity. If self-description inventories correlate with one another, this may mean only that people are consistent in applying misconceptions about themselves or that they are consistent in purposely distorting their own characteristics.

Most self-description inventories require an investigation of predictive validity (the term "prediction" being taken broadly to mean a functional relation with other forms of behavior either in the past, at present, or in the future). The great difficulty in validating many self-description inventories is that there is almost nothing available to predict. For example, what should the "friendliness" factor on the Guilford-Zimmerman inventory predict?

The adjustment-maladjustment inventories are in a better position to establish validity than are the inventories for social traits. A procedure which is often used to validate maladjustment inventories is to compare the scores of contrasting groups of persons—mental hospital patients with people outside, psychiatric rejects from the Army with soldiers in general, persons who suffer from psychosomatic ailments with people in general. Even if an inventory successfully distinguishes the members of contrasting groups, it might not be able to make precise distinctions in the borderline area between adjustment and maladjustment.

It is sometimes possible to validate social trait inventories with contrasting groups. For example, a "leadership" inventory can be used to distinguish persons who achieve positions of leadership from those who do not. In spite of the incompleteness of the "contrasted groups" design, it is one of the best methods of validation currently available for many personality inventories.

Personality inventories can be validated most easily when they are used to select persons for particular jobs, positions, and courses of training. If a reliable success criterion is available, it can be used to test the predictive validity of self-description inventories. For example, this can be done by correlating scores made on a self-description inventory by prospective salesmen with the amount of sales made later.

In those cases where the validity of self-description inventories can be determined either by the method of contrasted groups or by correlation with a continuous criterion, the inventories usually show disappointing results. There are isolated cases of self-description inventories which prove themselves valid to a reasonable extent, but these are few and far between. In addition to the generally low level of validity found for self-description inventories, the validity coefficients tend to change markedly with variations in testing circumstances. A common practice has been to administer self-description inventories to people who are already working on a job, and to validate the inventory by correlating it with measures of job success. A substantial correlation found in this way is no guarantee that the same results will be found when the inventory is used to select people for jobs. When people are applying for a job, they are eager to appear suited for the position, and the personality inventory is usually answered in such a way as to make the applicant appear in the best light. People who are already on the job are not under the same pressure to fake an inventory.

The responses that people give to personality inventories and the validity of inventories can change with subtle changes in the testing environment. The author [1] found that in military settings the responses to self-description inventories are sometimes different when they are administered by civilians rather than by officers and different when the respondents are told that the results will become part of their military records than when they are told that the results are to be used strictly for research purposes. Even if an inventory proves valid in one testing situation, it must be revalidated for any other situation in which it is used even if the two situations appear quite similar.

Self-description inventories have so far been of no practical aid in the prediction of school success. Although personality must certainly be an important element in school work, the author knows of no situation in which a self-description inventory has added materially to the predictive efficiency of conventional aptitude batteries. Self-description inventories work out better as aids to student counseling and guidance. The student who rates himself as unhappy, lacking in self-confidence, and without friends is likely to be in need of help. Persons who rate themselves as maladjusted are good prospects for more detailed study. There is no guarantee that the student who describes himself as happy, confident, and abundantly possessed with friends is really well adjusted. He may actually be well adjusted or he may be as sick or sicker than the person who relates his troubles.

The validity of self-description inventories in job selection varies considerably with the job (see **10**). The inventories perform moderately well in the selection of salesmen and sales clerks and have some validity for clerical workers and skilled trades; they work poorly in the selection of supervisors, foremen, and service workers (such as policemen).

Language difficulties. The validity of self-description inventories depends to a considerable extent on the clarity with which items are phrased. Consider, for example, a typical item such as "Do you usually lead the discussion in group situations?" Respondents must interpret what is meant by "usually"—60 per cent of the time, 75 per cent of the time, or 90 per cent of the time. Does the word "lead" mean to talk the most, make the most important points, or have the final say? Does the phrase "group situation" pertain only to formal groups such as club meetings, or does it include casual discussions among friends? This may be overdoing the difficulties of communicating social traits, but it illustrates the need for language clarity in the phrasing of self-description items.

In addition to the difficulty of wording items clearly, test constructors must be careful in describing the traits measured by inventories. This is true both of the inventories derived by factor analysis and those which are constructed on a "rational" basis. Some of the trait names appearing

[1] Unpublished research.

on current inventories are esoteric and confusing, such as "rathymia," and 'adventurous cyclothemia." A school psychologist who uses self-description inventories must know the meaning of the traits being measured before the results can be put to any valid use. The problem is not confined to self-description inventories. Aptitude factors like *verbal comprehension* and *perceptual speed* might be misunderstood by the test user, but there is more of a problem in communicating the meaning of personality factors.

Nunnally and Husek (15) studied the clarity of factor interpretations in three widely used multifactor inventories. They found that the factors in one battery were considerably less understandable than those in the other two. Because of the difficulties in communicating the meanings of personality traits, an attempt should be made to determine the clarity of factor interpretations before inventories are distributed commercially.

A serious consequence of the difficulty of naming and explaining personality traits such as those found in the multifactor inventories is that different inventories which purport to measure the same trait may have little in common. Correlations are sometimes very low between different inventories used to measure a trait such as introversion. Consequently, whether or not a person is said to be introverted depends on the inventory which is used.

Trait Clusters. Little is gained from knowing responses to particular self-description items unless the items evolve into more general clusters of traits. The hope is that there are a relatively small number of clusters or factors which underlie the many specific social traits. Factor analysis is the tool which is used most often to search for clusters of related traits. Unfortunately, the factor-analytic work with self-description items has not borne the useful results which have been found in studies of aptitudes, interests, and attitudes.

Correlations between self-description items tend to be low. Relatively unclear factor solutions are often obtained. Different investigators find different numbers of factors. The factors are often difficult to name, and different investigators use different names. Although there is still controversy about how many and what kinds of factors exist in human abilities, there is enough confirming evidence and agreement among investigators to talk as we did in Chapter 9 about the "structure" of human abilities. There is as yet no comparable factor structure which can be said to underlie self-description inventories.

The difficulty in finding self-description factors is not statistical but is due to the nature of social traits. Social traits are often combined in a highly individual manner. In order to find substantial factors, it is necessary for a group of traits to go together in the same way for all persons. If, for example, there is a general trait of dominance, the person who is dominant with women should be dominant with men, dominant at work and dominant at home, dominant when placed in one situation as well as in any other. However, people are often dominant and submissive in highly individual ways. The person who is dominant with women may be submissive with men, dominant at home, but submissive at work, dominant among strangers but submissive with people who know him well. The particularity of social trait patterns in individuals is not so marked as to spoil all efforts at determining trait clusters, but particularization is present to a degree that markedly hinders the successful use of self-description inventories.

The Acceptability Influence. More important than the other roadblocks to the construction of self-description inventories is the fact that the respondent can and usually does control the responses for his own ends. There is a strong drive in all of us to appear socially acceptable and acceptable to ourselves. Acceptability in our society means being intelligent, courageous, courteous, kind, dominant, and so on. It is extremely difficult for an individual to admit to himself that he is ignorant, cowardly, rude, mean, and submissive. It is even more difficult for an individual to admit these failings publicly. People in general tend to describe themselves in rosy terms, to an extent that lowers the diagnostic value of self-description inventories.

A study by Edwards (**6**) demonstrates the extent to which the "acceptability influence" dominates the responses made to self-description inventories. In the first part of his study, 152 subjects rated the social acceptability of each of 140 personality trait items on a nine-point scale. Scale values for the items were determined, showing the relative negative or positive social value attributed to the traits. Next, Edwards made the 140 items into a personality inventory. A group of students was asked to indicate "yes" for each item that characterized them and "no" for items that did not characterize them. The proportion of persons answering "yes" to each item was determined. Edwards found a correlation of .87 between the judged social acceptability of items and the proportion of people who endorsed the items. This is strong evidence that people generally try to describe themselves in a socially acceptable manner on personality inventories.

What is acceptable behavior for particular persons varies somewhat in terms of age, sex, vocation, and social position. The soldier needs to be tough and stern, whereas the minister is more in need of the virtues of kindness and patience. Respondents are usually aware enough of the characteristics needed in a particular situation to fake in the required direction.

The strength of the acceptability influence in self-description inventories depends on the degree to which the item alternatives differ in social acceptability and the punishments which result from not appearing socially acceptable. There is some variance in acceptability among the alternatives in attitude, opinion, and interest inventories, but not nearly so much as is involved in most self-description inventories. The punishment received for not appearing socially acceptable is either embarrassment or failure to obtain a sought-after job or position.

The acceptability influence is less strong when respondents mark inventories in private, when they do not put their names on the forms, when assurance is given that all results will be kept anonymous, and when the inventory is unconnected with selection procedures of any kind. This is the situation that prevails in most research studies, and it is in research studies that self-description inventories have their most valid use. The acceptability influence becomes particularly strong when the friends and acquaintances of a respondent will see the responses or when the respondent is applying for a particular job.

Efforts have been made to cancel out the acceptability influence by using alternatives of equal social acceptability. For example, the respondent is asked to rate whether he is more strong or intelligent, more impatient or distrustful, and more calm or friendly. Employing items of this kind is referred to as the *forced-choice technique*.

A forced-choice inventory which seems to meet with some success as a military screening aid is the Shipley Personal Inventory (16). The item alternatives were chosen to be of near social acceptability. A scoring key was derived by criterion keying to differentiate the responses of psychiatric patients from normal persons. A typical item is as follows:

I have felt bad more from head colds. _____
I have felt bad more from dizziness. _____

The forced-choice technique is a promising lead in the construction of self-description inventories but by no means a cure for all of their faults. Even with the best efforts to equate the social acceptability of alternatives, the discerning person can often recognize the most desirable responses.

Summary Evaluation. Extensive amounts of time, energy, funds, and hope have been invested in the construction of self-description inventories during the last thirty years. It is currently a major activity of many persons in psychology and kindred fields. The inherent difficulties of constructing valid inventories and the poor validities which the inventories usually produce make many psychologists feel that further work along these lines would be futile. The great need to measure personality characteristics and the paucity of adequate measures should make us cautious about disparaging any well-intentioned efforts. However, the author is among those who believe that the successful measurement of personality characteristics will rest largely on testing procedures other than self-description inventories.

REFERENCES

1. Allport, G. W., and Allport, F. H. *The A-S Reaction Study: Revised Manual.* Boston: Houghton Mifflin, 1939.
2. Bell, H. M. *The Adjustment Inventory: Manual for Student Form, 1934; Manual for Adult Form, 1938.* Stanford University, Calif.: Stanford Univer. Press, 1934, 1938.
3. Bernreuter, R. G. *The Personality Inventory: Manual.* Stanford University, Calif.: Stanford Univer. Press, 1935.
4. Burgess, E. W., and Cottrell, L. S. *Predicting success or failure in marriage.* Englewood Cliffs, N.J.: Prentice-Hall, 1939.
5. Cattell, R. B., Saunders, D. R., and Stice, G. *The Sixteen Personality Factor Questionnaire: Handbook.* Champaign, Ill.: Inst. Pers. Ability Testing, 1950.
6. Edwards, A. L. The relationship between the judged desirability of a trait and the probability that the trait will be endorsed. *J. appl. Psychol.*, 1953, **37**, 90–93.
7. Ellis, A. Recent research with personality inventories. *J. consult. Psychol.*, 1953, **17**, 45–49.
8. Ellis, A., and Conrad, H. S. The validity of personality inventories in military practice. *Psychol. Bull.*, 1948, **45**, 385–426.
9. Flanagan, J. C. *Factor analysis in the study of personality.* Stanford University, Calif.: Stanford Univer. Press, 1935.
10. Ghiselli, E. E., and Barthol, R. P. The validity of personality inventories in the selection of employees. *J. appl. Psychol.*, 1953, **37**, 18–20.
11. Gough, H. G. Minnesota Multiphasic Personality Inventory. In A. Weider (Ed.), *Contributions toward medical psychology,* Vol. 2. New York: Ronald, 1953.
12. Guilford, J. P., and Zimmerman, W. S. *The Guilford-Zimmerman Temperament Survey: Manual.* Beverly Hills, Calif.: Sheridan Supply Co., 1949.
13. Hathaway, S. R., and McKinley, J. C. *Minnesota Multiphasic Personality Inventory: Manual.* New York: Psychol. Corp., 1951.
14. Hathaway, S. R., and Meehl, P. E. *An atlas for the clinical use of the MMPI.* Minneapolis: Univer. Minn. Press, 1951.
15. Nunnally, J., and Husek, T. "Semantic clarity": One standard for factored tests. *Educ. psychol. Measmt,* 1958, **18**, 761–767.
16. Shipley, W. C., Gray, F. E., and Newbert, N. The personal inventory: its derivation and validation. *J. clin. Psychol.*, 1946, **2**, 318–322.
17. Super, D. E. The Bernreuter personality inventory: A review of research. *Psychol. Bull.*, 1942, **39**, 94–125.
18. Thurstone, L. L. *Thurstone Temperament Schedule: Examiner's Manual.* Chicago: Science Research, 1950.
19. Woodworth, R. S. *Personal data sheet.* Chicago: Stoelting, 1918.

CHAPTER 15

Projective Techniques

The projective techniques offer an approach to the measurement of personality which is interestingly different from that of the self-description inventories. Whereas the self-description inventories require the subject to describe himself, the projective techniques require the subject to describe or interpret objects other than himself. The projective techniques are based on the hypothesis that an individual's responses to an "unstructured" stimulus are influenced by his needs, motives, fears, expectations, and concerns.

If there is an agreed-on public meaning for a stimulus, it is referred to as a *structured* stimulus. If there is no agreed-on public meaning for a stimulus, and in consequence there is considerable latitude for individual interpretation, it is referred to as an *unstructured* stimulus. A structured stimulus is compared with an unstructured stimulus in Figure 15–1. First, what do you see in picture *A?* Nearly everyone will say that it is a house. A few people might call it a school or even a jail, but people will generally agree that it is a dwelling of some kind. The shape of a house is a highly structured stimulus. Now what do you see in picture *B?* There is no accepted common meaning for that stimulus pattern. It might be interpreted as a thunderstorm, a dog, or an artist's palette.

There is a considerable body of evidence to show that interpretations of relatively unstructured stimuli are related to moods, needs, and expectations. Studies of the effect of food deprivation show that hungry subjects more frequently interpret ambiguous drawings as representing food than do non-hungry subjects (9). In one study a completely blank screen was used and subjects were led to believe that faint images were being presented (10). It was found that the number of food responses increased as the interval of food deprivation lengthened. Other studies show that perception is influenced by values, social taboos, and personal conflicts (see 5). An experience common to most of us is the misreading of printed material in a way that indicates our concerns of the moment. For example, the student who worries over an examination coming the next day is likely to see in a hasty glance at the evening paper that "The police will give the examination tomorrow," whereas a careful reading will show that "The police will give the explanation tomorrow."

If the individual interprets picture B in Figure 15–1 as a thunderstorm rather than as a dog, this may indicate something about him personally. However, it is one thing to say that a response is significant and quite another thing to say just what it indicates about the person.

FIGURE 15–1. Comparison of a relatively structured stimulus (A) with a relatively unstructured stimulus (B).

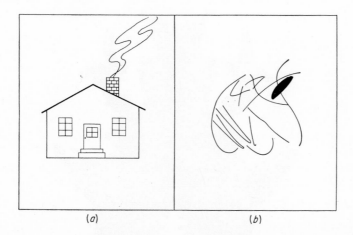

(a)   (b)

The instruments which will be discussed in this chapter are primarily based on the interpretation of personality characteristics from responses to relatively unstructured stimuli. The ultimate in unstructured stimuli is found in one of the pictures in the Thematic Apperception Test (TAT). The subject is asked to make up a story about a completely blank card. Other stimuli are structured to some extent to obtain information about particular needs and concerns. For example, in an instrument used to study attitudes, a picture which shows a white person and a Negro talking can be used. The stimulus is structured to that extent and in that manner in order to learn about attitudes toward Negroes.

The term "projective tests," which is used to refer to the kinds of instruments to be discussed in this chapter, is somewhat of a misnomer. The more strict meaning of the term *projection* is the tendency of an individual to see his own unwanted traits, ideas, and concerns in other people. For example, the individual who is himself a rather hostile person is often prone to see hostility in other people on the basis of little or no evidence. Here we will be concerned not only with projection in the stricter sense but with the many ways in which the interpretation of unstructured stimuli can be used to detect personality characteristics.

RORSCHACH TECHNIQUE

By far the most widely used projective technique is the Rorschach. It was developed during and after the First World War by Herman Rorschach, a Swiss psychiatrist. He experimented with different ink blots to find a set which would provide the most insight into the nature of

FIGURE 15–2. An ink blot of the type used in the Rorschach Test.

mental disorder. The 10 ink blots which he settled on are still in use. An ink blot like those used in the test is shown in Figure 15–2. Five of the ink blot cards are made in shades of black and gray only. Two of the remaining cards contain bright patches of red in addition to shades of gray. The three remaining cards employ various colors.

Administration. The Rorschach, like the other projective devices, should be administered only by a highly trained examiner. The results will depend very much on the examiner's skill. Although there are several schools of thought as to how the Rorschach should be administered and interpreted, a similar approach is used by most examiners. The most widely used approaches are those advocated by Beck (2) and by Klopfer and Kelley (8).

The usual procedure followed in administering the Rorschach is to talk with the respondent a minute or so to gain rapport, seat him with his back to the examiner, and then introduce the task with approximately the following instructions: "People see all sorts of things in these ink blot pictures; now tell me what you see, what it might be for you, what it makes you think of" (8, p. 32). The respondent is allowed to give as many interpretations as he likes. If he gives only one response and apparently tries to give no more, the examiner suggests that he look for other things, saying something like, "People usually see more than one thing." A typical series of responses to one card would be for the subject to report, "It all looks like a bat" and "This part looks like a vase." After looking at the card for a few more seconds, he might give as his final response, "This little bit looks like a nose."

After the respondent runs out of interpretations for the first card, he is handed the next one, and so on for all 10 cards. The examiner is kept busy ordering the materials, measuring the time taken to give each response, and writing down verbatim what the respondent says. After the series of ink blots is administered, the examiner conducts what is called the "inquiry." This consists of asking the subject questions about each of his responses to learn what part of the blot is involved in the interpretation and why the particular part gives rise to the response.

Scoring. There are a number of different kinds of scores given to each response. The major scoring categories relate to "content," "determinants," and "location." The interpretation of a response depends on the scores received from all three categories. Consequently, only very general implications can be given to scores in one category alone.

Some of the major categories of content are listed and illustrated as follows:

> *Human.* A response that would be scored *human* in content is "a man doing a dance."
> *Human Detail*, e.g., "a nose."
> *Animal*, e.g., "a bat."
> *Anatomy*, e.g., "bones."
> *Clothing*, e.g., "a nun's habit."
> *Nature*, e.g., "northern lights."
> *Sex*, e.g., "a woman's breast."
> *Landscape*, e.g., "a lake."
> *Food*, e.g., "a steak with mushrooms."

If a person gives almost all animal responses, this is taken as an indication of low "functioning intelligence." A predominance of anatomy responses is usually interpreted as an indication of depressive tendency or of overconcern with health. If an individual gives many more responses in one content category than in others, e.g., many food responses, this is taken as evidence of an especial personality need.

Location refers to the part of the ink blot which instigates a particular response. This information is usually obtained in the inquiry. The response is scored W if the whole blot is used in the response. Typical W responses are "a bat," "a sky full of dark clouds," and "a garden of flowers." The response is scored D if the location is a commonly perceived subdivision of the total blot. Typical D responses are to call a large part of an ink blot "a bird's head," and another part of the same blot "a statue." The response is scored Dd if the location is a small and usually unnoticed part of the ink blot. A typical Dd response is to interpret a small patch of gray off from the main figure as "a face."

The location of responses is thought to indicate the subject's mental approach to life, whether he deals in sweeping generalizations, considers details systematically, or gets lost in the compulsive consideration of unimportant side issues. The number and kind of W responses supposedly reflect potential intelligence. The intelligent, creative person is thought to give numerous, well-organized W responses. The person who emphasizes D responses is thought to have a common-sense, matter-of-fact approach to life problems. An emphasis on Dd responses is taken as an indication of compulsive tendency or mental disorganization. The Rorschach responses of the average adult contain approximately 6 W responses, 20 D, and 4 Dd.

The scoring of determinants is both more complex and more subjective than the scoring of content and location. If the response is determined by the shape or outline of either the whole or part of the ink blot, it is scored as a form response (F). Form responses are further scored either "plus," if they are adequate responses of the kind that normal and superior people would give, or "minus," if they are not adequate interpretations. A response is scored M if movement is seen in the interpretation, e.g., "two women dancing." If the response is apparently determined by the color of the part which is interpreted, it is scored C. If the response is "sea water," and in the inquiry the subject gives as his reason, "because it's green," it would be scored as a color response. A response is scored Y if it is determined by the shades of gray within a blot. A typical Y response is "dark clouds." It is usually the case that a response must be scored on more than one determinant. For example, an FC score means that the response is determined mainly by form and that color enters as a secondary determinant. A CF response means that color is the primary determinant and form the secondary determinant.

Form responses are thought to indicate a factual, rational approach to life. Color responses are thought to indicate emotional reactions. If a person gives considerably more form than color responses it is taken as a sign of emotional impoverishment and repression of feelings. If color predominates over form, it is said to indicate impulsiveness, lack of emotional control, and dominance of emotion over reason.

Movement responses are considered to be indicators of the richness of imagination and "inner" life. When movement responses predominate over color responses, the interpretation is that the individual is introversive. If color responses are more numerous than movement responses, the subject is said to be extratensive, more concerned with the "outer" rather than the "inner" life. Shading responses are taken to indicate uncertainty, worry, depression, and anxiety.

After each response has been scored in terms of content, location, and determinants, scores are added up over all responses, forming the "response summary." The total number of responses given and the time taken to respond are also considered in the summary.

Interpretation. Rorschach responses are interpreted in terms of psychoanalytic and other "depth" psychologies. The response summary alone is only a part of the material used in the interpretation. The trained examiner takes note of many complex relationships among content, location, and determinants. Thus, the movement response "children playing ball" might be interpreted quite differently from "men playing ball" in terms of the other responses in the record. A response that would be interpreted one way for a man is often interpreted differently for a woman. If a person who has never finished high school gives numerous anatomical content responses, it might be taken as an indication of morbid thoughts. If a college student gives many anatomical responses, it might be interpreted as interest in and familiarity with biology.

The interpretation of Rorschach responses is an extremely complex task. Although there are reasonably clear-cut rules for scoring individual responses, there are only general standards and examples to direct the final interpretation. The interpretation depends heavily on the subjective impression of the examiner. It takes about two years of practice, usually working in close collaboration with experienced examiners, to become proficient at interpreting Rorschach responses.

THE THEMATIC APPERCEPTION TEST (*TAT*)

The *TAT*, developed by Murray (12) and his associates, consists of pictures of people in various settings. One of the pictures is shown in Figure 15–3. Some of the pictures are more suited to young rather than older people, and some are more suited to men than women. The pictures are structured in such a way as to elicit responses concerning relationships between various social roles and responses relating to different emotions. The pictures are unstructured in the sense that a wide variety of interpretations can be given about the feelings and actions of the persons shown.

Administration. The examiner has a choice as to how many of the pictures and what kinds will be used with a subject. If the standard set of

FIGURE 15–3. One of the pictures used in the Thematic Apperception Test. (Reproduced by permission of Harvard University Press.)

20 pictures is used, it usually requires more than one testing session to complete the series. In many cases the examiner uses only the half-dozen or so pictures which he thinks will elicit the most pertinent information from a particular subject. The subject is told to make up a story about each picture in turn. The instructions are approximately as follows: "I am going to show you some pictures. I want you to tell me a story about what is going on in each picture. What led up to it, and what will the outcome be?" The responses are either written down verbatim or a phonographic recording is made.

Scoring and Interpretation. Murray originally scored *TAT* responses in terms of *needs* and *presses*. A *need* is something that the individual is trying to obtain. Some of the *needs* listed by Murray are achievement, aggression, nurturance, passivity, and sex. *Presses* are the outside influences which help or hinder the attainment of *needs,* such as aggression, dominance, and rejection by other persons. Each story can be inspected for the *needs* and *presses* which are portrayed.

Murray's system of scoring also considered the *hero* in each story and the *outcome.* The *hero* is the person in the story with whom the subject apparently identifies. For example, responses to Figure 15–3 could concern stories about either the older woman or the younger woman. Sometimes the *hero* is a person outside of the picture. For example, a story about Figure 15–3 could concern a relative of one of the persons in the picture.

Although *needs, presses, hero,* and *outcomes* are considered by most of the people who work with the *TAT*, apparently few examiners make detailed scorings of them. In fact, no formal scoring system of any kind is used by the majority of *TAT* examiners. The examiner interprets the responses in terms of his knowledge of personality and his experience with the instrument. Some interpretations are of a common-sense kind with which most examiners would agree. If a male subject imputes unfriendly motives and actions to all of the female characters, it strongly suggests that he is having troubled relations with women in real-life situations. If all of the stories end in disappointment, embarrassment, and failure, it is likely that the subject feels defeated and depressed. If the stories are lacking in passion and violence, even in pictures where strong emotion is the evident theme, it indicates that the subject is suppressing his own emotions. If any one type of social interaction, such as adultery, is seen in numerous pictures and in pictures where there is little to suggest it, this indicates that the subject is overly concerned about a particular issue. Although there is no standard procedure of interpretation, responses to the *TAT* pictures provide many hints about the subject's concerns, his conception of himself, and the way he views his human environment.

Special Uses for TAT Pictures. The original set of pictures developed by Murray and his coworkers is only one of many such sets of pictures that are presently in use. Pictures can be made for many different kinds of special studies. For example, a special set of pictures could be used to study the attitudes that management and labor hold toward one another. Pictures of persons dressed like foremen, workmen, union executives, and vice-presidents could be made. These persons could be posed in settings pertinent to the problems under study and structured to the extent that attitudes about certain kinds of social interactions would be elicited. Special sets of pictures have been composed for Negroes, Indians, and other racial and ethnic groups. Pictures of the *TAT* kind have been used to study anti-Semitism, family relations, attitudes toward military life, and many others.

Comparison of Rorschach and TAT. There is considerable competition between the Rorschach and the *TAT* as clinical instruments. Some psychologists prefer the Rorschach in general; other psychologists are equally biased toward the *TAT*. Most testers agree that there are some differences in the kinds of things which the two techniques measure, as well as some special advantages for each instrument with particular types of subjects.

Although both instruments require an expert examiner, it is somewhat more difficult to learn the administration and interpretation of the Rorschach. Although it is difficult for the subject to "fake" either of the techniques, it is probably more difficult to distort responses on the Rorschach.

The Rorschach is not primarily concerned with content. That is, it is not very important whether a particular part of the blot is referred to as a snake or a rope. The important thing is whether or not the percept is a sensible interpretation and whether the percept is determined by the form or color of the area. Content is the meat of the *TAT*. If a character is described as a detective rather than as a salesman, it will markedly affect the interpretation.

The Rorschach is thought to be valuable in getting at disturbances in the thinking processes, particularly in patients who are nearing psychotic breakdowns. The *TAT* is more concerned with social adjustment than with thinking processes. Although there is controversy about the point, there are many people who believe that the Rorschach is better for detecting and classifying psychotic disorders, and that the *TAT* is better with neurotic disorders and milder disturbances. In many cases both tests are given to a subject, and many clinical psychologists believe this leads to a better all-around diagnosis than could be obtained from either of the instruments separately.

OTHER PROJECTIVE TECHNIQUES

In addition to the Rorschach and the *TAT*, there are numerous procedures for evaluating personality which are best thought of as projective techniques. Almost anything that can be described, completed, or interpreted serves to some extent as a projective test. We tend to read our concerns and expectations into everything we do.

Word Association. An old technique for learning about personality is to have an individual associate words. Various lists of words (see **7; 13,** chap. 2) have been employed to get at particular kinds of reactions. The usual practice is to place certain emotionally tinged words among relatively neutral terms. The following list of words would be useful in studying the home and school adjustment of adolescents:

1. Hair	_____		7. School	_____
2. Mother	_____		8. Love	_____
3. Home	_____		9. Tree	_____
4. Desk	_____		10. Hate	_____
5. Book	_____		11. Paper	_____
6. Father	_____		12. Shoe	_____

13. Fight	_____	17. Body	_____
14. String	_____	18. Me	_____
15. Sister	_____	19. Brother	_____
16. Cake	_____	20. Friend	_____

The words are read to the subject one at a time. He is asked to give the first word that comes into mind. The examiner records the responses and notes the time taken to respond. There are several ways in which the results are interpreted. The words which are associated often indicate the subject's attitudes toward persons and activities. In obvious cases where, for example, the association to "father" is "spanking" and the association to "hate" is "father," there is the strong suggestion of a negative reaction to the father. Equally revealing as the associated words are the emotional reactions to the initial terms. If the subject takes a relatively long time to respond or gives signs of being embarrassed, a strong emotional reaction is suggested. Thus, even though the subject eventually supplies an innocuous association for "father," such as "hat," the long time taken to respond would suggest "blocking" and underlying conflict. A third type of information used in the interpretation is the tendency to give unusual associations. For example, most persons will associate "table" with "chair" or respond with some other related item of furniture. It is unusual to find the response "tiger" to "chair," and when numerous such associations are made, it might be related to mental illness.

Sentence Completion. A technique which is similar to word association is the use of incomplete sentences (see **14**). Examples are as follows:

1. I dislike most to _____
2. I wish that I had never _____
3. Most people are _____
4. I become embarrassed _____
5. The people I like most _____

The usual procedure is to have subjects write their responses, permitting the testing of a number of persons at one time. The sentences can be structured to provide information on different areas of adjustment. No effort is made to "time" the responses. Consequently, the subject has time to make up whatever responses he chooses. The responses are analyzed similarly to those on the *TAT*. That is, the moods, motives, solutions, and expectations portrayed in the responses are interpreted in respect to the subject's personality.

Play Techniques. A method which is especially useful with children is to employ play materials as a projective device (see **3**, chap. 22). Children betray their feelings quite readily in play activities of all kinds, and almost any set of play materials serves as a "test." Dolls and puppets are used most often for this purpose. The situation can be structured by, for example, naming the dolls "mother," "father," "little brother," "me," and so on. Also the environment for the dolls can be structured to some extent by having present toy implements, such as a baby bottle, a toilet, a bed, doll clothing, and others. The child is encouraged to play with the material in whatever way he chooses. A revealing set of actions would be for the child to place the doll for "mother" and "little brother" with their faces to the wall while "father" gives the bottle to "me." Play activity of this kind is usually very rich in suggestions about the feelings and concerns of children.

Drawings, Paintings, and Sculpture. Artistic productions can be used as projective devices. These may be almost completely unstructured like finger painting (see 1, chap. 14), or they may be structured to the point of asking for the drawing of a man (see 11). The advantage of the relatively unstructured task is that it is often not perceived as a test. A widely used procedure is to furnish clay to children and let them make whatever they like. The product can be analyzed for the symbolism apparent or simply in terms of the actions imputed to the clay figures. If the child makes a clay image of himself, it is important to note whether the bodily parts are in proper proportion. An outsized nose or excessively small arms might offer suggestions about the child's concept of himself. Children often manifest strong emotions in artistic productions that they would not talk about openly. For example, a disturbed child might make a clay figure of mother, then run over her with the toy car, tear off the arms, and finally throw her in the wastebasket.

Finger painting is used with both adults and children. The subject is presented with a variety of paints and encouraged to use his fingers to make whatever he likes. The way that the subject approaches the task is thought to be as important as what is drawn. Some persons are very reticent about putting their fingers in the paint or making a mess with the materials. Other subjects take a childlike glee in smearing the paints and making the biggest mess possible. The colors which the individual chooses are thought to be important. The proportioning, balance, and integration of the finished painting are also used in the interpretation. For example, it might be considered a sign of schizophrenia if the person makes only swirling smears with one color.

EVALUATION OF PROJECTIVE TECHNIQUES

Some adherents of projective techniques feel that their instruments lay open the depths of personality to observation. Rather sweeping generalizations are often made about the response to an unstructured stimulus. Before the reader becomes alarmed about his own personality as it might be mirrored in the projective techniques, a look should be taken at the factual basis for the instruments.

Reliability. The ordinary measures of reliability are difficult to obtain with projective tests. If, as on the Rorschach, component scores are obtained prior to the interpretation, the reliability of these can be studied by split-half, equivalent-form, and other techniques. The reliabilities of single components on the Rorschach, like number of W responses and number of color responses, are less than those obtained with most tests of human ability but not so low as to render the indices unusable (see **4**). There are two reasons why the reliability of projective techniques cannot be determined from component scores. First, most of the projective devices employ few, if any, scores for separate responses. Second, even if separate responses are scored, the interpretation is the final test result, not the initial scores. Consequently, it is necessary to test the reliability of interpretations from the test.

Before studies of the reliability of interpretations can be made, it is necessary to develop objective procedures for recording interpretation. One way to do this is to have the Rorschach examiner make ratings of the subject on various personality traits (a handy procedure for doing this called the Q-sort will be discussed in Chapter 17). Correlations can then be made between the interpretations given by one examiner on two occasions and between the interpretations given by different examiners. Very few studies of this kind have been done.

Beck [1] found correlations between the interpretations by two examiners on numerous cases to range from above .80 down to zero. One examiner repeated the ratings of 10 cases a year after the first ratings were made. He did not remember making the earlier ratings. The correlations between the two interpretations ranged from .50 to .89, with a mean of .70. Although these are only a drop in the bucket to the studies which are needed, they indicate that the reliability fluctuates considerably for different kinds of subjects. Thus, whereas a child's responses might be interpreted with low reliability, an adult's responses might be interpreted with high reliability; and the reliability of interpretations made about mentally ill persons might be higher or lower than interpretations made about normal persons. The problem is further complicated in that the kinds of cases with which reliable interpretations are obtained from the Rorschach may be cases for which only unreliable interpretations are obtained from the *TAT* or from other projective instruments.

Whereas it is expected and usually necessary that scores on most tests remain stable over moderate periods of time, it is not necessarily expected with the results of projective techniques. If the scores made by adults on an intelligence test fluctuate markedly over a period of six months or

[1] Personal communication from S. J. Beck.

even several years, the use of the instrument would be seriously impaired. However, it is to be expected that some of the personality attributes mirrored in the projective techniques should sometimes change substantially in relatively short periods of time. For example, the Rorschach or *TAT* responses of an individual would likely change from the beginning to the end of a successful psychotherapy. Instruments like the *TAT* are probably affected to some extent by day-to-day changes in moods and by good and bad turns of events. Consequently, it is difficult to untangle the expected changes in responses from the measurement error inherent in the testing procedures.

Much more research needs to be done on the reliability of interpretations derived from projective techniques. Equally important to learning the over-all reliability with which interpretations are made is the need to learn the kinds of traits which are more reliably rated and those which are less reliably rated. For example, it might be found for one projective technique that interpretations regarding moods are reliable (high agreement among examiners) and that interpretations regarding future actions are relatively unreliable. Studies of this kind would help define the kinds of traits which are most reliably interpreted from different instruments.

It is doubtful that any one test can make the sweeping observations about personalities which are often claimed. Different techniques probably have different strong and weak points as personality measures. Because an instrument is shown to be reliable, it does not necessarily mean that it is valid for any purpose; but if it can be shown that interpretations regarding certain kinds of traits are unreliable, it means that they cannot be valid in any sense. Systematic studies of the reliability with which different projective techniques lead to interpretations of various personality characteristics would help define techniques in terms of what they measure, at least reliably, and would narrow the field of investigation for subsequent studies of validity.

Validity. Projective techniques must be classified as predictors by default. It is difficult to argue that the projective techniques are assessments of personality. For example, if an individual calls an ink blot a butterfly, there is no reason to believe that this response represents anything about his personality unless evidence is provided to prove that such is the case. Consequently, the validity of projective techniques can be determined only by correlating interpretations with important behaviors outside the testing situation.

In comparison to the many applications of projective techniques, there are very few studies of predictive validity. Consequently, no firm statements can be made concerning the validity of projective techniques as a group or about the validity of particular instruments. One of the problems is finding assessments for the projective testers to predict. The contrasted-groups study has been used most often to validate projective techniques. In a typical study an examiner is given the Rorschach records of both normal persons and individuals who are diagnosed as schizophrenic. The examiner must decide from the test results alone whether each person is from the normal or the schizophrenic group. Studies of this kind indicate that the Rorschach and the *TAT* are moderately successful in differentiating normal persons from the mentally ill. However, it should be pointed out that this is a very weak test of validity. The instruments are often used to make fine distinctions between people in the normal range and to differentiate among types of mental illness.

One of the difficulties in validating and improving the projective techniques is an unwillingness on the part of some devotees to subject their instruments to empirical investigation. A kind of cultism which encourages faith in the instruments rather than a healthy scientific skepticism has arisen among some projective testers. They would like other people to accept their projective devices and the elaborate interpretations which they make as self-evidently valid. It is encouraging to see that many exponents of projective techniques are aware of the need for empirical investigations and are busily performing the necessary research.

Standardization. A test was defined earlier as a standardized situation which provides the individual with a score. Do the projective techniques meet the requirements? In comparison to most tests, the projective techniques are relatively unstandardized. Although efforts are made to standardize the presentation of material to the subject, there are inevitable differences in the approaches used by different examiners. Much apparently depends on the way the examiner acts and the kind of person he is. With an instrument like the Rorschach, some examiners typically obtain more responses than other examiners, and women examiners sometimes obtain responses different from those obtained by male examiners.

The final results of projective techniques, the descriptions of individual personalities, are highly dependent on the intuitive judgment of the examiner. Not only are examiners unable to catalogue all of the rules which they use in reaching interpretations, but they are probably not aware of many cues which they employ. The examiner is not a person who simply administers the test and as such plays a minor role in the result. The examiner is part of the projective technique and inseparable from the test materials. Some examiners are undoubtedly more effective than others in deriving personality descriptions. Consequently, the validity of the technique is interwoven with the ability of the examiner who uses it. As long as projective techniques depend so heavily on the intuitions of examiners, they will not be tests in the stricter sense. Projective testing is more of an art than a science, but this does not necessarily mean that the results are invalid. It does, however, force us to consider the validity of separate examiners, and that immensely complicates the development of projective techniques for general use.

Some efforts have been made to more fully standardize projective techniques, particularly the Rorschach. Several multiple choice Rorschach forms have been developed. A list of responses is presented with each ink blot. The respondent chooses the alternative response which most nearly matches what he sees in the ink blot. The alternatives for each blot were chosen from the records of both normal and abnormal subjects. Although the earlier forms provided only an over-all adjustment score, a more recent version (6) provides scores for different aspects of personality like those considered in the usual method of applying the instrument. Most Rorschach examiners prefer the traditional procedure to the multiple choice approach. There is not enough evidence to say how well the multiple choice instruments work in practice; but any systematic efforts to obtain more standardized procedures should be encouraged.

Special Advantages. One of the foremost advantages of projective techniques is that most of them are difficult to fake. The subject is usually unaware of how his responses will be interpreted. The person who tries to distort responses often gives himself away. It was mentioned earlier in connection with the word-association technique that an effort to cover up unpleasant feelings can usually be detected by the relatively long time taken to respond. Certain areas on Rorschach ink blots usually generate sexual associations. If a person avoids sexual responses, it might indicate that he is concerned about sex. There are many other ways in which the experienced examiner can detect what the subject tries to hide. Even professional testers find it difficult to distort their own responses to projective techniques.

An advantage which is shared by most of the projective techniques is that they can be administered to persons of all ages, ethnic groups, and intelligence levels. The instructions are very simple and, in most cases, neither reading nor writing is required. The projective techniques are particularly applicable to children. Children who are unable or unwilling to discuss their problems directly usually react to the projective techniques as though they were games.

Clinical Usefulness. The projective techniques are used primarily in clinical practice. They are not likely to receive wide use in school programs or in the selection of people for particular jobs. The examiner must be an expert, and there are not enough of these experts to fill the needs of large testing programs. It takes the better part of a day to administer and interpret responses on the Rorschach and the *TAT*; thus, it would be excessively expensive to test large numbers of subjects in this way.

Projective techniques are used in making decisions about people who seek psychiatric treatment and about mental hospital patients. Questions must be answered about the nature and severity of the patients' problems and the kinds of treatment which are likely to do the most good. These are very important questions concerning human lives, and all available sources of information should be used. Decisions about patients must often be based on no more than one or several interviews plus some background information. To the extent that the projective techniques actually help in making these decisions, they perform a very worthwhile service.

Summary Evaluation. The projective techniques are ingenious efforts to measure personality variables. Many of the interpretations that arise from them appeal to common sense and fit in with psychological theory also. Unfortunately, the techniques are relatively unstandardized, and it is difficult to determine how well they work. Some projective testers have made unwisely sweeping claims for particular instruments. The techniques are often said to measure the "whole personality" and the "total behavior pattern." It is doubtful that activities so circumscribed as responding to 10 ink blots or making up stories about particular pictures will lead to such broad conclusions about the complexities of human personalities. The indicated directions for future research are to standardize the projective techniques and to determine the kinds of personality attributes which each measures most effectively.

REFERENCES

1. Anderson, H. H., and Anderson, G. L. *An introduction to projective techniques.* Englewood Cliffs, N.J.: Prentice-Hall, 1951.
2. Beck, S. J. *Rorschach's Test. I.: Basic Processes; II.: A Variety of Personality Pictures.* New York: Grune and Stratton, 1944, 1945.
3. Bell, J. E. *Projective techniques.* New York: Longmans, 1948.
4. Hertz, M. R. The reliability of the Rorschach ink blot test. *J. appl. Psychol.*, 1934, **18**, 461–477.
5. Jenkin, N. Affective processes in perception. *Psychol. Bull.*, 1957, **54**, 100–127.
6. Kellman, S. Multiple Choice Rorschach. In A. Weider (Ed.), *Contributions toward medical psychology.* Vol. 2. New York: Ronald, 1953.
7. Kent, G. H., and Rosanoff, A. J. A study of association in insanity. *Amer. J. Insanity*, 1910, **67**, 37–96, 317–390.
8. Klopfer, B., and Kelley, D. M. *The Rorschach technique.* Yonkers, N.Y.: World, 1942.
9. Levine, R., Chein, I., and Murphy, G. The relation of the intensity of a need to the amount of perceptual distortion: a preliminary report. *J. Psychol.*, 1942, **13**, 283–293.
10. McClelland, D. C., and Atkinson, J. W. The projective expression of needs: I. The effect of different intensities of the hunger drive on perception. *J. Psychol.*, 1948, **25**, 205–222.
11. Machover, K. *Personality projection in the drawing of the human figure: A method of personality investigation.* Springfield, Ill.: Charles C. Thomas, 1949.

12. Murray, H. A. *Thematic Apperception Test Manual.* Cambridge, Mass.: Harvard Univer. Press, 1943.
13. Rapaport, D., et al. *Diagnostic psychological testing.* Vol. 2. Chicago: Year Book Publishers, 1945, 1946.
14. Rotter, J. B., and Rafferty, J. E. *The Rotter Incomplete Sentences Blank: Manual.* New York: Psychol. Corp., 1950.

CHAPTER 16

The Future of Personality Measurement

In the previous two chapters, we discussed the instruments which are currently being used most widely as measures of personality: self-description inventories and projective techniques. It was concluded that neither of these approaches to personality measurement has yet provided instruments of known validity. Whereas we have reasonably good measures of interests, attitudes, and opinions (which some authors would classify as personality variables), few, if any, proved techniques are available to measure social traits, degree of adjustment, and personality "dynamics." This leaves a great gap in the storehouse of measurement tools in an area where measurement methods are most needed. Personality traits are, of course, very much involved in success and happiness in vocational and social life. Consequently, there is an urgent need to develop adequate measures of personality traits. This chapter will discuss some of the directions in which the research in personality measurement seems likely to move.

Instead of looking for new approaches to personality measurement, it is possible that self-description inventories and projective techniques can be refined to the point of providing adequate instruments. It was said in Chapter 14 that the results of self-description inventories are probably most valid when they are administered in research studies and not used to evaluate people or make decisions about them in any way. Self-description inventories may prove useful in the search for more valid personality measures. For example, it may be found that a physiological attribute correlates with the results of a self-description inventory, say to measure "dominance," when the instruments are administered in a research setting. Whereas the self-description inventory would likely not be a valid measure in nonresearch settings, like personnel-selection programs, because of the need and ability of individuals to "fake" responses, the physiological variable might not be controllable by subjects.

In spite of the cleverness and good sense involved in some of the projective instruments, the administration, scoring, and particularly the interpretation are relatively unstandardized. They may provide valid results in particular settings, used by particular examiners, and in respect to particular traits; however, it is not known when and how they work best and which examiners are more proficient at interpreting the results of projective instruments. Consequently, projective techniques cannot be used for general-purpose testing until they are more fully standardized and their validity tested for particular uses.

Unfortunately, there seems to be only a moderate amount of research interest in the standardization of projective techniques. One attempt is the multiple choice Rorschach which was mentioned in Chapter 15. Many people feel that multiple choice forms and other standardized scoring procedures measure only the simpler human attributes and therefore lose much of the "richness" inherent in the free-response projective testing procedure. This criticism is probably justified in that it is much easier to invent objective tests for simple rather than complex attributes. But part of the criticism is probably due to a resistance on the part of some clinical psychologists to objective tests as such. The clinician prizes his intuitive ability and his function as an observer and interpreter of human behavior. If these functions are taken over in part by standardized tests, the clinician quite naturally feels that his particular usefulness is somewhat diminished. However, the more important problem of using measurement techniques to help unhappy people should receive precedence over professional likes and dislikes. Consequently, every effort should be made to refine and standardize the projective techniques.

OBSERVATION OF BEHAVIOR

Rather than infer personality characteristics from paper-and-pencil or projective tests, another approach is to observe people as they actually behave. As a simple example, a disturbed child can be observed as he plays with a group of children. If the observations can be reliably recorded and scored, they can be used as personality measures. The advantage of observational testing is that it has a real-life quality not shared by conventional testing instruments.

Many everyday decisions about people are, of course, reached by a form of observational analysis. The football coach observes the freshman quarterback to see how well he passes, kicks, and runs with the ball. The new bank teller is judged in terms of his promptness, accuracy in maintaining accounts, and courteousness to customers. The new cook is judged by her cakes and pies and by the neatness of the kitchen. The following sections will discuss some of the ways in which behavioral observation can be used to measure personality traits.

Ratings. Rating scales are used very widely as a means to record behavioral observations. Many industrial settings employ a standard rating form which foremen use to record their observations of individual employees. Office managers use rating scales to judge the promptness, neatness, and job proficiency of clerical workers. Candidates for graduate school training are rated by their professors in terms of general educational background, intelligence, initiative, emotional stability, writing skill, and other traits. Rating scales are used widely in military life to judge the suitability of men for promotions or for specialized training. A typical set of rating scales is shown in Figure 16–1.

FIGURE 16–1. A typical set of rating scales.

	Much below average	Below average	Average	Above average	Much above average
Courtesy					
Intelligence					
Moral character					
Personal appearance					
Health					
Ambitiousness					
Friendliness					
Creative ability					
General knowledge					
Writing skill					
Emotional stability					
Diligence					

Ratings are often said to be more objective than self-description inventories. It is certainly true that other people are less sensitive about recording an individual's shortcomings than the individual himself would be. However, there are numerous pitfalls that beset ratings, and only after these have been guarded against will ratings provide a valid picture of individual personalities.

One of the most common sources of error in ratings is lack of information about subjects. Ratings usually will not be valid if raters see the subject only on several occasions or if they see the subject only in restricted environments. Army officers are sometimes called on to rate as many as 100 men on the basis of two or three months' performance in training. College professors often have more than 60 students in a class, and the first-hand acquaintance with any one of them is likely to be slight. In these and many other circumstances, ratings are sometimes made with only a small amount of information about the persons who are rated. Typically, in situations of this kind, the rater is familiar with only the extremes. The very good and the very poor men catch the rater's eye, and he is able to make valid ratings about them. The majority of the people, however, do nothing either so meritorious or so wrong as to make their presence known, and therefore, only very unreliable ratings can be made about them.

In some situations the rater has considerable experience with subjects in a particular setting but little or no acquaintance with them in other settings. For example, a college professor may have a good opportunity to observe diligence in the classroom but no opportunity to judge social behavior outside the classroom. The first step in arriving at valid ratings is to make sure that raters have both an extensive acquaintance with subjects and that they have witnessed behavior in situations relevant to the traits being rated.

In addition to lack of information about subjects, a number of forms of bias often enter rating scales. One of these is personal bias toward particular individuals. It is difficult not to give better ratings to our friends than to people whom we do not know or do not like. Another source of error is a constant bias on the part of the individual rater to rate all persons generally high or generally low. If a number of raters are asked to rate 30 men, they will differ to some extent not only in their orderings of the men but also in their mean ratings. Some raters have a positive bias, tending to rate all persons near average or above. Other raters have a negative bias, giving a preponderance of low ratings.

A form of bias called the "halo effect" consists of giving all bad, all average, or all good ratings to people. Rather than thinking differentially about the strong and weak points in persons, we tend to develop general attitudes toward individuals. Consequently, the individual rater is prone to rate a person in much the same way on different rating scales even when that is not the true picture. For example, the soldier who is good in drill and maintenance of equipment is not necessarily good in marksmanship.

An important point to note about ratings is that they are often unreliable. The reliability of ratings can be studied by all of the methods discussed in Chapter 6 in the same way that the reliability of mental tests is determined. The preferred procedure is to have the same individuals rated by two raters either on the same or an equivalent rating form. The two sets of ratings can then be correlated to obtain an estimate of the reliability coefficient. The coefficients obtained for ratings in this way are seldom as high as .80, often run below .50, and go all the way down to zero in some cases.

A number of things can be done to improve ratings. One, which was mentioned previously, is to provide more and better opportunities to observe individuals. Secondly, raters should be trained for their jobs, told about the various forms of bias in ratings, and given extensive practice in observing and rating individuals. Thirdly, a substantially more accurate picture of the subject can usually be obtained by averaging the ratings of two or more raters. This serves to iron out the biases of individual raters and results in a more reliable measure. Using multiple raters improves the reliability in much the same way that increasing the number of items improves the reliability of tests. Nunnally [1] recently determined the reliability with which four psychiatrists rated the symptoms of 21 cases. The median reliability for individual psychiatrists was less than .40. When ratings were averaged over the four psychiatrists, the median reliability rose above .80.

Some personal skills, like military bearing, "bedside manner" of physicians, and leadership qualities, are probably so complex that they can best be measured by the equally complex judgmental processes of human observers. However, we often make decisions about people on the rather unreliable, often biased, judgment of only one rater. One rater is seldom sufficient. Two or three raters provide a more reliable measurement. The gain in precision from using more than four raters is seldom worth the effort.

Instead of having ratings made by experts or by administrative officials, another approach is to have the workers or trainees rate one another. This is usually referred to as the "peer rating" technique. In a typical use of peer ratings, officer candidates in the Armed Forces are required to rate the other men in their unit in terms of their abilities and leadership qualities. The advantage of the peer rating technique is that the men usually have a large amount of first-hand experience with one another. Validity studies indicate some promise for peer ratings.

Situational Tests. In addition to standardizing the rating of behavior observations, some efforts have been made to standardize the situations which are observed. One of the pioneer efforts of this kind was the screening program developed by the Office of Strategic Services during the Second World War (12). The purpose was to select men for military intelligence work, espionage, and other dangerous assignments. In addition to tests of intelligence, memory, and mechanical ability, each candidate was given a series of "situational tests." Each situational test involved a type of problem that might be encountered in actual duty. The candidate's performance was rated in terms of ability to think quickly and effectively, emotional stability, and leadership.

In one of the situational tests, the candidate was given the problem of constructing a 5-foot cube from wooden blocks, poles, and pegs. The candidate was told that, since it was impossible for one person to complete the task in the ten minutes allotted, he would be supplied with two

---

[1] Unpublished results found by Nunnally while working as consultant to Dr. Roy Grinker on a study of depressed patients.

helpers. Actually, the two "helpers" were psychologists whose purpose was not to help but to hinder in all possible ways. One "helper" acted lazy and confused; the other bickered, argued, and criticized. The "helpers" were so effective that no one ever completed the task. The real purpose was, of course, to observe the candidate's behavior in a tense, frustrating situation.

In another OSS situational test, the candidate was told to imagine that he is caught going through files marked "SECRET" in a government office, that he does not work in the particular building, and that he carries no identification papers. The candidate was given twelve minutes to construct an alibi for his presence in the suspicious circumstances. Then he was subjected to a harrowing interrogation, in which attempts were made to break his alibi and to make his statements appear foolish. The candidate was rated on the convincingness of his story and his ability to support it in the interrogation.

Because the OSS measurement program operated under considerable time pressure and because it had to fulfill the immediate task of evaluating men, some of the procedures were relatively crude. There was little opportunity to measure the effectiveness of situational tests as predictors of later performance. One of the difficulties was finding adequate criteria of performance against which to validate the tests. The major criteria were ratings by field commanders and by fellow workers. These ratings proved to be of low reliability, and consequently, correlations with situational test scores were quite restricted. The effectiveness of situational tests in the OSS program is still a matter of controversy.

The OSS selection program received wide attention, and since the Second World War, a number of attempts have been made to employ situational tests. One of the best known of these was a five-year project whose purpose was to develop instruments for selecting student trainees in clinical psychology (9). Potential trainees in Veterans' Administration hospitals came from 30 universities scattered across the country. They were housed at the University of Michigan during the testing period. In addition to tests of ability and personality, a number of situational tests were used.

The situational tests used in the Michigan study were modeled directly after those employed in the OSS program. One consisted of a discussion situation in which the candidates were told to act as a citizens' committee and discuss the use of a large financial bequest. A second situational test involved improvising responses in a social situation. A third consisted of a group problem-solving task involving the moving of a set of heavy blocks. The fourth test required the individual candidate to demonstrate the emotions expressed in poetry and in particular words, with gestures and facial expressions only.

Whereas there was little opportunity to study the validity of situational tests used by the OSS, an extensive study of validity was made in the Michigan project. Criterion ratings were obtained from university and clinical supervisors some three years after the original testing. Trainees were rated in terms of clinical competence and preference for hiring. The ratings made earlier in regard to performance in situational tests correlated .35 with clinical competence and .20 with preference for hiring. However, standard printed tests worked as well. Situational test results added nothing to the predictive efficiency which was obtained from objective test results and personal history information.

There are numerous practical drawbacks to the use of situational tests. They often require elaborate equipment, much work space, and many persons to administer the tests. It is often necessary to use trained actors in the tests and it is difficult to standardize their performance. Much pretesting must be done on the test design, and raters must practice their jobs. Only one or only a few men can be tested at once, and it is time consuming to place large numbers of men through the tests. It is difficult to hide the nature of the test situations from new subjects. The persons previously tested often pass on information to people who will later take the tests. If the situations are not changed often, with the result of much additional work, or if elaborate precautions are not made to keep secret the nature of the situations to be used, new subjects will "rehearse" their behavior prior to the tests.

In general, situational tests are cumbersome, expensive, and difficult to standardize. Only if they produce a marked gain in predictive validity over more conventional measurement techniques will they be worth the effort. The situational tests employed so far have not lived up to that standard. The evidence so far indicates that ratings made in respect to a longer-term general acquaintance with a person are more valid than ratings made about behavior in contrived situations.

Behavioral Tests. Another method of behavioral observation is to collect some objective product of activity in lifelike situations. The test concerns what an individual actually does rather than ratings of his behavior. One of the earliest and still the best-known use of behavioral tests was that of Hartshorne and May (8) of the Character Education Inquiry. They wanted to measure traits in school children, such as honesty, truthfulness, cooperativeness, and self-control. Rather than use conventional tests or ratings to measure these characteristics, they chose to observe the actual behavior of children in respect to the traits. The observations were conducted in the normal routine of school activities, in athletics, recreation, and classroom work.

Observations were made in respect to each trait in such a way as to provide an objective score. For example, one of the measures of cheating was obtained by allowing students to grade their own papers and noting the number of alterations of answers. Tests like vocabulary and arithmetic reasoning were administered in the classroom. The tests were collected and a duplicate copy made of each. The original unscored papers were returned to students along with a list of the correct answers. Children scored their own papers and either gave themselves the correct grade or altered answers to improve their standings. Scores reported by students were then compared with the scores students actually attained, as measured by the duplicate test copies. The amount of discrepancy between the two scores provided a measure of cheating.

Another of the Hartshorne and May tests concerned the trait of charity. Each child was given an attractive kit, including 10 articles such as pencil sharpener, eraser, and ruler. After the children had examined the materials for some time, they were allowed to give away some or all of the items to "less fortunate children." The children were not coerced to donate, and the donations were made anonymously. Each child was provided with a large envelope in which to put his donation, and the donations were dropped into a common box. Unknown to the children, envelopes had been marked in such a way as to identify the donations of each child. The number of articles donated served as a measure of charity.

When behavioral tests of the kind originated by Hartshorne and May can be used, they have a number of attractive advantages. The use of actual behavioral products frees the measurement procedure from the subjectivity of rating scales. If observations can be made in natural situations where the subject is unaware that he is being tested in any sense, the results are probably more valid. One of the faults of situational tests is that they are more like games than real-life situations, and subjects often regard them as such.

Other than the Hartshorne and May studies, there have been few attempts to develop systematic behavioral tests, although much the same thing is done informally in many evaluational efforts. The major uses of behavioral tests have been with children. This is because children are easier to find in group situations or easier to place in group situations without having them suspect an ulterior purpose. Also, the behavioral products of children are usually simpler and more easily measured than complex adult interactions. Behavioral tests are sometimes used with kindergarten and nursery school groups. Behavioral records can be kept either surreptitiously by an examiner, or the children can be watched through a one-way vision screen. Notes are made of the number of times a child offers a toy to others, the number of times he asks for adult help, and other relevant behavior. In order to get at more complex responses, it is sometimes necessary to use both direct recording of actions and ratings of behavior to measure such traits as "responsiveness" and "tendency to withdraw."

An adaptation of the behavioral type of test is presently being used to measure the social responsiveness of mental patients. The patient is placed in a standard interview situation and records are made of actual behavior. One such routine is referred to as the Minimal Social Behavior Scale (3). A typical "item" consists of offering the patient a pencil and noting whether or not it is accepted. In another "item" the examiner places a cigarette in his mouth and fumbles for a match. He stands up and looks through all of his pockets. A book of matches sits in plain view of the patient. The patient is scored "plus" if he mentions the matches on the desk or offers a match from his own pocket. A series of such behavioral observations provides a picture of the patient's social responsiveness.

MAXIMUM PERFORMANCE TESTS

It has always been hoped that one day we should have tests, in the stricter sense of the term, to measure personality characteristics instead of having to use instruments like self-description inventories, which are controllable by subjects. When an instrument concerns how much an individual knows, how many problems he can solve, or how well he performs, we tend to think of it as a measure of some intellectual characteristic as distinct from personality characteristics. However, it is entirely possible that personality characteristics are involved in what appear to be "ability," "cognitive," or "maximum performance" type tests.

Perceptual Tests. It has always been thought that perceptual tests, like those mentioned in Chapter 9, measure not only certain ability factors but relate to personality characteristics as well. One of the earliest attempts to test this hypothesis was Thurstone's (10, pp. 137–141) study of government administrators. He administered a wide variety of perceptual and other tests to both experienced government administrators and to relatively inexperienced officials. He categorized the subjects in each age group according to their salaries, assuming that salary related at least roughly to administrative competence and perhaps this in turn to leadership ability. He found that among other tests which served to differentiate the salary groups, one of the perceptual tests appeared to produce a significant differentiation. The particular test, the Gottshaldt Figures Tests, is concerned with the ability to detect visual patterns imbedded in more complex figures. The finding is now mainly of historical value, but it serves to illustrate the interest in relating perceptual functions to personality variables.

One of the most interesting studies relating perceptual functions to personality characteristics is the work of Eysenck (see 1) on "dark vision." Dark vision is, quite simply, the ability to see well at night, in contrast to the usual criterion of good vision, the ability to see well in the daytime or in lighted rooms. It has been known for some time that dark vision is not necessarily related to day vision. Persons who can see quite well in the daytime often have great difficulty in seeing well at night, and vice versa. Eysenck compared the dark-vision ability of 96 neurotic patients with 6,000 apparently non-neurotic members of the British RAF. On a scale ranging from 0 to 32, the neurotics had a mean score of 7.1 and the normals had a mean score of 19.3. Additional investigations showed that the dark-vision test tends to discriminate among neurotics in terms of the severity of their disorders.

Another perceptual measure which is currently receiving some attention as a possible test of personality characteristics is the color-form dominance test. The test consists of presenting on film visual images of a composite nature so that the subject can report a perception of movement which is determined either by colors or by form, or shape, only. It is found that some people characteristically see the color-determined percept and others characteristically see the form-determined percept. The evidence so far is insufficient to say whether or not color-form dominance relates to particular personality characteristics.

Persistence Tests. Tests of the maximum performance type have been used to measure how long individuals will work at difficult or even impossible problems. These supposedly measure a trait of persistence, which in everyday language means the tendency to stick with problems when the going is tough. In a typical test, the subjects are presented with a very difficult mechanical puzzle. Some subjects will give up after a few failures; other subjects will work on in spite of numerous failures. Similar tests can be constructed for perceptual, verbal, motor, and numerous other ability functions. Studies to date (see 2, pp. 284–290) indicate that there is a general trait of persistence underlying many of the tests. The trait correlates to some extent with intelligence test scores but correlates more highly with school grades; this indicates that an important personality attribute is at least being touched on in persistence tests.

Response Sets. It is possible to differentiate people not only in terms of the test scores which they make but in terms of the way in which they take tests as well. Regardless of what the test is about, people bring with them certain test-taking habits, or "response sets," which, in part, determine their scores. One of the oldest observations along these lines is that personality, or as it was called in older days, "temperament," is involved in psychophysical studies of judgment. The subject can be asked either to judge whether stimulus A is greater or less than B or he can be provided with a third choice, an "indifferent" category, in which the judgment is "neither less nor greater." It was noted early that some subjects use the "indifferent category" much more than other subjects do, regardless of the judgments being made, indicating the presence of a personality trait seemingly involving the "willingness to take a stand."

One type of response set which has received some attention lately is that of "acquiescence." Acquiescence is usually studied with either very ambiguous or very difficult statements like the following:

The moons of Saturn were first discovered by Gustav Whittenborn.   Yes _____ No _____
An excess of porthymadrone results
in dilation of the pupils.   Yes _____ No _____

Very few persons are likely to have any first-hand information about statements like those above. Although both of them are false, they might as well be true as far as most persons are concerned. When presented with a longer list of such questions, some persons characteristically agree (answer "yes") and others show a tendency to disagree. People who give a preponderance of "yes" answers are said to acquiesce. That is, they seem to be pushed into agreement by the force of the statements alone.

There are numerous other response sets which can be measured. When a rating scale is used instead of a simple "yes" or "no" answer, people tend to pile up their answers at different points on the continuum. If, for example, opinions are being studied with a seven-point continuum which ranges from "strongly agree" to "strongly disagree," some people will most often mark the extremes and some people will put most of their marks in the middle of the continuum.

Response variability is another type of response set which is currently being studied. This is measured by comparing scores made by the same people on the same or similar tests given on two occasions. The instruments can be either tests of the ability type or attitude, opinion, and personality inventories. Some persons will give much the same response on the first and the second testing; other persons will vary their answers considerably. There is some evidence (see 2, pp. 290–293) to indicate that response variability is related to neuroticism and other personality characteristics.

Knowledge Tests. One approach to the measurement of social traits is to test people's knowledge about particular kinds of social interactions. For example, rather than try to measure "friendliness" with a self-description inventory, subjects can be tested on their knowledge of courtesy, the meaning of certain social behaviors, and the needs of other people. Although instruments of this kind have not generally been successful, more systematic efforts might meet with success.

One example of an information test which proved useful in measuring personality functions is the Naval Knowledge Test developed by Glickman (**6**). The test was constructed for the purpose of predicting the success of naval officer candidates in training school. A battery of conventional tests of the aptitude type was being used successfully at the time, and it seemed that only by the addition of tests of the personality type could substantial gains in validity be made. Although the Naval Knowledge Test is ostensibly a measure of factual information about naval customs, equipment, and history, it apparently measures some components of personality and interests. The sort of person who would interest himself in facts about the Navy and naval history before entering the service is likely to be someone who will like naval life and perform at least moderately well on actual duty. The test added substantially to the predictive efficiency which was obtained from the aptitude battery alone.

Suggestibility Tests. It has long been thought that there is a connection between suggestibility and neurosis. One of the most widely used measures of suggestibility is the "body sway test." In the test, the subject stands blindfolded, and the experimenter says, "You are falling forward, you are falling forward . . ." Under these conditions some people will sway very little or not at all and others will sway to the extent of actually falling. The amount of sway is measured by mechanical equipment. Using this type of testing procedure, Eysenck (**2**, pp. 296–299) found a definite relationship between suggestibility and neuroticism. Not only was there a significant mean difference in suggestibility between neurotics and normals, but amount of suggestibility differentiated among neurotics in terms of the severity of their disorders.

PHYSICAL AND PHYSIOLOGICAL MEASURES

It is a truism to say that the way a person is physically constituted has a strong influence on his personality. Although much of what we call personality is the result of long and complex learning experiences, much also is apparently determined by the particular muscular, neural, and chemical make-up of the individual. In so far as relevant physical and physiological traits can be measured and validated, they can be used as tests.

There is a wealth of evidence to demonstrate connections between physical states and personality. When people are sick, they seldom behave the same as when they were well. They are often more easily disturbed, quick-tempered, and depressed. Ordinary medicines which are taken for "colds" and other disorders affect our moods and social behavior. Different drugs tend to have different effects. One drug tends to make people elated and another tends to depress. The impact of neural functions on personality is often witnessed in the altered behavior of people with brain damage. Even the relatively mild physiological impact of the changing weather seems to alter our moods and social behavior.

Physique. It has long been thought that different types of body build accompany different types of personalities. The prevalent social stereotype is that short, fat people are friendly and jolly, whereas tall, thin people are thought to be shy, and "serious." There have been numerous investigations during the last half-century (see **2**, chap. 5) both to catalogue body types and to relate these to personality characteristics. The typology which is used most often is that of the endomorph, or short, fat build, the ectomorph, or tall, thin build, and the mesomorph, or athletic build. Very few persons fall neatly into one of the types, and consequently, each person must be considered some compound of the three.

Whereas there are evidently some relationships between body type and personality characteristics, the relationships are not as strong as was originally supposed. One of the major findings is that, among the mentally ill, schizophrenics tend to be ectomorphs and manic depressives tend to be endomorphs (**2**, chap. 5). There is also some support for the oft-held contention that ectomorphs are more often introverted and endomorphs more often extraverted (**2**, chap. 5). Perhaps the next decade of research will show more clear-cut relationships between physique and personality characteristics.

Autonomic Activity. The autonomic nervous system regulates the varying states of bodily alertness, reaction to fear, accommodation to sleep, and many others. In spite of the many suggestions that people differ in autonomic characteristics and that these in turn are related to social behavior, there has been only a relatively small amount of research in this area. This is probably because autonomic and related physiological variables require rather elaborate and time-consuming measurement procedures.

Some of the autonomic and related physiological variables which have been studied so far are electrical skin resistance, blood pressure, metabolic rate, rate of salivation, muscular tonus, respiration rate, and pulse rate. The two kinds of studies which have been employed so far are 1) to determine individual differences in autonomic activity at one period in time and 2) to determine individual differences in autonomic response to experimental variables, such as emotional situations, thirst, and electrical shock.

The evidence is yet too meager to say with any conviction how personality characteristics relate to autonomic activity (see **2**, chap. 6). The following suggestive results are offered mainly to indicate what is being attempted.

In terms of the first type of study mentioned above, there is some evidence to indicate that mobilized autonomic states (high blood pressure, salivation, muscular tonus, etc.) are related to neuroticism and personality inventory measures of shyness, introversion, and emotional instability. In an interesting study of experimental changes in autonomic activity, Freeman and Katzoff (5) measured the effect of sudden loud noises, electrical shock, and others on autonomic mobilization and recovery. They found rate of recovery to be significantly related to psychiatric ratings of emotional stability.

Blood Chemistry. The blood stream carries not only the nutrients and regulators of bodily activity but substances which influence our moods and social behavior. In so far as chemical differences among people can be shown to relate to personality differences, a "blood test" might prove to be a perfectly sensible approach to predicting certain kinds of social behavior. Most of our knowledge about the relationship between social behavior and blood chemistry comes from introducing chemicals into the blood and noting their effect. Experimental studies of the effect of drugs and glandular injections on social behavior exemplify this approach. However, it is more interesting, from the standpoint of psychological measurement, to search for existing chemical differences among people and to relate these to social behavior.

The use of chemical indices to measure personality characteristics has received great encouragement from recent findings about schizophrenia. A number of independent investigators (see 11) have isolated a copperish substance which is present to a marked degree in the blood of most schizophrenic patients but present to only a slight extent in most normal individuals. Other studies show that when a substance from the blood of schizophrenic patients is injected into normal persons that a transitory state of schizophrenia develops which is indistinguishable from the behavior of real patients. These findings may lead not only to new methods of treating schizophrenia but to a method for detecting schizophrenia as well.

Summary of Physical and Physiological Measures. It is doubtful that the fine points of personality will be measured by strictly "physical" variables alone. The evidence so far is that physique, autonomic activity, and blood chemistry may eventually define some broad personality tendencies in people. As the present findings regarding schizophrenia indicate, physical measures may prove useful in predicting whether or not people will develop severe mental disorders. However, it is doubtful that physical measures alone will be the most efficient way to make more complex predictions, such as whether two people will make good marriage partners or whether an individual will succeed as a physician.

BIOGRAPHICAL AND PERSONAL DATA INFORMATION

As a final approach to the measurement of personality, we can return to the common-sense method that is used in everyday life. Without any more direct way of forecasting how an individual will behave in the future, the best bet is that he will continue behaving in the same manner that he has in the past. This is the principle upon which so much of our knowledge of other people is based. By observing our family and friends in many situations, we gradually learn to predict how they will behave in new situations. The person who has behaved shyly in numerous social situations in the past is not likely to switch to being the "life of the party." The individual who has a long history of fights and arguments is likely to continue in that vein. The person who has shown jealous behavior in numerous previous situations is likely to act jealous in new situations. People do change, of course, but seldom so markedly or so rapidly as to render them grossly unpredictable to friends and family.

Although we seldom keep systematic records of the validity with which we can predict the behavior of others, at least we feel that our forecasts are fairly accurate. There are, of course, many exceptions, which are evidenced in the oft-heard phrase, "I didn't think he would do that." It would be an odd world, and a frightening one too, if we were not able to predict the behavior of others with some accuracy. We can depend partly on cultural mores and customs, which force most of us into relatively narrow channels of social response. For example, if you say "Good morning" to an acquaintance, it can be predicted with fair accuracy that he will say "Good morning" or some variant of it in return. If he replied with "Fish for sale" or some other highly unpredictable response, you would probably attribute it to mental illness. Beyond the confines of culturally defined actions, we also learn to predict with some accuracy the idiosyncrasies of particular persons. We do this mainly through numerous observations of behavior in different situations.

Rather than accumulate information about people on an informal basis, a systematic accumulation of facts can be made. Either the person can be "investigated," or the individual himself can be asked to supply pertinent information. This is essentially what is done in many job application blanks. The individual gives information about places of residence, health, work history, military experience, hobbies, personal accomplishments, and others. Although the application blank is usually not employed as a test, it can be standardized and scored.

Although it might prove useful in the future to collect biographical information to measure general personality traits, most of the uses so far have been in selecting personnel for particular jobs. The "test" is constructed much like any other predictor instrument. A large collection of "items" is made. Each item concerns a personal history event, action, or accomplishment. The items would, of course, likely be different for different personnel-selection situations. Some items which might be useful to predict the success of real estate salesmen are as follows:

1. How many jobs have you had during the last five years?   _____
2. How long were you employed in your last job?   _____
3. How many years of schooling have you completed? _____
4. Do you own your own home?   _____
5. How long have you lived in this city?   _____
6. Are you married?   _____
7. Do you belong to a fraternal organization or club? _____
8. How much money do you have in the bank?   _____

Here we are only guessing what might be important characteristics of a successful real estate salesman. The real "proof of the pudding" is to learn which items differentiate successful salesmen from unsuccessful salesmen. A longer list of biographical items like those above could be administered to job applicants. One or several years later, measures of job success could be obtained, which might include ratings, amounts of property sold, and other pertinent indices of success. Then item-analysis procedures like those discussed in Chapter 8 could be performed on the biographical items to obtain an efficient predictor instrument. This might show that successful salesmen are usually married, own their own homes, and have been residents of the particular city for a long time. The most valid items can then be used to form a test, which can henceforth be used to select personnel. The finished product is called a biographical inventory, personal data form, or personal history record.

Biographical inventories have been employed successfully in a number of selection programs. One of the most striking examples is that of the Aptitude Index (see 4, pp. 282–286) developed by the Life Insurance Agency Management Association to select prospective insurance salesmen. Part I of the Index consists of 10 biographical items concerning net worth of the applicant, age, social affiliations, and others. Weighted scores on the 10 items are averaged and transformed into letter grades ranging from A through E. Validation studies (see 4, pp. 282–286) show that applicants who score A on the test sell between 300 and 400 per cent more insurance during the first working year than applicants who score E.

Biographical inventories were among the most valid predictors of the successfulness of pilot trainees in the Army Air Force during the Second World War (see 7, chap. 27). The inventories concerned background information on parents, social affiliations, employment, hobbies, athletic accomplishments, and schooling. One form correlated .42 with the success of pilots in training.

You might wonder why a self-report test like the biographical inventory works well as a selection instrument whereas self-report instruments of similar appearance, such as self-description inventories, generally do not work well. Biographical inventories have a number of advantages over self-description inventories. It is difficult to construct unambiguous items for self-description inventories, but it is relatively easy to construct meaningful biographical items. The subject is asked his age, how long he has been married, and other understandable questions. It is apparently easier to hypothesize and compose valid biographical items than valid self-description items. The research effort needed in the former is therefore considerably reduced. Most important, whereas self-description inventories are quite often invalidated by the amount of faking in selection situations, biographical inventories are affected little by faking. The reason for this is that most of the biographical items are factual matters of the kind that can be checked on by others. An applicant who might be perfectly willing to say that he loves his father more than his mother in order to appear in the best light would be quite reluctant to say that he is married when he is not or that he belongs to the Elks Club when he does not. There is some stretching of facts, such as the addition or subtraction of years from one's age, on biographical inventories, but this is seldom so gross as the amount of distortion encountered in self-description inventories.

The biographical inventory is probably the best measure of "personality" presently available for selection programs. Although it is not certain what kinds of personality attributes they measure, the inventories often add substantially to the predictive efficiency which can be obtained from tests of intellectual functions and special abilities.

SUMMARY

It is easy now to see that the early workers in personality measurement anticipated achieving their goals more quickly and more easily than has actually been the case. This was probably due in large measure to the comparative ease with which the early tests of human ability were constructed and the many successful applications which have been encountered. In this chapter we saw that there are some hopeful approaches to personality measurement, but these are mainly complex procedures which require a relatively large amount of work both in their construction and their application. The need, however, for adequate personality measures is so acute that even expensive, laborious techniques would be worth the cost.

REFERENCES

1. Eysenck, H. J. *Dimensions of personality.* London: Routledge, 1947.
2. Eysenck, H. J. *The structure of human personality.* New York: Wiley, 1953.
3. Farina, A., Arenberg, D., and Guskin, S. A scale for measuring minimal social behavior. *J. consult. Psychol.,* 1957, **21,** 265–268.
4. Ferguson, L. W. *Personality measurement.* New York: McGraw-Hill, 1952.
5. Freeman, G. L., and Katzoff, E. T. Individual differences in physiological reactions to stimulation and their relation to other measures of emotionality. *J. exp. Psychol.,* 1942, **31,** 527–537.
6. Glickman, A. S. The Naval knowledge test: construction and validation. *Technical Bulletin 54–7.* Washington: Bureau of Naval Personnel, 1954.
7. Guilford, J. P. (Ed.) Printed classification tests. *AAF aviation psychology program research reports, Rep. 5.* Washington: GPO, 1947.
8. Hartshorne, H., May, M. A., and Shuttleworth, F. K. *Studies in the Organization of character.* New York: Macmillan, 1930.
9. Kelly, E. L., and Fiske, D. W. *The prediction of performance in clinical psychology.* Ann Arbor, Mich.: Univer. Mich. Press, 1951.
10. Thurstone, L. L. A factorial study of perception. *Psychometr. Monogr.,* 1944, No. 4.
11. Blood tests in mental illness. Papers and discussions presented at the Annual Scientific Conference of the Brain Research Foundation, 1957. Chicago: Brain Research Foundation, 1957.
12. OSS Assessment Staff. *Assessment of men: selection of personnel for the office of strategic services.* New York: Rinehart, 1948.

CHAPTER 17

Selected Techniques for Psychological Experiments

There are many psychological studies in which individual differences among people are of only secondary interest. In Chapter 1, a distinction was made between studies of individual differences and studies of psychological processes, a process being defined as a set of systematic changes within the individual. Studies of psychological processes are usually referred to as *experiments*, in distinction to the more general term *research* which is used to refer to systematic observations of all kinds, including studies of individual differences.

The purpose of this chapter is to consider some of the measurement techniques that are currently receiving wide use in psychological experiments. In addition to their use in experiments, some of the techniques to be discussed are useful in "descriptive" studies, where the effort is to determine the mean responses of a group of individuals. The opinion poll is an example of a descriptive study.

Little attention will be given in this chapter to measurement methods for studies of physiological psychology, perception, and learning. These are treated adequately in available texts. The emphasis will be on measurement in social psychology and the study of personality.

In its simplest form, an experiment involves two variables or measures. One variable is manipulated by the experimenter, or the experimenter waits for the variable to change by natural causes. The variable which changes in this way is called the independent variable. The experimenter then determines the influence of the independent variable on a second measure, the dependent variable.

The simplest form of experimentation can be illustrated with the well-known laws of gases. The problem is to determine the influence of pressure on the temperature of a gaseous body. A gas, say ordinary air, is enclosed in a cylinder. A gauge on the cylinder tells the pressure of the gas. A thermometer notes the temperature inside the cylinder, and temperature is the dependent variable. Pressure is the independent variable. A plunger in the cylinder is slowly forced down, raising the pressure of the gas inside. It is found in this way that temperature is a linear function of pressure. An experiment in which change in the independent variable has no influence on the dependent variable can be found in Galileo's laws of falling bodies. If, as story has it, Galileo dropped a small and a large stone from the Leaning Tower of Pisa, he demonstrated that weight, the independent variable, has no influence on the velocity of falling bodies, the dependent variable.

Nearly all of the test and measurement techniques which have been described in previous chapters can and are used as variables in psychological experiments. Some examples are as follows:

1. *Psychophysical judgment.* The purpose of the experiment is to determine the influence of alcohol on sensory discrimination. Subjects are given an ounce of alcohol each fifteen minutes over a period of an hour and a half. Five minutes after each "cocktail," the *threshold* for faint light signals is tested by the *method of limits.* Amount of alcohol consumed is the independent variable and height of threshold is the dependent variable.

2. *Achievement testing.* The purpose of the experiment is to determine the differential amount of learning from two methods of teaching statistics. Six instructors each teach two sections of statistics. One section is given three lectures per week. In addition to the three lectures, the other section is given a laboratory session in which statistical problems are discussed and worked through. In this experiment, the independent variable is expressed as a qualitative distinction between two methods of instruction. The dependent variable consists of a standard achievement test which is given to all students. An analysis is undertaken to determine which method of instruction produces the higher scores and to find the kinds of items which are more often correctly answered by the students in one or the other circumstance.

3. *Intelligence testing.* The purpose of the experiment is to determine the influence of distraction on intelligence test scores. A group of 300 college students is randomly divided into three subgroups of 100 each. One of the group intelligence tests is given to each subgroup in a separate room. Group A is tested in a quiet room as free as possible from distractions. Group B must work while a phonograph record plays lively music. Group C is bombarded with noise. The same phonograph record used with Group B is played along with the noise of sawing wood coming from a *buzz saw* in the back of the room and the heavy pounding of a bass drum from the front of the room. Amount of distraction is the independent variable and intelligence test score is the dependent variable.

4. *Attitude measurement.* The purpose of the experiment is to determine the influence of living in a Northern city on attitudes of Southerners toward Negroes. The dependent variable, a measure of attitude toward

Negroes, is given to 1,000 migrant Southerners who have lived in the North from one month to thirty years. The independent variable is the number of months' residence in the North. The independent variable is correlated with the dependent variable.

5. *Projective testing.* The purpose of the experiment is to determine the personality changes that go on in two different kinds of psychotherapy. In one type of therapy, the patients are seen in individual sessions. In the other, patients meet as a group and talk over mutual problems. All patients are given Rorschach tests before and after the treatment. Expert examiners rate the Rorschach records for amount of anxiety, insight into problems, severity of illness, and other attributes. Comparisons are made to see which type of therapy produces the most change and the kinds of changes that go on in each. The independent variable is the qualitative distinction between kinds of therapy. The dependent variable is the amount of improvement shown by the examiners' ratings.

The Validity of Experimental Variables. The validity of measures of individual differences was discussed in Chapter 4. The distinction was made between predictors and assessments, and rationales were presented for validating each type of measure. Although the rules given there are not completely airtight for all testing problems, they are sufficient guides for the major uses of psychological tests—in vocational guidance, school management, classroom testing, and personnel selection.

How can the validity of experimental variables be determined? In other words, how can it be determined whether or not an experimental technique measures what it is purported to measure? The rules which will be given here for the validation of experimental variables are less definite than those given in Chapter 4 for the validation of individual difference measures. As a first principle, there is usually more difficulty in validating dependent rather than independent variables. Independent variables are usually real-life things such as amounts of time, kinds of training, and other variations of circumstances. There is often considerable difficulty in determining whether dependent variables are what they are purported to be. The examples, 1 through 5 above, of psychological experiments were ordered in terms of the difficulty with which their dependent variables could be validated.

Any experimental variable which can be considered an assessment in terms of the rules given in Chapter 4 can be judged by the standards for assessments. Such measures are either reasonably self-evident measures of what they purport to measure, such as sensory threshold in the first example, or measures founded on the principle of content sampling, such as the achievement test in example 2. It is not with measures of the assessment type that particular difficulty is met in the validation of experimental variables. Assessments used as experimental variables can be validated with equal ease, or difficulty, as those used in studies of individual differences.

The difficulty in validating experimental variables comes with the use of instruments that are tests of the predictor type. Examples 3, 4, and 5 above all use dependent variables which the author would classify as predictors. The function of the dependent variable is not to predict some future behavior outside of the experiment but to *measure* the change that goes on within the experiment. Consequently, experimental variables should all be assessments. Unfortunately, either nothing is known or nothing is feasible to use in many experiments except measures of the predictor type.

Whenever experimental variables consist of predictor measures, the experimental results are open to interpretation and, more or less, to uncertainty as to what they mean. In example 4 above, the experimental results would show only that people *express* different attitudes after they have been in the North for a considerable period of time. Verbal behavior is important, and in some studies this is all that is meant to be measured, but in many experiments the object is to show that *attitude* in some more basic sense has changed. It would be hoped that the changes in response to the attitude-measuring device reflect real changes in the social response to Negroes rather than only a change in verbalized attitudes.

The meaning of the results in the fifth example above are directly dependent on the Rorschach test and its use by experienced examiners as a *measure* of personality attributes. Because of the generally unanswered questions about validity, most psychologists would view the results of the experiment with some skepticism.

The validity of predictor measures in psychological experiments is dependent on what the study purports to show. The purpose in some experiments is to show that predictor measures are influenced by the circumstances in which they are administered. Example 3, above, is meant to show that distraction in the testing situation influences scores on intelligence tests. No one would interpret the results of the experiment as showing that distraction influences intelligence but only the testing of intelligence.

Some of the experimental variables which will be discussed in the following sections can be used either to record what the subject *says* that he likes or that he thinks, or they can be used inferentially to *measure* what he likes and thinks. In the former usage, when the intention is only to determine what the subject is willing to say about himself and others, the results can usually be taken at face value. In the latter case, when an experimental variable purports to measure underlying tendencies in the individual, not just verbal report, the validity of the variables is open to question.

When instruments of the predictor type are used as experimental variables and the intention is to measure something more than verbal report, the principal validation procedure is that of construct validity as it was discussed in Chapter 4. That is, a measure of the predictor type gains meaning of its own through continued use and research. That is why the intelligence test in example 3 above can be considered to have more construct validity than the attitude-measuring instrument in example 4. And similarly, the attitude-measuring instrument in example 4 has more construct validity than the Rorschach test in example 5. The building-up of construct validity for an instrument is a slow process, and no instrument in psychology has been studied sufficiently to say unequivocally that it has a specified degree of construct validity. However, for many of the experimental variables that are in use, validity can be known only by the slow building-up of connections with other human attributes.

It would be unduly restrictive to expect that researchers who are working on the "cutting edge" of psychological science should use only experimental variables of known validity. In the beginning stages, a new measure is more a hunch than a proved instrument. But it is also incumbent upon psychological investigators to keep their measures open to continuous research and not simply to retain measures because of faith, fiat, or fashion.

THE Q-SORT

The Q-sort rating technique is most prominently identified with the work of William Stephenson (see **23**) and his colleagues. The particular rating scheme is only one aspect of a more general methodology for the study of personality. Stephenson's methodology will not be discussed here, only the handy Q-sort rating procedure, which lends itself to a wide variety of studies.

The Q-sort was developed as a means of recording and measuring multiple judgments, preferences, and impressions. In a typical study, subjects are asked to rate 100 photographs of art objects in terms of their preferences. Instead of rating each of the photographs separately, the subject is asked to "sort" them in terms of a forced-normal distribution. A typical forced-normal distribution for 100 items is shown in Table 17–1.

TABLE 17–1. TYPICAL FORCED-NORMAL Q-SORT RATING DISTRIBUTION
FOR 100 ITEMS

Number of items

	2	4	8	12	14	20	14	12	8	4	2	
Prefer least	0	1	2	3	4	5	6	7	8	9	10	Prefer most

Pile number

In the forced-normal distribution shown in Table 17–1, the subject is first required to pick the two photographs which he likes best and place them in pile 10. Then he chooses the 4 photographs which he likes next best of the remaining 98 photographs and places them in pile 9, and so on to the 8 photographs in pile 8, and the 12 photographs in pile 7. The pile numbers are written separately on file cards and spread out on a large table or desk. The subject literally sorts out the photographs to demonstrate his preferences.

The most widely used approach is to have the subject work from both extremes of the distribution toward the middle. That is, he first sorts the items into the several "most prefer" categories, say in this case working down as far as pile 7. Then he switches to the "least prefer" end, working down from pile 0 to about 3 in the present example. Finally the items are placed in the remaining middle piles. One reason why this approach is used is that extreme likes and dislikes are usually easier for the subject to rate. A second reason for working from the extremes to the middle of the continuum is that the extremes are much more important than the middle piles in determining the size of correlations and other statistical measures. Therefore, it is more important to have reliable ratings on the extremes than on the middle piles.

A forced distribution can be constructed quite simply for any-sized item sample being used. This can be done by referring to the areas under different sections of the normal distribution (see Appendix 3). A simpler procedure is to make up a distribution which looks like the normal curve without going to a more rigorous effort to fit the normal distribution form. It matters very little whether the distribution is precisely normal or only approximates the normal distribution.

The number of categories, or piles, varies in different studies in accordance with the size of the item sample. A rule of thumb is to use 9 piles with 60 to 80 items, 11 piles with 80 to 100 items, and 13 piles with samples of more than 100 items. Most persons prefer an odd rather than an even number of piles. An odd number of piles provides a middle pile that can be used for "neutral" items or items that are unrelated to what is being rated.

Item Universes and Item Samples. One of the appealing features of the Q-sort is its ability to handle a wide variety of item material. All things that can be photographed, drawn, or written on cards can be used as items. This provides a means of studying many kinds of materials that would otherwise be experimentally unmanageable.

One of the praiseworthy features of the Q-sort is that it emphasizes the sampling of item content. The collection of items actually used in the Q-sort, 100 photographs in the example above, is referred to as an item sample, or it is variously called a "trait sample," or a "stimulus sample."

When properly done, the item sample should be as representative as possible of a specified "item universe." Content sampling was discussed previously in respect to achievement tests and assessments generally. A rating method like the Q-sort also has more meaning when the items range broadly across a larger body, or universe, of possible items.

Analysis of Q-sort Data. The completed Q-sort represents the subject's preferences for or judgments about the things in an item sample. The simple description of peoples' responses may be all that the research seeks to accomplish, but in most cases the object is to compare the responses of subjects with one another or to compare the responses of subjects before and after an experimental treatment. The correlation coefficient is the statistic which is used most often in the analysis of Q-sort data. One sort can be correlated with any other that is made with the same item sample. This provides a correlation between two persons rather than the more conventional correlation between two tests. The correlation between two sorts is an index of the similarity of the item placements either by two persons or by the same person on two occasions. Because of the forced distribution that is used for all sorts made with the same item sample, a short-cut correlational formula can be applied. The formula is presented in Appendix 7. It allows the computation of correlation coefficients in only a fraction of the time that is required by conventional formulas like those presented in Chapter 5.

Correlations among sorts are often carried on to a factor analysis. The correlation matrix contains all of the intercorrelations among the sorts of a number of persons; or in a few studies (see **14, 15**), the correlation matrix is filled with the intercorrelations of a number of sorts made by only one person. Conventional factor-analytic techniques (see **10**) can be applied to the intercorrelations among Q-sorts as well as to the intercorrelations among tests. Each factor represents a common way of ordering the items by a number of persons.

In the illustrative study mentioned earlier with the 100 pictures of art objects, the preferences of some subjects might be determined by realism, by the extent to which the art objects accurately represent real-life forms. The subjects whose choices are made in this way will tend to correlate with one another. Other subjects may sort the 100 pictures in terms of their impressionistic value, regardless of how well the items picture real-life forms. The sorts of the impressionists will tend to correlate more with one another than they correlate with those of the realists. These are the conditions under which clusters arise in the correlation matrix, and the impressionists and realists are likely to be separated as factors in more formal factor-analytic treatment. Most persons are usually found to have a mixture of factors rather than to have one factor only. That is, a subject's sort can be determined both by realism and impressionism. The loadings which the subject has on the different factors show the extent to which the factors determine his preferences or judgments.

Evaluation of the Q-sort. One point of criticism which has been leveled against the Q-sort concerns the forced-normal distribution. The rating technique assumes without any formal proof that a normal distribution fits the ratings of different subjects. The forced distribution requires all subjects to have the same mean, the same standard deviation, and the same distribution form. It is possible and quite likely that if subjects are left to use whatever distribution they like, they will differ from one another in the way in which they distribute the items.

It can be counterargued that the forced distribution is only a convenience which does little injustice to the data one way or the other. If, as is usually the case, correlations among persons and subsequent factor analysis are the major statistical treatments, the forced distribution distorts the data almost not at all. It was shown in Chapter 5 that the correlation coefficient automatically equates means and standard deviations of two sets of numbers. The correlation coefficient is insensitive to even marked changes in the distribution form. If two normally distributed variables correlate a particular amount, say .50, the correlation will usually not change by more than .01 or so if both distributions are flattened to a complete rank-order. Likewise, skewing the distributions or even making them bimodal usually brings about only small changes in particular correlations. The forced distribution then saves a great deal of time in performing correlations (see Appendix 7) when only adding machines and desk calculator equipment are available.

The Q-sort is a relative rating technique. It requires the subject to decide which things he likes better or to judge which things possess more of a stated attribute. Some persons have criticized the Q-sort on this basis, claiming that absolute ratings should be used instead. An example of an absolute rating is the conventional rating scale, in which each item is rated separately: either into one of two categories or along a continuum. Absolute ratings could be used in the illustrative study of art objects mentioned earlier. Each photograph could be rated separately on a seven-point scale ranging from "like very much" to "dislike very much."

The people who criticize the relative ratings in the Q-sort evidently fail to consider that almost all of the traditional psychophysical methods are relative ratings also. Looking back to the discussion of psychophysical methods in Chapter 2, it can be seen that the methods of constant stimuli, rank-order, and pair comparisons are all relative ratings. Either rank-order or pair comparisons could be used to study judgments or preferences with respect to item samples, but both of these are far more laborious than the forced distribution with little gain in precision.

Rather than argue that absolute rating methods are better in general than relative rating methods or vice versa, it is more fitting to consider them as alternative techniques for handling different kinds of problems. Relative ratings make more sense with certain kinds of studies and absolute methods are more sensible for others. Relative ratings, like the Q-sort, should be used only when the items are all from some common frame of reference. To take an extreme example, it would be incorrect to have the subject sort 100 pictures, half of which are photographs of automobiles and half of which are photographs of houses. In making the Q-sort the subject would have to decide not only which houses he likes better and which automobiles he likes better, but whether he likes automobiles better than houses. This would make for a very ambiguous rating task.

Relative rating techniques, like the Q-sort, must be used when there is no concrete basis on which absolute ratings can be made. For example, no one would seriously consider using absolute ratings in a study of lifted weights. It would make little sense to have the weights judged on, say, a seven-point scale ranging from "very heavy" to "very light." Similarly in many studies of preferences and impressions, there is little concrete basis on which absolute ratings can be made. For example, the individual can feel quite safe in his choice between steak and lamb chops but have difficulty in deciding how much he likes either in an absolute sense. Such preferences are inherently comparative. On the other hand, there are many studies in which absolute ratings are essential. This is so in most studies of attitudes. For example, it might be of some interest to learn the individual's relative feelings about Negroes as opposed to Jews and Orientals; but the major purpose of such studies is to learn the degree of favorableness of the individual's attitudes toward different groups.

As a final point of criticism about the Q-sort, there has been some controversy about the objectivity of such ratings. People who have used the technique in clinical study, particularly projective testers, have spoken of the Q-sort as being objective, whereas critics of the method say that it is subjective. A distinction needs to be made between objectivity and validity. The Q-sort provides a means of objectifying impressions, but they are impressions nevertheless and not necessarily correct or valid until proved so. The important point is that rating techniques like the Q-sort provide the first step in studying the validity of impressions.

Illustrative Studies. The Q-sort rating technique is not an adjunct to any one field of psychology. It is a method for investigating a wide variety of problems. The following illustrative studies are presented to show the range of topics that have been studied.

Personality. Nunnally (14) studied the changing self-conceptions of one subject over a period of two years' time. The item sample was obtained from a three-months prestudy of the individual. Items were distilled from protracted discussions with the subject and with family and friends. Additional items were suggested by projective and aptitude test results. The 60 items used in the *Q*-sort were meant to cover a broad range of the things that the subject says about herself or might say under appropriate conditions. Some of the statements are as follows:

   a. I sometimes think of myself as being neglected and unloved.
   b. I feel pleasantly exhilarated when all eyes are on me.
   c. I sometimes feel that I could run out of the room I am in, scream, or burst into tears.
   d. When at a party I can get quite drunk to escape the monotony.

The subject used the item sample to describe herself, sorting the items from "most characteristic of myself" to "least characteristic." She made 15 separate *Q*-sorts to describe her behavior in different social settings. A factor analysis showed three factors, representing three different modes of behavior. Predictions were then made about how the individual would sort and how the three factors would change after psychotherapy. The main purpose of the experiment was to demonstrate ways of studying self-conception.

Communications. Swanson [1] carried out a series of *Q*-sort studies concerning the readership of magazines. In one study he was interested in the effect of title pages on the readership of different articles. One hundred title pages were sampled from the issues of a particular magazine over several years. These were placed individually on cardboard squares and used as the items for *Q*-sort ratings of preference. The responses of 20 subjects were factor analyzed. The four factors which were obtained reflected interestingly on why different people read different kinds of articles. Illustrating the type of results which he obtained, one of the factors is a clear measure of sensationalism. The title pages relating to the factor contain pictures of corpses, daggers, guns, voluptuous women, and the like. The titles themselves contained terms like B-girl, bloodhound, murder, FBI, and sex.

Psychotherapy. The field of psychotherapy abounds with different theories about the therapeutic process and about methods of treatment. Fiedler (6) performed a *Q*-sort study of the viewpoints of therapists about the therapeutic process. The item sample contained statements concerning a wide variety of ways in which the therapist might interact with the client. The therapists included 20 practitioners each of psychoanalytic, nondirective, and Adlerian schools. Ten members of each school were expert psychotherapists and ten were relatively inexperienced, nonexpert therapists. Each therapist was asked to sort the item sample in such a way as to describe his behavior in therapeutic interview situations. Correlational analyses showed that experts in the three schools of thought

[1] Personal communication from C. E. Swanson.

gave Q-sort descriptions which were more alike than were the descriptions of experts and nonexperts within any one school. The results suggest that therapists become more alike in their practice with continued experience and that differences between schools of psychotherapy are not as marked as they would seem.

Esthetics. Stephenson (**23**, pp. 128–144) used the Q-sort technique to study the esthetic values of art students. The item sample consisted of 120 cards containing various arrangements of colored rectangles. The rectangles were arranged in such a way as to be either overlapping or nonoverlapping and to form either regular or irregular designs. The hypothesis was that experienced artists would prefer irregular and overlapping designs and that artistically untrained persons would not prefer that combination. Stephenson's interest in the problem was largely methodological, to show how the Q-sort could be used in studies of esthetics. A small-scale investigation with 18 subjects tended to uphold the hypothesis.

THE SEMANTIC DIFFERENTIAL

The Semantic Differential rating instrument is most prominently identified with the work of C. E. Osgood (see **19**) and his associates. It grew out of the need for a measure of "meaning," for a way of indexing the manifold implications of objects, persons, and ideas for the human observer. Perhaps no other construct is as inextricably interwoven with psychological and philosophical theory as is meaning. It is axiomatic that human behavior is determined by the meaning of events rather than by intrinsic properties of events. The baby reacts approvingly to its mother's voice because that has acquired the meaning of nourishment, warmth, and protection. A soft buzzing sound will strike fear in the experienced outdoorsman for whom the meaning is rattlesnake and danger. On a more complex social level, different people harbor different meanings of concepts like Republican Party, Jew, Protestant Church, Cadillac, college, and even chop suey.

The fundamental hypothesis underlying the Semantic Differential is that certain important components of meaning can be measured by the rating of objects or ideas in respect to bipolar adjectives. Bipolar terms like good versus bad, strong versus weak, and intelligent versus ignorant are continua along which everyday meanings are expressed. On a metaphorical level, we may, for example, speak of a person being cold rather than warm. The implication is that the cold individual is an unpleasant person rather than that his bodily temperature is below normal. The American culture as well as a number of other cultures studied to date (see **19**, pp. 170–176) have a common metaphorical usage of a wide variety of bipolar terms. It seems to be almost universal that "good" things imply white instead of black, high instead of low, and full instead of empty.

Each set of bipolar adjectives is called a *scale* on the Semantic Differential. The number of scales in most studies ranges from a half-dozen to more than thirty. The customary approach is to use a seven-point continuum for each set of bipolar adjectives. The thing to be rated, the *concept*, is placed at the head of a page above the bipolar scales. An abbreviated form is shown in Figure 17–1. A list of scales is presented in Appendix 8 which contains the bipolar adjectives which have been most widely used in studies to date. The same set of scales is used to rate all of the concepts in a particular study. The pages of the rating form differ only in terms of the concept at the top of each sheet.

FIGURE 17–1. A Semantic Differential form for rating the concept Napoleon.

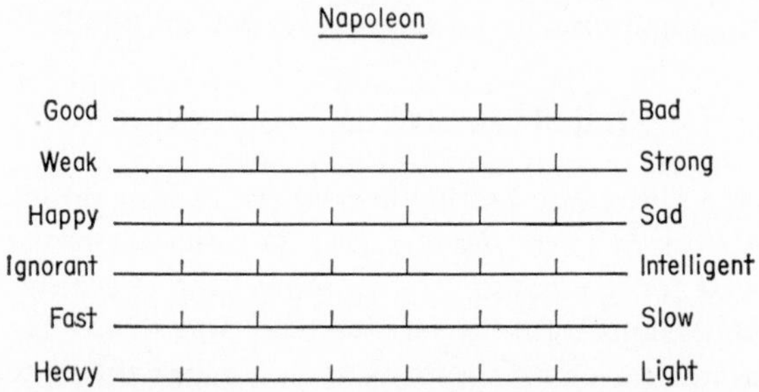

Napoleon

Good	_____⌐__⌐__⌐__⌐__⌐__⌐_____	Bad
Weak	_____⌐__⌐__⌐__⌐__⌐__⌐_____	Strong
Happy	_____⌐__⌐__⌐__⌐__⌐__⌐_____	Sad
Ignorant	_____⌐__⌐__⌐__⌐__⌐__⌐_____	Intelligent
Fast	_____⌐__⌐__⌐__⌐__⌐__⌐_____	Slow
Heavy	_____⌐__⌐__⌐__⌐__⌐__⌐_____	Light

Multidimensional Meaning. Basic to the use of the Semantic Differential is the hypothesis that meaning is multidimensional, that there are a number of facets of meaning rather than only one continuum along which things are ordered. At the rawest level, each scale can be taken as a separate facet of meaning. Two concepts can be said to have similar meanings if they are given nearly identical scores on a wide variety of scales. If two concepts have similar scores on some of the scales and not on others, this provides a way of charting the ways in which their meanings are similar and different. But if each scale must be considered a separate facet of meaning, this provides little understanding of the nature of meaning and also makes the results of any one study dependent on the particular scales which are used. Fortunately, bipolar scales like those used in the Semantic Differential evolve into a relatively small number of common factors. Factor-analytic studies by Osgood and Suci (**18**) and by others of a wide variety of scales applied to a wide variety of concepts have agreed on the following factors:

1. *The Evaluative Factor,* most prominently identified by scales like good-bad, valuable-worthless, kind-cruel, bitter-sweet, clean-dirty, fair-unfair, and pleasant-unpleasant.

2. *The Potency Factor,* most prominently identified by strong-weak, large-small, heavy-light, and thick-thin.

3. *The Activity Factor,* most prominently identified by active-passive, fast-slow, hot-cold, and sharp-dull.

The three factors above are ordered in terms of the variance that they account for in the scales which have been studied to date. The evaluative factor is by far the most prominent of the three. It appears to measure "attitude" much like that which is tested by conventional attitude scales. Most scales have at least moderate loadings on this factor and many have loadings well above .80. Some of the scales are mixtures of the factors rather than measures of one factor only. For example, hard-soft is a mixture of evaluation and potency, and relaxed-tense is a mixture of evaluation and activity.

The three factors described above are useful in classifying scales. Thus, rather than include a large number of scales which are known to be highly evaluative in a rating form, only a smaller number of the most highly loaded scales need be used. Similarly, a few scales can be included to represent potency and activity. This will provide ample room for including additional scales that have particular relevance to the concepts being studied.

By averaging scores on the most highly loaded scales for each factor, an approximate factor score can be obtained for each individual. Exact factor scores require more complex statistical treatments (see **27,** chap. 15). For example, if an individual rates the concept *labor union* on four of the purely evaluative scales at positions 4, 5, 6, and 5 respectively, the average of these, 5, can be taken as his over-all evaluation of *labor*

FIGURE 17–2. The scores for one person on the evaluative and potency factors for the concepts God, My Father, Satan, and Beggar.

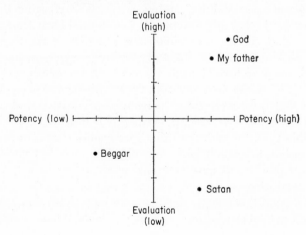

union. In a similar way, factor scores on the potency and activity factors can be found for *labor union* or any other concept in the particular study. The resulting scores can be pictured geometrically in what is called a semantic space. Each factor is used as an axis, resulting in a three-dimensional scattering of points. The position of each point in the space and the proximity of points to one another can be used to understand the meaning of particular concepts either for one individual separately or for the average responses of a group. A two-dimensional example is shown in Figure 17–2.

Illustrative Studies. A great deal of empirical work has been undertaken in recent years with the Semantic Differential (see **19**), ranging from studies of dream symbolism to cross-cultural studies of language. The following studies were selected to illustrate the wide variety of applications for the measuring instrument.

Psychotherapy. Because of the traditional interpretation of psychotherapy as a way of changing attitudes toward or meanings about one's self and the surrounding human environment, the Semantic Differential has a welcome place in understanding the psychotherapeutic process. One of the most interesting studies of this kind concerned the now famous case of triple personality first reported by Thigpen and Cleckley (**26**). They made a protracted study of a psychotherapy patient who periodically displayed such marked changes in attitudes, gestures, voice quality, and general behavior as to suggest an almost complete movement from one personality to another. The subject's customary "personality" was given the pseudonym of Jane, and the less frequent alternative modes of behavior were referred to as Eve White and Eve Black respectively. Thigpen and Cleckley followed the case until psychotherapy "killed off" the two Eves, leaving only the behavior typical of Jane.

The Semantic Differential entered the study as an independent measure of the different "personalities" and as a means of charting the changes brought by psychotherapy. A Semantic Differential form concerning concepts in the patient's life was administered to each of the three "personalities" as they occurred in different psychotherapy sessions. The same three measures were taken later in therapy, and follow-up measures were taken over the subsequent months. With little knowledge of the case other than that there were three "personalities," Osgood and Luria (**17**) attempted a *blind* analysis from the Semantic Differential data. They were not only able to distinguish the three "personalities" and to provide considerable insight into the behaviors involved in each, but they also made some correct predictions about the final personality which would be evidenced in the ratings.

Developmental Psychology. Following the hypothesis that meanings are learned and not inborn in the child, there should be an increasing tendency for children to agree with one another about meanings as they grow up. For example, four-year-old children are likely to hold different meanings about the word *lion* or a picture of the animal. One child will think of the lion as a pretty pussycat and another child will consider the animal as an immediate danger, lurking just beyond the cellar door. Older children and adults are more likely to agree with one another that the lion is powerful, dangerous, and remote from the immediate environment.

Donahoe (see **19**, p. 289) used a Semantic Differential form to study the movement toward agreement in meanings of common objects as a function of age. Using a standard set of concepts and scales, subjects were tested at four age levels ranging from the first grade to the college level. He found, as predicted, an increasing tendency toward agreement among subjects going from younger to older ages.

Learning Theory. A number of studies have been undertaken to relate responses on the Semantic Differential to typical measures of learning and habit formation. Osgood and his colleagues (see **19**, pp. 155–159) studied the relationship between *latency*, how long the subject takes to respond, and the extremeness of ratings on Semantic Differential scales. They found that when a subject marks a concept on the extremes of a scale, on the 1 and 2 or 6 and 7 positions, he makes up his mind more quickly than if the mark is made toward the center of the scale.

Staats and Staats (**22**) have recently used the Semantic Differential in an experiment of the classical conditioning type. They simultaneously presented names of countries along with either positively or negatively evaluative words. Subjects then rated each of the countries on the scale *pleasant-unpleasant*. Those who had received positive evaluation terms in conjunction with the name of a country rated the country as more *pleasant* than subjects who had received negative evaluation terms in conjunction with the country. This suggests, quite interestingly, that meanings as measured by the Semantic Differential can be conditioned like other stimulus-response connections.

Public Attitudes. The Semantic Differential lends itself readily to studies of public reaction to social issues, minority groups, and commercial products. Adherents of the technique feel that more is learned from the many scales on the Semantic Differential than from the one over-all score obtained with most conventional attitude measures. Nunnally [2] used the Semantic Differential to study public attitudes toward mental disorders and toward various social and family roles. The form was administered to 200 members of an opinion *panel*, a group of individuals chosen in such a way as to resemble the whole United States population in terms of a number of demographic characteristics. Scale profiles for three of the concepts are shown in Figure 17–3. It was found that indi-

² Unpublished research.

viduals with a mental disorder are viewed as relatively bad, weak, and inactive, in comparison to normal people. The scale which best differenti- ates public attitudes toward mental disorders from attitudes toward nor-

Figure 17–3. Semantic Differential profiles for the concepts Me (___), Old Man (_ _ _), and Neurotic Man (...). Each point represents the mean rating of 200 subjects.

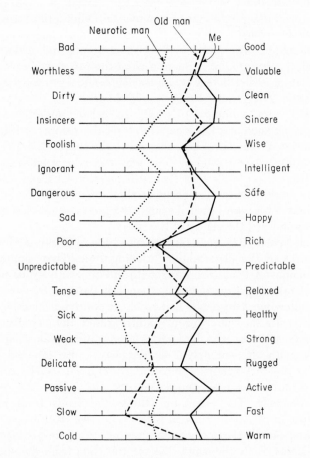

mals is tenseness. Evidently "nervousness," or anxiety, is the cardinal sign of mental disorder in public thinking. Psychotic disorders are differen- tiated from neurotic disorders by being rated more strong, less pre- dictable, and more dangerous.

Evaluation of the Semantic Differential. One of the major questions to ask about the Semantic Differential is, "Does it measure meaning?" The concepts *father* and *mother* receive similar ratings by most subjects, with some consistent differences. Does this imply that father and mother mean the same thing to most subjects? Of course, fathers and mothers are not completely similar in all the ways that the term meaning can be construed. But in another sense they are much the same, providing love, guidance, security, and also discipline. It is best said that the Semantic Differential measures some components of *connotative* meaning rather than meaning in all of its aspects. It measures the implications of objects rather than the total perceptual reaction to objects. Another way of explaining it is to state that the Semantic Differential is concerned with metaphorical meaning.

Some people wonder whether sensible ratings can be made with some of the scales that are applied to particular concepts. For example, what sense does it make for an individual to rate the Empire State Building on the scale hot-cold or on the scale friendly-unfriendly? There is no concrete way in which subjects can be told the basis for making such ratings, but practical experience has shown that they can do it anyway. A very detailed series of reports on reliability (cf. **19**, chap. 3) shows high reliabilities for factor scores and even surprisingly high reliabilities for individual scales.

Here in its purest form is exemplified the difficulty of validating an experimental technique. There is little else with which to measure connotative meaning and certainly no more dependable index with which Semantic Differential scores can be correlated. In cases of this kind the only appeal is to construct validity as it was discussed previously. The many researches that are being undertaken with the instrument (see **19**) and the many relationships which are being shown with other variables are gradually demonstrating what the instrument can and cannot measure. Considering the wide use of the instrument and the string of interesting research results, the Semantic Differential gives real promise as a measure of connotative meaning.

SIMILARITY JUDGMENTS

A number of rating techniques (see **12**, pp. 246–251; **13**) are available that depend entirely on judgments of similarity and differences among persons, objects, and concepts. The most widely used procedure of this kind is the method of triads. In a typical problem the investigator studies the relationships among a dozen stimuli. The stimuli can be anything from the names of persons to geometrical forms. The stimuli are presented to the subject three at a time, and he is asked to judge which two are more similar. Next, the subject is asked which two of the three stimuli are most different. The subject is presented in turn with all possible triads of the stimuli, or he is presented selectively with as many triads as are necessary to ensure that each stimulus appears at least once with all others.

The analysis of similarity judgments depends on the percentages of times that objects are judged to be similar to or different from one another. The percentages can be obtained either by repeating the whole set of triads many times with the same person, or more typically, the percentages are calculated over the response of a group of subjects. Statistical procedures are available (see **1, 13, 21, 28**) for determining the positions of the experimental stimuli on the continua which underlie the judgments. A number of other methods of similarity judgment (see **12**, pp. 246–251) provide much the same results as the method of triads.

Perhaps the best illustration of similarity judgments can be given with a type of study which, to the author's knowledge, has not yet been undertaken. The problem is to learn how a group of industrialists in a particular city judge members of the United States Senate. Twenty senators are selected in such a way as to cut broadly across what are thought to be dimensions of political and governmental philosophy. The name of each senator is typed separately on a file card. One hundred industrialists are used as subjects. Each is required to make similarity judgments by the method of triads. The responses of all subjects are placed together in a table, showing the per cent of times that senator A is judged to be more similar to B than to C, and so on.

The data can be used to deduce a number of things about how the industrialists view the senators. Primarily it can be determined which senators are viewed as being more similar in their political behavior. Secondly, an analysis will indicate the number of underlying dimensions along which the senators are judged. For example, it might be apparent that one underlying continuum concerns foreign policy, a second concerns fiscal policy in the United States, and a third concerns social welfare legislation. The analysis would provide a means of locating each of the 20 senators on the three dimensions. In general, the study should provide a better understanding of how senators are judged by the particular group of subjects.

Evaluation of Similarity Judgments. One obvious feature of similarity judgments is that they are very laborious. If there are 20 stimuli as in the example above, there are 1,140 possible triads. If the subject makes even a fraction of these judgments, the gathering of data is time consuming. The subsequent task of statistical analysis is difficult and still somewhat controversial.

It may help to understand the method of similarity judgments by comparing it with the Q-sort and Semantic Differential. The Q-sort could be applied to the hypothetical problem above by having each industrialist describe each senator with, say, a sample of 50 items. The items would be such as "favors more financial aid to England," "supports high tariffs," and "wants more federal aid to education." The Semantic Differential would use each of the senators as a concept with scales like strong-weak, liberal-conservative, wise-foolish, kind-cruel, and safe-dangerous.

The judging of objects in terms of similarity is both an advantage and a disadvantage. Similarity is a primitive idea that is difficult to explain to subjects, and it is easy to imagine experiments in which judgments of similarity would be hard to make. The use of similarity judgments also provides little information for interpreting the results. It can be determined that certain objects or concepts are judged as similar but an interpretation must be made of the underlying characteristic which makes for similarity. In both the Q-sort and the Semantic Differential the respective items and scales indicate more directly the way in which things are viewed as similar. On the other hand there are advantages to the similarity concept in ratings. It is not dependent on any set of items or scales, and thus the results often have a broader generality than those found with the Q-sort or Semantic Differential. Similarity judgments have to this time and will likely continue to have the most value in dealing with stimuli for which items or scales are very difficult to devise. The major studies to date have largely dealt with perceptual objects, geometrical forms, colors, and stimuli of that kind.

TECHNIQUES FOR STUDYING INTERPERSONAL RELATIONS

Much of psychology and particularly that branch called social psychology is concerned with the relationships between people and the ways that people behave in group situations. Because of the complexity of human interactions and the difficulties of measuring interpersonal responses, studies in this area have lagged behind most other branches of psychological investigation. This section will consider some of the more promising inroads into the measurement of group and interpersonal behavior.

Sociometry. One of the earliest and most widely used methods for understanding relationships within a group is based on choices of the group members for participation with one another. The method can be illustrated with a hypothetical situation in which 12 high school students are being divided into subgroups for work on a class project. The first step would be to ask each of the students to note, in private, the one or several persons with whom he would rather work. The choices can then be plotted as a diagram, or a *sociogram* as it is often called. This is done by drawing arrows from person to person showing the choices. Figure 17–4 shows a typical situation in which each student is asked to give a first and second choice for a work partner.

The sociogram contains no new information over what is known from the choices of individuals for one another, but it does provide a way of picturing and understanding the groupings of people. Looking at the sociogram in Figure 17–4, we find that persons 5, 8, 11, and 12 form a group, or clique. All of the first choices and all but one of the second choices stay within the group. Person 12 is especially popular in the group, receiving the first-choice nominations of the other three members. Persons 1, 6, 7, and 9 form a second group. Persons 2, 4, and 10 form a completely closed group, in which all choices remain among the three

FIGURE 17–4. Sociogram showing the choices for work partners in a group of 12 students.

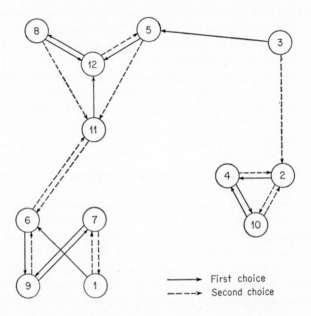

First choice
Second choice

persons. Person 3 is an isolate, and for that reason might have difficulty in working with any of the individuals. Persons 6 and 11 serve as inter-mediaries between their respective groups. Their relationship might be used to get better communication between the two groups or help in getting them together on mutual projects. Relationships of the kinds shown in the sociogram would prove useful in dividing the class into subgroups, either placing individuals into the natural groups which they form or improving relationships between certain individuals to allow new groupings of the students.

The sociogram technique can be applied to a wide variety of inter-actions including systems of leadership and communications. For exam-ple, in a study of military leadership, it would be expected that a hier-archy would be formed in which each individual receives his orders from someone above him, leading to the officer who is in over-all command of an operation.

In addition to the simple pictographic inspection of the sociogram, there are a number of indices that can be applied to sociometric data (see **20**). In the case where each individual makes only one choice, an estimate of an individual's popularity in the group can be obtained as follows.

$$\text{Choice status of } P_i = \frac{\text{no. of persons choosing } P_i}{N-1}$$

where P_i stands for person i

 N stands for the number of persons in the group

Because the individual is not allowed to choose himself, the denominator of the fraction is $N - 1$ rather than N.

If individuals are allowed to choose as many persons in the group as they like, an index of over-all liking of the group members for one another, or what has been called "positive expansiveness," is obtained as follows.

$$\text{Positive expansiveness of } P_i = \frac{\text{no. choices } P_i \text{ makes}}{N-1}$$

Indices are also available (see **20**) for describing the group as a whole. The following formula gives an indication of the extent to which all of the group members are incorporated, or integrated, into the group.

$$\text{Group integration} = \frac{1}{\text{no. of isolates (individuals receiving no choices)}}$$

The most important use of sociometry and sociometric analysis is in measuring experimental changes in group structures. For example, it might be hypothesized that a certain type of leadership will alter the interrelationships of group members in a particular manner. An experiment is undertaken in which the special type of leadership is instituted. Sociometric analysis is made before and after the experiment to measure the change in group structure.

Interpersonal Perception. It is a truism that much of human social behavior is determined by how the individual regards other people, how well he understands the feelings of others, and the contrast between what the individual thinks of himself and of other individuals. Empathy, or the ability to understand others, is a variable that has been studied extensively in this regard. In the psychotherapy situation it would be expected that the effective therapist could understand well how the patient thinks and feels. It might also be expected that adjustment in marriage would depend in part on how well the individuals understand each other's thoughts and feelings. A suggested measure of empathy is obtained by having an individual judge how another person will describe himself. This can be done with interest tests, self-report inventories, the Q-sort, the Semantic Differential, or other methods of personality description. The judge fills out the form in the way that he thinks the person to be predicted will fill out the form. The judge's marks are then compared with the actual ratings of the other person. If the two sets of marks correspond closely, it is said that the judge has high empathy, at least for the one person being judged. A statistical comparison of the two sets of ratings can be made either with the correlation coefficient or, better, with the D statistic discussed in Chapter 7.

In addition to measures of empathy, techniques have been proposed for measuring a number of other aspects of interpersonal perception. Fiedler (7, 8) has performed extensive investigations with a measure named "assumed similarity of opposites" (ASO). The subject is asked to rate two persons with the Semantic Differential: one individual whom he likes or with whom he works well and another individual whom he dislikes or with whom he works poorly. Fiedler employs the D statistic between the two sets of ratings as a measure of ASO. The larger the D, the more dissimilar are judged the high-preference and low-preference persons.

Fiedler (8) found a relationship between the ASO scores of pilots and the effectiveness of bomber crews and between the ASO scores of tank commanders and the effectiveness of tank crews. Measures of effectiveness consisted of expertness in bombing and tank gunnery respectively. Each leader was asked to predict the self-ratings of an individual with whom he worked poorly and the self-ratings of an individual with whom he worked well. Fiedler found that the leaders of effective crews tended to regard their most and least preferred coworkers as relatively dissimilar.

Measures of interpersonal perception have not yet met with substantial success. Many different kinds of rating forms and questionnaires have been used in the studies, and it would not be expected that all would produce the same results. It is unreasonable to think that an individual's ability to judge the ratings of another person on, say, an interest inventory will be the same as the ability to judge another person's ratings on the Semantic Differential. As is true in all measures of similarity, it is meaningless to speak of similarity between persons or between ratings in general. There is a current trend toward the use of factored tests rather than the use of a miscellaneous collection of items. This will permit a more concrete statement of the ways in which sets of ratings are similar and will permit a more direct comparison of the results obtained by different investigators.

Measures of interpersonal perception meet with a number of statistical and conceptual difficulties. There has been considerable dispute (see 4) regarding the proper statistical procedures for analyzing the research data. Although the *D* statistic is presently the most logical and the most widely used, the conglomerate nature of the statistic makes the results somewhat difficult to interpret in many studies. One of the conceptual difficulties is that some of the measures of interpersonal perception, such as the *ASO* measure, are so complicated, that even if significant results are obtained, it is hard to understand what they mean. Another difficulty in the measurement of interpersonal perception is the confusion of accuracy in the understanding of others with the individual's knowledge of general social stereotypes. The "acceptability influence" was discussed in Chapter 14, where it was said that there is a tendency for all persons to give similar and culturally favored ratings of themselves. Therefore, what may appear to be accuracy in the understanding of specific persons may be only a knowledge of cultural stereotypes, a knowledge of how people in general rate themselves. Current methodological and empirical investigations (see 3, 11) are endeavoring to clean up the statistical and conceptual ambiguities in this area, and it is hoped that measures of interpersonal perception will eventually be of substantial use.

MEASUREMENT TECHNIQUES FOR COMMUNICATIONS STUDIES

The field of human communications is rapidly developing as a meeting ground for diverse scientific disciplines and research techniques. Broadly considered, much of human behavior can be subsumed under the term communications. The basic ingredients in a communications system are a source, a person or device that determines the message; a set of signals or signs into which the message is encoded; a method of transmission; and a receiver, either human or mechanical, that takes in and decodes or gives meaning to the message. The system of events takes place in ordinary conversation when first an individual has an idea; the idea is formulated in terms of verbal language; the sounds carry to the other person's ears; and the human brain acts as the decoding mechanism.

Each step in the communications process offers many possibilities for research, and many of the instruments discussed earlier in this chapter and in previous chapters can be applied. A vocabulary test measures, in part, the range of language signs in the individual repertoire. Achievement tests can be used to measure the differential effectiveness of different ways of encoding and transmitting messages. For example, it would be useful to know whether college classes conducted via television promote the same amounts and kinds of learning which are obtained from ordinary classroom participation. Traditional methods of measuring attitudes are useful in learning the differential effectiveness of different messages and different media of communication.

One of the primary stumbling blocks in communications studies is the lack of effective methods for the description of written and spoken messages. For example, if it is found that a particular type of written message is effective in either conveying information or changing peoples' attitudes, the finding is of no general use unless the message itself can be concretely described. An adequate description must consider some of the important message characteristics, and only a scanty knowledge is presently available about the important ways in which messages vary.

"Message anxiety" is a characteristic which is receiving wide attention in communications studies. A communication is said to have message anxiety if it tends to frighten the audience, uses inflammatory statements, and goes into detail about the dire consequences of particular events. At present, characteristics like message anxiety rest largely on intuitive grounds. It is difficult to state explicitly when a communication has message anxiety or any of the other characteristics being used in communications studies. Even the few characteristics of messages that are presently available must be documented intuitively on a "more and less" basis rather than measured directly. It can be expected that further developments in the field of communications will depend heavily on the invention of measures of message content. The following sections discuss some of the measurement methods currently under investigation.

Readability. One of the primary needs is a measure of the simplicity and ease with which messages can be understood. It is common knowledge that there are different ways of writing the same set of facts, and that some ways are more conducive to the reader's understanding than others. A number of formulas have been developed (see **5, 9**) which purport to measure the readability of written messages. The formulas mainly depend on counts of the length of words, either in letters or syllables, the frequency with which words occur in English writing, and the length of sentences. The following example shows two ways of stating essentially the same facts, the first sentence having low readability and the second high readability:

The primary consequence of protracted cerebration on profound and enigmatic problems, if not interspersed systematically with less involved, quiescent diversions, is a reaction of tedium.

Thinking for a long period of time about difficult problems will make you feel tired.

Numerous examples have been shown (see **5, 9**) in which the formulas correlate well with intuitive estimates of readability (see Table 17–2). However, the concept of readability is difficult to define and somewhat misleading. It should not be assumed that readability as measured by current counting methods necessarily means good writing. Scientific articles are necessarily less readable in terms of readability formulas. In scientific writing, complex words must often be used to convey complex thoughts. "Mary had a little lamb" is more readable in terms of the readability formulas, but it is not likely a better poem than Gray's "Elegy."

A message is readable in terms of the readability formulas if it is simple and can be understood easily even by persons with relatively little education. The readability formulas are most important when the message is intended to convey specific information to a wide audience. They would be useful, for example, in constructing government pamphlets for the general public, dealing with child care, farming methods, safety precautions, and the like.

TABLE 17–2. READABILITY SCORES FOR VARIOUS KINDS OF WRITTEN MATERIAL
(From Flesch, 9, pp. 6)

Reading ease	Description of style	Typical magazine	Syllables per 100 words	Av. sentence length
90–100	Very easy	Comics	123	8
80–90	Easy	Pulp fiction	131	11
70–80	Fairly easy	Slick fiction	139	14
60–70	Standard	Digests, *Time,* mass nonfiction	147	17
50–60	Fairly difficult	*Harper's, Atlantic*	155	21
30–50	Difficult	Academic, scholarly	167	25
0–30	Very difficult	Scientific, professional	192	29

Cloze Procedure. The incomplete sentence is an old device for testing the intelligence of children. Taylor (see 24, 25) has developed a similar procedure for the study, not of individual differences among subjects, but of differences among messages. His method begins with the deletion of a certain number of words from the written material. This is done either by deleting words randomly or by removing every *n*th word systematically. (A series of empirical studies [3] suggests that a good approach is to delete every fifth word in a message.) The mutilated messages are then given to a group of subjects. They are told to fill in the blanks as best they can. The score for each person is the number of correct words placed in the blanks. The score for the message is the mean number of correct words obtained by the group of subjects.

The two mutilated messages below illustrate the use of *Cloze* procedure. The first is a low *Cloze* score ("hard") message and the second is a high *Cloze* score ("easy") message:

During the conjugation of _____ coli in the chimpanzee _____ micronucleus undergoes two maturation _____ to form

[3] Personal communication from W. L. Taylor.

four nuclei, _____ which three degenerate and _____ fourth
divides to produce _____ stationary and migratory pronuclei.
_____ the exchange of nuclei, _____ exchanged nuclei fuse
and _____ divide to form a _____ and a large nucleus.

The boy picked apples _____ a tree in the _____. He gave
them to _____ farmer's wife. She baked _____ apple pie for
the _____. He ate two big _____. Then the boy helped
_____ farmer milk the cow.

Taylor considers the *Cloze* procedure to be a new approach to the
measurement of readability, which he regards as having certain advantages over older methods. Suci and Nunnally [4] found correlations of .42
and .48 of *Cloze* scores with Flesch (9) readability scores and Dale-Chall
(5) readability scores respectively over a diverse sample of 70 messages.
This shows that *Cloze* is related to conventional readability formulas; but
the correlations are far enough from perfect to raise the question as to
what additional variable or variables are being measured by the *Cloze*
procedure.

Regardless of whether or not *Cloze* procedure proves to be a useful
approach to the measurement of readability, it has interesting properties
in its own right. *Cloze* seems to measure the psychological redundancy,
or repetitiousness, in writing messages. If everyone can correctly fill in a
deleted word, the word is completely redundant in the message. This is a
way of saying that the particular word supplies no new information over
the rest of the message. *Cloze* procedure and the concept of redundancy
can be applied to auditory and visual patterns as well as to written material. Notes or melodic phrases can be either systematically deleted or
deleted on a random basis from musical selections. Subjects can be asked
to "fill in," either hum or play, the missing parts.

Taylor [5] is presently applying *Cloze* procedure to paintings. He sections
the painting into a large number of square areas. A fraction of the areas
are removed on a random basis. Subjects are asked to fill in the missing
forms and colors. By this method he hopes to find systematic differences
among different styles of painting.

Redundancy and its measurement by *Cloze* procedure might eventually prove to be an interesting psychological variable. In some forms of
written material, redundancy is a desirable characteristic. This is so when
the purpose of the message is to "hammer in" a few important facts or
instructions. The interestingness of written messages, paintings, and musical compositions might be dependent on optimal levels of redundancy.
That is, it may be that a certain amount of redundancy is necessary to

---

[4] Unpublished research.
[5] Personal communication from W. L. Taylor.

make a stimulus pattern pleasing. A musical composition in which each succeeding note and pattern of notes is completely unpredictable from previous notes sounds chaotic. On the other hand, a composition so repetitious that each succeeding note and phrase can be anticipated with very high accuracy proves to be dull and uninteresting to the sophisticated ear.

Content Analysis. A simple way of describing the communication process is to say that it concerns *how who* says *what* to *whom*. *Who* and *whom* are the source and audience in the communication process. The readability formulas and *Cloze* procedure are concerned with *how* the message (*what*) is phrased. Although the term "content analysis" is often used to speak in general about methods of analyzing the properties of messages, it will be used more specifically here to refer to the information or meanings which the message embodies.

Content analysis came into prominence during the first twenty years of this century as a means of studying the content of American newspapers. Journalists were interested in the subject-matter coverages which provoked the most public interest. Sociologists were interested in the influence of newspaper content on the changing political and legal forces on the American scene. Content analyses during this century ranged into the hundreds (see **2**) and varied from the "dominant images" in Shakespearian plays to the analysis of propaganda during the Second World War.

TABLE 17–3. CONTENT ANALYSIS OF NEWSPAPER TREATMENT
OF A MURDER TRIAL

(Adapted from Berelson, **2**, p. 41)

	Morning Sun, per cent	News-Post, per cent	Evening Sun, per cent	Afro-American, per cent
Helpful to James's case	0	4	10	78
Destructive to James's case	34	46	40	3
Neutral	66	50	50	19

The results of a typical content analysis are shown in Table 17–3. The analysis concerned the differential treatment by a number of newspapers of a Negro, accused of murder, before his trial. The content of the four papers was searched for material relevant to the case. Judgments were made about the relative favorableness or unfavorableness of each article. The number of "helpful," "destructive," and "neutral" materials were then transformed to percentages. The results show, among other things, that the *Morning Sun* had more space devoted to "neutral" content but nothing that could be construed as "helpful" to the accused. The *Afro-American* was the most one-sided of the four papers, the content being predominantly "helpful" to the accused.

Table 17–4 shows an analysis of the literature of the Boy Scouts of America and of Hitler Youth. The content was scored in terms of the ends that were recommended to the youths. The emphasis in Hitler Youth was on the development of the individual as a member of a national community, whereas in the Boy Scouts the emphasis was on improving the individual as a person.

TABLE 17–4. CONTENT ANALYSIS RESULTS OF THE GOALS RECOMMENDED IN THE LITERATURE OF HITLER YOUTH AND THE BOY SCOUTS OF AMERICA

(Adapted from Berelson, 2, p. 38)

Justification	Hitler Youth, per cent	Boy Scouts, per cent
As a member of national community	66	25
As a member of face-to-face group	19	28
Essential for individual's own satisfaction or perfection	15	47

A third illustrative content analysis is shown in Table 17–5. The problem was to determine the amount of cooperation between the propaganda agencies of Italy and Germany. Content analyses were undertaken of the replies made by Radio Berlin and Radio Rome to a speech made by Roosevelt. Counts were made of the number of references to each country, to the collaborating country, and to the joint effort of the two countries. The content of the two radio stations proved to be so different regarding self-references as to suggest strongly that little cooperation went on between the propaganda efforts of the two countries.

TABLE 17–5. CONTENT ANALYSIS OF PROPAGANDA REFERENCES BY RADIO BERLIN AND RADIO ROME IN REPLY TO THE ROOSEVELT SPEECH OF SEPTEMBER 11, 1941

(From Berelson, 2, p. 73)

Self-references in reply to Roosevelt speech	Radio Berlin, per cent	Radio Rome, per cent
Germany	96	22
Italy	0	1
Axis	4	77

Measurement methods for content analysis have been dominated by counting techniques. The experimenter seeks something to count that will have a bearing on a more general issue. In each of the three examples above, something was counted as a way of getting at a broader problem. In some studies the simple counting of things supplies all the information that is needed, such as would be the case in learning the different amounts of newspaper space or radio time devoted to news, sports, drama, and advertisement. In other cases, the issue being studied is much more complex, and the units which are counted are only tangentially related to what will be inferred from the results.

After a decision is made as to what is to be counted or observed in message content, a number of steps must be undertaken to effect a systematic content analysis. If the content analysis is to describe the treatment of a topic in a broad range of messages rather than in several particular messages, a sampling of messages and message sources must be undertaken. If, for example, the problem is to study the different amounts of time given to different subject-matter categories in United States television programs, a broad sample of programs from United States television networks must be analyzed. In addition it would be necessary either to draw randomly or vary systematically the number of programs analyzed during different periods of the day. A thorough sampling of this kind is a large-scale operation.

After messages are chosen for a content analysis, judges, usually referred to as coders, must be selected and trained for the work. The type of coders chosen depends on the purpose of the study. For example, if the analysis concerns how housewives react to romance magazines, the coders would necessarily be drawn from a representative cross section of "homemakers." If the work of the coders is concerned with analyzing what is in the message rather than reacting to the message, the coders are likely to be sophisticated persons who have some training in communications studies.

A third step in the organization of a content analysis is the training of coders. This may be a relatively easy job if a simple count is being made of readily observed content characteristics. If coders must make complex judgments about the characteristics of content, a considerable training period may be required. For example, in a recent study in which the author participated (16), coders were required to judge the presence or absence of 10 factors concerning beliefs about mental health as they are portrayed in radio, television, newspapers, and magazines. It was necessary to use psychology majors as coders, and considerable training was necessary to teach the meanings and implications of the content factors.

One essential step before the content analysis is undertaken is to test the reliability of coders. This can be done quite simply by comparing the judgments or counts made by several coders on the same material. If the coders agree on, say, only 25 per cent of their judgments, either the study should be abandoned or additional training should be given the coders. Unless the judgments or counts are so simple as to be agreed upon almost perfectly by all coders, it is wise to use either two or several coders for each message that is analyzed. As is usually the case in the averaging of ratings or judgments, a much more reliable set of results will be obtained by the use of more than one coder.

The major snag in the use of content analysis comes when the question being studied is complicated to the point where simple counts or judgments cannot be used. To illustrate this point, consider the following excerpt from the analyses of Wolfenstein and Leites (**29**) of the characters and themes in American motion pictures:

It is probably a characteristic American conviction that suffering is pointless and unnecessary. In keeping with this, love in American films rarely involves suffering. . . . Dangers in American films tend to take the form of external violence, not inner conflict. (**29**, pp. 94, 99)

Insightful and interesting as are such analyses, it is difficult to see how they could be substantiated by measurements or counts of message characteristics.

Content analysis is essentially what is intended in many of the instruments of clinical psychology. Projective tests, particularly the *TAT*, are concerned with message content and the inferences which it provides about the individual's personality. Here, as in numerous other content analyses, the questions under consideration are complicated beyond the use of simple counts and judgments about content characteristics. New and more powerful methods of content analysis are badly needed in many areas of research; but for some time to come it can be expected that many issues about message content will be studied by an intuitive approach rather than with explicit, standardized techniques.

REFERENCES

1. Attneave, F. Dimensions of similarity. *Amer. J. Psychol.*, 1950, **63**, 516–556.
2. Berelson, B. *Content analysis in communications research.* Glencoe, Ill.: Free Press, 1952.
3. Cronbach, L. J. Processes affecting scores on "understanding of others" and "assumed similarity." *Psychol. Bull.*, 1955, **52**, 177–193.
4. Cronbach, L. J., and Gleser, G. C. Assessing similarity between profiles. *Psychol. Bull.*, 1953, **50**, 456–473.
5. Dale, E., and Chall, J. A formula for predicting readability. *Educ. Res. Bull.*, 1948, **27**, 11–20; 37–54.

6. Fiedler, F. E. A comparison of the therapeutic relationships in psychoanalytic, non-directive, and Adlerian therapy. *J. consult. Psychol.*, 1950, **14**, 436–445.
7. Fiedler, F. E. Assumed similarity measures as predictors of team effectiveness. *J. abnorm. soc. Psychol.*, 1954, **49**, 381–388.
8. Fiedler, F. E. The influence of leader-keyman relations on combat crew effectiveness. *J. abnorm. soc. Psychol.*, 1955, **51**, 227–235.
9. Flesch, R. *How to test readability.* New York: Harper, 1951.
10. Fruchter, B. *Introduction to factor analysis.* Princeton, N.J.: Van Nostrand, 1954.
11. Gage, N. L., and Cronbach, L. J. Conceptual and methodological problems in interpersonal perception. *Psychol. Rev.*, 1955, **62**, 411–422.
12. Guilford, J. P. *Psychometric methods.* (2nd ed.) New York: McGraw-Hill, 1954.
13. Messick, S. J. Some recent theoretical developments in multidimensional scaling. *Educ. psychol. Measmt*, 1956, **16**, 82–99.
14. Nunnally, J. C. An investigation of some propositions of self-conception: the case of Miss Sun. *J. abnorm. soc. Psychol.*, 1955, **50**, 87–92.
15. Nunnally, J. C. A systematic approach to the construction of hypotheses about the process of psychotherapy. *J. consult. Psychol.*, 1955, **19**, 17–20.
16. Nunnally, J. C. The communication of mental health information: A comparison of the opinions of experts and the public with mass media presentations. *Behav. Sci.*, 1957, **2**, 222–230.
17. Osgood, C. E., and Luria, Z. A blind analysis of a case of multiple personality using the semantic differential. *J. abnorm. soc. Psychol.*, 1954, **49**, 579–591.
18. Osgood, C. E., and Suci, G. J. Factor analysis of meaning. *J. exp. Psychol.*, 1955, **50**, 325–338.
19. Osgood, C. E., Suci, G. J., and Tannenbaum, P. *The measurement of meaning.* Urbana, Ill.: Univer. Illinois Press, 1957.
20. Proctor, C. H., and Loomis, C. P. Analysis of sociometric data. In M. Jahoda, M. Deutsch, and S. Cook (Eds.) *Research methods in social relations, Part II.* New York: Dryden, 1951, chap. 17.
21. Richardson, M. W. Multidimensional psychophysics. *Psychol. Bull.*, 1938, **35**, 659.
22. Staats, C. K., and Staats, A. W. Meaning established by classical conditioning. *J. exp. Psychol.*, 1957, **54**, 74–80.
23. Stephenson, W. *The study of behavior.* Chicago: Univer. Chicago Press, 1953.
24. Taylor, W. L. "Cloze procedure": A new tool for measuring readability. *Journ. Quart.*, 1953, **30**, 415–433.
25. Taylor, W. L. Recent developments in the use of "Cloze procedure." *Journ. Quart.*, 1956, **33**, 42–48.
26. Thigpen, C. H., and Cleckley, H. A case of multiple personality. *J. abnorm. soc. Psychol.*, 1954, **49**, 135–151.
27. Thomson, Sir Godfrey. *The factorial analysis of human ability.* London: Univer. London Press, 1951.
28. Torgerson, W. S. *A theoretical and empirical investigation of multidimensional scaling.* Princeton, N.J.: Educ. Testing Serv., 1951.
29. Wolfenstein, M., and Leites, N. *Movies: A psychological study.* Glencoe, Ill.: Free Press, 1950.

CHAPTER 18

Establishment of Testing Programs

So far in this book, psychological measurement has been discussed in the abstract, without considering the real-life world in which measurement methods must be applied. The best efforts of the psychological laboratory can be thwarted by the unknowing or unsympathetic test user, and the instruments which are founded on the best of theory may be impractical and too expensive for general use. The person who is well grounded in the principles of test construction may lack the personality and the know-how needed to educate the test consumer, establish congenial relations with administrative officials, and organize a testing program. The purpose of this chapter is to discuss some guideposts for applying psychological measurement methods.

The Measurement Specialist in an Applied Setting. Large-scale testing programs are employed most often in vocational guidance, psychological counseling, school programs, and personnel selection. Special problems encountered in each of these settings will be discussed in turn. Regardless of where the measurement specialist applies his skills, there are some general principles that he should follow in order to establish friendly relations.

It is not uncommon for the measurement specialist to meet with considerable suspicion in the applied setting. The plant manager, for example, might regard the introduction of a testing program as a challenge to his authority to select and supervise personnel. The workers may fear that tests will be used to deprive them of their jobs or to shift them to less desired tasks. School teachers often react negatively to disruptions of schedule by psychological testing. The measurement specialist applies esoteric procedures like multiple correlation, item analysis, and factor analysis. These procedures tend to create difficulties in communicating research findings, and administrators often feel insecure in the face of statistical mumbo jumbo.

The first requirement for getting along well in an applied setting is to communicate frankly about the methods and purposes of testing. It should be made clear that the measurement specialist intends to fit in with existing programs and work toward the goals of the group. The testing program is intended to supply administrators with information which can then be used in behalf of their own goals. Eventually, the testing program may have an impact on the goals of an organization and point to better ways of doing things; but this is likely to come about only if administrators understand the research evidence and are able to feel that they are not being pushed into decisions.

Although the measurement specialist may take pride in teaching testing procedures to others, his responsibility is principally to speak the language of the organization with which he deals or in which he is employed. Statistical findings can usually be communicated without recourse to mathematical intricacies, by the use of simple graphs and diagrams. Rather than provide the organization with only statistical results, however, the specialist should also be able to explain the practical implications of measurement findings.

One of the jobs of the measurement specialist is to explain to administrative officials what tests can and cannot do. People in general tend to overestimate the power of psychological tests. Administrators will eventually be disappointed in the results of a testing program if they think that psychological tests will be a cure-all for their personnel problems. The proper point of view is that psychological tests are far from perfect but that they are quite often better than any other method of evaluating people.

Many administrative officials are not at all familiar with the construction and validation of tests. It is sometimes assumed that the psychologist can make up a test on his own without studying particular jobs or performing research. Consequently, administrative officials are sometimes surprised to learn that it will be necessary to interview personnel (workmen, students, soldiers), give them tryout tests, and perform follow-up studies later. The administrator may be sincerely interested in establishing a testing program but have little idea that it will require rearrangement of schedules and the absence of men from the job or classroom. These matters should be explained to administrators in advance to avoid later sources of misunderstanding.

Confusion between tests of the predictor and the assessment type often hinders the development of a testing program. The measurement specialist is often asked to construct a predictor test when there is no assessment available. For example, a request may be made for a selection device for taxicab drivers. While discussing the problem with administrative officials, the specialist may learn either that no indices of job performance are available or that the available indices are unreliable. If he then proceeds to construct predictor tests, there will be no way to measure their predictive efficiency. It is often necessary to explain that predictor tests cannot be constructed and put in use before more dependable assessments of job performance are obtained.

A second point of confusion involved between predictor and assessment tests is the assumption that the measurement specialist can, completely on his own, manufacture job or classroom performance assessments. Using the example above, it would not be unexpected to receive a request for tests to measure the efficiency of taxicab drivers who are presently on the job. It must be explained that assessments concern human values, and although the measurement specialist can help implement the values, the values themselves must come from those who have the responsibility to make decisions.

Above all, the measurement specialist must steer clear of factionalism and dispute within an organization. A testing program can be used punitively to try to show, for example, that one administrator is more efficient than another. The measurement specialist should retain his standing as a scientist and gather facts in an impartial manner; otherwise he will lower his value as a research worker and his results will be trusted by few.

Vocational Guidance. Vocational guidance may be incorporated in a school program, a psychological clinic, or in a separate government or commercial organization. People usually seek vocational guidance on their own or at the suggestion of an employer or teacher. The younger people come because they are unfamiliar with job opportunities and because they are not sure of their own aptitudes. Older people come because they are dissatisfied with their present positions or because their physical disabilities necessitate a change of jobs.

A wide variety of tests is needed in a vocational guidance setting. It is particularly necessary to measure different aptitudes rather than to measure general intelligence only. Two persons with the same over-all level of ability may have very different strong and weak points in particular aptitude factors. Tests must also be available for the "special abilities," such as the mechanical aptitudes. Interest tests are also widely used in vocational guidance, and they apparently serve their purpose well. Because of the variety of tests which must be employed with most subjects, it requires as much as one or two whole days to complete the testing and subsequent discussion of results. A thorough vocational guidance program is rather expensive to maintain.

In addition to a thorough knowledge of psychological tests, the vocational counselor must have a wide acquaintance with job requirements and employment opportunities. It would, for example, be incorrect to suggest a particular vocation which would utilize an individual's interests and abilities if there is a severe shortage of jobs in that line.

The counselor does not tell the individual what job or vocation he *should* enter. Tests are not sufficiently exact or all-inclusive to be able to make a decision for the person. Often extraneous factors outweigh the test results. A person may appear best suited for a career as a painter or actor; but, if he has several dependents, the immediate need for a steady income may necessitate the choice of another vocation. The needs of a person's family, the values of his subgroup, and the desire to live in a certain locality will all affect decisions about jobs and professional training. The purpose of vocational guidance is to furnish the individual with information about himself and about occupations which, when added to what he already thinks and feels, will help him arrive at wise decisions.

Psychological Counseling. Here we will consider the use of tests to aid in making decisions about maladjusted persons. The setting may be a psychological or psychiatric clinic or a mental hospital. The purpose is to diagnose the source of maladjustment and to decide the kinds of treatments that will do the most good. Whereas most of the instruments used in vocational guidance are group tests, individual tests predominate in clinical settings. Individual tests are used because the nature of the person's maladjustment may make it difficult to use group tests, and because the individual testing situation provides many opportunities to observe the person. Group tests could not be used with a person who is so mentally retarded that he cannot read the instructions or follow directions without assistance. Similarly, group tests cannot be used effectively with persons who are severely depressed or withdrawn.

The opportunity to watch a person take an individual test is often as rich a source of information as the test score. Two children may make low scores on a test like the Stanford-Binet for very different reasons. One child may try hard, in a slow, strained manner. Another child might give wrong answers with a sly look in his eyes and intersperse his wrong answers with highly intelligent remarks about the testing situation. Being able to note differences of this kind is very helpful in detecting sources of maladjustment.

The highest level of testing skill is required in the clinical setting. It is usually more difficult to give an individual test, like the Rorschach, to a disturbed person than to a normal individual. Sometimes it is difficult to establish contact at all or to get a single response. Whereas the normal individual can be expected to respond to a polite approach and a sensible explanation of the test, maladjusted individuals will often remain suspicious and uncooperative. Clinical examiners must be prepared for adults who grow angry or begin to weep in the middle of the testing session. The severely disturbed child may refuse to enter the testing room or, after being coaxed inside, hide under a table or tear up the testing materials. Disturbed individuals are not always so recalcitrant or hostile, but the examiner must be prepared for and capable of handling such situations as they arise.

The range of tests employed in a clinical setting is usually not as broad as that required in vocational guidance. Reliance is placed principally on measures of general ability, particularly on the Stanford-Binet and the Wechsler scales, and on the Rorschach and *TAT* as measures of personality. Although there is occasional use of personality inventories, such as the Bernreuter and the *MMPI*, these are less favored than the projective instruments.

Psychological counselors differ in the extent to which they employ psychological tests. Some counselors believe that the use of tests starts treatment off on the wrong foot. They feel that tests encourage the individual to think that the counselor is going to give him the "answers" to all his problems. Counselors with this point of view prefer to foster the individual's independence of thought, work with him in solving his own problems, rather than advise, manage, and direct. However, most counselors feel that tests are very useful in conjunction with treatment. Some counselors would prefer not to give and interpret the tests themselves, because they think that it will foster an unhealthy dependence. They would prefer to have the tests administered by some other psychologist and, to the extent that it is advisable, have the examiner explain the results to the individual.

School Programs. The emphasis in testing programs changes from elementary to advanced education. In elementary and high school, the testing program is usually tied directly to classroom instruction and the management of students. The measurement specialist is usually referred to as a school psychologist and usually has extensive training in educational methods. He helps compose examinations for particular courses, selects achievement tests, and performs diagnostic testing for those children who are meeting with difficulties. It is becoming popular to give all children a standard battery of tests, usually consisting of a group intelligence measure, interest inventories for older children, and sometimes attitude and personality inventories.

Contrary to the procedure used in some other countries, there are no formal selection procedures in the United States to decide who can and who cannot enter grammar school and high school. Anyone can go on to a higher grade if he passes the next lower one. Consequently, tests are very seldom used for selection in elementary and high school. Tests are becoming increasingly popular in educational research, to find better methods of instruction and better ways of organizing curricula.

In the late years of high school and in college, one of the major functions of a testing program is to aid vocational guidance, which was discussed in a previous section. Selection is one of the primary jobs in many college and university testing programs. Many private colleges and some state-supported institutions admit only those applicants who show promise of doing well scholastically. In conjunction with high school grades, psychological tests are the major selection instruments. Tests for selecting college freshmen are used very widely and they serve the purpose well. The predictive efficiency of the tests can be measured straightforwardly by correlating scores with grade point averages obtained later. Because the number of college applicants is steadily increasing beyond the facilities of educational institutions, it is expected that psychological tests will come even more prominently into play as selection instruments.

Personnel Selection and Management. Tests are being used widely in military, civil service, and industrial work to decide which persons will be given particular jobs or positions and to organize working conditions for maximum efficiency, safety, and pleasantness. Specialists who concern themselves with these matters are usually referred to as personnel psychologists.

Some of the strategy of selecting people for particular jobs was discussed in Chapter 5. The efficiency of selection depends not only on how well predictor tests correlate with the assessment of job performance but on the selection ratio and the success ratio as well. Even the most valid predictor test will be of little use if the number of applicants for a job is hardly more than the number of vacancies. Even with a low (favorable) selection ratio, a test or test battery will serve little purpose if the success ratio is very high. That is, if the job is so simple that almost anyone chosen at random could perform satisfactorily, there is little need for psychological tests.

The personnel psychologist usually must perform more research and usually needs more training in measurement research methods than persons who work in vocational guidance, clinics, and school programs. In personnel selection it is often necessary to construct and validate tests for the particular employment setting. Jobs that have very similar titles may differ in their actual duties, and consequently, specialized selection instruments are often required. This means that the personnel psychologist must either try out a range of commercially available tests or construct tests for his particular purpose. Even if commercially distributed tests are used, it is often necessary to invent special test instructions and procedures of administration and to gather norms in the local setting.

Successful performance in a particular job is only one of the criteria for selecting personnel. Equally important is whether a particular person will rise to higher positions in the institution. A test which may be only moderately predictive of success in a low-level job may work very well as a predictor of long-range achievement. Table 18–1 shows the relationship between intelligence test scores and job levels reached by clerical workers. Whereas 87 per cent of the persons with lowest scores on the

TABLE 18–1. RELATIONSHIP BETWEEN INTELLIGENCE TEST SCORES OF CLERICAL WORKERS AT TIME THEY WERE HIRED AND JOB LEVEL THEY ACHIEVED LATER

(Adapted from Pond and Bills, **9**)

Intelligence test score	Low job, per cent	Middle job, per cent	High job, per cent
180 and above	4	42	54
160–179	9	71	20
140–159	33	59	8
139 and below	87	13	0

test remained in a low-level job, only 4 per cent of the persons with highest test scores failed to move up to higher positions.

One of the major variables to consider in selecting personnel for some jobs is labor turnover. That is, the job may be easy to learn and most persons may perform well enough, but many employees leave the job after a short time. Because it is expensive to "break in" new employees and because a high turnover disrupts operations, it is important to select persons who are likely to remain on the job for a relatively long time. Tests can be used to predict the likelihood that an individual will remain on a job. Table 18–2 shows the relationship between intelligence test

TABLE 18–2. RELATION OF INTELLIGENCE TEST SCORES TO LENGTH OF SERVICE FOR A GROUP OF CASHIERS AND INSPECTOR-WRAPPERS

(Adapted from Viteles, **10**)

Test score	Average length of service, days
90 and above	35
80–89	87
70–79	96
60–69	100
50–59	107
40–49	142
30–39	91
20–29	91
10–19	3

scores and length of service in one job setting. In that instance, people in the middle intelligence range are more likely to remain on the job for a long period. It is likely that interest, attitude, and personality tests will also be useful in predicting job turnover.

In selecting individuals for some jobs, the major concern is how safely the individual will perform. This is particularly so when the individual will be responsible for the lives of other persons, as is the case with bus drivers, train engineers, and airplane pilots. Tests can be used to predict the tendency to have accidents on a particular job. Table 18–3 shows the

TABLE 18–3. THE VALIDITY OF VARIOUS TESTS IN THE PREDICTION OF ACCIDENTS OF TAXICAB DRIVERS

(Adapted from Ghiselli and Brown, **6**, p. 349)

Type of test	Validity coefficient
Dotting	.35
Tapping	.47
Judgment of distance	.18
Distance discrimination	.20
Mechanical principles	.11
Arithmetic	−.09
Speed of reaction	−.04
Interest	.28

validity of various tests as predictors of accidents by taxicab drivers. In that instance the two motor skills of dotting and tapping (both concerned with the rapid and precise use of finger and arm muscles) are the best predictors. The most predictive tests tend to be different for different jobs, and in only a few cases have tests been successful in predicting who will have accidents.

SOURCES OF TEST INFORMATION

Although numerous tests have been used in previous chapters to illustrate principles of human measurement, this book is not intended to be a complete reference source for available tests. Many tests are developed each year, and it is nearly impossible to be well informed about even a sizable percentage of the new instruments. Therefore, the person who works with psychological tests needs to be familiar with lists of commercially available tests, digests of research findings, and reports on new methods and procedures.

Available Tests. A list of the most prominent test publishers is presented in Appendix 1. It is the usual practice of each company to distribute a yearly catalogue of available tests. The person who works in a testing program will want to request test catalogues from some or most of the major commercial firms. The catalogues give price lists and short descriptions of the tests. Most companies will send a *specimen set* of any printed test. Prices range from less than a dollar up to several dollars, depending on the test. Test catalogues are very helpful for keeping informed about new tests. It is too much to expect that the test publisher will be completely unbiased in the claims for a new instrument. Critical evaluations are best obtained from some of the research reports which will be discussed in the following sections.

In addition to the test catalogues, a number of test bibliographies are available. Hildreth (7, 8) published a list of 5,294 tests, covering the major instruments that had been developed up to 1945. The tests are listed by topic, in order that a person who is interested in, say, manual dexterity tests can most easily find the instruments that are available. No effort is made to present research findings in respect to the tests or to evaluate them in any way. References as to where the test is published or where it is described in some detail are given for each test. Other lists have been prepared for special testing areas.

Administration and Use of Tests. After one or several tests are selected as likely candidates for use in a particular setting, it is necessary to learn how the test is administered and scored. This information is usually supplied by test manuals, which can be purchased along with or separately from particular tests. Manuals usually describe how the test was constructed, provide some norms, and in many cases report research findings on reliability and validity. The amount of research evidence given in the manual and the nature of the findings will often provide helpful suggestions as to whether or not a test should be tried in a particular situation.

A particularly useful publication for all those who deal with psychological tests is "Technical Recommendations for Psychological Tests and Diagnostic Techniques" prepared by the Committee on Test Standards of the American Psychological Association.[1] It provides numerous suggestions for the development, validation, commercial distribution, and use of psychological tests.

Research Evidence. It is important before accepting a test to examine the research evidence which has accrued from applications to different measurement problems. Although a test may look quite promising when it is published, it takes several years or more to judge how well it works in practice. One source of research findings is the *Journal of Applied Psychology.* You would search there if you were interested, for example, in the ability of the Strong Interest Inventory to select salesmen. The *Journal of Consulting Psychology* has reviews of new tests and research reports on older tests, primarily those instruments which are used most widely in clinical psychology. Summaries of research in whole areas of testing, such as the application of personality inventories in military psychology or the use of tests to measure brain damage, appear occasionally in the *Psychological Bulletin.*

The most detailed sources of research information about tests are the

[1] The publication appeared as a supplement to the *Psychological Bulletin,* 1954, **51,** Part 2. A copy can be obtained by mail for $1 from the American Psychological Association, 1333 Sixteenth Street, N.W., Washington 6, D.C.

Mental Measurements Yearbooks prepared by Buros (**2, 3, 4, 5**). The four Yearbooks currently available were published in 1938, 1941, 1949, and 1953 respectively. (The gap between 1941 and 1949 was due to the Second World War). Each *Yearbook* is a large volume containing research findings and critical reviews of many different tests. The most prominent tests receive reviews by several experts. In addition, the *Yearbooks* supply considerable factual information about most tests: administration time, cost, scoring procedures, and populations for which the instruments are most suitable. Numerous references are provided to other publications that report research evidence on particular tests. The *Yearbooks* are a "must" for any person who deals extensively with psychological tests.

Research Methodology. Equally important to keeping up with new tests as they are developed is staying abreast of new logical and statistical developments in psychological measurement. Information concerning many of these developments can be obtained from current textbooks on psychological measurement. Some of the professional journals also report recent advances in methodology. *Educational and Psychological Measurement* is primarily concerned with new conceptions in human measurement, new outlooks on test reliability and validity, new methods of test construction, and practical problems of using tests. *Psychometrika* is devoted largely to measurement logic and mathematical statistics, much of which is pertinent to the development and use of psychological tests.

PRACTICAL ARRANGEMENTS

When tests have finally been selected for use in a measurement program, there are numerous practical considerations which will govern the efficiency and economy of their use. Many of the practical problems are specific to particular testing situations; however, there are some rules and procedures that will generally help in maintaining a smoothly operating measurement program.

Physical Setting. A primary consideration is to obtain an adequate testing room. It should be well lighted, free from noise and other distractions, and equipped with the necessary number of desks or tables. If possible, it is best to have a particular room permanently assigned for testing, so that it can be equipped for the testing program. Special equipment, such as wiring for electrical devices, cabinets for storing test material, movie projectors, public address systems, and others, may be required.

Administration and Scoring. In most cases the examiner explains to the examinees why particular tests are being administered and how the forms should be completed. The instructions should be sufficiently detailed to cover most of the problems that will come up. For example, if a particular kind of pencil is used with the test, the subjects should be informed that

more pencils are available if a point breaks. If the examinees are allowed
to ask questions during the test, they should be told the kinds of questions that will be permitted and also how to summon the examiner. When
a large number of persons are being tested at one time, it is usually better
to inform them that it will not be possible to answer questions once the
testing is under way. Subjects must be told what to do when they complete the test or tests: go back and work on the problems some more, leave
the room, or remain seated without looking back at the materials.

It is usually necessary to employ several assistants when testing a large
group of persons. They can answer questions if questions are permitted.
They can help direct people to their proper work spaces, give out materials, and collect them when the testing is over. Assistants are also helpful
in preventing cheating. They need have little knowledge about the nature
and purpose of the tests being used.

It is very helpful to "role play" the administration procedure before testing groups of subjects. This consists of going through all of the administration routine with a few people acting as subjects. They are asked to
note any point at which the testing procedure is unclear. One subject may
notice that at the bottom of the first page there is no information to indicate whether to go on to the next page or stop there. Another subject may
not know whether or not he is to guess when unsure of the answers. A
trial run of this kind will offer many suggestions for clarifying the administration routine.

Analysis of Test Data. High-speed computational machines are rapidly
replacing the relatively slow human hand and human mind. Special
answer sheets are now widely used for testing large groups of subjects.
The answer sheets can either be scored with a stencil or, much faster, by
machine (International Business Machine Corporation is one of the best-
known distributors of such equipment). Hundreds of answer sheets can
be scored in an hour's time.

It facilitates the subsequent analysis of test results if scores are recorded
on punch cards. One card can store a considerable amount of information
about a person: scores on a number of tests; assessment scores, such as
job ratings and production records; and personal data, such as years of
experience and marital status. High-speed computational equipment can
then be used to find particular kinds of persons, such as those who score
above a certain level on a test, those who have three years of experience,
and those who are unmarried. Also, it is even more important that
machine computers can make relatively fast work of the complex statistics which are often required in the construction and use of tests. A few
years ago it would have been prohibitively laborious to undertake a
factor analysis of 100 test items. Now it requires only several hours of
digital computer time to complete the job.

THE USE OF HUMAN SUBJECTS

The life sciences (including the biological and social sciences) and physical science have many points in common. Both search for lawfulness in nature, value objectivity above opinion and desire, and employ many of the same conceptual and mathematical tools. They differ mainly in that the life sciences deal with people whereas physical science is mostly concerned with inanimate objects or subhuman animals. Thus, the working routine of the psychologist is vastly more difficult than that of the physical scientist for two reasons. First, human behavior obeys no simple laws, and consequently, progress in psychology is often slow. Second, the psychologist must consider the feelings, needs, and safety of his human subjects. The physicist who is interested in the structure of crystals can pound them, burn them, freeze them, and work without considering their "feelings." The psychologist must be very careful not to harm or, in many cases, even discomfort his human subjects. This section will discuss some of the ground rules for dealing with human subjects in psychological experiments and testing programs.

The Use of Disturbing Materials. It is often necessary to frighten, embarrass, or disturb people in order to carry out an experiment or test a particular attribute. For example, if you want to learn the effect of anxiety on memory, it is necessary to create human anxiety to perform the experiment. This might be done by an electric shock, a series of embarrassing questions, or a film of a surgical operation. In some studies it is necessary to hypnotize a subject, isolate an individual in a dark room for several hours, or have someone act out the part of a murderer. The first rule in dealing with material that is likely to create strong disturbance is that all subjects should be informed of the nature of the materials before the experiment. They need not necessarily be told what the experimenter hopes to find or all of the conditions of the study, but they should at least be told about the source of disturbance which will be employed. Secondly, the subjects should all volunteer without undue pressure from the examiner, and they should be allowed to discontinue the experiment if they so desire.

Obtaining Subjects. One of the primary difficulties in performing experiments or in developing tests is to obtain enough subjects. Whereas the physical scientist can often obtain large quantities of the material he needs, and procurement is only a financial problem, it is often difficult to contact human subjects and persuade them to participate in studies. They are often not interested in the study, or, like most people, they are busy with jobs, home life, and recreational pursuits. Consequently, many studies are performed on college students, simply because they are the most available subjects. There is a growing awareness that many research findings are different when the subjects are recruited from the community at large rather than from students only.

It is generally bad practice to rely on volunteers for developing tests and for research studies, although, as was said in the previous section, volunteers should be used when disturbing materials are part of the study. The people who volunteer are usually more knowledgeable about the research area, women tend to volunteer more often than men, and it is likely that the personalities of volunteers and nonvolunteers are somewhat different. In some cases it is possible and not unethical to assign whole groups of individuals to an experiment. This can be done in some school, industrial, and military situations. When subjects are not obligated to participate in a study, as would be the case in studying the attitudes of a particular church congregation, the experimenter should try to enlist as many of the people as possible. There will always be some people who either cannot or will not participate, but if as many as 80 or 90 per cent are obtained, the results will probably not be strongly influenced by "volunteer bias."

Giving Information. People are sufficiently curious to want to know what a research study is about; and when psychological tests are used, they will want to know how well they perform. It must be decided prior to a study just how much information can be given to subjects. The subjects should be informed before the experiment what they can be told later about the results.

One place in which decisions must be reached about providing information to subjects is in the routine administration of a testing program. There are certain testing situations in which the subject is usually informed in some detail about the test results, as would be the case in vocational guidance. At the other extreme, the subject is usually not told the results of personality tests given in a clinical setting. The information might disturb him and raise more questions than are answered. In between these extremes there are situations in which it is difficult to decide how much information should be supplied to the subject and to other people.

Subjects generally should not be told the results of tryout instruments whose worth has not yet been established. The experimenter may think that he is employing a measure of neuroticism, but subsequent research studies show that it does not measure what is intended. It would be a real injustice to inform a subject that he has a high neurotic tendency on the basis of the test. In general, the less known about the validity of the instrument, the fewer are the grounds for informing subjects of test results.

Disguising Materials. Participants in psychological studies are often wary that some trick is involved, that the real purpose of the study is disguised. Many research studies and many tests would not be successful without either omitting information about the experimental purpose or purposefully misinforming subjects. For example, in a study of visual illusions, the subject is not told that the purpose is to study distortions in perception. If subjects are informed of the illusion, they will not report what they see but what they think they *should* see. It is often necessary to disguise the purpose of attitude and personality measures. A good example is the situational test described in the previous chapter. The subject is told that two men will *help* solve the problems, whereas their real purpose is to hinder and distract.

The border line between harmless disguise and harmful deception is sometimes difficult to define. Surely there should be no more deception than is necessary for the experiment. If the deception is of a kind that may cause lingering worry for the subjects, they should be informed later of the deception and told why the deception was necessary. It is much easier to defend disguise in the experimental material than deception regarding the use of measurement results. For example, most psychologists would consider it highly unethical to tell subjects that test results will be kept anonymous and then disclose them later, or to tell subjects that test results will be used for research purposes only and later use them for personnel selection.

Human Reaction to Human Measurement. Finally, we should return to a point mentioned in the first pages of this book, that psychological measurement is often reacted to as an unfriendly intrusion into human lives. There is a wide range of reaction from people who take psychological tests or participate in research studies; but it is often easy to detect an underlying tension in even the outwardly most casual subject. Most of us cherish the belief that we are somehow better than our reputations and gifted beyond our positions in life. Psychological tests often represent an ego challenge, a type of objective evidence which may unveil our inabilities and personal deficiencies. Although we can rationalize our everyday failings, it is hard to argue with test scores.

A typical question asked of psychologists is, "I made a low (or high) score on a manual dexterity test in high school. What does that mean?" Instances of this kind show that people are sensitive to the scores made on psychological tests, and test scores may influence people's viewpoints about their own abilities and personalities. Another place in which it is easy to see the popular anxiety over human measurement is in the classroom examination situation. Although some students may be casual and unconcerned, the majority show obvious signs of tension, such as frowning, nail biting, gritting teeth, and other forms of "nervousness." The tension is even higher when the graded examinations are returned.

The person who is new in the field of human measurement may be surprised at the amount of hostility sometimes shown by subjects after a research study or after taking tests. For example, after administering a tryout personality test, a number of the subjects are likely to come up afterwards and say that the test is no good (they hope) or that the study will show nothing. This is often a way of blowing off steam because of the tension brought on by the test, and it is part of the experimenter's job to accept the hostility and even encourage its free expression. A special follow-up meeting is often used, called a "cathartic session," to allow people to vent their feelings about a study. This allows a give-and-take discussion between experimenter and subjects, lets the subjects feel that they are more than "guinea pigs," and usually reduces tension considerably.

The importance of human measurement far outweighs the tension and embarrassment that is sometimes generated. We may all be created equal in the social sense but we are not all equal in terms of abilities and personality characteristics. It would be a great social waste not to help the talented achieve as much as they can, and a great social harm to encourage unsuited individuals to labor in ventures that will bring failure and discouragement. Taking a frank look at our own abilities and personality characteristics is not always pleasant at the moment, but it is necessary for long-range achievement and happiness.

REFERENCES

1. Beckman, A. S. Minimum intelligence levels for several occupations. *Personnel J.*, 1930, **9**, 309–313.
2. Buros, O. K. *The 1938 mental measurements yearbook.* New Brunswick, N.J.: Rutgers Univer. Press, 1938.
3. Buros, O. K. *The 1940 mental measurements yearbook.* Highland Park, N.J.: The Mental Measurements Yearbook, 1941.
4. Buros, O. K. *The third mental measurements yearbook.* New Brunswick, N.J.: Rutgers Univer. Press, 1949.
5. Buros, O. K. *The fourth mental measurements yearbook.* Highland Park, N.J.: Gryphon Press, 1953.
6. Ghiselli, E. E., and Brown, C. W. *Personnel and industrial psychology.* (2nd ed.) New York: McGraw-Hill, 1955.
7. Hildreth, G. H. *A bibliography of mental tests and rating scales.* New York: Psychol. Corp., 1939.
8. Hildreth, G. H. *A bibliography of mental tests and rating scales. 1945 supplement.* New York: Psychol. Corp., 1946.
9. Pond, M., and Bills, M. A. Intelligence and clerical jobs. *Personnel J.*, 1933, **12**, 41–56.
10. Viteles, M. S. Selection of cashiers and predicting length of service. *J. Personnel Res.*, 1924, **2**, 467–473.

APPENDIX 1

Test Publishers and Distributors

Acorn Publishing Company, Rockville Centre, N.Y.

Association Press, 291 Broadway, New York 7, N.Y.

Bureau of Educational Measurements, Kansas State Teachers College of Emporia, Emporia, Kans.

Bureau of Educational Research and Service, Department of Publications, State University of Iowa, Iowa City, Iowa.

Bureau of Publications, Teachers College, Columbia University, New York.

California Test Bureau, 5916 Hollywood Boulevard, Los Angeles 28, Calif.

Educational Test Bureau, 720 Washington Avenue, S.E., Minneapolis 14, Minn.

Educational Testing Service, 20 Nassau Street, Princeton, N.J.

C. A. Gregory, 345 Calhoun Street, Cincinnati, Ohio.

Grune and Stratton, Inc., 381 Fourth Avenue, New York 16, N.Y.

Harvard University Press, 79 Garden Street, Cambridge 38, Mass.

Houghton Mifflin Company, 2 Park Street, Boston 7, Mass.

Doncaster G. Humm Personnel Service, P.O. Box 1433, Del Valle Station, Los Angeles 15, Calif.

Marietta Apparatus Company, Marietta, Ohio.

University of Minnesota Press, Minneapolis 14, Minn.

National Institute for Industrial Psychology, Aldwych House, London, W.C. 2, England.

The Psychological Corporation, 522 Fifth Avenue, New York 36, N.Y.

Public School Publishing Company, 509 North East Street, Bloomington, Ill.

Science Research Associates, 57 West Grand Avenue, Chicago 10, Ill.

Sheridan Supply Company, P.O. Box 837, Beverly Hills, Calif.

Stanford University Press, Stanford University, Calif.

C. H. Stoelting Company, 424 North Homan Avenue, Chicago 24, Ill.

Teachers College, Columbia University, New York, N.Y.

Western Psychological Services, Box 755, Beverly Hills, Calif.

Williams and Wilkins Company, Mt. Royal and Guilford Avenues, Baltimore, Md.

World Book Company, 313 Park Hill Avenue, Yonkers, N.Y.

APPENDIX 2

Scale Transformations

A problem that is often encountered in using psychological tests is that of transforming an obtained set of raw scores to a set with a particular mean and standard deviation. For example, it might be found that the mean of the obtained raw test scores is 40 and that the standard deviation is 5. In order to compare scores on the test with scores on another test, or in order to place the scores in an easily interpretable form, it might be desired to transform the raw scores in such a way that the new scores have a mean of 50 and a standard deviation of 10. Transformations of this kind can be performed with the following formula:

$$X_t = \frac{\sigma_t}{\sigma_o} X_o - \left[\frac{\sigma_t}{\sigma_o} M_o - M_t \right]$$

where X_t = scores on the transformed scale
  X_o = scores on the obtained scale: raw scores
 M_o, M_t = means of X_o and X_t respectively
  σ_o, σ_t = standard deviations of X_o and X_t respectively

The formula can be applied to the problem illustrated above as follows:

$$X_t = \left(\frac{10}{5} \right) X_o - \left[\left(\frac{10}{5} \right) 40 - 50 \right]$$
$$= 2X_o - 30$$

By this transformation a raw score of 40 would be transformed to a score of 50, and a raw score of 25 would be transformed to a score of 20. Because the formula is a linear transformation, it does not change the shape of the score distribution.

Proportions of the Area in Various Sections of the Normal Distribution *

	z Standard score (x/σ) (1)	Area between (2)	Area beyond (3)
+ and −	0.00	0.0000	1.0000
	0.05	.0392	.9602
	0.10	.0796	.9204
	0.15	.1192	.8808
	0.20	.1586	.8414
+ and −	0.25	.1974	.8026
	0.30	.2358	.7642
	0.35	.2736	.7264
	0.40	.3108	.6892
	0.45	.3472	.6528
+ and −	0.50	.3830	.6170
	0.55	.4176	.5824
	0.60	.4514	.5486
	0.65	.4844	.5156
	0.70	.5160	.4840
+ and −	0.75	.5468	.4532
	0.80	.5762	.4238
	0.85	.6046	.3954
	0.90	.6318	.3682
	0.95	.6578	.3422

* If, for example, in a normal distribution of test scores, you want to estimate the number of persons who make scores between plus one standard deviation of the mean and minus one standard deviation of the mean, you would look opposite 1.00 in the first column at the proportion in the second column. There it is seen that the proportion is .6826 or, in other words, approximately 68 per cent. This means that approximately 32 per cent of the individuals make scores either greater than one standard deviation above the mean or less than one standard deviation below the mean. If you want to determine the proportions of people who lie within or beyond certain standard score units above the mean only or below the mean only, the proportions in columns 2 and 3 should be halved.

z Standard score (x/σ) (1)	Area between (2)	Area beyond (3)
+ and −		
1.00	.6826	.3174
1.05	.7062	.2938
1.10	.7286	.2714
1.15	.7498	.2502
1.20	.7698	.2302
+ and −		
1.25	.7888	.2112
1.30	.8064	.1936
1.35	.8230	.1770
1.40	.8384	.1616
1.45	.8530	.1470
+ and −		
1.50	.8664	.1336
1.55	.8788	.1212
1.60	.8904	.1096
1.65	.9019	.0990
1.70	.9108	.0892
+ and −		
1.75	.9198	.0802
1.80	.9282	.0718
1.85	.9356	.0644
1.90	.9426	.0574
1.95	.9488	.0512
+ and −		
2.00	.9544	.0456
2.05	.9596	.0404
2.10	.9642	.0358
2.15	.9684	.0316
2.20	.9722	.0278
+ and −		
2.25	.9756	.0244
2.30	.9786	.0214
2.35	.9812	.0188
2.40	.9836	.0164
2.45	.9858	.0142
+ and −		
2.50	.9876	.0124
2.55	.9892	.0108
2.60	.9906	.0094
2.65	.9920	.0080
2.70	.9930	.0070
+ and −		
2.80	.9948	.0052
2.90	.9962	.0038
3.00	.9973	.0027
3.10	.99806	.00194
3.20	.99862	.00138

	z Standard score (x/σ) (1)	Area between (2)	Area beyond (3)
+ and −	3.40	.99932	.00068
	3.60	.99968	.00032
	3.80	.999856	.000144
	4.00	.9999366	.0000634
	4.50	.9999932	.0000068
	5.00	.9999942	.00000058
	6.00	.999999998	.000000002

APPENDIX 4

Derivation of Measurement Error Formulas

Currently there are two mathematical models from which measurement error statistics can be derived. Although the same statistics are developed from both models, the models make different assumptions about the data. The first model to be examined considers any particular test as one from a universe of possible tests. The following assumptions are made in the model:

1. All of the sample tests in the universe of tests have the same variance.

2. All of the sample tests correlate the same with one another. That is, the correlation of test 1 with test 2 is the same as the correlation of test 1 with test 3, and the same as the correlation of test 2 with test 3, and so on.

3. All of the tests correlate the same with some outside variable (a criterion to be predicted, a test from another universe of content, or any other variable).

If the above assumptions hold, the correlation of the sum, or average, of all the sample tests in the universe (which is usually spoken of as the set of "true" scores) with the criterion variable is obtained as follows:

$$r_{y(\Sigma x)} = \frac{\Sigma z_y(z_1 + z_2 + z_3 + \cdots + z_n)}{\sqrt{\Sigma z_y^2}\sqrt{\Sigma(z_1 + z_2 + z_3 + \cdots + z_n)^2}}$$

where $r_{y(\Sigma x)}$ = the correlation of the criterion variable, y, with the sum of the standard scores on all sample tests in the universe

z_1 = standard scores on sample test 1

z_n = standard scores on test n

The equation above can be expanded as follows:

$$r_{y(\Sigma x)} = \frac{r_{y1} + r_{y2} + r_{y3} + \cdots + r_{yn}}{\left[\sum_{i=1}^{n}\sum_{j=1}^{n} r_{ij}\right]^{1/2}}$$

where the denominator is the square root of the sum of all the coefficients in the square matrix of intercorrelations of sample tests.

Because of assumptions 2 and 3 in the model:

$$r_{y(\Sigma x)} = \frac{nr_{yi}}{\sqrt{n + n^2 r_{ij} - nr_{ij}}} \qquad i \neq j$$

$$= \frac{r_{yi}}{\sqrt{\frac{1}{n} + r_{ij} - \frac{1}{n} r_{ij}}}$$

$$\text{Limit, as } n \to \infty, r_{y(\Sigma x)} = \frac{r_{yi}}{\sqrt{r_{ij}}} \qquad i \neq j$$

What the formula says is that, if the assumptions in the model hold, the correlation between a criterion and a set of "true" scores is obtained by dividing the correlation between a particular test and the criterion by the square root of the correlation between the particular test and any other test in the universe. The reader will recognize this as the correction for attenuation in one variable.

The correlation of any particular test with the sum of all the sample tests in the universe can be obtained as follows:

$$r_{i(\Sigma x)} = \frac{\Sigma z_i (z_1 + z_2 + z_3 + \cdots + z_n)}{\sqrt{\Sigma z_i^2} \sqrt{\Sigma (z_1 + z_2 + z_3 + \cdots + z_n)^2}}$$

and because of the assumptions made in the model:

$$r_{i(\Sigma x)} = \frac{1 + (n-1)r_{ij}}{\sqrt{n + n^2 r_{ij} - n r_{ij}}} \qquad i \neq j$$

$$= \frac{\frac{1}{n} + r_{ij} - \frac{1}{n} r_{ij}}{\sqrt{\frac{1}{n} + r_{ij} - \frac{1}{n} r_{ij}}}$$

$$\text{Limit, as } n \to \infty, r_{i(\Sigma x)} = \frac{r_{ij}}{\sqrt{r_{ij}}}$$

$$= \sqrt{r_{ij}}$$

What the formula says is that, if the assumptions of the model hold, the correlation of a set of test scores with the sum of all of the scores from the tests in the universe equals the square root of the correlation between any two sample tests. Usually the two tests which are correlated are referred to as equivalent or comparable forms. The correlation of any two sample tests, r_{ij}, is usually symbolized as r_{11} and is called the reliability coefficient. Because the square root of the reliability coefficient equals the correlation of either of the sample tests with "true" scores, r_{11} is said to equal the per cent of non-error variance.

The model also allows the derivation of the standard error of measurement and the other statistics which are needed in the study of measurement error. Of course the conditions of the model will not hold exactly in any domain of tests. Sample tests (equivalent forms) will have different variances, they will correlate differently with any outside variable, and their intercorrelations will not all be equal. Consequently, the reliability coefficient is only estimated by the correlation of two particular sample tests, or equivalent forms. The advantage of the model is that it shows what assumptions must be met in determining measure-

ment error statistics, and it provides an indication of the way in which depar-
tures from the model can be studied.

There are several disadvantages of the above model for determining measurement error statistics. One difficulty is that the model is based on a sampling
theory, which considers any particular test as one from a universe of possible
tests. It is difficult to define universes of test content and difficult to ensure that
all tests are from the same universe of content. Another disadvantage of the
model is that it requires an infinite number of sample tests, and in consequence,
the infinity sign appears in the derivation of measurement error statistics. Infinity
is, of course, only a handy fiction when discussing empirical data. However, the
model should hold with good accuracy if a large number of sample tests, say
100, is studied. Although studies of this kind have not yet been undertaken, it
would be possible to develop 100 similar tests, such as 100 short spelling,
vocabulary, or arithmetic tests and study the extent to which the model fits
empirical data.

The second model which is used for the derivation of measurement error
statistics begins by defining an obtained score as the sum of a "true," or universe score, and an error score:

$$x = x_u + e$$

where x is the score obtained by an individual on a particular test

x_u is the individual's true score

e is the error or chance portion of the obtained score

The first assumption in the model is that the error scores are uncorrelated with
true scores. Therefore

$$\sigma_x{}^2 = \sigma_u{}^2 + \sigma_e{}^2$$

If there are two measures of the same trait, the true score is expected to be the
same in both measurements, but the error scores are not necessarily the same.
The two obtained scores can then be broken down as follows:

$$x_1 = x_u + e_1$$
$$x_2 = x_u + e_2$$

The two measures are usually spoken of as equivalent forms, or sometimes they
are called parallel or comparable forms.

The reliability coefficient is defined as the correlation between two equivalent forms:

$$
\begin{aligned}
r_{11} &= \frac{\Sigma x_1 x_2}{N\sigma_1 \sigma_2} \\[2mm]
&= \frac{\Sigma (x_{u_1} + e_1)(x_{u_2} + e_2)}{N\sigma_1 \sigma_2} \\[2mm]
&= \frac{\Sigma x_u{}^2 + \Sigma x_{u_1} e_2 + \Sigma x_{u_2} e_1 + \Sigma e_1 e_2}{N\sigma_1 \sigma_2}
\end{aligned}
$$

Several assumptions are then made:

1. As in the first model, it is assumed that the two equivalent forms have
equal standard deviations, and, consequently, equal variances.

2. It is assumed that error scores on each test are uncorrelated with true scores on both tests.

3. It is assumed that error scores on one test are uncorrelated with error scores on the other test.

If assumptions 2 and 3 hold, three of the terms in the numerator of the above expression vanish, and the correlation between equivalent forms reduces to the following:

$$r_{11} = \frac{\sigma_u{}^2}{\sigma_1 \sigma_2}$$

Because of the assumption that the standard deviations are equal on the two equivalent forms, the reliability coefficient may be expressed as

$$r_{11} = \frac{\sigma_u{}^2}{\sigma_x{}^2}$$

What the formula says is that, if the assumptions in the model hold, the correlation of two equivalent forms equals the ratio of the "true" variance to the variance of either measurement or, regarding the ratio as a percentage, equals the per cent of non-error variance. This is the same conclusion that we obtained from the first model.

The standard error of measurement can be obtained through the following developments:

$$\sigma_x{}^2 = \sigma_u{}^2 + \sigma_e{}^2$$

Both sides of the equation can then be divided by the standard deviation of x:

$$\frac{\sigma_x{}^2}{\sigma_x{}^2} = \frac{\sigma_u{}^2}{\sigma_x{}^2} + \frac{\sigma_e{}^2}{\sigma_x{}^2}$$

$$1 = r_{11} + \frac{\sigma_e{}^2}{\sigma_x{}^2}$$

$$\frac{\sigma_e{}^2}{\sigma_x{}^2} = 1 - r_{11}$$

$$\sigma_e{}^2 = \sigma_x{}^2(1 - r_{11})$$

$$\sigma_e = \sigma_x \sqrt{1 - r_{11}}$$

In the text the more explicit symbol, σ_{meas}, was used rather than σ_e. In a similar way the model can be used to derive the correction for attenuation and the other measurement error statistics.

The advantage of the second model presented here is that it is not explicitly dependent on a sampling theory as is the case with the first model presented. However, this apparent advantage is not all to the good. The statistical results— the reliability coefficient, the standard error of measurement, etc.—are likely to be somewhat different if a test is compared with a number of different equivalent forms instead of only one. There is then some confusion as to the correct statistical results, and the model itself is unable to deal with the inconsistencies. One can always say that the reliability coefficient obtained from correlating any two equivalent forms is only an estimate, but the second model gives no hint as to what is being estimated nor any means for studying the accuracy with which estimates are made in general. Consequently, advocates of the second model have begun to think in terms of the relationships among collections of equivalent forms, all of which have the same variance and all of whose intercorrelations are equal. Therefore, a sampling theory is creeping into the second model; and, as the necessity for considering any test as one from a possible universe is brought into the model, the second model presented begins to collapse into the first model presented.

There are other reasons why the first model presented is probably better than the second. In particular, some of the constructs in the second model cannot be measured directly. Neither "true scores" nor "error scores" can be measured directly and can only be inferred from correlations among equivalent forms. The first model presented does not require these nonoperational constructs. Another mark against the second model is that some of the assumptions are probably not true in particular testing situations. On some occasions it is likely that errors will be correlated with "true" scores and errors on one test will be correlated with errors on another test. The first model does not require either of these assumptions.

It is comforting to know that two different, or apparently different, models arrive at the same formulas. This gives us some confidence in applying the standard measurement error statistics, such as the correction for attenuation and others. Future research should indicate which of the two models is more generally useful in studying the effect of measurement error in psychological tests.

APPENDIX 5

The Influence of Test Length on Reliability

If reliability is determined by the split-half method, the correlation between the split-halves is the reliability of half the test rather than the reliability of the whole test. Of course the whole test is employed in applied work, and the reliability of the whole test is larger than that of the half-tests. The reliability of the whole test can be estimated as follows:

$$r_{11} = \frac{2r_{hh}}{1 + r_{hh}}$$

where r_{11} is the reliability of the whole test
r_{hh} is the correlation between the split-halves

The formula is referred to as the "Spearman-Brown prophecy formula." The use of the formula can be illustrated with a correlation between split-halves of .80:

$$r_{11} = \frac{2(.80)}{1 + .80}$$

$$= \frac{1.60}{1.80}$$

$$= .89$$

Thus the best estimate of the reliability of the whole test is .89.

What the Spearman-Brown formula does is to estimate the reliability of a test twice as long (twice as many of the same kinds of items) as the test from which the reliability is actually computed. The formula can be extended to estimate the reliability of a test lengthened by any particular amount:

$$r_{nn} = \frac{nr_{11}}{1 + (n-1)r_{11}}$$

where r_{nn} = the reliability of a test n times as long as the original test
r_{11} = the reliability of the original test

If the reliability of a 20-item test is .70, and if 40 items very similar to the first 20 items are added to the test, the reliability of the 60-item test is estimated as follows:

$$r_{33} = \frac{3(.70)}{1 + (3-1).70}$$

$$= \frac{2.10}{1 + 1.40}$$

$$= \frac{2.10}{2.40}$$

$$= .88$$

Some cautions should be heeded in applying the formulas for estimating the reliability of a lengthened test. The formulas assume that when the test is lengthened the new items will be of the same kind as the original test items. If the new items relate to factors other than those in the original items or if the new items are generally easier or more difficult than the original items, the formulas will give misleading estimates. However, in spite of the assumptions which the formulas make, they provide a very useful, and usually a reasonably accurate, estimate of the gain in reliability that will come from lengthening a test. The formulas are also useful in estimating the amount of reduction in reliability that will follow from shortening a test. It may be desirable to use a shorter version of a particular test in order to reduce the time for administering test materials. For example, if the reliability of a 100-item test is known, and it is desired to use only 50 of the items, say, choosing only the odd-numbered items, the reliability of the 50-item test can be estimated by substituting ½ for n in the equation above and substituting the reliability of the 100-item test for r_{11}.

Sampling Error of Percentages

In opinion polling or in any other use of samples of persons, the results obtained are only estimates of the true population values. Sampling error was illustrated in Chapter 13 by considering the results of polling 1,000 persons, in which it is found that 55 per cent of the people say that they will vote for candidate A and the remaining 45 per cent say they will vote for candidate B. Before it can be safely said that candidate A has an edge over candidate B, it must be ensured that the apparent difference in voting sentiment is not likely to be due to sampling error only. If more than 50 per cent of the population actually vote for A, he will be elected. Consequently, the question is whether the sample value of 55 per cent who say they will vote for A is significantly greater than 50 per cent. This can be determined by the standard error of the percentage, which is obtained as follows:

$$\sigma_p = \sqrt{\frac{PQ}{N}}$$

where P = the hypothetical population percentage
$Q = 100 - P$
N = the number of persons in the sample

The formula is applied to the illustrative problem as follows:

$$\sigma_p = \sqrt{\frac{50 \times 50}{N}}$$

$$= \sqrt{\frac{2,500}{1,000}}$$

$$= \sqrt{2.50}$$

$$= 1.58$$

What this means is that, if samples of 1,000 persons are drawn at random from the population, the expected standard deviation of percentages in this problem is 1.58. This offers a way of determining the likelihood that sample values differ from the population percentage by particular amounts. This can be determined by subtracting the hypothetical population value from the sample value and dividing the result by the standard error of the percentage, as follows:

$$z = \frac{55 - 50}{1.58} = \frac{5}{1.58} = 3.16$$

The resulting value is a standard score, and its significance can be found in Appendix 3. There it is seen that a standard score of 3.20 is nearest to the obtained value of 3.16. Only .00138 of the cases lie above and below 3.20 standard scores. Here we are interested only in the proportion of people in one tail of the distribution. Our only concern is whether the population per cent is greater than 50 per cent. If it is, it makes no difference whether the population per cent is actually larger than the sample value of 55 per cent. Therefore, the value found in Appendix 3 should be divided by 2, which gives .00069. In other words, with a population per cent of 50 and with samples of 1,000 each, less than one time in a thousand would we expect to find sample values of 55 per cent or greater.

Another problem in which sampling error formulas are needed is in determining the significance of the difference between the results obtained from two independent samples. For example, the results of one poll might show that 55 per cent of the people intend to vote for candidate A, and a later poll, using a different sample of persons, shows that 60 per cent of the people intend to vote for A. It is tempting to interpret the results as showing an increased popularity of candidate A. However, before this can be done, it is necessary to test the significance of the difference between the two sample results. Formulas for the significance of the difference between two percentages and for more complex sampling error problems can be found in standard statistical texts.[1]

[1] See A. L. Edwards, *Experimental Design in Psychological Research*, New York: Rinehart, 1950; Q. McNemar, *Psychological Statistics*, 2d ed., New York: Wiley, 1955; Helen M. Walker and J. Lev, *Statistical Inference*, New York: Holt, 1953.

APPENDIX 7

Computation of Correlations among Q-sorts

One of the handy features of the Q-sort rating scheme is that it permits the computation of correlation coefficients with a minimum of labor. Because the same distribution is used for all *sorts* in a particular study, the following formula can be used:

$$r = 1 - \frac{\Sigma d^2}{2N\sigma^2}$$

where r = the product-moment correlation between two sorts

N = the number of items in the sample (100 in the illustrative sample of photographs of art objects mentioned in Chapter 17)

σ = the standard deviation of the forced distribution, which is the same for all *sorts* using the distribution

d^2 = the squared difference between the pile number for an item in two *sorts;* thus, if a particular item is placed in pile 7 in one *sort* and pile 9 in another, the d^2 is 4. The sum of d^2 is taken over the N items

The term $2N\sigma^2$ is a constant for all correlations computed with a particular forced distribution. After the constant is determined, it is only necessary to obtain the sum of squared differences between item placements to compute the correlation. For any particular Q-sort distribution, a table can be composed to transform sums of squared differences directly into correlation coefficients. The formula effects a great time saving for the individual who does not have high-speed computers available. A correlation can be determined by the formula in a small fraction of the time it takes to use the customary product-moment formulas.

APPENDIX 8

Some Semantic Differential Scales Which Have Been Used in Various Studies

1. angular-rounded
2. bass-treble
3. beautiful-ugly
4. black-white
5. blatant-muted
6. boring-interesting
7. brave-cowardly
8. bright-dark
9. calm-agitated
10. calming-exciting
11. chaotic-ordered
12. clean-dirty
13. clear-hazy
14. colorful-colorless
15. concentrated-diffuse
16. controlled-accidental
17. deep-shallow
18. definite-uncertain
19. deliberate-careless
20. dull-exciting
21. dull-sharp
22. emotional-rational
23. empty-full
24. even-uneven
25. expensive-cheap
26. fair-unfair
27. familiar-strange
28. fast-slow
29. ferocious-peaceful
30. formal-informal
31. fragrant-foul
32. fresh-stale
33. gentle-violent
34. genuine-artificial
35. gliding-scraping
36. good-bad
37. happy-sad
38. hard-soft
39. healthy-sick
40. heavy-light
41. high-class–low-class
42. high-low
43. honest-dishonest
44. hot-cold
45. humorous-serious
46. important-trivial
47. intimate-remote
48. kind-cruel
49. labored-easy
50. large-small
51. long-short
52. loose-tight
53. loud-soft
54. lush-austere
55. masculine-feminine
56. meaningless-meaningful
57. mild-intense
58. modern–old-fashioned
59. near-far
60. nice-awful
61. obvious-subtle
62. pleasant-unpleasant
63. pleasing-annoying
64. powerful-weak
65. pungent-bland
66. pushing-pulling
67. rumbling-whining
68. red-green
69. relaxed-tense
70. repeated-varied
71. repetitive-varied
72. resting-busy

73. rich-poor
74. rich-thin
75. rough-smooth
76. rugged-delicate
77. sacred-profane
78. safe-dangerous
79. simple-complex
80. sincere-insincere
81. solid-hollow
82. static-dynamic
83. steady-fluttering
84. strong-weak
85. superficial-profound
86. sweet-bitter
87. sweet-sour
88. tasty-distasteful
89. thick-thin
90. unbelievable-believable
91. unique-commonplace
92. usual-unusual
93. vague-precise
94. valuable-worthless
95. vibrant-still
96. wet-dry
97. wide-narrow
98. yellow-blue
99. young-old

APPENDIX 9

The Influence of Reliability
on Predictive Validity

In Chapter 6, we discussed the correction for attenuation, which estimates how highly a test would correlate with an assessment if both were made perfectly reliable. A more useful formula is that for estimating the validity of a test if the reliabilities of the test and the assessment are raised or lowered by particular amounts. The formula is as follows:

$$\bar{r}_{12} = \frac{r_{12}\sqrt{r'_{11}}\sqrt{r'_{22}}}{\sqrt{r_{11}}\sqrt{r_{22}}}$$

where r_{11} and r_{22} = the original reliabilities of the predictor test and the assessment respectively

r'_{11} and r'_{22} = the new reliabilities of the predictor test and assessment

r_{12} = the original correlation between the test and the assessment

$\bar{r}_{12}$ = the estimated correlation between the test and the assessment after their respective reliabilities have been increased or decreased

The formula can be illustrated in a situation in which a test is used to predict ratings of performance. Assume that the original reliabilities of the test and the assessment are .64 and .49 respectively and that the correlation between the test and the assessment is .36. Suppose that, by improving the test and the assessment, their reliabilities are raised to .81 and .64 respectively. The estimated validity of the test after the reliabilities are increased is obtained as follows:

$$\bar{r}_{12} = \frac{.36\sqrt{.81}\sqrt{.64}}{\sqrt{.64}\sqrt{.49}}$$

$$= \frac{.36(.9 \times .8)}{.8 \times .7}$$

$$= \frac{.2592}{.56}$$

$$= .46$$

The formula will also serve to estimate the validity of a test if the reliabilities of the test and the assessment are decreased or if one is increased and the other decreased.

436

Name Index

437

Subject Index